The Churches in England
from Elizabeth I to Elizabeth II

Kenneth Hylson-Smith

The Churches
in England
from Elizabeth I
to Elizabeth II

Volume II: 1689–1833

SCM PRESS LTD

(cased) 0 334 02667 9

(limp) 0 334 02668 7

First published in Britain 1997
by SCM Press Ltd
9–17 St Albans Place, London N1 0NX

Typeset by Regent Typesetting, London
and printed in Great Britain by
Biddles Ltd, Guildford and King's Lynn

Contents

Preface

This is the second of a three-volume history of the churches in England from the reign of Elizabeth I to the present day, and it covers the period from the Glorious Revolution to 1833, the date which can be reckoned as marking the beginning of the Oxford Movement. It stands as an independent work, complete in itself, but it is intended to take up the story where the first volume finished, and to lead on to the third volume which is due to be published in 1998.

Since the 1960s there has been a massive and dramatic expansion in the scale and breadth of work on late seventeenth, eighteenth and early nineteenth-century history in general, and on the history of the churches in particular. Nevertheless, despite the veritable explosion of information, analysis and comment, no attempt has been made to draw together the many and most valuable theses, articles and books and to provide a judicious, informed and comprehensive overview embracing the Church of England, all the Dissenting bodies and the Roman Catholics. The present book seeks to fill this gap.

Six themes help to give the book coherence and structure. The first is the way the English religious scene became increasingly complex with the emergence or consolidation of High Churchmanship, Evangelicalism and Liberalism within the Church of England; with the evolution of Dissent into Nonconformity, as the various Dissenting bodies grew in numerical strength, and in political, social and religious importance; with the emergence of new denominations such as Methodism in its various forms, the Catholic Apostolic Church and the Brethren; and with the transmutation in the status and standing of Roman Catholicism. The second is the attempt by the churches to come to terms with unprecedented urbanization and industrialization, which transformed not only the face but the very nature of the country. The third is the origin, development, character and effects of the evangelical revival. The fourth is the extent to which the Protestants in England contributed to the growing sense of Britishness among the population. The fifth is the emergence of overseas missionary work. The sixth is the increasing importance of such rivals and enemies of orthodox Christianity as 'secularization', 'rationalism', 'radicalism', Unitarianism, Socinianism and atheism.

In the acknowledgments for the first volume I expressed my indebtedness to numberless scholars who have contributed to our understanding of the history of the churches in England in the period 1558 to 1688, and I sincerely reiterate my appreciation of those who have fulfilled a similar task for the long eighteenth century. The bibliography and notes for the present work attest in some small way to my dependence on the excellent work of others.

For this volume I am most grateful to Dr Henry D. Rack and Dr Mark Smith for their most helpful comments. The Revd Dr John Bowden, the Managing Director of SCM Press, has continued to provide encouragement and support, and Margaret Lydamore and Susan Molyneux have been invaluable in the typically efficient and courteous assistance they have given.

Introduction

Historiography

Until the 1920s the nineteenth-century Whig interpretation of eighteenth-century English history held sway. It was dominated by notions of continuous human progress. It abounded in grand generalizations. It was the tradition of W. E. H. Lecky, S. R. Gardiner and G. M. Trevelyan, Wallace Notestein and Sir David Lindsay Keir. For all the whig or liberal historians the century and a half from the time of the Revolution, as indeed all history, was part of an irresistible process; the unstoppable progress towards ever greater liberty in English society. It was 'the unfolding of parliamentary liberties, the rule of law, and representative institutions'.[1]

Then, from the publication of *The Structure of Politics at the Accession of George III* in 1929, Sir Lewis Namier and his school dominated the field. In place of Whig generalizations Namier substituted rigorous attention to detail, and a concentration on the world of high politics as exemplified in the lives and careers of a small number of politicians. Although he was fully aware of the complex psychological forces which influenced people's actions he was primarily concerned with structure. He was later criticized for this, and for ignoring the role of extra-parliamentary groups and opponents of the governing elite, as well as the political views and actions of the lower socio-economic groups and the impact of political writers and the press.[2]

In the 1960s and 1970s there was 'a dramatic expansion in the scale and breadth of work on eighteenth-century British history'.[3] There was not a common approach, but the new perspectives frequently stressed ideology. And much of this vibrant historiography was firmly placed within the framework of assumptions and priorities established in earlier generations by writers such as the Webbs, the Hammonds, R. H. Tawney, Harold Laski, Graham Wallas and G. D. H. Cole. Particular mention should be made of E. P. Thompson and E. J. Hobsbawm, who focussed their attention on the eighteenth and nineteenth centuries; while for the seventeenth century a similar Marxist interpretation was provided by Christopher Hill. Capitalism and the history of the 'working class' assumed centre stage, and in place of the former pre-eminence of Protestant morality and the inevitability of progress the concepts of economic and historical determinism and economic reductionism supplied the theoretical guidelines. The general picture conveyed was of a dynamic and confident society, with an increasingly empowered and assertive working class coming into its own and preparing to dismantle Britain's *ancien regime*. But in its turn this interpretation was implicitly or explicitly rejected or revised; and the most radical new appraisal was offered by J. C. Clark.

In addition to those historians already mentioned, Clark singled out for attack his former teacher Sir John Plumb and Lawrence Stone. All of them according to Clark had been so biased by their Marxist, radical or liberal presuppositions that they had ignored pertinent evidence and were disastrously wrong in their understanding of history. In opposition to them Clark asserted that there is no necessary direction in history. This not only precludes Marxist historical determinism. Democracy also should not be perceived as the ultimate ideal towards which the eighteenth century was inexorably moving. The overthrow of monarchs and all forms of traditional authority was not inevitable; and hierarchy and deference were in any case as 'natural' as any other form of political organization. Indeed the *ancien régime* in Britain continued, largely unimpaired until the triple hammer blows of the Repeal of the Test and Corporation Acts in 1828, the Catholic Emancipation Act of 1829 and the Reform Act of 1832. Until that time the country was a confessional state in which the most important elements, politically and culturally, were the monarchy, the aristocracy, which was no less dissolute than in France, and the clerical intelligentsia. There was no Industrial Revolution in Britain in the period, in the sense that there was no sudden surge of growth which constituted 'a technological-industrial Prometheus bursting the bonds of traditional society and transforming 'the world we have lost' into 'the world we have'.[4] Likewise, in his view class, or at least class consciousness in the presently accepted sense of the term, did not exist in Britain before Victorian times, and so it cannot be used to explain political developments in Britain in the one-hundred-and-seventy years after the Civil War and Commonwealth. There was no rising middle class throughout the seventeenth and eighteenth centuries which formed a challenge to the aristocracy, either politically or culturally, and which spearheaded the march towards democracy. Lastly, and from our point of view most importantly, Clark attempted to counter the tendency of Marxist and liberal historians to downplay the vital importance of religion in the history of the eighteenth century, or the practice, when they had given attention to the church, of portraying it as reactionary. He declared unambiguously that one of his main aims was to re-integrate religion into an historical vision which had become almost wholly positivist.[5]

Clark expounded his approach, and set forth his rewriting of eighteenth-century British history, in the most widely influential work on the eighteenth century for two decades, *English Society 1688–1832* (1985), and in its companion, *Revolution and Rebellion: State and Society in England in the Seventeenth and Eighteenth Centuries* (1986). They are well-written, highly stimulating, and have been found by a host of readers to be either of seminal importance or exceedingly irritating.

Some historians, although irritated, have responded with reasoned arguments. Let one of these, Joanna Innes, speak for the rest.[6] She refutes Clark's claim to have provided a new agenda for the social history of the eighteenth century. She claims that Clark does not fairly characterize other people's work; he does not identify and address real deficiencies in the historiography, and he does not provide an account which substantially contributes to our knowledge and understanding of eighteenth-century Britain. He misrepresents the stance of other historians, as when he portrays E. P. Thompson as one of the Marxist 'Old Guard' who produced teleological, materialist and determinist histories, when in fact he devoted much of his intellectual career 'to an assault upon teleology and determinism, and to an impassioned defence of the role of creative imagination in shaping the course of history'.[7] Innes reckons that Clark has an extraordinarily blinkered view of intellectual history. In many instances his presumed innovative ideas are merely restatements of what has already been widely accepted. His message that political and intellectual life are not straightforwardly determined by social and economic factors 'is the cry of a man who has just discovered America'. She adds that in 'the late 1980s it seems fair to ask for a little more'.[8] Methodologically she faults Clark for inconsistency and failure to integrate the study of the social and economic with the study of the political and intellectual aspects of history, once determinism is ruled out. She is no less severe in her judgment about the substance of his account of the eighteenth century. In his consideration of industrialization, urbanization and secularization she identifies a tendency to present an extreme variant of a familiar tale and to lean heavily on one side of a set of sociological categories, so that he effectively distorts or exaggerates the difference between his interpretation and that of other historians. He is 'too brusque in his dismissal of historians who, sharing certain of his interests, have not reached the same conclusions as he'.[9] She criticizes him for setting an unacceptable and too narrow agenda for the social history of the eighteenth century, and she suggests a series of more pertinent and potentially more fruitful questions to address.

Since Clark wrote the two works I have cited, and after a long time of relative neglect compared with the academic focus on the centuries on either side, the eighteenth century has returned to the foreground of historical scholarship. In social history there has been new interest in the whole area of social protest and crime, which itself has posed larger questions about social relations and the exercise of power; there has been a strong challenge to the traditional views of economic 'revolutions', provoked in part by the re-estimation of rates of change in output in both manufacturing industry and agriculture; there has been the significant use of new methods and new data in population history; and there has been a revival of urban and trade union history. Of particular importance have been the challenging, provocative and insightful works of Paul Langford, in which he portrays the multi-faceted Georgian world with its disorder and vulgarity as well as its stability and elegance, and its saga of remarkable contrasts and changes;[10] the revived interest in Jacobitism, with the light that casts on the history of the long eighteenth century;[11] the fascinating and penetrating work on 'Britishness' by Linda Colley;[12] and the multiplication of works on the church during the long eighteenth century, which I am about to consider. 'Gone are the days when "keeping up with the literature" was easier for eighteenth-century historians than for most of their colleagues.'[13]

Turning to the history of the eighteenth-century churches, the outstanding contribution in the early twentieth century was made by Elie Halévy. In his massive, detailed and original works on the general history of England in the eighteenth century he gave prominence to religion, and he propounded his controversial but influential analysis of the link between the Methodist revival and the absence in England of revolution, which was so prevalent on the continent. But despite such fructifying thinking, by the mid-twentieth century the conventional view of the Church of England, and more generally of the churches in England other than the Methodists, as moribund and soporific was still widely accepted. Lytton Strachey repeated it when he asserted that 'for many generations the Church of England had slept the sleep of the . . . comfortable.'[14] In his much read *History of the Church of England*, H. O. Wakeman remarked that when 'the bells range out in 1714 to welcome the accession of George I, they sounded the death-knell of her [the Church of England's] high ideals and vigorous life for more than a century . . . Quiet and satisfaction reigned supreme.'[15] Accomplished and fair-minded historians as a whole had consistently and persistently drawn a gloomy picture of the eighteenth-century church. In their late Victorian classic *The English Church in the Eighteenth Century*, C. J. Abbey and J. H. Overton maintained that the church was flourishing in 1702, when Anne ascended the throne, and there were signs of revival by 1800, but in the intervening decades it 'partook of the general sordidness of the age; it was an age of great material prosperity, but of moral and spiritual poverty, such as hardly finds a parallel in our history'.[16] F. Relton joined Overton in beating the same drum. They portrayed the eighteenth century as an era of decline for the church, a period 'of lethargy instead of activity, of worldliness instead of spirituality, of self-seeking instead of self-denial, of grossness instead of refinement'.[17]

Since Victorian times the historiography of the eighteenth-century church has also often had a strongly judgmental slant. High Churchmen have been biased by their resentment at the expulsion of the Nonjurors, and have tended either to ignore the eighteenth century or to portray it as the dark era before the dawn of the Oxford Movement. The assessment of evangelicals has been coloured by their condemnation of the Church of England for its rejection of the revival movement. There were also other ways in which the history of the eighteenth-century church tended to be distorted. 'In the ecclesiastical version of the whig interpretation, the Tories and High Church Anglicans were always the reactionary villains, and the Dissenters and Whigs were invariably the moral, farsighted heroes.'[18]

The Victorian depiction of the eighteenth-century church was clearly in serious need of revision.

The process began with the publication in 1934 of arguably the most important work on eighteenth-century church history to appear in the twentieth century, Norman Sykes' *Church and State in England in the Eighteenth Century*. Sykes insisted that it was anachronistic to use nineteenth-century standards to make pronouncements on the Georgian church.[19] Many of its failings were not peculiar to that time. Pluralism and non-residence, to which reference was so frequently made, were familiar in the Middle Ages, and also among the much admired Caroline clergy. Hanoverian prelates may have been regularly absent from their sees for parts of the year while they attended Parliament, but they could be matched in this by their mediaeval forebears who went on service in the royal household. The record of the life and service of Hanoverian Churchmen was reasonable in view of the post-Revolutionary problems caused by the policy of religious toleration, and the later unprecedented challenge of urbanization and industrialization. It was not an heroic era for the church, and its worship and witness rarely rose above the ordinary, but Sykes concluded that a body of dutiful and conscientious Churchmen were trying to do their work according to the not over-demanding standards of the day. He also helped to rescue the Tories and High Church Anglicans from the role assigned to them by Whig interpreters of the eighteenth century as conservative bigots, unjustly opposing democratically minded Dissenters.

Although other church historians have built upon the fine analytical and descriptive detail provided by Sykes, his conclusions have not been universally accepted. The debate between the optimists and the pessimists continues. The overall assessment remains inconclusive. Jeremy Gregory,[20] J. C. D. Clark,[21] Peter B. Nockles,[22] P. Rycroft,[23] Mark Smith,[24] Albion M. Urdank[25] and Arthur Warne,[26] for example, present a fairly favourable picture, and W. R. Ward draws attention to the contemporary peons of praise for the eighteenth-century Church of England from the continent,[27] whereas Peter Virgin, in his important book, *The Church in an Age of Negligence*, is cautiously pessimistic. But the debate is much better informed. To take but a few examples. There have been sophisticated studies of church and society, such as those of A. D. Gilbert[28] and E. R. Norman;[29] works on church and state;[30] studies of the church in relation to the Enlightenment, including those of John Gascoigne;[31] works on Jacobitism which have cast further light on the religion of the period;[32] studies of various aspects of High Churchmanship,[33] Whig churchmen or 'liberal Anglicans'[34] and Evangelicals;[35] works on the Dissenters and the Roman Catholics;[36] studies of the revival, of which those by J. D. Walsh,[37] W. R. Ward[38] H. Rack[39] and C. J. Podmore[40] are of particular value; and a proliferation of local studies[41] and other research on specific and pertinent topics.[42] Remarkably, with such an abundance of information, analysis and comment there has been little attempt to present an overview. Perhaps it is because the surface has still only been scratched, and to try to provide a comprehensive analytical account is merely to step in where wiser historians fear to tread. But that is what is being attempted in this volume.

Themes

With such a rich and abundant crop of relevant works, but with no consensus on even the main contours of the picture which emerges, the present synthesis could well degenerate into a welter of complex and confusing facts. As a guard against this I will identify a few themes: threads which will run through the narrative and comment. To some extent these will take up the lines of thought enunciated in the first volume of this present trilogy,[43] and this is as it should be because any point in history, or any period, is unavoidably and intricately linked with the preceding period and leads on and into what follows: starting and finishing points are always somewhat arbitrary.

My first theme is pluralism. By this I mean not the holding by an incumbent of more than one living, but the process whereby the Protestant scene in England became ever more varied and multi-faceted with the passage of time. One aspect of this was the extent to which the great convulsions of the Civil War, Commonwealth, Restoration and Revolution had profoundly modified the ancient allegiance between church and state.[44] In the early years of the reign of Elizabeth I the Protestant religion in England was represented by the single, largely unified 'Church of England'; but by 1688 the established church was confronted by four major Dissenting groups – the Presbyterians, the Congregationalists, the Baptists and the Quakers – and there were certain sects remaining from the confusing Commonwealth period, such as the Muggletonians. With the Toleration Act of 1689, the emergence of the Methodists, the secessions among the Methodists in the late eighteenth and early nineteenth centuries, the appearance of additional bodies such as the Catholic Apostolic Church and the Brethren, and the incorporation of pluralism into the law of the land through the repeal of the Test and Corporation Acts in 1828 and the Catholic Emancipation Act of 1829, the confessional state, with one national church working in harmony with the state in a fruitful partnership, had become well and truly a thing of the past, if it had ever existed. 'Traditions of religious dissent in English society go back to the Reformation and beyond, but it was only in the century after 1740 . . . that popular extra-Establishment religious movements arose which were capable of challenging and ultimately subverting the traditional monopolistic role

xvi The Churches in England from Elizabeth I to Elizabeth II

of the Church of England.'[45] As a corollary it will be seen that Dissent
was transmuted into Nonconformity, and the various Nonconformist
bodies became increasingly consolidated into national, and indeed international, institutions. Prima facie this seems to be the story of a growth
in Nonconformist denominational strength, unity and coherence; but
the process may hide a decline in dynamism, dedication and the pursuit
of clearly recognized goals. 'Puritanism – Dissent – Nonconformity: the
decline collapses into a surrender. *Dissent* still carries the sound of resistance to Apollyon and the Whore of Babylon, *Nonconformity* is self-
effacing and apologetic: it asks to be left alone.'[46] An examination of
what really happened and how it should most accurately be interpreted
will constitute my second theme; and in this analysis the conceptual
framework provided by the sociological distinction between church,
denomination and sect, expounded by Max Weber, Ernst Troeltsch,
Richard Niebuhr, and such recent sociologists as J. M. Yinger, David
Martin and Bryan Wilson, will be of considerable help.[47]

Within Roman Catholicism different forces were at work. There was
a marked change in the number and the distinctive features of the
Catholic community in England. I will trace this transformation as my
third theme.

Meanwhile, the Church of England will be seen struggling to come to
terms both with this pluralism and with the unprecedented urbanization
and industrialization which so radically changed the character of the
country during the one hundred and fifty years covered in this study.
I want to present an accurate portrayal of the church as it tried to contend with the various forces waged against it, and as it tried to be the
'church in the world' in the midst of changing and not easy circumstances. I want to weigh the evidence; not to take a 'pessimistic' or
an 'optimistic', but a realistic view. The Church of England was
increasingly hampered by a combination of the effects of toleration,
legal restrictions, its own corruption and complacency and its slowness
to adapt to the new and ever changing economic and social conditions.
In its struggle to be true to its calling we will encounter many failings,
but we will discover triumphs, and much worthy of praise in its life and
witness. It may not have been among the most glorious epochs in its
history, but it was not as dark and dismal for the Church of England as
it has frequently been painted. To give a more balanced and fairer
account of its history during the period than has often been given, and
to help make a re-evaluation of the 'pessimistic thesis' will constitute the
fourth theme.

Then, inevitably, one of the major themes must be the origin, development, character and effects of the evangelical revival. This of all eighteenth-century church history topics invites partisanship. I write as a long-standing and active Evangelical, but also as an historian concerned to exercise integrity in both description and analysis. A re-appraisal of the revival is timely in view of much recent work on the subject. Here I have a fifth theme.

Taking Protestantism as a whole, and taking my lead mainly from Linda Colley, I will examine the degree to which the Protestants in England contributed towards a developing sense of Britishness among the population, and to what extent Protestantism itself was coloured by this increasing national consciousness. This will be my sixth theme.

Lastly, as the seventh theme, I will consider the rivals and enemies of orthodox Christianity: among which I will cover 'secularization', 'rationalism', 'radicalism', Unitarianism, Socinianism and atheism. There was a distinct change in the religious climate over the one hundred and fifty years covered by my survey. For a combination of reasons which I will be examining, there was an increase in the number of people, albeit still a small minority of the total population, who treated religion, and of course the Christian faith in particular, as irrelevant. Newtonian concepts of the universe; the philosophies of Thomas Hobbes, John Locke, David Hume and others; the doctrines of theism, of the Socinians and the Unitarians; radical political and social theories; and the impact of urbanization and industrialization, all combined to produce a corrosive effect upon the churches, and to undermine Christian teaching. Ideas of providential intervention in mundane affairs became less tenable for a small, but increasing, number of people. 'The notion of a moral universe, where natural events became acts of God intended to warn men by afflicting providences, became less and less convincing to the educated laity.'[48]

Part 1

The Churches in Confusion and Decline

I

The Post-Revolution Church of England

A new era

The English Revolution of 1688–9 was a pivotal event in English history. 'No one who studies British history before and after the years 1688–9 should fail to be aware that in passing from one period to the other we are crossing one of the great divides on the entire landscape of "early modern" and modern times'.[1] In the scale of key turning points in the history of England the Revolution of 1688 and the arrival of a new monarch whose right to the throne was severely questioned by many in the population, must, by any reckoning, assume high ranking. Most historians acknowledge this.[2] Others have questioned the significance accorded to those few, drama-filled months.[3] But all are agreed that to some extent they represent a landmark. It is possible, as J. C. D. Clark argues, that the Revolution only secured the hegemony of the largely Anglican aristocracy and gentry in the face of the threat apparently posed by a Roman Catholic monarchical bureaucracy, and thereby only preserved what 1660 was supposed to have re-established; and that 1688 did not represent a fundamental discontinuity. But surely that in itself makes it of crucial importance? The degree to which the beating off of the Jacobite and radical challenges ensured the continuance of the 'old' Anglican, aristocratic, monarchical, confessional society for a further one hundred and forty years is questionable. Maybe former 'whig' historians have overstated the case by claiming massive 'progress' towards democracy during the long eighteenth century, and the transformation of society as a consequence of a series of 'revolutions'. Nevertheless, I maintain that these years did in fact see such significant political, constitutional, economic, social and religious changes that the *ancien régime* at the very least underwent major modification; and to a great extent the changes began with the bloodless Revolution.

Politically perhaps the most dramatic transformation resulting from the events of 1688 and 1689 was the redisposition of England within the European scene. 'It brought to this island a Dutchman whose knowledge of continental politics and experience of continental diplomacy surpassed by far that of any English king since the Middle Ages, and whose whole commitment to the Revolution stemmed in the first place from his determination that Britain should no longer evade her European responsibilities.'[4] He had for a long time fought for the Protestant cause, and he had established himself as the foremost Protestant champion among the nations of continental Europe. In accepting the crown of England he was resolved to continue his Protestant crusade. He was determined that his new kingdom should play the role for which he was convinced her growing wealth, her strategic position, her militant Protestantism and above all her sea power fitted her. Those who invited him to invade their country and to become its monarch were not duped; they were aware that they were 'committing England to participation in his life-long struggle to contain and reduce French power'.[5] Nonetheless, neither William nor those who welcomed him to England could have foreseen the long-term transforming effect upon the country of what they were undertaking. In effect they were taking a decisive step in the creation of the modern British nation, and preparing it for the part it was to play on the world, and not only the European, stage. The prolonged conflict with Roman Catholic France was a crucial element in defining England, and then, after 1707, Britain, as a bastion of Protestantism, and a country whose destiny and whole character were identified with Protestant Christianity. The Revolution was a critical event in the forging of a distinctive, self-conscious, Britishness, in which Protestantism was an essential ingredient.

William had a suitably impressive pedigree to qualify him to be a Protestant protagonist. He was the grandson of England's revered martyr king, Charles I, and the great-grandson of William the Silent, the widely-admired champion of Dutch Protestantism. He had assumed some prominence in European politics as a consequence of his heroic defence of the Dutch Republic against the onslaught of France. For seventeen years before he was crowned king of England he had waged an unremitting military, diplomatic, political and ecclesiastical war against the might of Louis XIV's France. It was fundamentally a matter of territorial control and religious allegiance. Louis was rapidly becoming the 'Master of all Christendom'. It was feared that such aggrandizement included designs on Protestant England. Francophobia and anti-popery became ever more closely linked with one another in

England, especially when James II appeared to be steering the country in a Roman Catholic direction. The saviour of the Protestant Dutch Republic, and the leading Protestant opponent of Catholic France seemed the ideal candidate to come to the rescue. 'William's purpose in mounting his expedition to Britain was to reinstate the despised Protestant interest in government, to investigate the disputed issue of the succession to the crown, and to enlist the major Protestant monarchy in Europe, with its considerable revenues and enviable fighting power, as an ally in the armed struggle against Louis XIV and French aggression.'[6] In all these objectives he was fully supported by his most able wife, Mary, who with her profound devotion to Protestantism played her part in moulding the religious life of post-Revolution England.

It was fortuitous that William's expeditionary force landed, unopposed, in Torbay on 5 November 1688 – the day set apart each year for Protestant thanksgiving for the nation's earlier deliverance from the machinations of popery in 1605. The Whigs were better placed and better qualified than their Tory rivals to work with William in overthrowing James II. They had never wanted James to be king; and they 'were neither compromised by association with the discredited Stuart regime, nor inhibited by scruples over resisting the Lord's Anointed'.[7] But William tried to woo both parties. Although the political nation was sharply divided between Whigs and Tories, 'this was on the basis of past controversies which were made less relevant by the emergence of new issues. By establishing a mixed administration of whigs and tories William initiated a process of regrouping. Both parties began to split into court and country sections.'[8]

It was also in the post-Revolutionary era that this re-alignment assumed a distinctly religious complexion. The difference between Whig and Tory was most frequently couched in religious terms. 'In the early eighteenth century politics and religion were indistinguishable.'[9] The Exclusion crisis and the events surrounding the Revolution had bound the interests of Anglican Whigs to those of the Dissenters. They 'advocated contractual kingship, ardently supported both the Revolution and the Protestant succession, were anxious to defend Dissenters against the arbitrary exercise of its legal power by the Anglican church, and backed with increasing conviction England's commitment as a major power to the system of alliances built up in Europe to contain Louis XIV'.[10] The Tories were associated with the High-Anglican tradition and the Whigs were generally composed of the more moderate churchmen. The Tories were identified with the Stuart dynasty, with Jacobitism, with the doctrines of Divine Right, Passive Obedience and Non-Resistance. They were at least uneasy about the Revolution if not actually hostile to it and all that it came to represent; while the Whigs were the party in support of the Revolution and all the principles it enshrined, and of the new King and all he represented, and this included the Low Church tradition combined with toleration and support for the interests of Dissenters. Such a political-religious linkage persisted until the mid-century party crisis with its re-definition of policy and allegiances which we will encounter in chapter 3.[11]

The most delicate question in 1689 was the degree of toleration to be allowed to Dissenters. Since the Restoration they had suffered under the Clarendon Code and the protracted hostility of the established church. As we have just noted, they were an important component of the Whig party which had been instrumental in facilitating and supporting the Revolution, and in providing a welcome to the new King. How were they to be rewarded without unduly alienating those in the Church of England who were antagonistic to any form of Dissent? The answer was the Toleration Act of 1689. It was a strangely unsatisfactory solution.

The Earl of Nottingham introduced two bills into the House of Lords which were designed to go together.[12] One was for comprehension, and laid down generous terms by which Dissenters might be admitted to the Church of England. The other was for toleration, and carefully specified limited terms for the toleration of the anticipated relatively small number who would not agree to participate in such comprehension. Both bills received a second reading. But the King then blundered. Without any testing of the opinion of his Tory ministers, he appeared in the House of Lords and proposed that the Test and Corporation Acts (passed during the reign of Charles II, imposing severe restraints on Dissenters) should be abolished. There was almost unbounded Anglican anger and alarm. The King's proposal was overwhelmingly defeated, the Comprehension Bill was lost, and the Toleration Bill alone went on to become law. The result was that the new Act, which had been designed to deal with a small number of intransigent nonconformists, now had to apply to nearly half a million sober and respectable citizens. It granted Dissenters the right to worship separately in their own meeting-houses on condition that they took the oaths of supremacy and allegiance and made the declaration against transubstantiation. Dissenting ministers had to affirm those of the Thirty-nine Articles which did not concern church government; all places of worship had to be registered with a bishop or the Quarter Sessions, and services had to be conducted with the doors unlocked. The Dissenters still laboured under the disabilities of the Test and Corporation Acts; and the Toleration Act specifically declared that the old laws about attendance at church on a Sunday continued to apply to those who did not resort to a licensed meeting-house.

In the face of such stringent provisions Nottingham tried to revive his former comprehension project, and he set up a royal commission to this end. But the ordinary parish clergy were fearful of any such changes, and they successfully blocked the legislation when it came before the Convocation.

The result of all this confusion was that the meaning of the Toleration Act was always in doubt. It was interpreted in different ways by the clergy, the government and by the great majority of ordinary lay-people. Some churchwardens insisted on regarding the Act as a statutory continuation of the state of affairs which had existed since James II's Declaration of Indulgence. It was all very unfortunate, and perhaps the most regrettable aspect of the whole saga of muddle was that the authority, status and standing of the Church of England was undermined, while, at the same time, substantial and lasting rights were not granted to the Dissenters. In this chapter we will look at the Church of England in the forty-five years after the Revolution, and in the next at the Dissenters.

The Church of England

The Revolution wrought fundamental short, medium and long terms changes in the Church of England. The 1689 Toleration Act produced a sea change, and pointed forward to ever-increasing religious pluralism. The Church of England was demoted from 'the national church' to 'the established church', and she took it badly. A number of churchmen persisted in preaching against toleration, insisting that Dissenters remained guilty of schism, whatever Parliament might enact. But however much they might protest, and however much they might lament the changed status of the Church of England, the transmutation which was taking place was evident to all who had eyes to see it, and the honesty and courage to admit it. Not only was the Toleration Act a major stride in the march towards pluralism, but it was yet one more episode in the metamorphosis of Anglicanism itself.

The Revolution had compromised the fundamental principles of the Restoration Church of England. The Restoration ideal of a single, all-inclusive, national church had been repudiated; and the vision of the complete Christian life, which had complemented that ideal, had been tarnished and diminished. The ecclesiological consensus of the Restoration church – her sense of being both Reformed and Catholic and her refusal to follow through the implications of her own episco-palianism – faltered and, with the departure of the Nonjurors, began to collapse. The Revolution had set in train the eventual fragmenta-tion of Anglicanism.[13]

The involvement of Anglicans in rebellion against James II, whether it was done actively or passively, called into question the previous cherished principle of a divinely-ordained authority in the state. It broke down that special relationship of the Church of England with the monarchy, and via the monarchy with the whole apparatus of state, which had been a central feature in its character and one of its greatest strengths. The Revolution, the accession of William and the Revolution Settlement 'reduced to tatters the whole Anglican concept of an indis-soluble link between the altar and the throne'.[14] The church could not remain untouched by such a blatant denial of its political creed, or hope to preserve even outward unity. The imposition on the clergy of sacred oaths of allegiance to William and Mary, although with the use of words obligingly trimmed by Parliament, led to a devastatingly harmful open schism: the Nonjurors went out into the wilderness, and for the next few decades they were a powerful presence in the wings.

The Nonjurors

'The occasion of the non-juring scheme was simple. It was the refusal of the Archbishop of Canterbury and a group of his episcopal colleagues to swear allegiance to the intruding William and Mary, on the ground that they had already sworn inviolable oaths of allegiance to James II. In consequence they were first suspended and then deprived of their offices, as were some 300–400 inferior clergy and an unknown number of laity who followed them.'[15] The Nonjurors were important in their generation, and their successors continued to exercise a considerable influence, but recent scholarship has questioned the previous assessment of the extent of their impact upon the conforming Church of England. Their departure undoubtedly inflicted damage on the church, but the amount of the damage should not be overstated. It did not 'open the sluice-gates to let a flood of Whig latitudinaries' into William III's episcopate. It was also not the ideological disaster it was once thought. The loss of godly priests with a high sense of calling, some of whom were men of high ability and influence, was very wounding to the church; and the deprivation of Sancroft alone was a heavy blow. John Tillotson, who was Primate until 1694 and Thomas Tenison, who succeeded him, were both energetic and gifted leaders, but 'with a question-mark against their legitimacy lingering in many minds, they could never aspire to the firm authority which Sancroft had enjoyed at Canterbury nor to the loyal support which he had commanded almost universally among the clergy'.[16] Indeed, although for about thirty years there was a very identifiable group of Nonjurors with their distinctive ideology and theology, it was the loss of individuals which was probably more serious than the success of a group *per se* and its continuance outside the pale as a separatist church. And this damaging effect was reinforced by 'the influence which the martyr's crowns of the Nonjurors and their skilful publicists gave them subsequently over the mass of conforming clergy'.[17]

The Nonjuring communion was based on clergymen. They were a loose confederation of mostly ordained men with a very impressive array of erudition. The degree to which they were Jacobites is uncertain, and has been a matter of academic debate. It has been claimed that the 'Nonjuring schism was the clerical counterpart of Jacobitism'.[18] But most of the Nonjurors were not Jacobites, Jacobite agents or conspirators. Neither, however, were they all patristic scholars. Most of them were ordinary working clergymen. They were united in a refusal to accept the legitimacy of the new regime and to swear oaths to the ruling monarch. They were adamant and forthright in affirming that William and Mary, Anne and the Georges had less right to their allegiance, and to the throne, than the exiled Stuarts. 'In an age that took oaths very seriously, Nonjuring was a very strong political statement.'[19] The Nonjurors asserted that the established church which had been born of the Revolution of 1689 was as illegitimate as the new political regime.

Although there were varieties and even conflicts of opinion among the Nonjurors, it is not unreasonable to discern two distinct clusters of ecclesiastical and political views. There were those who wished to retire into seclusion, and who did not want to be active in the ecclesiastical and political arena. They were the more passive and irenic of the Nonjurors. They were headed by Robert Frampton, Bishop of Gloucester, who belonged to the Sancroft generation; but their spiritual mentor was the saintly Bishop Ken, and they included influential laymen like Robert Nelson and Francis Cherry.

Thomas Ken (1637–1711) has always been acknowledged as a shining light among the Nonjurors; and later High Churchmen were to regard him as perhaps the most significant Nonjuring contributor to the High Church tradition. His particular type of spirituality was demonstrated in his *Manual of Prayers*, his *Exposition of Divine Love* and his *Practice of Divine Love*, the latter being a classic expression of Laudian doctrine in which he clearly reveals his Catholicism as firmly Anglican and non-Roman.

As Bishop of Bath and Wells he had exhibited those pastoral qualities which were characteristic of the best of the Nonjurors. He had organized relief for persecuted Huguenot refugees; established schools for poor children; and adopted such personal measures as having twelve poor men or women to dine with him on Sundays. He was one of the seven bishops who had reluctantly withstood James II in his demand that his second Declaration of Indulgence should be read in all the churches in 1688; but, despite that act of confrontation, he had remained unflinchingly loyal to the King who had given him so little cause for such loyalty. He resolutely adhered to his understanding of the divine right of kings and the practice of passive obedience, determined to resist any deposition of the King or choice of any other King, or to assent to any breaking of the link in the royal chain. He lived in retirement, and even in 1703 when Kidder who had held the see of Bath and Wells since Ken's disposition, died, he refused the offer of reinstatement. He maintained his consistent stand, and when he died in 1711 he was the last survivor of the original Nonjuring bishops.

The more outspoken, uncompromising and, some would say, more spleeny Nonjurors were led by the dour Yorkshireman, George Hickes. From the moment of his deprivation he was forthright in his views and did not 'mince words or dodge the logic of his principles'. Of the conforming clergy he said:

> They can perform no valid acts of priesthood: their very prayers are sin: their sacraments are no sacraments: their absolutions are null and void: God ratifies nothing in heaven which they do in his name upon earth: they and all that adhere to them are out of the church.[20]

He was fierce in his condemnation not only of Gilbert Burnet and John Tillotson, whom he blamed for the schism, but also of those who, like Thomas Ken and Henry Dodwell, were prepared to bring it to an end. He was the most formidable Nonjuring leader, and with such dedication to the Nonjuring cause and unflinching assertion of Nonjuring principles it is not surprising to find that it was he who carried out the negotiations with the exiled James II for the perpetuation of episcopal succession which led, on 24 February 1693, to the establishment of a separate, Nonjuring, episcopal structure. He was consecrated Suffragan Bishop of Thetford and Thomas Wagstaffe was consecrated Bishop of Ipswich.

The more the Nonjurors undertook the search for religious purity the more they advanced the process of separation; and 'they came close to removing themselves from even a liturgical resemblance to the established Church'.[21] But this ever more introverted band of idealists experienced the fate of many such intense groups; they found issues on which they were passionately divided among themselves.

The most bitter dispute was over the so-called 'Usages' of Edward VI's first Prayer Book: the oblation of the elements in the eucharist; the invocation of the Holy Spirit upon the elements; the removal of the word 'militant' so that the prayer for the whole estate of the church might include both the living and the dead; and the mixing of wine with water in communion. Those who regarded these four usages as necessary or essential became known as 'essentialist' Nonjurors; and those who totally opposed them as 'Non-Usagers'. Although a compromise was eventually reached, the favour shown for the first Prayer Book, which was less strongly Protestant than later versions, made the Nonjurors appear to be crypto-Catholic. This impression was reinforced by the open attack some of them made on the liturgical competence of the English Reformers, and by the assertion that the liturgy of Cranmer and Ridley had been perverted by the influence of such continental divines as Martin Bucer and Peter Martyr.

It is, however, clear that the Nonjurors as a whole shared with the great majority of their fellow countrymen a Protestant, anti-Roman Catholic outlook. Archbishop William Sancroft was at pains to urge the bishops to take every opportunity of declaring their loyalty to the Reformation, and their implacable opposition to the errors, superstitions, idolatries and tyrannies of the Church of Rome. Most of the succeeding Nonjurors did not depart from such views, although this only heightened their sense of isolation. 'Utterly opposed to Rome, detesting the Lutheran and Reformed Churches, counting the English Dissenters as little better than heathen men and publicans, the Non-

Jurors found it difficult to give practical expression to their zeal for the unity of all Christians'.[22]

It is sad to learn of the divisions, wrangles, nasty gossip and intrigues which bedeviled relations between the leading Nonjurors, but they did not exhaust their energies in internal controversy. In addition to the devotional works of Ken, some of John Kettlewell's tracts helped to nourish the eucharistic devotion of churchmen, as did those of Nathaniel Spinckes; Robert Nelson issued works on worship, with his *Companion for the Festivals and Fasts of the Church of England* being particularly popular; and William Law, if he is accepted as a Nonjuror, exercised special and widespread influence mainly through his *Practical Treatise upon Christian Perfection* (1726) but supremely through his masterpiece *A Serious Call to a Devout and Holy Life* (1728). Then there were the liturgical studies of Bishop Brett and Thomas Deacon which transcended in importance and influence what they achieved in their own day and generation.

The Nonjurors were a beleagured minority; a proscribed community on whom the authorities might swoop at any time. Some met in their own assemblies, with notable concentrations in London and Manchester. But not all of them abandoned the institutional church. Some of the outwardly conforming clergy and lay people had most uncomfortable consciences, and took the oaths with considerable reservations, while others were explicitly nonconformist. At least ten English peers became Nonjurors after 1688 as well as about sixty present and former Members of the House of Commons. In the 1690s there were possibly about one hundred Nonjuring gentry families. Although they were not all strict Nonjurors, and most probably attended the established church, nevertheless their actions excluded them from any public office, and could have had a severe effect on their family fortunes. After the death of James II in 1701 many lay Nonjurors agreed to take the oaths, but others persevered in their refusal. It is difficult to gauge the Nonjuring strength both numerically and in terms of vehemence of commitment among the lower and middling classes, as the oaths were not required of them, but it was they who provided the bulk of worshippers in Nonjuring conventicles. It can be reckoned as a minor success of the Nonjurors that they managed to draw laymen of humble backgrounds into the work of their church.

It is arguable that with their uncompromising separation from the juring church, their anti-Erastianism, their increasing religious 'purity' and their distinctive liturgy, the Nonjurors quite rapidly transformed themselves into a nonconformist sect. It was ironic and tragic that their strict loyalty alienated them more and more from the ecclesiastical establishment which they both loved and hated. In the meantime the church which they disavowed was having a difficult and fraught time.

Conflict in the church

'In the generation after the revolution the Church of England was torn apart by a great conflict of parties. It was clear even to the most detached observer that her clergy and laity were involved in a radical reappraisal of the whole role of the national Church in English society.'[23] It was a period of crisis for the national church as it attempted to weather the traumatic transition from the personal kingship of the Stuart regime, with the culminating crisis of the reign of the 'Romanizer' James II, to the new age of party management, the Toleration Act and seething discontent among the ordinary priests. But of particular importance were the devastating conflicts caused by the clash of church parties, with the High Church, the Low Church and the Latitudinarians at loggerheads, the inroads made by the teachings of Arians, Socinians and Unitarians and Deists, and the undermining effects of resurgent Dissent.

The modern High Church tradition in the Church of England went back to the Elizabethan era, although, of course, High Churchmen would trace their roots as far back as the early church, and ultimately to Christ himself. Such a tradition may be seen in embryo, ill-defined and imprecise in the latter half of the sixteenth century.[24] Among those who championed some features of the pre-Reformation 'Catholic' church in opposition to Puritanism were Anthony Corro, William Barrett, Peter Baro, Richard Hooker, Richard Field, Bishops Richard Cheyney of Gloucester, Edmund Guest of Rochester and John Overall of Norwich, and Samuel Harsnett, Archbishop of York. To this list may be added two lay members of Parliament, Francis Alford and James Dalton. Three Archbishops of Canterbury, Matthew Parker, John Whitgift and Richard Bancroft also, in different ways, tried to retain links with the 'Catholic' past, and strove to preserve the 1559 settlement from further changes in a Protestant direction. Although he was one of the intellectual leaders of the reforming party, the teaching of John Jewell, especially as it was expounded in his masterly defence of the Church of England *Apologia Ecclesiae Anglicanae*, may also be said to have contributed to a 'Catholic' tradition. Lancelot Andrewes not only gave expression to this tradition in his writing and sermons, but exemplified it in his life and ministry. With William Laud and the Laudians the Church of England 'Catholic' teaching was implemented in a full ecclesiastical and political programme. The distinctive theological teaching of High Churchmanship was expanded and amplified by the Caroline divines. It found poetic form with John Donne, Richard Crashaw and George Herbert, and was expressed ascetically in the life of Nicholas Ferrar and the Little Gidding Community. In the late seventeenth and early eighteenth centuries it was perpetuated by conformists like Bishop Francis Atterbury and Nonjurors such as Bishop Thomas Ken.

High Churchmanship, like any of the other church traditions of the eighteenth century we are considering, does not lend itself to neat definition. For one thing it contained a range of emphases and interpretations, so that any one individual, or even group, within the tradition might well differ from others. Nonetheless, it is possible to identify the main lineaments.[25]

Eighteenth-century High Churchmen tended to uphold some form of the doctrine of apostolical succession, and to have a strong attachment to the catholicity and apostolicity of the Church of England as a branch of the universal catholic church, from which they excluded those reformed bodies which had wilfully abandoned episcopacy. Consequently, they ascribed great important to episcopacy, to the authority and to the role within the church of bishops and priests. They believed in the supremacy of the Bible, but generally insisted that it needed to be interpreted in the light of such authoritative standards as the Prayer Book, the Catechism and the Creeds. They set varying degrees of value on the testimony of tradition. They tended to value the writings of the early Fathers, especially as witnesses to, and commentaries on, biblical truth. They emphasized the doctrine of sacramental grace, both in the eucharist and baptism, but were inclined to eschew the principle of *ex opere operato*.[26] Great stress was laid upon the cultivation of a practical spirituality based on the sacraments and nourished by acts 'of self-denial, rather than upon any subjective conversion experience or special personal and corporate manifestations of the Holy Spirit. They were zealous in upholding the importance of a religious establishment, and they insisted on the responsibility of the state, as a divinely ordained rather than secular entity, to protect and promote the interests of the church. Taken in its totality, and allowing for variations in the extent to which the features identified were held more explicitly and unequivocally by some than by others, this profile distinguishes a recognizable eighteenth-century type of churchmanship which, until quite recently, has not been fully acknowledged, or has been misrepresented, by historians.

High Churchmanship was bound up and infused with political Toryism; but this became less so as the century progressed. As we have seen, it was a marked feature of the High Churchmanship of the first fifteen years of the century at least, when it was defined as much in political as in sacramental terms. The Frewen dynasty of clerics well illustrates this.[27] From the time of Laud until well into the eighteenth century they were staunchly of a High Church temperament, and indeed adhered to Laudianism when this hue of churchmanship had become outmoded. 'In the highly charged first decade and a half of the eighteenth century, they consistently lined up on the Tory/High Church side of the conflict. Their voting pattern in Sussex from 1705 to 1741 was consistently Tory, with only one exception.'[28] At the core of the Frewen family's Toryism was concern over Nonconformity, which they thought should be prohibited, for they regarded toleration towards it under the Toleration Act as at best ill-advised, and at worse woefully destructive, for it threatened the state and society as well as the church. They upheld such Anglican practices as wearing the surplice, signing the cross in baptism and kneeling at the sacrament, and considered that the Dissenters, and any who sympathized with them, were guilty of impiety in opposing such reverential conduct. This fear of Dissent, and contempt for it, contributed to the perpetuation of their High Church/Tory perspective until late in the eighteenth century.

The Frewens were also not happy with the Hanoverian accession. None of the family was in orders at the time of the Revolution. Both Thankful Frewen and Stephen were ordained within the next ten years, but it is not clear with what measure of seared or uneasy consciences they struggled over subscription to the oaths before taking such a decisive step. They were probably 'sentimental' Jacobites. 'They opposed the Whig oligarchy and fought against any further relief for Dissenters, but when the moment of decision came in 1745, they preferred to be resigned and wistful, rather than to gamble on a military venture to restore the Stuarts. They lived in a Whig world, and, though they deplored Whiggery and all it stood for, they coped with its existence and even befriended its proponents.'[29]

It is instructive to observe that although the Frewens maintained an emphasis on sacramentalism, and on the importance of communion, with exhortations to their parishioners to partake frequently, they, like the majority of other Georgian clergymen, only made it a quarterly practice. The decision to do so appears to have been the result of practical considerations of who would come and how it was to be paid for, and was not an indicator of decreased ministerial sacramentalism. Small parishes did not usually find it feasible to provide more frequent communions. It was much easier to do so in the larger centres of population.

In their sacramentalism the Frewens also stressed the other supremely important holy occasion for them when God touched human life in a special way: baptism. For Thomas Frewen baptism was the regenerating sacrament, when children were 'born again of the water and of the Holy Spirit and so made Christians'. Grace came to people through the mystery of baptism before it ever reached them through logic and closely reasoned sermons. Not that they despised sermons: far from it, for their sermons were usually steeped in scripture, rational and well argued, and yet quite frequently emotional as well.

The High Church and Low Church parties among the clergy which emerged between 1697 and 1702 disagreed over the correct relationship of the church with the state. By the time Anne came to the throne in 1702, High Churchmen were becoming convinced that a political solution to most of the problems of the Church of England was the only way ahead. They favoured a close partnership between Convocation and a favourably disposed Parliament. The Low Churchmen, on the other hand, were profoundly sceptical about political action and political panaceas. They accepted the need for state assistance in certain administrative and financial matters, but in general they thought that the church needed to work out her own destiny. The church should accept two unpalatable truths: it had only survived in 1688 by turning its back on political principles, and in 1689 it had, in effect, been partially disestablished. The clash of views was publicly and painfully demonstrated in the 'Convocation controversy'.

When the Lower House of the newly summoned Convocation of 1689 expressed furious opposition to the proposed measures for Comprehension and Toleration the Convocation was prorogued. 'Thenceforward, while Parliament grew daily in stature and prestige, it seemed that Convocation must wither away, leaving the lower clergy with no medium to express their convictions and get rid of their frustrations.'[30] This gave scope for Francis Atterbury to display his journalistic flair, and to assume a central role as the stormy petrel of the

High Church revolt. By doing so he helped in the formation of a new High Church party as one aspect of a new Tory party which remorselessly attacked William's ministers.

His opening salvo, which began the Convocation controversy, was the publication in 1696 of a pamphlet entitled, *A Letter to a Convocation Man*. It rehearsed, in a pungent and highly readable style, all the grievances of the church, and demanded as the sole remedy an active and effective Convocation. The reply from William Wake, Canon of Christ Church and Rector of St James's, Picadilly, which was requested by Archbishop Tenison, was long and tedious, and in the event disastrous for the case it presented, for it appeared to be a completely Erastian argument, and it aroused widespread anger. It provoked Atterbury to a reply which only emerged after two years of study and research. *The Rights, Powers and Privileges of an English Convocation* (1700), was a *tour de force* which, in combination with his previous work on the subject, helped to establish him as the champion of Convocation against the crown, and of the clergy against the bishops. His whole purpose was to make Convocation a means whereby 'urgently needed measures could be taken to restore the authority and status of the Church'.[31] But he was also the champion of the High Church party, and by 1702, in the short span of about five years, party lines were clearly drawn. 'High and Low Church parties had consolidated in and out of Convocation with these labels firmly attached, in much the form they were to retain for the rest of Queen Anne's reign.'[32]

Within Convocation itself there was a protracted struggle between the bishops in the Upper House and the High Church majority in the Lower House. Party division was also manifested in the matter of preferments, which were quite frequently viewed and discussed in terms of party ambitions. The greatest tragedy was that church party politics became the subject matter of preaching. 'Clerics who conducted their quarrels with so much license in print were not likely to keep them out of the pulpit. And so it proved. The least edifying of all the spectacles presented by a Church divided into High and Low factions was the prostitution of the pulpit, particularly in Queen Anne's reign, to blatantly party ends. Henry Sacheverell's crime of 1709 was but the offence of hundreds of his fellow-divines writ large.'[33]

Dr Sacheverell was a High Church Anglican clergyman, a Tory zealot, a Fellow of Magdalen College, Oxford, and somewhat of a firebrand. 'Strikingly handsome, fastidiously dressed, he seemed always in evidence about college and university business. Contemporaries testified to his impressive appearance in the pulpit and his strong, clear voice. But virtually no one in Oxford appears actually to have liked him; indeed he was universally recognized as overbearing, ambitious and avid for personal publicity. What attracted the ordinary MAs to him was the constant zeal with which he propagated his violent tory opinions. He had the temerity to assert openly what others said in private company.'[34] He had obtained a reputation for turbulence, passion and arrogance, and was marked out as a reinforcement to be reckoned with on the side of the High Church-Tory controversialists as a consequence of some vehement sermons and pamphlets before he preached his seditious sermon on Guy Fawkes' Day, 1709, at St Paul's Cathedral, on the text, 'In peril among False Brethren'. It was a diatribe in which he 'launched himself into a furious rant against dissenters, occasional conformists, unlicensed schools, "moderate" bishops, Burnet, Hoadley and all who gainsaid the primitive doctrine of loyalty and obedience'.[35] It was explosive material when seen against the back-cloth of party political strife and the contention between High and Low churchmen which we have just considered, and an incredible hundred thousand copies of the sermon were sold. Nonetheless, the whole affair may have passed off as a seven days' wonder if the government had not decided to impeach the preacher, and to bring him to trial in a most public way in Westminster Hall before the House of Lords in March 1710. In doing so the Whigs hoped to initiate a grand national debate on the nature of the Revolution and of political authority. It could have been an astute move whereby the stigma of Jacobitism was branded clearly and lastingly on the Tories, the majority of whom were not Jacobites but squires, parsons and others of a similar social standing who were concerned to preserve a way of life, and were not zealous for a Stuart succession. No one anticipated the remarkable and universal popular clamour which would be engendered in favour of 'the Doctor'.

The trial took place amidst much public turmoil. Pamphlets, broadsheets and cartoons abounded. The cry went up that the church was attacked and a priest was being persecuted. There were riots throughout the country. Crowds shouted for 'High Church and Dr Sacheverell' as Lords and Members of Parliament made their way to and from the trial. Francis Atterbury and Sir Simon Harcourt took over the entire case and its advocacy; and they provided a brilliant defence. They claimed that Sacheverell was 'an ordinary priest grievously misrepresented by spiteful opponents; he had done nothing more than proclaim that teaching on loyalty and obedience which had ever distinguished

Anglican beliefs; he did accept the Revolution as a providential work of Almighty God; he prayed for the Queen with his whole heart; and he looked to the House of Hanover as the only safeguard for the Protestant religion'.[36] It was a triumph, and at the end of the speech for the defence Tory peers wept openly. The doctor was found guilty, but by the narrow margin of seventeen votes. He escaped with the derisory sentence of three years' suspension from preaching; and there were rejoicings throughout the length and breadth of the land. Church bells sounded out, and toasts were drunk. Low churchmen and Whigs expediently remained indoors. The hero of the hour went on a triumphal tour through the Midlands and was received rapturously by the Tory mob.

High Churchmen began to feel that their day had at last come. Politically the Dr Sacheverell affair paved the way for the defeat of the Whigs in 1710, and their replacement by the last truly Tory ministry the country was to experience for a hundred years. The victory was a culmination rather than a dawn in the feverish search by the High Church clergy for a political solution to their problems. The Tory ministry was short-lived, the surge of popularity quickly waned, and the high hopes of High Churchmen soon ended with frustration and inertia. Francis Atterbury had been an extreme example of hitching the High Church star to the Tory, and even Jacobite, waggon, but many late seventeenth-century and early eighteenth century High Churchmen did likewise. It proved to be a religio-political identity which was to contribute to their waning influence during the next half century and more.

It was not long before another sermon ignited further party conflict within the church, and also within the wider political community. It was on 31 March 1717 that Benjamin Hoadly preached before the King on John 18.36, 'My kingdom is not of this world'. It vies with the sermon by Sacheverell as the most famous, or notorious, example of eighteenth-century pulpit oratory.

Benjamin Hoadly was a Low Churchman. 'His was a Latitudinarianism from which the mystical element had gone, leaving only the rationalism and moralism.'[37] He was the very antithesis of Sacheverell, not only in his theology and churchmanship, but in his physique, being a little man and a cripple compared with the tall, imposing stature of the Doctor; but they were both masters of the ambivalent and enigmatic. Hoadly was a poor preacher but an able pamphleteer. He could clothe his ideas in written language which attracted widespread attention in the coffee houses of the country.

The sermon which caused such a rumpus was based on an examination of the fate of the word 'kingdom'. Through constant usage and with the passing of time, it had acquired connotations which contradicted its original meaning and significance. Hoadley attempted to pin down its true biblical meaning:

> The *Kingdom of Christ*, is the same with the *Church of Christ* . . . He himself is King . . . He is himself the sole *Law-giver* to his Subjects: . . . the sole *Judge* of their *Behaviour*, in the affairs of *Conscience* and *Eternal Salvation* . . . in the affairs of Conscience and Eternal Salvation he hath left behind him no visible, humane *Authority*, no *Vice Gerents*, who can be said properly to supply his Place – no *Interpreters*, upon whom his Subjects are absolutely to depend: no *Judges* over the Consciences of Religion of his people . . . to set up any other *Authority* in *His* Kingdom, to which his Subjects are indispensably and absolutely obliged to Submit their Consciences, or their Conduct, in what is properly called Religion [destroys the authority of Christ . . . Christ is] *King* in his own Kingdom: he is sole *Law-giver to his Subjects and Sole Judge* in matters relating to salvation.[38]

Hoadly, in common with others such as A. A. Sykes, was primarily concerned to restrict the power of civil and ecclesiastical rulers, but especially the latter, and to serve the interests of religious toleration.[39] What especially attracted criticism was his apparent assertion that 'sincerity' was the sole criterion of religion. In his defence, it is significant that he 'spoke in terms of christianity, not of any truth there might be in other religions or atheism. Within christianity, he was attempting to ensure toleration in the same way as Locke, by arguing that true religion cannot be created by external sanctions or persecution.'[40] Criticism of him secondly focussed upon his imputed denial of all authority in the church. He claimed that he always qualified any statement on the subject with such words as 'proper' and 'absolute'. He also claimed that he was only concerned in his description of the church with matters of 'conscience' and 'eternal salvation'; and the church to which he mostly referred was 'invisible'. He denied that his strictures affected the existence or powers of 'visible' churches such as the Church of England; but he was vague in defining the powers which are proper to a Christian church and ministry; and indeed he failed to distinguish clearly between an 'invisible' and a 'visible' church.

Convocation, the Lower House of which was antagonistic to him because of his previous utterances, and above all for his work against the Nonjurors, which was in effect an assault upon High Church principles, condemned Hoadly as 'tending to subvert all government and discipline in the church and to reduce this kingdom to anarchy and chaos'.[41] He was charged with denying the royal supremacy; taking away all authority from the church; and contradicting the visibility of the church as affirmed in Articles 19 and 20 of the Thirty-Nine Articles. It was also widely agreed that Hoadly's sermon was designed to make way for the repeal of the Test Act. The most devastating reply to Hoadly was furnished by the then quite unknown William Law in his celebrated *Three Letters to the Bishop of Bangor*. It was a masterpiece of lucid and flowing prose; ruthless in its argument, and among the most noteworthy of a fairly small group of theological polemics in English literature. But it misrepresented Hoadly, took texts out of their context, and drew outrageous conclusions from statements which were never intended by the original author.

Hoadly attracted intense venom in part because he was seen as a prominent representative of the much maligned Latitudinarians. The Latitude Men had affinities with the Cambridge Platonists[42] but need to be distinguished from them. Both groups were latitudinarian in temper, but many even of the first Latitudinarians, such as John Tillotson and Simon Patrick, were not Platonists. The Latitudinarians eschewed extremes. Their watchword was 'Let your moderation be known to all men' (Phil. 2.5) 'They emphasized the relationship between religion and morality, between piety and civic virtue. They were tolerant of differences, stressed the common core of Christianity and placed the creeds and dogma at the margins of their concerns.'[43]

But caution is needed in using the term. It was rarely used by contemporaries, and church historians are now less confident than Norman Sykes and scholars of his time in writing of 'the dominance of the Latitudinarian tradition in the Hanoverian Church' as if it was a truism.[44] It is not clear if it has much validity as a historical label to be applied to a group of churchmen in the late seventeenth century and throughout much of the eighteenth century; and if so to whom it refers. It is no longer perceived as having the cohesion and distinctiveness which was formerly attributed to it. It can no longer be viewed as describing a homogeneous block of clerical opinion, which was rational, informed by natural philosophy and science, opposed to patristic studies, sat loose to church doctrines, favoured a comprehensive inclusion of Dissenters in the establishment, and was Low Church and politically Whig. It can be seen as containing these elements in varying proportions according to its particular manifestation, but should it be given a wide or narrow definition? Should it be restricted to the theological liberalism of Tillotson and his followers, or given a broad connotation to denote 'little more than a low-key piety, whose tone was "homespun and practical", "rational and ethical rather than emotional, dogmatic, or mystical", adjectives which could fit the preaching and pastoral outlook of a vast number of priests over the centuries'.[45] It has been treated as a theological position, and even a movement; a school of liberal religious thought with well-defined tenets,[46] while others have presented it as merely a state of mind.[47] Norman Sykes correctly pointed out that because latitudinarianism was a 'theological temper' it could transcend 'differences of political persuasion'.[48]

Perhaps it is best not to be mesmerized by a single word description, but to recognize that in the hundred years after the Revolution there was a category of broad churchmen, as to some extent there has been in every generation since then, who helped more than in some other ages to set the tone of church life, but who did not dominate the scene. They were not of a single type, with identical views; they differed in the things they stressed, but they had certain characteristics in common which differentiated them from other churchmen. They believed in the importance of free enquiry; they laid great store by toleration; they were not prepared to fight over theological niceties, and in fact preferred to keep their theology uncomplicated; they gave a prominent place in their hierarchy of values to good works; they found any form of 'enthusiasm' obnoxious, and especially religious enthusiasm; and they supported the concept of a comprehensive, inclusive Church of England. The 'Latitudinarians' not only shared certain fundamental beliefs, but they represented an attitude of mind which was a fusion of various elements. 'First, there was an emphasis on simplicity and rationality; second, there was the belief that reason and revelation spoke the same language, and produced the same enlightenment, for the "understanding of man is the candle of the Lord"; third, that the essential truths were contained in the Bible; fourth, the optimism that these essential truths were accessible to all men; fifth, that apart from these truths, all other truths were matters of opinion; finally, that men may know God in various ways, and that God would not be offended by a belief sincerely held.'[49] Here was a blend of Protestantism and Christian humanism; an approach which ran counter to the religious absolutism of the Roman Catholics and the Puritans but which, nevertheless, had its own synthesis of faith and logical consistency.

Arians, Socinians and Unitarians

The emergence of Arians, Socinians and Unitarians in the late seventeenth and early eighteenth centuries needs to be placed within a philosophical context in which the dominant figures were Thomas Hobbes and John Locke.

The shadow of Thomas Hobbes hung over post-Revolution England and lingered for the remainder of the long eighteenth century. In particular it was his theories as expounded in *Leviathan* which were at the core of his influence.[50] The book was published in 1651 and immediately caused a stir. Even some of his former admirers were affronted, and one of his old acquaintances, the Anglican theologian Henry Hammond, described it as 'a farrago of Christian Atheism'. Hobbes shared with Descartes an acceptance of the sceptics' argument that we can have no direct and truthful experience of the external world. They both considered that all we can perceive is the internal activity of our own brain. Nonetheless, unlike Descartes who suggested that in fact there might not be an external world, and we could be like dreamers who only think that what they experience is real, Hobbes asserted that the mind can be satisfied that there are material objects outside itself. But here we start to touch upon what was so controversial in his philosophy, for he maintained that the experiences of the mind were caused by the motion of external objects, and there was no need to invoke the idea of God. There could be no question of words referring meaningfully to any features outside the experiences of a human mind; so the traditional scholastic idea that words might refer to abstract 'essences' or 'universals' was meaningless. He was a latter-day nominalist.[51]

For Hobbes the only principle on which all men would spontaneously agree was the right to preserve ourselves. He believed that the basic self-protective instinct of men would make them pacific towards one another, but their independency of judgment about the world would lead to conflict. Independent judgment about most matters of fact must therefore be eliminated. In cases of uncertainty independent judgment must be transferred to a common decision-maker: the sovereign. This sovereign would induce his subjects to agree on what they termed 'good' and 'bad'; and would in effect possess unlimited ideological authority on issues of morality and religion as well as day-to-day politics. Here, in such transfer of power, was the second cause for alarm at his theories. Furthermore, as Hobbes expounded his philosophy,

'Christianity became merely another socially sanctioned way of expressing the feelings of natural religion, and the sovereign could interpret
Scripture or determine doctrine without paying any attention to
ordained clergymen.'[52]

If Hobbes cast his shadow over the eighteenth century, John Locke
was a most powerful presence. He was instrumental in promoting the
radicalism in politics and religion which was a characteristic facet of
life throughout the century, in the periodic surge of theism, Arianism
and Socinianism, and in the pervasive influence of rationalism which
attracted the sobriquet 'Age of Reason' to describe the essential tone
of the period. Locke's philosophy permeated the whole of society. It
profoundly affected the mind of Wesley, and it found various literary
expressions, as in the novels of Lawrence Sterne. The work which
probably more than any other had such potent ramifications and
repercussions was *An Essay Concerning Human Understanding*. It
'exerted a tremendous influence on theological and metaphysical
debate amongst the Hanoverian clergy, an influence which allows the
intellectual historian to find a way into the cast of the clerical mind'[53]
from Locke's time until the late eighteenth century.

'It is', said Locke, 'an established opinion amongst men that there are
in the *understanding* certain *innate principles*, some primary notions
. . . characters, as it were, stamped upon the mind of man, which the
soul receives in its first being and brings into the world with it.'[54] He
then provided cogent arguments in an attempt to convince unprejudiced
readers of the falseness of this supposition. Having dismissed the concept of innateness in general, he went on to consider particular implications of such a denial. He dismissed the innateness of the conviction that
God is to be worshipped. He proceeded to an even more crucial denial
of the innateness of belief in God.

> If any *idea* can be imagined *innate*, the *idea of God* may, of all
> others, for many reasons be thought so, since it is hard to conceive
> how there should be innate moral principles without an innate *idea* of
> *deity*. Without a notion of a law-giver, it is impossible to have a
> notion of a law and an obligation to observe it. Besides the atheists
> taken notice of amongst the ancients and left branded upon the
> records of history, hath not navigation discovered, in these latter
> ages, whole nations . . . amongst whom there was to be found no
> notion of a god, no religion.[55]

In Book II Locke further examined the validity of the belief in innateness. He postulated a blank mind, without any *ideas*, and asked how it came to be furnished with ideas and all the materials of reason and knowledge. He answered his own question in one word, *experience*. 'This great source of most of the *ideas* we have, depending wholly upon our senses, and derived by them to the understanding, I call SENSATION.' The other fountain from which experience furnishes the understanding with ideas is 'the *perception of the operations of our own minds* within us, as it is employed about the ideas it has got . . . But as I call the other *sensation*, so I call this REFLECTION'.[56]

Locke's philosophy in general, and in particularly his religious ideas which he developed in *The Reasonableness of Christianity as Delivered in the Scriptures* (1695), provided a framework of thinking for two of his associates, John Toland and Anthony Collins, who were to become eminent Deists. He also greatly influenced William Whiston and Samuel Clarke, who were to play leading roles in the promotion of 'Arianism' from within the Church of England fold. Locke maintained that the only secure basis for Christianity is reasonableness, although he accepted the biblical miracles as proofs of the divine origin of the scriptures. Reason was, however, the final arbiter in the acceptance of the supernatural and in the interpretation of scripture. The core of Christianity is the acknowledgment of Christ as Messiah, who was sent into the world mainly in order to spread the true knowledge of God and of our duties; and all other doctrines are of secondary importance and incapable of conclusive proof. But Locke was not a deist. He acknowledged that there were things which were beyond reason, and which came within the province of special revelation. He conceded that there are

many things wherein we have very imperfect notions, or none at all; and other things, of whose past, present, or future existence, by the natural use of our faculties, we can have no knowledge at all: these, as being beyond the discovery of our natural faculties and above *reason*, are, when revealed, *the proper matter of faith*.[57]

Sir Isaac Newton also had a massive impact on the process of rationalization which was about to invade the church from within as well as from without. Newton remained an active member of the Church of England, but he departed from orthodoxy; and his insistence on the unity of the one God, the Governor of the Universe, stimulated and encouraged the 'Arians'.

William Whiston was a leading proponent of Lockean and

Newtonian rationalism in the post-Revolution Church of England, and one of the early Anglican Arianizers. He was a highly intelligent Cambridge academic who combined feeble judgment with utter faith in the soundness of his own opinions. In his *New Theory of the Earth* (1696) he provided 'an explanation of the Deluge on Newtonian lines, which foundered on a howler about hydrostatics'.[58] He succeeded Newton in the Lucasian chair of mathematics, but it .was in the field of theology and church history that he aroused high dudgeon. He conferred on the fourth-century *Apostolic Constitutions* an apostolic authority of canonical status. Then, more disconcertingly, and in defiance of history and the teaching of his own church, he declared that the true christology of the fourth-century was not that of Athanasius. He ascribed the truth if not to Arius, then at least to Eusebius.[59] He was deprived of his chair and banished from the university. In further writings he aroused the ire of Convocation with his unwelcome view of the nature of the primitive church. For a time he was friendly with Samuel Clarke who was to be the foremost 'Arianizer' in the early eighteenth-century church, and the chief target of those who opposed the view that Christianity could largely be derived from the exercise of human reason.

The tenor of Clarke's theology became evident in 1709 in his choice of disputation topics for his Cambridge doctorate of divinity: 'No Article of the Christian Faith delivered in the Holy Scriptures is Disagreeable to Right Reason' and 'Without the Liberty of Human Actions there can be no Religion'.[60] His methodology was governed by the conviction that 'the central truths of Christianity were evident to anyone willing to examine the evidence impartially in the same way that a natural philosopher could appeal to the accuracy of his data'. In his 1704 Boyle lectures, and elsewhere, he 'stated plainly his desire to follow a method as near as possible to that of mathematics and hence he adopted a deductive structure, each demonstration having its own propositions and proofs'. He was concerned 'to minimise as much as possible those elements of Christianity which could not be reconciled with reason'.[61]

In Clarke's scheme of theology there was little emphasis on revelation as separate and distinct from natural knowledge. The primary end of Christianity was to promote adherence to the natural moral order. In common with the prevailing views of the age in which he lived, Clarke believed in the verbal inspiration and infallibility of scripture, in the literal fulfilment of the Old Testament prophecies, and in miracles; and these were, in fact, the most certain demonstrations of the truth of the Christian revelation. 'In addition, he was convinced that the Gospels set forth a fully rational religion which was entirely congruent with man's natural reason, and only went beyond it to give information that was outside the range of such reason.'[62] It was not, then, that he discarded the bedrock on which the theology of the church was built; but he went beyond mere acceptance of theological doctrines. He sought to scrutinize doctrines and to make them acceptable to reason. In so doing, he was considered by some to have overstepped the accepted bounds and to have fallen into heresy.

There were two issues which particularly engaged Clarke's attention, and which established his reputation as a heretical 'Arian': his view of the accepted doctrine of the Trinity, and his opinion on submission to the Thirty-Nine Articles as required of Church of England clergy.

It was after he had delivered the 1704 Boyle lectures that Clarke's thought turned to the doctrine of the Trinity; and he began to have doubts concerning the official teaching on this central topic of the Christian religion. As a consequence of his study of the primitive church, and in part as a result of the influence of Sir Isaac Newton, he started seriously to question the pronouncement of the Council of Nicaea, and the definition given by the Athanasian Creed of the Trinity. It was not a propitious time to have such doubts. Feeling ran high on the matter at the beginning of the eighteenth century, and there was a very decided public hostility to any unorthodox views on such a key tenet of belief. The second half of the seventeenth century had seen a revival of the Trinitarian controversy. Heretical views emanated from Poland, where Faustus Socinus taught what was essentially an Arian doctrine, that Christ was a creature and not the Son of God in the sense stipulated by the Council of Nicaea. Unlike the Arians, he denied that Christ had any pre-existence before his incarnation; Christ was simply a man whose life showed exemplary obedience to the will of God. Socinus rejected the doctrine of vicarious atonement. By the early eighteenth century anti-Trinitarian teaching was rife, with Arians, Socinians and Unitarians vigorously proclaiming their unorthodox doctrines. The Unitarians would have nothing to do with the doctrine of the Trinity or with belief in the divinity of Christ. They favoured a concept of the unipersonality of God. It is not surprising that in England, as elsewhere, such views were seen as destructive of the distinctive dogmas of Christianity, and were roundly and firmly repudiated. The church and the state were clear and determined in their official opposition to such heresy. The Toleration Act of 1689 had not extended its beneficial provisions to those holding anti-Trinitarian views, and by identifying with them Clarke was inviting fierce and unmitigated opposition and abuse.

Clarke maintained that the Athanasian Creed was wrong and that its declaration of three co-equal and co-eternal Persons in the one Trinity was unscriptural. He concluded that scripture presented a supremacy in the Father, who alone fulfilled all that was contained in the very concept of the godhead. He alone could properly be called God. The Son and the Spirit were subordinate to him, and those who asserted that the Son and the Spirit, together with the Father, constituted the self-existent being, had fallen into the heresy of Sabellianism (a second and third century heresy which asserted that in the Godhead the only differentiation was a succession of modes or operations). He was forthrightly condemned in Convocation and by orthodox writers, most notably by the formidable and persistent Daniel Waterland. By his learning, and to some extent by his arguments, Waterland rallied the clergy to the Nicene and Athanasian Creeds, and helped to rescue the ancient rationale and long tradition of God as Trinity in Unity.

The practice of imposing tests and requiring subscription to the Thirty-Nine Articles continued into the eighteenth century despite considerable doubts concerning its value. Clarke objected mainly on the ground that both the Articles and the Creeds were the creations of men. It was nonsense to insist on subscription to what were fallible human formularies when at the same time the perfect and infallible word of God was available. Subscription to the Bible alone was justified and sensible.

As we have noted, Clarke was in many ways orthodox. Perhaps his main failing was that he allowed rationalism to dominate. 'The weakness of Clarke's rationalism is that it does not do justice to the element of the numinous in religion, the feeling of awe in the presence of the deity, the transcendence of the divine nature beyond anything we can conceive. Nor does he appreciate the strength of feeling and dedication that can be found in devotion to a personal Saviour.'[63] He spoke from within the church as a churchman concerned to promote the Christian faith in a form, and in a way which he thought right. During his time there were others who turned their brand of rationalism against the church. 'While Socinianism and Arianism were Christian heresies, Deism was essentially anti-Christian and, in addition, ruthlessly anti-clerical.'[64]

Attack from without – the 'sceptical crisis', Deism and Atheism

By the end of the seventeenth century the Church of England was facing a 'sceptical crisis'. But its severity must not be overstated. I have already considered the potentially erosive effects of the philosophy of Hobbes and Locke on the fundamental presuppositions of Christianity, and I have touched upon the consequences of Newtonian science. I will now look at the latter a little more closely.[65]

In late seventeenth England there was not the same gulf as in France and other countries between a group of self-consciously enlightened thinkers and the defenders of established tradition. There was a considerable measure of harmony which was underpinned by 'the *rapprochement* that had been achieved between secular learning, notably science, and the established Church of England'.[66] In England, in contrast to France, neither Francis Bacon nor Isaac Newton were widely invoked in a campaign to undermine Christian faith. There were no English encyclopaedists. During the half-century after the Restoration, or perhaps more pertinently the foundation of the Royal Society in 1660, an alliance was forged between Newtonian natural philosophy and Anglican apologetics which remained an important aspect of English intellectual life until the mid-nineteenth century. As we have seen, all was not calm and unruffled within the Anglican fold as some of the 'apostles of reason' strove to reconcile Christian faith with the demands of reason, but such heated debates were conducted within the overall framework of this underlying alliance. The onslaught of Deism, which I am about to consider, was a severe trial for the church; but again its advocates could not build upon a basic disharmony, or battle, between 'science and religion'. There were times when it appeared that the anti-Christian forces might be heading towards victory, but these were short-lived, and their defeat was decisive.

The same may be said for the confrontation of the church with the new 'science of religion', which recent scholarship has unearthed as a significant feature of late seventeenth and early eighteenth-century intellectual and ecclesiastical life. One aspect of the Enlightenment was the emergence in Western thought of the concepts of 'religion' and 'religions' as we now understand them. 'The great revolutions in science and religion which took place in the sixteenth and seventeenth centuries thus paved the way for the development of a secular study of the religions, and equally importantly, of a concept of "religion" which could link together and relate the apparently disparate religious beliefs and practices found in the empirical "religions".[67] This particular 'sceptical crisis' had been developing in the first half of the seventeenth century, when a debate was generated about responses to the poly-genetic and polytheistic evidences. The new data seemed to show that the varieties of mankind were not consistent with the picture presented by biblical history, either chronologically or geographically; and like-wise that the wide range of beliefs throughout the world was not com-patible with the biblical account. Serious questions were thus raised concerning the whole Jewish and Christian framework.[68]

Given such sixteenth and seventeenth century developments in philosophy and science, the relationship between science, scientific philosophy and religion, and the appearance of biblical criticism and the 'science of religion', it was inevitable that at some time there would emerge ideas, and even a body of opinion, of the type which has been designated Deism. The term itself, like Latitudinarianism, is difficult to define or to pin down historically. It was, 'like Gnosticism in the early Church . . . rather a tendency of thought than a consistent body of opinions'.[69] In essence it was an attempt to synthesize some or all of the trends I have just reviewed. It was the proclamation of the superiority of universal natural religion over the traditions of revelation. It was an appeal 'to the general religious consciousness of mankind as furnishing the few essential doctrines necessary for the conduct of man in society and the education of his soul for the future state of rewards and punishments'.[70] Ancillary to this attack upon the fundamental premises of revealed religion was the heaping of ridicule upon the different theo-logical creeds which were formulated by the various Christian sects, which manifestly demonstrated that Christians were not even able to agree on the exegesis of their inspired biblical oracles. The Deists poured scorn on the idea of God as the author of a revelation which provoked such bitter disputes over its interpretation as that between Calvinists and Arminians.

'The first clear pointer after the Revolution to the fact that Deism was on the march was the publication by Charles Blount of a book signifi-cantly titled *The Oracles of Reason*.'[71] In it he argued that the only true beliefs were those which derived from experience or from propositions which were self-evidently demonstrable by reason. Blount was dis-missed by many as blasphemous but lightweight. The same could not be said of John Toland, and both Anglicans and Nonconformists conceded that Deism was a threat to be taken very seriously when he published *Christianity not Mysterious* in 1696. It was a frontal assault upon

Christianity and one of the most sensational books to issue from the press in England in the entire seventeenth century. Toland stripped so much away from Christianity that there was in effect nothing left. He argued that revelation must be intelligible and what is revealed must be possible, whether God or man is the revealer. He went on to declare that if revealed religion contradicted human reason, as he made plain he thought it did, then the pronounced 'truths' must be false. Although he did not specify particular dogmas of religious revelation, the implications of his premises for such fundamental 'mysteries' as the incarnation and the resurrection were only too evident. The book caused an uproar. Even a pronounced liberal like Thomas Firmin was scandalized. The book was in effect the opening salvo in a protracted controversy. Pamphlets poured from the press. A number of academically distinguished Anglican, Nonjuror and dissenting controversialists entered the lists against those who attacked Christian orthodoxy, including Francis Atterbury, Richard Bentley, George Berkeley, Joseph Butler, Edward Chandler, Samuel Clarke, William Law, Thomas Sherlock, Arthur Sykes, William Warburton and Daniel Waterland.

Other Deists, including Anthony Collins, Thomas Woolston and William Wollaston, joined in the battle of words and arguments. Collins concentrated on questioning the credibility of the biblical records. In his book *A Discourse upon the Grounds and Reasons of the Christian Religion* he took up the argument from prophecy. 'To his mind it was a clear case that the prophecies which were supposed to refer to Christ had a relation only to contemporary events, that none of them had been literally fulfilled, that it was only by the use of the allegorical method of interpretation that any allusion could be found in them to the being whom the Christians claimed as Messiah.' Woolston endeavoured to dispose of the historical character of miracles in his *Six Discourses on the Miracles*. He tried to do so by 'a fanciful process of allegorizing and of mystical interpretation, combined with a peculiarly blasphemous and scurrilous method of treating the subject'. Wollaston took a different line in his attempt to undermine the Christian doctrinal superstructure. His book *The Religion of Nature Delineated* (1724) was a closely argued treatise, considered by some as perhaps the most impressive intellectual performance of the whole Deist output. The climax was reached with the publication in 1730 of Matthew Tindal's provocative book *Christianity as Old as the Creation*. The author declared roundly that 'the religion of nature is absolutely perfect; Revelation can neither add to nor take away from its perfection'. If the law of nature is perfect it cannot receive, and does not need, any additions; if it is not, 'does it not argue want of wisdom in the Legislator in first enacting such an imperfect law and then letting it continue imperfect from age to age, and at last thinking to make it absolutely perfect by adding some merely positive and arbitrary precepts ?' For Tindal there was no problem of a contradiction between natural and revealed religion; he simply identified Christianity with the law of nature. 'God never intended mankind should be without a religion, or could ordain an imperfect religion; there must have been from the beginning a religion most perfect, which mankind at all times was capable of knowing; Christianity is this perfect, original religion.' To the extent that the creeds and theologies of the churches did not concur with this simple religion they were at fault; they were corrupt declensions from the pure original, or spurious additions to it. It was the theological parallel to the political philosophy of Rousseau, with his noble savage, whose original capacity for perfect citizenship had been corrupted by the retrogressive influence of civilization. The spiritual understanding of the simple believer in natural religion had been well nigh extinguished by the immoral inventions imposed upon the pure original faith by a self-seeking priesthood.[72]

'In the battle thus joined between the champions of natural and revealed religion, the defenders of Christianity essayed the dual strategy of demonstrating that natural religion was neither so clear, so perfect, nor so universal as the Deists professed, and that the evidence of the divine commission to Moses and Christ, the authors of the Old and New Covenants of the Jews, was sufficient for belief in the doctrines of their proclamation.'[73] In his anonymously issued *Scripture Vindicated* Waterland attempted to reply to Tindal in a work which was learned but hardly devastating. He tried to demonstrate from a wide range of modern and patristic biblical teaching that the God depicted in the Old Testament, and in the orthodox doctrine of the atonement, is indeed perfect in truth, justice and mercy.

A more impressive, but perhaps too intricate riposte came from the pen of William Law. In a closely argued work, *The Case of Religion and Reason or Natural Religion fairly and fully stated* (1731), he defended both natural religion and, within limits, the use of reason. But he also 'defends God from the charge of caprice and arbitrariness, and revealed religion in its doctrine of God and our redemption in Christ, and especially in the doctrines of a vicarious atonement and sacrifice'.[74] He attacked Tindal's arguments at their most vulnerable spot: their almost exclusive focus upon rationality, and their failure to take account of the irrationality of much human behaviour, and the corruptions of the human heart.

The most telling response to Deism came in the form of a work which established itself as a classic of orthodox apologetic: Bishop Joseph Butler's *Analogy of Religion* (1736). It transcended in importance what it achieved in its day. It was perhaps the one hammer-blow which, more than any other, caused the rapid and almost complete demise of Deism. It was a work of major and permanent significance philosophically and theologically. Butler accorded a central place of honour to reason as 'the only faculty we have wherewith to judge concerning anything, even revelation itself'. 'First. It is the province of reason to judge of the morality of the scripture . . . whether it contains things plainly contradictory to wisdom, justice or goodness; to what the light of nature teaches us of God . . . Secondly. Reason is able to judge, and must, of the evidence of revelation, and of the objections urged against that evidence.'[75] Nonetheless, although he elevated the faculty of reason to such a high level, he was insistent on its limitations, on its function to serve an overriding moral purpose, and on its supreme purpose as a means whereby we apprehend transcendent truth. In this respect, as in others, his view contrasted with the secularized notion of reason propagated by Locke and his devotees.

In his argument with the Deists Butler also developed his lastingly influential concept of probability. By means of it he attempted to hold together the rational and the moral. He came to consider probability as the guide to the interpretation of life, and the way of providing at least limited assurance in our earthly state of moral probation. What appealed to contemporaries in such a notion, and has continued to make Butler's philosophy attractive to countless people in the succeeding centuries, is his honesty and realism. He wanted to satisfy his own mind and conscience, and in so doing he acknowledged that there is a scepticism which is inseparably bound up with the Christian faith. The concept of probability was an attempt to face up to the whole matter of doubt which Butler saw as inherent in life, and to which the Christian was not immune. It was part of a comprehensive philosophy which seemed to many to address the real difficulties of life; and, in the short term, it effectively met the Deist challenge not just in specific ways on particular points at issue, but at a more fundamental level. It was a triumph, but it did not herald the total and final collapse of deism. The underlying religious and philosophical orientation of the Deists lingered on, and it reappeared in the sceptical views of individuals throughout the century. It manifested itself in a precise and public way in the late eighteenth-century teaching of Tom Paine, with his alliance of infidelity and radical politics.

Butler's philosophy provided an orientation and a framework for thinking which was received by many as expressing the essential ethos of Anglicanism with its restraint, its steady and cautious approach and its determination to continue quietly and humbly serving others and doing good, but not prying into mysteries too deep for us. As such, it served to set the prevailing tone of the Hanoverian church.

Some late seventeenth century and early eighteenth-century observers saw 'Arianism and Socinianism as half-way houses, and Deism as a later staging-post, along the road to "plain Atheism".'[76] Churchmen of all hues believed that atheism was advancing malevolently in the 1690s. During the reign of James 11 the prevailing fear had been of the advance of Roman Catholicism. This was replaced as the dominant concern of some churchmen by the more insidious progress of disbelief. 'Instead of Popery', wrote William Sherlock in 1697, 'men are now running into the other extremes of atheism, Deism, and a contempt for all reveal'd religion.'[77] There was perhaps a rapid progression from anti-Trinitarian thinking to atheism or infidelity. Until the late seventeenth century Socinian thinking merely had a precarious toehold in England; until after the Revolution it had been all but imperceptible to the literate public. But in the history of the Church of England and of the Dissenting denominations from the 1690s to the 1730s purveyors of heterodox doctrines keep appearing on the scene. It is as if a fifth column within the orthodox bodies was there awaiting every opportunity to declare itself. For perhaps the first time in English church history there is a sense of threat from within: not the threat of one theological view in opposition to another, or even of a particular heresy re-appearing. Rather it was the questioning from within of the very fundamentals of the faith. It appears that 'anti-clericalism, religious deviationism in all its forms, and even bare-faced irreligion all gained ground in the years immediately after the Glorious Revolution . . . And while Unitarians and Trinitarians belaboured each other, a small but flamboyant minority of the educated elite grew yearly bolder in denying the existence of any God at all, at least of a God with any meaningful, overseeing function. Two years before the end of formal press censorship in 1695 a future bishop of Peterborough could already observe with consternation that "Socinianism and atheism drive furiously on".'[78]

The Toleration Act seemed to herald a free market in religious opinions; and this included the propagation of atheism. As Humphrey Prideaux expressed it, toleration 'hath almost undone us, not in increasing the number of dissenters but of wicked and profane persons'.[79] The lapsing of the Licensing Act in 1695 opened the way to endless public controversy, sometimes on matters which the orthodox found scandalous. What in the past had seemed axiomatic and beyond attack was now openly debated and derided.

The Principal of Jesus College, Oxford, commented in 1693 that since 1689 'Socinian books . . . swarm'd all upon a sudden, and have been industriously dispers'd through all parts of the kingdom, whereby many weak and unstable souls have been beguiled, and their minds corrupted from the simplicity which is in Christ'.[80] Such penetrating observers as Gilbert Burnet commented on the disturbing presence of blasphemers, or those who scoffed at the church or at Christianity. The clergy were shocked to find themselves becoming targets of derision as much as objects of contempt. There was a widespread concern that the church was loosing its grip on the minds and hearts of the population.

The 'competition' from Dissent

However serious the threat from these variegated assaults on Christian orthodoxy may have been, churchmen as a whole, and clergymen in particular, were more immediately concerned about the 'competition' from Dissent. It was 'not long into William III's reign before many Church of England divines, including even leading moderates like Edward Stillingfleet, the new Bishop of Worcester, who had worked to produce such a settlement in the Convention, began to feel that, almost by an oversight, charity had gone much too far in 1689'.[81] They were alarmed at the way Dissent was gaining ground at the expense of the establishment. They heard of Dissenting academies, such as those at Exeter, Stoke Newington and Attercliffe (Sheffield) which displayed a disconcerting educational prowess, were deflecting the sons of some Anglican parents away from Oxford and Cambridge and providing training for a new generation of Dissenting pastors. They were staggered by the sheer volume of licences for meeting-houses taken out under the Toleration Act's provision: just over 3,900 by 1710, with well over 300 for new permanent structures. Some of the urban congregations seem to have exceeded a thousand 'hearers', with as many as 2,000 reported in Taunton.[82] By 1718 there were roughly 2,000 Dissenting congregations compared with 1,200 or so whose meetings were granted licences in the first year of the Toleration, and although this included a substantial number of small gatherings of Baptists or Quakers, it was a very visible sign of religious pluralism. It was indicative of the unexpected social influence, material prosperity and numerical strength of Dissent, and it was viewed as a distinct threat to the established church.

It is within this setting that one must view the whole controversy over occasional conformity; the practice whereby some Dissenters paid a single visit to the parish church and received the sacrament and a certificate in order to meet the requirements under the Test and Corporation Acts for appointment to a place of trust under the crown or to any municipal office, and thereafter went regularly and cheerfully to a meeting-house. It was another invasion of the Anglican monopoly enjoyed by the Church of England, and the High-flying clergy fought against it with vigour. In each of the years 1702 to 1704 a bill was introduced which would have made it a penal offence to attend a Dissenting place of worship after receiving the sacrament in an Anglican church for the purpose of qualifying for office. Each time the bill was strongly opposed by the Whigs, the Dissenters, and a substantial body of 'moderate' and Low Churchmen. It was a very emotive and deeply divisive issue. In 1704 there was even an attempt to 'tack' such a bill to the Land Tax Bill. The fourth Occasional Conformity Bill only became law as a consequence of a deal between the Junto and the Tory Earl of Nottingham in 1711. The culmination of this series of anti-Dissenting legislative measures was the vicious Schism Act of 1714, which was intended to cut the tap roots of Dissent by forcing the closure of their separate schools and academies.

But the time of the Whigs was at hand. With the accession of George I, and the coming to power of the Whigs, there was a refusal to enforce the measures, and in 1719 both the Occasional Conformity Act and the Schism Act were repealed. In the meantime, effectively in 1717, the decision was made to suspend the deliberations of the provincial Convocation of Canterbury. Although the ostensible occasion for this was the Bangorian controversy, which has already been considered in detail, it was part of a series of actions which established the Whigs in power during the reigns of George I and George II. The Riot Act, the Septennial Act, the repeal of the Occasional Conformity and Schism Acts, and the silencing of Convocation were of a piece: they were a prelude to an extended period of Whig rule. 'The silencing of

Convocation did not require statutory intervention, nor was it the occasion of a parliamentary debate. But its significance soon became obvious. It removed the principal mouthpiece of the High Church clergy; it liberated latitudinarian propagandists of the regime from potential restraint; above all it materially assisted Whig governments in one of their principal objectives, the avoidance of a "Church in Danger" crisis such as that which had accompanied the impeachment of Sacheverell and threatened to follow the provocations of Hoadly.[83]

The life, witness and worship of the church

Although the church of the late seventeenth century, and of the eighteenth century, 'was a slow-moving institution, its characteristic forms deeply influenced by the past and compounded of constant compromise mixed with seemingly perpetual precedent',[84] it continued to play an important part in the life of the nation at every level, and in countless and varied ways. It arguably remained more relevant to the daily round of communities and individuals throughout the length and breadth of the land than any other institution. It was far from being the spent force which some of its detractors have been prone to depict.

The Revolution of 1689 certainly introduced important changes in the relationship of the church to the state, but the presence of the established church was still very much in evidence throughout politics, law and society. At the top level in politics, the 26 bishops in the House of Lords had a vital block of votes. In 1714 the Lords comprised 213 members, and this had only increased to 224 by 1780. Even in crucial divisions the number present was rarely in excess of 120 to 145, so that the bishops' votes mattered, and on some occasions saved the government from defeat. And the intertwining of church, state and society was demonstrated in local affairs in every corner of the country. It was the prerogative of the crown to appoint all the bishops and deans, and to make nominations to 1,048 livings; and the patrons of over half the livings in England were laymen.

The parish was, of course the setting for the most intimate and sustained connection of the church with society. Until well into the nineteenth century the parish was, without exception, far more than a mere unit of local and church government. In all cases, and especially in rural parishes which predominated, it was a most intricate complex of legal obligations and property interests, with the gentry playing a dominant role. The description of Sir Roger de Coverly by Addison, with his paternalistic concern to beautify the church, increase the stipends of the vicar and the clerk, provide the vicar with the best sermons to be read Sunday by Sunday, and preside over the Sunday congregations with rigorous eccentricity, capture the essence of rural parochial life as it was found throughout most of the long eighteenth century, even allowing for its pronounced idealization.[85] By 1689 the Church of England had survived many ordeals and had assumed a shape and identity which was accepted by the vast majority of the population as a vital part of their lives. They felt an affinity with what the building, the liturgy and the ministry represented. The great majority of Anglican churches were mediaeval inheritances, and they stood in the midst of communities as symbolic of tradition, continuity and stability.[86]

Since the upheavals of the sixteenth century, and these arguably had not produced very extensive and permanent structural changes, there had not been much of note to change the outward appearance, let alone the bodily structure, of the established church. The random nature of diocesan geography had persisted since pre-Reformation times. Between the Reformation and the end of the eighteenth century the list of permanent improvements was not impressive: five new dioceses; a sixteenth-century, unamended, statute restricting pluralism; a new version of Canon Law; and the institution of Queen Anne's Bounty are the only noteworthy landmarks. It is a somewhat uncoordinated selection of changes, which does not imply any strategic planning in the context of considerable political, economic and social change, and of the emergence of 'rival' denominations; and it left the Church of England with the central problems of its own domestic life largely untouched. 'The church of Joseph Butler, of Warburton, of Gibson and of Hoadly was pretty well continuous with the church of Burnet, of Laud, of Andrewes and even of Hooker; and it was this church which was destined to come face to face with all the difficulties, and all the problems, unavoidable in any society striving to work its way through a period of profound change and equally profound discontent.'[87]

At the top of the ecclesiastical hierarchy in post-Revolution England stood the 27 English and Welsh bishops.[88] Their dioceses varied greatly in size, as did their emoluments. Rochester had fewer than 150 parishes, while Lincoln had over 1,500; the Archbishop of Canterbury received £7,000 per annum, the Bishop of Lincoln £1,500 and the Bishop of Bristol £450. And these sizes and rewards took little account of the changes in distribution of the population. In a large and demanding diocese especially, the ability of the bishop to exercise a pastoral role in his allotted territory was severely curtailed by the political demands made upon him. Court attendance and participation in the affairs of central government were expected of bishops. Even a most conscientious bishop 'found his purpose to cease following a court in order to devote the whole of his time to the government of his diocese could not be realized without a violent breach with the secular English episcopal tradition. At the heart of the problem of episcopal administration lay the distraction from the proper business of diocesan oversight involved in the residence of bishops in London during the greater part of each year; and it is in the light of this circumstance that all estimates of the diligence of their pastoral care must be made.'[89] Such residence in the capital was important, and some would say essential, if the episcopate was to maintain an interest and concern in public affairs, and to exercise an influence in those affairs, especially in the absence of a sitting Convocation after 1717; the church had no other central 'political' voice. This duality of duty often meant that they could not respond as they might wish to local opportunities and possibilities for evangelistic and pastoral service.

There is evidence that despite these required duties, and in the face of appalling conditions for travelling between their dioceses and London, as well as within their sees, there were many bishops who were competent administrators, and who diligently discharged the episcopal tasks of visitation, confirmation and ordination. Writing in 1718, Archbishop Wake declared that he 'believed the confirmations had never been so regular throughout the kingdom as within the last thirty years, nor the episcopal visitations and that by the bishops in person, so constant'.[90] To take but one specific example, it seems that in Devon at the beginning of the eighteenth century the 'bishop's triennial visitation together with the archdeacon's and the rural dean's annual visitations formed the keystone of ecclesiastical administration'.[91] Several months in advance of the bishop's visit the clergy were obliged to answer a series of written questions giving detailed information about each parish. This was supplemented by the rural dean's report on each incumbent's church and parsonage. During his visitation the bishop progressed from centre to centre, and the clergy and churchwardens in neighbouring rural deaneries were then summoned to him by citation. Non-attendance, except as a result of sickness, called for discipline in the bishop's consistorial court. The archdeacon's annual visitation followed the same pattern, with the clergy and churchwardens being under obligation to attend; and in many dioceses this was preceded by the rural dean's visitation, in the course of which he covered every parish in his deanery and gave a report to the archdeacon or bishop on the lives and morals of the clergy and people in his district, as well as on the condition of churches and parsonages. In a useful and enlightening study of the eighteenth-century Church of England in Devon, Arthur Warne describes the ministry of a number of conscientious bishops, and he concludes that previous blanket condemnations need at least to be modified. 'The eighteenth-century episcopate deserves a juster measure of appreciation than has been their lot at the hands of many historians, for there is no reason to consider the record of the Exeter bishops as untypical. They strove, on the whole, with diligence, and not without a good measure of success, to discharge the spiritual administration of their office.'[92]

In a study of eight Hereford and thirteen Oxford seventeenth- and eighteenth-century bishops, W. M. Marshall came to the firm opinion that they 'fulfilled their episcopal functions, with a few exceptions, to a high standard, even when judged by the criteria of any age'. He unhesitatingly supported 'the re-evaluation of the 18th century begun by Professor Sykes in his studies based on a number of dioceses and followed by other historians since'. He concluded that in every area so far investigated by research 'the Church was led by men who saw its weaknesses and did their best to correct them. In places the church was very much alive and even vigorous. Its worst failings were in its social welfare and in the tedium of its worship for the mass of the people, but it was neither asleep nor decadent.'[93]

This is all very impressive and convincing, but it is difficult to extrapolate from such anecdotal and regional evidence and make general statements about the episcopate as a whole, whether in this period or more generally throughout the eighteenth century. Such has tended to be the practice of historians; but actual 'hard' evidence is thin. The problems I have discussed, and others such as frequent episcopal translations, and the obdurate assertion of the parsons freehold, were hindrances to the fulfilment of anything approaching an ideal episcopal ministry within the dioceses themselves. It can, for example, be pointed out that in general visitations, which were usually combined with confirmations, occurred every three or four years, and that bishops turned such visitations into more effective tools of pastoral oversight and tried to make confirmation more orderly, and thus more spiritually edifying.[94] On the other hand, the pessimists such as Virgin can assert, with supporting evidence, that episcopal administration was frequently poor, and pastoral care minimal.[95] Perhaps the wisest, most honest, albeit somewhat embarrassing thing to do is to admit that there has been insufficient research to allow any very firm conclusion to be reached on this topic, not only for the fifty-year period after the Revolution but for the whole of the rest of the eighteenth century.

When we turn to the lower clergy we are on slightly firmer ground. Although even here, despite some local studies and research on specific relevant matters, simple, categorical, generalizations are unwise and unwarranted, some trends and features are discernable.[96] There were immense variations in the degree of wealth and the status of livings, but the records of the Queen Anne's Bounty Board, on which we rely for most of the statistical evidence on clerical pay matters in the early eighteenth century, reveal a high level of poverty among a large proportion of the clergy.[97] They show that 5,082 livings out of a total of about 10,500 benefices were worth under £80 a year. According to J. Ecton, in a report of 1721, 3,826 livings were worth less than £1 per week, and this included 1,216 benefices worth under £20 a year. This compares with an average income for shopkeepers and tradesmen of about £45 per annum, for artisans and handicraftsmen of approximately £40, and labouring people and outservants about £15.[98] In fact these figures understate the extent of clerical poverty. For various technical and procedural reasons, they did not include a considerable number of poor livings, and they do not reflect the plight of the unbeneficed curates. There is even less evidence for the richer livings, although it appears that there were more rich and less poor livings in the south and east compared with the north and the west. As we will see later, by the 1830s the incomes of the clergy overall had increased dramatically.

By the beginning of the eighteenth century a high proportion of the newly-ordained clergy were graduates. Of the 31 ordained to the diaconate in 1702 in the diocese of Exeter only one was a non-graduate; and the universities were probably providing a better quality of education at this time than their critics claimed.[99] Although the local incumbent was better educated than any of his forebears, and was a focal point for local community life, he did not necessarily have a high social status.[100] The church drew a high proportion of its clergy from clerical families, but it seems that there were fewer from gentry families than there were to be in the latter part of the eighteenth century.[101] Tithe commutation at enclosure was to make more of them substantial landowners, and clerical JPs were to become increasingly common. But the age of the Georgian 'squarson' had not yet arrived. Nonetheless, it appears that there was possibly less pluralism and non-residence than in the latter half of the eighteenth century. This would not necessarily have resulted in greater pastoral care, but it did, perhaps, result in the average early eighteenth-century country incumbent having a greater degree of integration into the communal life of his more lowly parishioners than was the case with his successors, despite the natural barrier created by his greater education. From a sample of 445 beneficed clergy in returns made by bishops to Queen Anne's Bounty in 1705, Virgin found that pluralism and non-residence were not frequent, and there was not much regional variation. About 16% of the sample held more than one living and, among them, only one incumbent had aggravated the offence by adding a third benefice to the second.[102] Pluralism was to increase substantially throughout the first three quarters of the eighteenth century; but most of the instances of pluralism involved neighbouring parishes, in many cases only a mile or less apart, or at least in the same diocese or even deanery, so that the parishioners were able to see their incumbents quite frequently, especially as many of them in fact shared their time between their two benefices. Non-residence in many cases resulted from the parish being too small to give full employment to a minister, or from the pressures of financial necessity placed upon the ordained man; and neither of these in themselves meant inevitable pastoral neglect.

As there is some evidence that pluralism and non-residence was less rife in the post-Revolution half-century than has formerly been assumed, so too the presumed rather undynamic, soporific and somewhat lethargic state of parochial life in that period must also be questioned. Mark Smith encourages such questioning as a result of his most illuminating study of Oldham and Saddleworth.[103] What he has to say about the local situation which commanded his attention seems to have wider relevance, and to apply in a variety of other localities. Various 'strategies were available for dealing with non-residence and at a local level there is remarkably little evidence of total neglect'.[104] A further study of the clergy in the diocese of London similarly concludes that one 'can be cautiously optimistic about religious practice and clerical professionalism in the eighteenth century. Large cities like London and its immediate surroundings in Middlesex were well provided for.' And although country livings continued to suffer from such long-lamented evils as pluralism, non-residence, poverty and depopulation, there was not universal defeat, degeneration and decline. In many parishes 'solutions were found – not all simple or easy, but warranted by old custom, and made possible by local conditions such as the high density of churches, the proximity of villages and the small number of inhabitants, as well as by the low level of the demands of laity and church authorities alike'.[105] Again, as with many other aspects of church life in the eighteenth century the picture was patchy, making generalizations difficult and dangerous.

In view of the former pessimistic view of the Church of England in this period and in the eighteenth century in general, it is noteworthy how many recent local studies reveal healthy growth and adaptation to the changing demands of an increased population and rapid industrial and social change. Let us take the example of Saddleworth again. Faced with a sudden increase in its population Saddleworth and its satellite villages initially made a more intensive use of existing structures. At the beginning of the century, the ancient parochial chapel seems to have provided seating for about 260 people, or about 20% of the population of the district. When this was found to be inadequate, a gallery was erected in 1711 at the west end of the church. This was followed over the next few years by an extension of the seating along the ground floor of the building until the chancel was crowded with seats almost to the communion rail, and a second gallery was constructed along one of the chancel walls. Finally, in 1728, two further galleries were built along the north and south aisles and a loft was constructed for the choir and organ. 'The result by 1730 was a doubling of seating capacity in the church and an increase in the proportion of the population accommodated to around 30 per cent – all achieved without troubling the church building statistics.'[106] In the forty parishes of the south Lancashire deaneries of the diocese of Chester seven new churches were built or rebuilt between 1690 and 1704, twelve in each of the next two periods of fifteen years, and fourteen more between 1740 and 1754. I will have occasion to return to this study when I consider parochial life during the remainder of the period up to 1833.

The services conducted within the parish churches of the post-Revolution period were more or less uniform throughout England. 'The morning service on Sundays consisted of matins, ante-communion, that is, the communion service to the end of the prayer for the Church, and a sermon. Evening prayer was said in the afternoons, usually without a sermon if one had been preached in the morning, though sometimes the catechism was expounded.'[107] In London in 1723 about 44% of parishes had only one service each Sunday; and very few parishes troubled with a week-day service, except in London, in Middlesex and the country towns.[108] The custom of frequent communion had not yet been established, but the ante-communion served to remind people that the liturgy was intended to culminate in the full eucharist. Most country churches 'had Holy Communion three or four times a year, while only in cities and some market-towns was it offered every month, and in London every Sunday'.[109] The principal method by which the Anglican clergy tried to establish the most simple and rudimentary understanding of their faith and its obligations to parishioners who for the most part were not very literate was through catechizing. In essence this consisted of a series of questions and answers designed to teach basic tenets of the faith.[110] It seems to have persisted throughout the eighteenth century. One study of Oxfordshire clergy concluded that, 'far from dying out at the end of the century catechizing still held an important place in the parochial work, and was a duty to which a number of the clergy were devoting thought as well as time'.[111]

It seems that music became increasingly significant in Church of England worship as the eighteenth century progressed. This was a period when parish churches began to instal organs. Small churches used the bass viol, and gradually, as the century wore on, other instruments were added, so that by the beginning of the nineteenth century some country churches had four- or five-piece bands to accompany the singing. It all helped to make services more 'congregational' and more attractive to the worshippers.

Criticism of the eighteenth-century Church of England has been levelled not only at the bishops and clergy, and the church services they conducted, but also at the low level of 'discipline' which was exercised. It was a vexed issue which was of concern to many contemporary church leaders: they knew that it touched Anglicanism at a vulnerable spot. 'The legislation of the cavalier parliament had restored the diocesan courts, but it had left the church still without any effective means of chastising sinners, of correction by means of canonical penance, or of fencing the lord's table from the hardened and unrepentant. This lack of "discipline" was a weapon for the church's enemies; it was a continual source of embarrassment and regret to churchmen themselves.'[112] The courts were not powerless, and the 'censures of the church, far from being ignored',[113] but the kind of godly discipline of which the communion service spoke seemed to many to be slipping out of the hands of the church. And the problem was exacerbated by the post-Revolution legislation. The Toleration Act of 1689 did not 'cause the ecclesiastical jurisdiction to collapse or even reduce its remaining volume of business, but it did effectively ruin the cause of Anglican uniformity and discipline and took from the spiritual courts what had been their principal activity. Without a part to play in the high politics of church and state, the activities of ecclesiastical affairs were pushed more and more to the margin of national life.'[114]

On the other hand there were local situations, which may have been typical of many, and possibly the majority, where the courts were surprisingly vital until almost the end of the century. This appears to have been the case in Craven where 'the sanctions wielded by the Church courts seem to have been treated with respect without the backing of the civil authorities'. The people demonstrated their acceptance of the power of the local church courts in a most practical and public manner.

> To avoid the ecclesiastical punishment of excommunication, the majority of those prosecuted chose to absolve themselves by performing a penance, a humiliating ceremony which involved the recital of the offence before the assembled congregation in church, whilst wearing a white sheet and carrying a lighted taper.[115]

As Rycroft rightly comments, such a system 'could only operate in communities in which the role of the Church in the maintenance of communal values was accepted'. He goes on to observe that the 'proportion of offenders who chose to perform a penance remained high into the 1790s, suggesting that the sharp fall-off in the number of cases was not due to inability to enforce the authority of the courts, but to official decisions to stop using the courts to judge moral offenses'.[116]

An important aspect of the life of the Church of England in the post-Revolution half century was the part played by Anglicans in those non-denominational bodies which were to be so significant as path-blazers for the evangelical revival: the societies for the reformation of manners and the religious societies. The momentous foundation of the Society for the Promotion of Christian Knowledge and then of the Society for the Propagation of the Gospel also took place in this period, but I will delay any consideration of them until chapter 9, simply remarking that any church which spawned such societies as these must have had some measure of vitality and vision.

In the main contemporary account of the early years of the religious societies, *An Account of the Rise and Progress of the Religious Societies*, the author, Josiah Woodward, traced their origin to 1678 or there-abouts, when anxious young men in London approached the Revd Anthony Horneck, preacher of the Savoy Chapel, for spiritual advice.[117] The enquirers were organized into small societies restricted to members of the Church of England. They met under clerical supervision for set prayers, the discussion of religious books and the occasional exchange of spiritual experiences; and frequent communion was encouraged. They also engaged in some charitable work. In their regular weekly gatherings they were first and foremost concerned to apply themselves to 'good discourses, and things wherein they might edifie one another'.[118] They remained staunchly Anglican, the members assiduously guarding against any semblance of schism or fractiousness by adhering to monthly Church of England communions, by attending public prayers and by obtaining the explicit approval of their super-intendent Church of England clergymen for the introduction of any new rule, prayer or practice. They represented a continuing possibility with-in the established church of a more profound and intense religious awareness and personal experience than was generally to be obtained through the regular parish ministry.

After 1688 the London societies multiplied, and other societies were established in the provinces. The situation became somewhat compli-cated with the rise of the societies for the reformation of manners. These worked largely in London and its environs, although they also spread to other parts of the country. They specifically concentrated on a campaign for the prosecution of moral offenders before the magistrates. Although the relationship between the two types of society has been a matter of dispute, it does appear likely that they were complementary, and worked in concert. The reformation societies undertook to meet on the first Monday of every month and 'to consult and resolve upon the best methods for putting the laws in execution against houses of lewdness and debauchery and also against drunkenness swearing and cursing and profanation of the Lord's day'.[119] They were composed almost entirely of men, most of whom were tradesmen or skilled craftsmen. They did not eschew unpopular methods, such as the use of informers, or the derision of others. They were convinced that there was an urgent need to intervene actively in the lives of others. 'The service required was to fight for God against his permanent opponent, the Devil, in the eternal battle for men's souls. Since sin was the mark of the Devil's Kingdom, the fight must be against sin. Moreover, since this battle was the crucial factor in the lives of every person – far over-riding, for example, mere differences between Anglican and Dissenter – it was absolutely impossible for anyone to be neutral.'[120] This point was made and sharply hammered home by Daniel Williams:

> Any man's neutrality between these engaged parties and opposite rules and designs is altogether impossible . . . Some please themselves with a conceit, that they are not of a Party with the Devil against Christ, 'tho' they are conscious they are not engaged on Christ's side – But the vanity of it is apparent from this, that their very surmized neutrality is really their being a party with Satan . . .'[121]

Both these types of society, and perhaps especially those which met for private devotion, were part of the drawing up of battle lines for the impending evangelical revival. 'The movement was not marked by an evangelistic zeal to bring vast numbers of persons into the societies. Indeed, their approach was aimed more towards quality than quantity and was grounded more in the process of nurture than conversion.'[122] But, with the stimulus they provided for 'mutual encouragement in the development of devotional piety based on a study of the Bible and other works of divinity', and with their ability 'to assist the promotion of a life of personal holiness and morality'[123] they offered a structure and framework for the forthcoming revival, and a channel through which it could flow, especially in its early phase.

'Popular religion'

Before leaving the Church of England in the post-Revolution era it is well to acknowledge that acts of Parliament, the machinations of church parties, and the public activities of the church at national and local levels, do not tell the whole story of what 'religion' meant for many of the formally 'Church of England' members of English society. For a large proportion of Church of England members 'religious belief' consisted of an ill-defined mixture of orthodox Christianity, superstition and social mores. But it has to be recognized that it is exceedingly difficult to discover what was the essential character and content of this late seventeenth-century and early eighteenth-century 'popular religion', which provided the milieu for the more formal, public and historically acknowledged acts and activities of the churches in these years. To attempt to do so is to attempt a 'history of the people who have no history'.[124] Such history from below 'is in fact no more "real" than history from above; but it is still largely true that "the people" in this sense are a dimension missing from many interpretations of the past.'[125]

In all types of community in late seventeenth- and early eighteenth-century England, and especially in rural villages and hamlets which remained untouched by any form of 'industrialization', and in which the vast majority of the people spent all their domestic and working lives, social and economic relations 'were conducted within a contractual framework which was both universally understood and held to be binding'.[126] What is more, this social and economic hierarchy and framework, which dictated every aspect of the lives of all citizens, was almost unanimously accepted as divinely ordained. It was not man but God who had created social inequality, and who had assigned everyone to their particular and various social positions. This was well expressed by one writer in 1681:

> There is nothing more plain nor certain, than that God Almighty hath ordained and appointed degrees of Authority and Subjection; allowing Authority to the Master, and commanding obedience from the servant unto him; for God hath given express commands to Masters to govern their Servants, and to Servants to be subject to their Masters . . . Christians in all Ages have asserted and owned this distinction; some of them having been placed as Masters, and others as Servants, and according to the Station which it hath pleased God to allot them, they have performed their mutual dutys . . .[127]

This almost universal acceptance of God's benign and rational plan, and of his essential beneficence in so ordering the affairs and inter-relationships of men, women and children in society, resulted in widespread conservatism. It also tended to produce religious conformism. The established church 'promoted obedience, submission, orderliness, respect for authority, patience in suffering, civility, restraint and loyalty'.[128] It continued to be intimately involved in every aspect of the life of the community through its 'uncontested monopoly over the rites of passage, its provision of welfare and education, its widespread distribution of popular forms of religious literature and its thorough identification with the political, legal and social institutions of the State both at the centre and in the localities'. It 'was not simply the religious arm of the State, but rather offered a framework of loyalty and allegiance within which other activities had their meaning'.[129]

Alongside this, however, there was much folk religion which in many cases was far from orthodox in belief or practice. In the largely familiar, routinized and repeated daily round the common tasks of life, the weekly, monthly, seasonal and yearly cycle of events, various layers and forms of religious or quasi-religious belief and conduct emerged. In every community there were folk tales; there was received wisdom passed on verbally from one generation to another; there was a 'popular morality' consisting of maxims of practical conduct and inherited customs; and there was a mixture of religion, astrology and magic which all 'purported to help men with their daily problems by teaching them how to avoid misfortune and how to account for it when it struck'.[130] This is not to trivialize religion, or to place it on a par with astrology or magic. 'Popular magic in England discharged only a limited number of functions; it provided protection against witchcraft, and various remedies for illness, theft, and unhappy personal relationships. But it never offered a comprehensive view of the world, an explanation of human existence, or the promise of a future life. It was a collection of miscellaneous recipes, not a comprehensive body of doctrine. Whereas the faith of the Christian was a guiding principle, relevant to every aspect of life, magic was simply a means of overcoming various specific difficulties.'[131]

Throughout the whole of the long eighteenth century it appears that magic was adopted in an attempt to combat illness, and for purposes of divination, in rituals intended to foretell the future, or even to affect future events. Although such magic was becoming less significant in the lives of communities and individuals in the post-Revolutionary age than it had been in the sixteenth century and the earlier part of the seventeenth century, it remained a vital element in the total world view and daily experience of ordinary people until well into the nineteenth century. Magical techniques and rituals continued to be practised by a wide range of people and, as in the past, there were specialists in magic, known as wise men or women, white witches, conjurers or cunning men, who were thought to possess special powers in managing and interpreting those mysteries which baffled people in everyday living.

English labouring people in particular, in a pre-scientific, predominantly oral culture, were constantly and strongly aware of a spiritual (or supernatural) reality, in which supernatural interventions in secular affairs were thought to be routine occurrences. The world was seen as a mysterious and often somewhat awesome place, abounding in unexplained catastrophes. Sudden death, unexpected disasters, epidemics, crop failures, pain and suffering, as well as the stresses of what was for most people a hard and frequently short life, led people to look for aid in whatever solace was at hand. In trying to cope with the harshness, uncertainties and tribulations of life it is not surprising that ordinary, ill-educated, people drew upon a range of resources which were on offer. It is also understandable that there was much popular irreligion combined with ignorance of the basic tenets of Christianity, a considerable amount of indifference to religion, and some outright hostility or scepticism.[132] Religion, irreligion, magic, orthodoxy, folk religion and the teaching of the Church of England were all bound up in local communities in the bundle of local life. The difficulty facing the Church of England, as well as other churches, 'was not simply ignorance of its doctrines, but the fact that popular culture surrounded orthodox religious practice with a penumbra of folklore and magic'.[133]

Many of the practitioners of magic were women; but it is significant that in the late seventeenth and early eighteenth century there was little change in the Anglican attitude towards women. Church of England thought on the family, the place of women within it, and on the role of women in society as a whole was dominated by the concept of sub-ordination. But the strong element of patriarchalism regarding the government of the country as well as conduct and relationships within the family, which characterized the Anglican cast of mind, was modified during the eighteenth century. In the immediate post-Revolution years there were signs of a loosening of attitudes both in church circles and in the political arena. The Revolution itself had severely dented the theory of absolute patriarchal monarchy; the controversial Benjamin Hoadly drew attention to the implications of a female supreme governor of both church and state; and women such as the Anglo-Saxon scholar Elizabeth Elstob and the intellectually wide-ranging writer Mary Astell set an example of what women could achieve if given the opportunity. The seeds were being sown for the ensuing Enlightenment which was to witness a massive step forward in the liberation of women. A more liberal attitude to the role of women in the family and in society as a whole was to go hand-in-hand with increased lay participation in the affairs of the church at every level.[134]

2

Dissenters in an Age of Toleration

The Toleration Act

The hopes of Dissenters were raised by the Revolution and the replacement of James II by William III. It is undeniable that when he set out for England the Prince of Orange was sincere in his desire to promote in his new kingdom that religious toleration which was already enjoyed in Holland. In the Declaration which he published before his departure he had promised 'to endeavour a good Agreement between the Church of England, and all Protestant Dissenters'.[1] Dissenters had become part of English life, and they could not be effectively uprooted. They hoped that the new regime would recognize this by appropriate policy and legislation. Dissenters had co-operated with Anglicans in paving the way for William's accession to the throne, and this created a rare sweetness in the relations between Conformists and Nonconformists. Expectations among Dissenters were high. A group of them, led by the venerable John Howe, joined Henry Compton, the Bishop of London, and a number of his clergy to welcome the liberator to London. William met a specifically Nonconformist deputation which expressed their sense of gratitude for his coming, and in his reply he spoke of his desire to promote 'a firm Union among Protestants'.[2] It all seemed to augur well for the expectant Dissenters.

But this pleasant atmosphere, and this Nonconformist euphoria did not last long. The rejection of the Comprehension Bill was a cruel blow to the Presbyterians, whose leaders had harboured great hopes that the terms of conformity might be so stretched that they could take their place within the established church.[3] The 1689 Toleration Act did not herald the dawn of paradise on earth for Dissenters. It was, as we have previously noted, the result of a peculiar concatenation of circumstances and not part of an evolutionary process of planned and deliberately increased toleration. To many of those who were instrumental in its introduction and implementation, including William himself, its importance was political rather than religious. 'Dissenters were to be tolerated since persecution was unnecessary and even counter-productive, not because they were co-religionists.'[4] In any case the Act was hardly a generous one. By it the penal code was not repealed: the Act merely excused the Dissenters from the code's penalties. The freedom granted was carefully hedged about with oaths, prohibitions and declarations. No Dissenting meeting could be held without the appropriate certificate having been obtained. The Church of England continued to exercise its financial hold over Dissenters, as tithes and parochial dues had still to be paid. A range of civil offices were barred from Dissenters, or only made accessible by means of a qualifying participation in Church of England communion. The Dissenters remained second-class citizens. Perhaps all this was inevitable, as comprehension on a broad doctrinal and ecclesiological basis, or complete toleration, were probably steps which were unrealizable at that time, in one giant move. The theoretical advocacy of toleration was much more widespread, and more closely linked than in the past to major trends in contemporary statecraft, but this did not mean that it was generally in the ascendant even in north-western Europe. The fierce High Church counter-attack against toleration, which we have already witnessed, was evidence of an underlying intolerance in at least some sectors of the population. Despite the multiplication of those advocating toleration, the issue remained contentious, and the political battle continued to rage at least until the second decade of the eighteenth century. The 1689 Toleration Act was a milestone, but its significance must be seen within a long timescale. It represented a tentative departure from long-accepted intolerance, and the changes it introduced, although they greatly improved the standing of most Dissenting bodies, were fragile and vulnerable.

The Dissenters at the time were aware of the very considerable limitations in what had been granted to them, and of the precarious nature of their new-found freedom. 'The trust deeds of meeting-houses built in the reigns of William and Mary and Anne contained provisions that, in the event of the proscription of Dissenting worship, the buildings should be sold and the proceeds used for the benefit of the poor.'[5] It was no mean thing that Presbyterians, Independents, Baptists and Quakers all gained the right, by law, to worship freely. But the reassurance given to Dissenters was undermined by the verbal assaults of Henry Sacheverell, himself the grandson of an ejected Presbyterian minister who had died in Dorchester gaol, who railed against Dissenters as 'miscreants begat in rebellion, born in sedition, and nursed in faction';[6] by the placing of Daniel Defoe in the pillory in 1703 for satirizing such views; by the attacks on Dissenting meeting-houses by a Tory mob celebrating the death of William III; by the further such plunder at the impeachment of Sacheverell; and later, in 1715, by the Jacobite celebration of the Pretender's birthday. They were made acutely aware that intolerance was widespread; and that even among some of the tolerant it was little more than skin-deep. Limited religious liberty had been conceded to Dissenters, but rigid Anglicans were extremely reluctant to grant them civil equality. Quakers continued to be fined and imprisoned for non-payment of tithes and for refusing oaths, despite their right under an Act of 1696 to make an affirmation instead of swearing an oath; and of course there was the protracted attempt to defeat occasional conformity, which I have already described.

It was only from 1719 onwards, with the repeal of the Occasional Conformity Act and the Schism Act, and with the ascendency of the Whigs, that the Dissenters began to think that toleration as a policy was secure, and there to stay. After 1719 the sacramental test was still required, but if a Dissenter could reconcile the practice of occasional conformity with his religious convictions, then no office under the crown was barred to him. Dissenters could even qualify for holding corporation offices without taking the sacrament as a result of the 1719 Act for Quieting and Establishing Corporations, which provided that anyone who was elected to a town corporation was freed from the need for any sacramental qualification and from any fear of prosecution if his tenure was not questioned in the six months after his election. The first Indemnity Act of 1726 introduced a further legal loophole, in that it allowed a person to qualify for office by receiving the sacrament after taking office rather than one year before election to corporate office, as under the Corporation Act.

The cynic might well say that the intolerant, let alone the tolerant, had little option but to accept the Dissenters; after all there were so many of them, and they were thoroughly entrenched in English society. It has been estimated that in the last four decades of the seventeenth century Dissenters, excluding Quakers, numbered 150,000–250,000, and in the first four decades of the eighteenth century 250,000–300,000.[7] Another calculation arrives at a figure, including Quakers, of 338,120 in the early eighteenth century. Of these, Presbyterians were far and away the most numerous (179,350), almost three times the number of Congregationalists (59,940).[8] Presbyterians were scattered in significant numbers everywhere; Baptists were thinly dispersed in the North, and Congregationalists made little impression there or in the West

Midlands, but the greatest strength of both was in the Home Counties. Quakers were widely, though more thinly, spread, with their greatest concentration being in the north-western area from which they originated, in Bristol, London and the northern Home Counties. By 1715 almost 65% of Dissenting congregations overall were located in towns. London was a major focus for Dissent, as were Exeter, Tiverton, Taunton, Colchester, Norwich, Coventry, Leeds, Manchester, and a host of the smaller cloth-working towns.

But the Dissenters, and most particularly the Presbyterians, experienced numerical decline from the third decade of the eighteenth century onwards. Of particular note was their decrease relative to the population as a whole.[9] Taken together, the Presbyterians, Congregationalists and Baptists dropped from about 5% of the population in 1715 to 4% or less in 1773.

Nonetheless, even with this decrease the Dissenters remained politically influential. This was partly because they were deeply involved in local politics, but it was also because, as a disciplined electoral block, they provided a core around which Low Church Anglicans could rally, and because they formed a unified Whig electoral interest group. I have already had occasion to comment on the close association of Dissent with the Whigs, and one reason why the Whigs did much better in contesting the borough seats in General Elections than in fighting the counties in the first generation after the Revolution was the strength of the Dissenting vote in numerous boroughs. Indeed, by the beginning of Anne's reign occasional conformity had enabled Dissenters to get a grip on many corporations, and this allowed them to influence parliamentary elections in the Whig interest, especially in some of the limited corporation boroughs. But even among the Whigs there was some support for the civil barriers which continued to keep the really conscientious Dissenters (who refused to avail themselves of the benefits of occasional conformity) out of municipal office, out of the universities, the civil service and the army, and which made it difficult, even if not entirely impossible, for them to become physicians or barristers. Some of the landed gentry, who had once been the great champions of Puritanism, became disenchanted with a Dissenting religious allegiance which carried such a marked social stigma. 'By 1720 the sects, with their increasingly urban image, were still holding adherents among the pseudo-gentry; but the pattern of the future, with their main strength overwhelmingly based on the middling and lower-middling strata of society, including the yeomanry, and their strong support, lower down, from the "mechanic trades" and other "plain people of no education" was already well established.'[10]

The Dissenters were quintessential Whigs partly because of two pivotal doctrines which they held in common irrespective of denominational allegiances: the authority of the Bible, which they consciously or unconsciously set against the authority of tradition, and the concept of the gathered church which was independent of the Establishment. The shared congregational polity provided an orientation which was in stark contrast to the hierarchical conception of society, and in favour of egalitarianism. This common theological heritage, combined with their shared political experience under the Stuarts, helped to weld them together and shape them into a single, well-defined, religious tradition.

But the post-Revolution period was a strange mix of expansion and a spiritually healthy life of worship and witness, and theological disputes, internal squabbles and evidence of decline. On the one hand there was the mushroom growth in the number of meeting-places, and the greater freedom to worship and to participate in the life of the community. For instance, in Devon the granting of toleration inaugurated a thirty-year period of great prosperity. It has been calculated that almost one person in five in Devonshire in 1715 was a Dissenter, and this may be a conservative estimate.[11] The Dissenters in that part of the country at least were not solely, or even largely, the economically deprived. In 1698 it was observed that at Ashburton the Dissenters included 'the most considerable persons in the town'. And Daniel Defoe found that the meeting-house at Bideford was filled with people of 'the best fashion'.[12] Socially, Dissent in Devonshire 'was very much the religion of the economically independent. There was a solid core of "Gentlemen" and tradesmen in both town and country meetings with farmers and yeomen in close alliance with them.'[13] On the other hand, as we will soon see, in a number of ways Nonconformity, at least at the national level, was in a parlous state. It lacked a sense of vision, and it, like the Church of England, was enervated by its struggle with Deism and atheism from without, and by Socinianism, Arianism and Unitarianism from within. Both these aspects will be evident as we turn to a close examination of the main Dissenting denominations of the day.

The Presbyterians

The moment of potential glory for the Presbyterians had come in the mid 1640s.[14] It was then that the determination of the shape of the national church seemed within their grasp, for Parliament had been ready to impose a Presbyterian discipline upon the nation. Thereafter, except for a further brief period of eminence when their authority revived in the last months of the Commonwealth, and they participated in actions surrounding the Restoration and the Restoration Settlement, it was increasingly the Independents, or Congregationalists, who took the lead among the Dissenters. Nonetheless, there was nothing to suggest that within fifty years the Presbyterians would have experienced a virtual collapse, with their discipline in tatters, their former reformed theology largely replaced by liberal unorthodoxy, and many of their churches converted to Calvinist Congregationalism or Unitarianism.

With the new regime of William and Mary it might have seemed that a new and better era was dawning for the English Presbyterians. After all William had been brought up as a Presbyterian and was greatly attracted by its simple worship; and Mary, though she had grown up in a Roman Catholic atmosphere, had not only abjured Roman Catholicism but had learned to communicate as a member of the English Presbyterian Church at the Hague. Nonetheless, when they arrived in England both of them readily conformed to the Church of England, partly because they seem to have found it congenial, and partly because it was politically expedient to do so. It soon became apparent that there was no intention of allowing any church or group of churches to qualify as a serious rival to the established church. With the abandonment of the possibility of comprehension any hope of incorporating the Presbyterian system in the Church of England appeared to be gone for ever. The Presbyterians unostentatiously dropped their proposed scheme of national synods and became congregational in polity; their distinguishing mark henceforth among fellow Dissenters was reduced to the ordination of ministers.

The post-Revolution decades were for Presbyterians more than for any other religious group the meeting-house building era. Between 1689 and 1710, when the High Church reaction set in so strongly in the last four years of Queen Anne's reign, well-nigh a thousand meeting-places seem to have come into use. The largest number of these by far belonged to the Presbyterians. England had never witnessed such a rapid surge of ecclesiastical building. Being constructed almost entirely within one generation they were of a similar pattern; and with the funding being dependent upon the sacrificial giving of mostly simple and quite poor people, they were unembellished and of little architectural distinction. They were plain-looking square or oblong buildings of stone, or of brick with stone facings. Their main and most noticeable feature was the very high-pitched hip-roof with curved or corrugated tiles, called pantiles. The focal point inside was the pulpit, with its heavy canopy or sounding-board, planted sometimes against a gable, sometimes against the side-wall, and not infrequently surmounted with a dove and olive leaf, the only emblematic figure which was permitted. On the back-board of the pulpit there would have been the nail or peg for the preacher's hat; by the pulpit rail a hoop or brass rail would have been provided for the baptismal basin; and in a prominent position at the front there would have been the precentor's desk, or, more commonly, the great 'table pew', with the communion table in the middle, the seats around it being used by the singers. Deep heavy galleries sometimes ran along all four sides, and the whole of the congregational space was filled with rows of stiff high-backed pews, often including great, square, family pews, lined with green baize, studded with rows of brass nails, for the use of those of greater affluence and higher social rank in the congregation.[15]

The sense of insecurity under the Toleration Act, and the precariousness of the liberty enjoyed, is inferred by the fact that many of these meeting-houses were thrust away behind the main streets, in order not to give unnecessary provocation to their opponents, and to screen them to some extent from pillage or destruction. With the accession of the Hanoverians, and the ascendency of the Whigs, some very substantial Presbyterian places of worship were erected on open and more accessible sites, and some of the existing frail or dilapidated meeting-houses were rebuilt.

The Presbyterians were to be found all over England, but they were especially numerous in Lancashire, Cheshire, Devon, Dorset, Northumberland, Berkshire, Derbyshire, Essex, Nottinghamshire and Staffordshire; these being approximately in descending order of density. They were also particularly prolific in the city of Bristol.[16] About 63.2% of Presbyterians were to be found in cities, boroughs or market towns; and it was at this local level that new initiatives were taken in the 1690s in an attempt to establish union with other Dissenting bodies, and especially with the Congregationalists.

In their local life Presbyterians found that they had much in common with Congregationalists. Presbyterian and Congregational ministers also realized that there was a shared concern to relieve some of their more impoverished fellow pastors and to assist congregations which could not support ministers from their own resources, of which the majority were in rural areas. This led in 1690 to the establishment of a Common Fund by a group of Presbyterian and Congregational ministers in London. The failure of the Comprehension Bill of 1689 was a spur to the promotion of schemes for union. The most ambitious of these was inaugurated in March 1691, when the so-called 'Happy Union' was formed with the adoption of a set of proposals known as the 'Heads of Agreement' by most of the Presbyterian and Congregational ministers in and about London. Associations of Presbyterian ministers in Devon, Hampshire, Cheshire, Lancashire, the West Riding, and probably elsewhere, subsequently endorsed these proposals.

The core element in the Heads of Agreement was the ideal of a voluntary association of ministers. This satisfied the Presbyterian need for regular meetings of ministers without infringing the Congregational belief in the independence of the local church. The Presbyterian term 'classis' was resurrected to describe these gatherings, but they contained no lay elders, and they confined their activities largely to licensing candidates for the ministry, arranging ordinations, and giving advice on the removal and settlement of ministers. Nevertheless there were issues which continued to divide the two denominations. The Presbyterians retained the marks of their parochial structure, the Congregationalists clung to their conception of the gathered church, which was composed of true believers and was self-governing under the Lordship of Christ. Presbyterians admitted to communion respectable people with some knowledge of the Christian religion, while Congregationalists restricted participation in the communion, and church membership, to those who could give an account of the work of God's grace in their lives. Presbyterians also restricted their ministry to well-educated candidates, and positively tried to exclude the unlearned. The Congregationalists, though they did not despise education, were more concerned to ensure that candidates for the ministry were spiritually gifted and qualified, even if they were somewhat academically deficient. The differences between the two bodies were also compounded by theological controversy, with the Presbyterians being taxed with rank Arminianism, while they retorted with charges of Antinomianism and moral laxity against their Congregationalist accusers. The attempted union unfortunately foundered.

Indeed, even while they were striving for a harmonious relationship with another Dissenting denomination, the Presbyterians were themselves encountering internal tensions and problems which were soon to tear them asunder.

The first indication of serious doctrinal defection appeared in Exeter in 1717. The theological orthodoxy of three local ministers, James Pierce, Joseph Hallett and Mr Withers, was brought into question, and the particular focus of attention was the learned and able Pierce. He was charged with the new, but in some quarters fashionable, modern manifestation of Arianism. He seems to have asserted that belief in one God required that the Son and the Holy Ghost, although divine persons, must be subordinate to the Father. When he was requested by the Trustees to clear himself from suspicion by an avowal of the orthodoxy of his faith, he refused, considering that such a suggestion was intrusive and oppressive. 'This was the ground generally taken by numbers of ministers all over the country who were conscious of departing more or less from the old doctrines, and who were ever ready with the plea of their liberty being in danger from inquisitorial requirements.'[17] The three non-complying Exeter ministers were ejected, and in 1720 opened a new meeting-house, where they preached to a congregation of about 300, notwithstanding the laws against Unitarianism. But now the controversy moved into a new phase, as it shifted to London, and to Salters' Hall, in February 1719, with a second meeting in March of the same year.

The issue at stake was not essentially theological. The first meeting had resolved by 57 votes to 53 that no human compositions, or interpretations of the doctrine of the Trinity, should be made a part of articles to which subscription was required. Henceforward the matter of contention between what became known as the Subscribers and the Non-subscribers was not, ostensibly, their orthodoxy or heresy on the question of the Trinity. The Non-subscribers disowned Arianism, and declared their belief in 'the doctrine of the blessed Trinity, and the proper divinity of our Lord Jesus Christ'. They also agreed that if a minister preached certain doctrinal errors, then his congregation was justified in withdrawing its support of him. Nonetheless, they were adamant about 'the Protestant principle that the Bible is the only and perfect rule of faith', and they refused 'to condemn any man upon the authority of human decisions, or because he consents not to human forms or phrases'.

Among the Subscribers were thirty Presbyterians; among the Non-Subscribers, forty-seven. This meant that the majority of Presbyterians took their stand on the sole sufficiency of scripture, without the necessity of subscription. In this they were joined by the General Baptists. The Non-subscribing Presbyterian ministers showed a tendency towards the reception of new ideas. To a far greater extent than with the Subscribing ministers they adapted themselves to current speculations, and to the spirit of the age. 'This was the section that slowly found themselves drifting away from former moorings, though they neither intended nor admitted to themselves that they were doing anything else than protesting against narrow, illiberal, and bigoted notions.'[18] And it is worthy of note that within a century most Presbyterian meetings and many of the General Baptist churches connected with the General Assembly had become Unitarian, whereas the churches of the main Subscribers, that is the Congregationalists and the Particular Baptists, remained Trinitarian, and furthermore continued to honour the theology of John Calvin.[19]

But this declension proceeded in parallel with much that was thoroughly orthodox in late seventeenth and early eighteenth-century Presbyterianism, and with evidence of spiritual vitality. After all this was an era of powerful Presbyterian preaching and teaching. There was Dr Samuel Annesley, a former lecturer at St Paul's, and rector of St Giles', Cripplegate, who was pastor of the Presbyterian Church at Little St Helen's; Matthew Sylvester, Richard Baxter's biographer, and one of the most profound theological thinkers of the age, who was minister at Carter Lane; Dr Daniel Williams, pastor of the New Broad Street Church, a controversialist of considerable ability, a man of eminent scholarship who combined candour and charity in a remarkable way in his advocacy of the faith, and who established a library which has been an invaluable aid to research ever since; and Matthew Henry, the founder of the Chester Presbyterian Church, a devoted pastor whose fervency of preaching perhaps excelled that of any other contemporary minister, and whose commentary on the Bible has earned him the highest reputation in every succeeding generation.[20] These, and others not mentioned, constituted a formidable array of talent, and this has to be set against the doctrinal drift, and the devastating dissention and division which wrought such havoc in the Presbyterian fold. The doctrinal turmoil may have had the greater short, medium and long-term effect on the course of Presbyterianism, but the solid evangelical teaching was of considerable importance at the time, as a factor in preparing the ground for the forthcoming evangelical revival, and as a spiritual resource for a century and more to come.

The Congregationalists

The Congregational churches had suffered grievously throughout the Restoration period. For some it had been a refining, purifying and strengthening experience, but other churches disappeared altogether, and a third group was in sore straits by 1689. The Congregational church at Keswick must have been typical of many of them. A contemporary observer remarks: 'There was a Church of wch mr Cane was Pastor but ye graue and ye Church of England haue Swallowed up all ye members but one or two.'[21] But however devastating and detrimental was the effect of protracted persecution, or perhaps the equally destructive effect of partial tolerance, by the middle of the second decade of the eighteenth century the Congregationalists were the third largest Dissenting group, measured by number of congregations, well after the Presbyterians, but almost equal to the Particular Baptists.[22]

They were not, like the Presbyterians, to be found in considerable numbers throughout the country. They were strongest in the counties which had formed the nucleus of the Elizabethan Puritan movement and which had upheld the parliamentary cause during the Civil War. They appear to have constituted over 3% of the population of Essex, Hertfordshire and Northamptonshire, almost 3% of Bedfordshire and Cambridgeshire, and more than 2% of Huntingdonshire, Suffolk and Hampshire.

The Congregationalists were more urban-based than any other denomination, with 69.5% of them located in cities, boroughs or market towns. It is possible that as the age of religious enthusiasm during the Interregnum and the testing but exhilarating years of persecution gave way to the more ordered, and less threatening, age of toleration, so this tendency for Dissenters to live in urban rather than rural areas intensified.

But whether they lived in town or country, the worship of the Congregationalists remained simple. As with the Presbyterians their meeting-houses were unpretentious buildings hidden discreetly behind rows of respectable houses with but a narrow alley for worshippers to enter. Although there were such separate, dedicated places of worship in existence before the Toleration Act, in many cases private houses, barns and outbuildings were used. The post-Revolution meeting houses had a very distinctive atmosphere. Externally they were plain, with an almost domestic appearance. Internally they were dominated by the pulpit with the clerk's desk below it. The whitewashed walls and the flat ceiling, together with the white-painted woodwork and the many windows, made the buildings light and pleasant. They were functional, but congenial places for worship, with a certain simple dignity, although not very comfortable. It seems that the average number of 'hearers' per church was about 300.[23] And, as with the Presbyterians, a large proportion of those found worshipping in these meeting-houses were broadly within the category of the economically independent. The merchant, the 'gentleman', the 'tradesman', and to a slightly lesser extent the farmer and the yeoman, were prominent members. Not infrequently the meeting-house congregation reflected the early eighteenth-century social stratification. It was not considered inappropriate for the important and wealthy members to have pews which hid them from public view, or for seats to be allocated according to social status. Thus, in the meeting-house of Isaac Watts, which was completed in 1708 the 'seats occupied by Sir John Hartopp and Lady Abney would cost 40s. and were situated near the pulpit on the ground floor. Apprentices would be allocated the 12s. 6d. or 15s. seats at the back row of the galleries to the left and to the right of the pulpit while the maidservants occupied the 7s. 6d. seats in the top row of the gallery facing the pulpit.'[24] As a general principle the nearer the seats were to the pulpit, the more expensive they were.

The services themselves were simple and dignified. In towns it was customary to have two services on the Lord's day (the phrase very frequently used by Congregationalists and Dissenters in general to describe Sunday), whereas in the country one had to suffice. Prayer, psalm-singing, and sometimes hymn-singing, the public reading of the Bible, an exposition of scripture and a sermon were the usual components of a morning service, with the sermon taking a central part; but the scripture exposition was frequently omitted in the afternoon service. Evening services only became common after the evangelical revival, and this innovation was not always approved of by those who favoured the older tradition, largely because it hindered family piety and religious education during the evening. It is an indication of the intensity of the full Congregational regime, and of the fact that there was often a high standard of religious devotion among Congregationalists in this period, that, in addition to the Sunday services and family devotions there was often a week-night preparation meeting in readiness for the Sunday communion; and sometimes week-night sermons or 'lectures'. It was a well-established practice to hold a communion service on the first Lord's day of the month.

During the post-Revolution period very important changes were taking place in Congregational worship. In 1707 Isaac Watts published his *Hymns and Spiritual Songs*, and a second edition followed two years later which incorporated many improvements suggested by his friends, as well as 145 new hymns. Hymns had been composed and used before this time, but they were of low quality, and the singing indifferent. There were exceptions, as with the hymns of the High Church Anglicans, Thomas Ken, William Barton, John Mason, the Independent, Richard Davis, and the Baptist Benjamin Keach, but they were neither good enough nor sufficiently popular to oust the widely-liked, traditional psalm-singing, or to dispel the strong prejudice against the adoption of works of 'human composition'. 'To Watts more than to any other man is due the triumph of the hymn in English worship.'[25] And he enhanced his eminent place in the evolution of English worship by his pioneer work in the interpretation of the psalms, which was more thorough than had ever been achieved before in the quite long history of metrical psalm composition. Much of the writing of hymns and metrical psalms which preceded Watts was 'crabbed, allusive, tortuous prose and verse'.[26] Watts, even more than Charles Wesley, the other great hymn-writer of the eighteenth century, went beyond his concern for the drama of God's manifold relationship with the soul of man, their estrangement, their reconciliation and their union, and set this, and supremely the cross, against a cosmic background. 'Watts sees the Cross, as Milton had seen it, planted on a globe hung in space, surrounded by the vast distances of the universe. He sees the drama in Palestine prepared before the beginning of time and still decisive when time has ceased to be. There is a sense of the spaciousness of nature, of the vastness of time, of the dreadfulness of eternity . . .'[27]

The contribution Watts made to the development of Congregational worship did not end with his hymns and version of the psalms. The publication of *A Guide to Prayer* in 1716 was a notable event in the refinement of Congregational devotion. Although he was by no means opposed to the occasional use of precomposed forms of prayer, he was convinced of the crucial part that the cultivation of extemporary prayer should play in Congregational worship if it was to retain and improve on its spiritual vitality. Lastly, with his wide perspective, it is not surprising that Watts helped to free ministers from the insularity which had so easily beset them as a consequence of their education and the somewhat beleaguered nature of their chapel life. He gave them a new awareness of a larger potential membership beyond the confines of the meeting house.

The preaching tradition of Congregationalism was retained in the post-Revolution years. A half-hour scripture exposition, followed after a psalm or hymn by a sermon, as in the services of Watts, was the rule.

The preaching in general was, however, affected by the dominance of John Tillotson in setting an accepted standard for Anglican sermons. The plain, carefully modulated prose of Tillotson, with its precision and concern for morality rather than dogma, which we have already encountered, had an influence beyond the Church of England, and was consonant with the prevailing demands of the new science and the rational philosophies of the age. But, like the whole life of the churches in England in these years, it was not as vacuous as it has sometimes been portrayed. 'Taken all in all the preaching of the generation immediately preceding the Evangelical Revival may not have been very exciting; but what it lost in vitality and personal appeal it gained in strength. In its favour it may be claimed that it was sound in its doctrine, dignified in delivery, intellectual in appeal and clear in diction.'[28]

It was the Dissenting academies which did so much to train and educate the ministers who undertook the preaching, and who led these local congregations; although it is arguable that they were also a seedbed for theological ferment. It was in certain respects their golden age. Despite the fact that many of those founded in the seventeenth century had ceased to exist by the early eighteenth century,[29] others came to replace them. They had their deficiencies, such as inadequate resources, limited library facilities, and poor locations, as well as discontinuity in a number of cases as a consequence of a large degree of dependence upon particular tutors. Any change of pastorate meant that pupils were obliged to uproot themselves; and the death of a tutor not infrequently meant the end of the academy. Notwithstanding these shortcomings and hazards, there were some outstanding institutions. The academy at Hoxton (1701–1785) achieved excellence as a centre of learning under Isaac Chauncey, Thomas Ridgley, John Eames and David Jennings, and none of the academies had so many distinguished students as Samuel Jones' at Tewkesbury from 1708 to 1724. One, the academy under John Lavington's supervision, opened in 1752 at Ottery St Mary, was specifically established and funded by the Congregational Fund Board as part of a programme to preserve Congregational churches from the inroads of heterodoxy. Others were distinctly liberal. Thomas Rowe conducted an academy at Newington Green in London from 1678 to 1705 in which he encouraged 'freedom of enquiry' by his students; and his most distinguished pupil, Isaac Watts, wrote in 1696 that he had sometimes 'carried reason with [him] even to the camp of Socinus', though Paul had borne him back again 'almost to the tents of John Calvin'.[30] Another distinguished example of a liberal academy was that which was opened at Kibworth Beauchamp in Leicestershire in 1715 by John Jennings, and made famous by its most notable student, Philip Doddridge. The influence of this academy in helping to mould the mind of Doddridge was about as profound for him as was the influence of John Locke's philosophy. If 'we define a liberal in terms of an undogmatic temper of mind, then Doddridge was one of the most liberal Dissenters of the early eighteenth century. Moreover, he kept the liberal temper alive at a time when in Dissenting circles opposition forces were becoming increasingly active and increasingly oppressive'.[31] In 1729 Doddridge became the Principal of Jennings' Academy; and later on in the same year he moved it to Northampton when he took charge of a large Independent congregation there. It was typical of him that, whatever his own theological opinions, he put the difficulties fairly before his students. Like Jennings he painstakingly represented the arguments and referred to the authorities on both sides, and then left the students to judge for themselves. It was this same open, enquiring man who left for posterity the thoroughly orthodox hymns 'Hark the glad sound! the Saviour comes', 'My God, and is Thy Table spread', 'O God of Bethel, by Whose Hand' and 'Ye servants of the Lord'. It was, perhaps, symbolic of the age in which he lived.

The Baptists

Both the General and the Particular Baptists have, until quite recently, been portrayed as in a perilous state of decline in the post-Revolution decades. 'Baptists were now in a backwater,' writes one such historian, 'well off the main channel of national life. Whether in State Papers or in private correspondence, they simply disappear henceforward, or at most appear as obscure satellites, to be discerned occasionally, among the "Dissenters".'[32] Another comments that soon after the Toleration Act it appeared 'that the Baptist body was . . . in a remarkably depressed state . . . From the year immediately succeeding the passing of the Toleration Act to the end of the reign of William the Third the history of the Baptist denomination, as a whole, was not a history of progression.'[33] And a more recent historian has said that although the Baptists, in common with other Dissenters, were glad, after thirty years of inter-mittent hardship and persecution, to see the dawning of a more tolerant age, when, once again, 'they could meet freely, no longer threatened by well-rewarded informers or irate magistrates', they 'were unable to respond adventurously to the challenge of a new opportunity'. Although the story of General Baptist life in the early eighteenth century was 'relieved by positive achievements' it was 'rarely inspiring', and 'as the years went by, their disunity and fragmentation became worse rather than better'. The 'late seventeenth-century "expectation of great things" did not immediately issue in effective mission on any meaningful scale and it was not until the closing decades of the new century that churches of both groups [General and Particular] were diverted from arid controversy to fruitful expansion.'[34]

There is some truth in all of this, but it needs to be highly qualified. The Baptists were not an insignificant minority.[35] In the second decade of the eighteenth century the General and Particular Baptists in total numbered about 49,320, and they worshipped in about 328 congregations. Both the General Baptists (who were distinguished from the Particular Baptists by their more open, less rigidly Calvinist, doctrinal stance) and the Particular Baptists were concentrated in the southern half of England. The General Baptists were most numerous in the counties where Lollardy had been most abundant, such as in the Chilterns and the Weald, and the Particular Baptists tended to be best represented in the same counties as the Independents from whom they had originally sprung.

The Particular Baptists closely resembled the Congregationalists both in theology and polity, and they believed strongly in leaving the local fellowship of believers to pursue their independent life unimpeded by any central body. Their annual assemblies from 1689 to 1692 were beset by controversy, and were in fact the first and last to be held before 1813. At the initial one in 1689 they made a point, as good independents, of insisting that 'we disclaim all manner of superiority, superintendency over the churches; and that we have no authority or power to prescribe or impose any thing upon the faith and practice of any of the churches of Christ'.[36] A fund was established to supplement inadequate stipends, to prepare men for the ministry, and to support evangelists. All was fairly harmonious up to that time, but at the gathering in 1692 it was agreed to divide the annual national meeting in two, with the eastern churches meeting in London, and the western in Bristol; and controversy broke out especially in London about the propriety of hymn-singing in churches. It is difficult to determine how far such contention percolated down to the local churches and adversely affected their worship and witness, but there was a distinct sense that strife was at least marring much devotion and outreach. 'It was the twilight for the Calvinistic Baptists in a special sense: the heroic age of the persecution was over and instead had come the time of half-hearted institutionalization and internal doctrinal dispute.'[37]

The General Baptists had annual national assemblies and paid less regard than the Particular Baptists to the independence of local churches. Whether it was in part at least a result of this or not, it is a fact that they experienced major schisms in the last quarter of the seventeenth century. For one thing it was easier for the Assembly to pass resolutions than it was to enforce them, and churches which disliked the Assembly's decisions had only to withdraw from membership.

This is exactly what happened during the protracted controversy over the views of Matthew Caffyn which racked the denomination from the 1670s to 1731. Caffyn was born in 1628, the son of a yeoman farmer. After adopting Baptist views during the first Civil War he returned to become a farmer in Horsham and to be the pastor of the town's General Baptist church, with responsibility for evangelism in Sussex and Kent. It appears that Anabaptist views persisted in the area, and that Caffyn was attracted to the christological beliefs of Melchior Hofmann.[38] In the mid 1680s he was accused of denying not only the humanity but also the divinity of Christ. The accusations were repeated in 1693, when the General Assembly condemned Melchiorite views but acquitted Caffyn of subscribing to them. When the Assembly refused to reopen the question a minority of churches seceded and met in 1697 as a rival General Association. For the next thirty-four years, until 1731, there were virtually two General Baptist denominations, for it was only then that the two groups, somewhat uneasily, reunited.[39]

Preoccupied as they were with their own internal matters, the Baptists as a whole were little involved in local or national political affairs. Few of them cherished political ambitions. Only one Baptist is known to have practised occasional conformity, and he was promptly cast out of his church for profaning the sacrament by using it as 'the stepping-stone to office, and the picklock of a place'.[40]

At the local level the concern of all Baptist congregations was with the continuance of their inherited pattern of religious life: radicalism may have reared its head, with quite devastating effect, in the assemblies, but conservatism reigned almost supreme in most of the individual churches. 'Most churches were in rural areas; insularity was inevitable.'[41] There were some large congregations in the towns, but the average size was probably less than fifty, and the typical worshipping body was to be found in the scattered hamlets, villages and small market-towns of the English countryside. 'It had its roots in an agrarian society with stability, dependability, integration, continuity and insularity as part of its mingled strength and weakness. Generations of inter-marrying meant that members of such churches were closely related. Lay leadership was often confined to privileged families who had served for many generations. The closeness provided strength, but . . . the church's horizons could become limited. Corporate life degenerated into self-regarding independence, even doctrinaire superiority.'[42]

The political indifference of Baptists at the local level was shared by the Quakers; but at the national level they were as effective as any of the Dissenting denominations in making their case known in courtly circles.

The Quakers

The hopes of the Quakers were severely dashed by the Revolution, but they showed characteristic adaptability to changed circumstances, and by various means retained their accustomed political influence.[43] From their beginnings they had looked for protection to the court: first to the court of the Lord Protector, for whom George Fox had a strange fascination; then to that of Charles II; then, after 1675, to Parliament as well; and finally under James II, once more to the monarch. The Revolution brusquely severed the hot line to the throne which the Quakers, and more particularly William Penn and Robert Barclay, had established and kept open. It was a blow from which they did not take long to recover. They mobilized their well-organized system for obtaining evidence of their 'sufferings' throughout the country, and then used it the moment the Toleration Act was passed to attempt to extend their statutory protection.

The Toleration Act anyhow made considerable and special concessions to the Quakers. It not only removed the penalties attached to former legislation in the way I have already described for Dissenters in general, and gave them freedom of public worship, but it additionally and specially relieved Quakers from subscription to any of the Thirty-Nine Articles, allowing them instead to subscribe to a general declaration. As a further bonus, it respected their conscientious objection to swearing oaths, and allowed them to make a simple declaration of loyalty to the new monarchs instead of swearing the Oaths of Supremacy and Allegiance. From the point of view of Quakers the Act was defective in that it did not exempt them from oaths which had to be sworn before magistrates in civil affairs; but they promptly set in motion their well-tried machinery to rectify this. They lobbied Parliament successfully, and won the support of the King to such an extent that they secured most of what they wanted in the Affirmation Act of 1696, with its renewal in an Act of 1702, and its modification in their favour in 1722. Even as the period I am at present reviewing came to an end, around 1735, they were agitating still further, with the support of 'evidence' they had collected, in a well-organized campaign to modify the provisions of the Toleration Act relating to the payment of tithes. It was an impressive record of political achievement.

In certain respects the Quakers in 1689, as indeed throughout their history, stood apart from the other Dissenting bodies. After all it was only about forty years since they had been founded and had received their normative shape amid the astonishing middle decades of the seventeenth century. They alone among the proliferating new sects of that period of religious ferment had survived. The English Presbyterians, Congregationalists and Baptists were already well established, with fifty years of history behind them, when the Quakers appeared on the scene. And what is more, three of the key leaders of this nascent religious fellowship were still alive: George Fox, the founder, Robert Barclay, the most weighty of all the Quaker theologians, and William Penn, a figure of monumental importance to the new movement as it attempted to establish itself. Even though Fox had only two years to live, and Barclay only one, the three of them helped to give a sense of continuity and rootedness to such a young, yet still vibrant, body of believers. Fox was almost seventy years of age, and was showing the effects of years of imprisonment and suffering; but he remained as ardent as ever. No man living had done more than he to propagate the faith and to build up Christian communities. He was a man of commanding stature and presence, and age had helped to mellow his previously somewhat brusque manner. The pioneer period, when he 'could sniff the battle from afar, and would stride into parish churches determined to make his witness in an angry dialogue at the end of the sermon'[44] were passed, but he was still the revered leader of his devoted people.

Of the other two, Robert Barclay had provided a defence of the Quaker doctrines (*Apology for the True Divinity*, 1676) which has not been superseded. No similar Quaker work can match it in quality and scholarship.

Among the new cluster of leaders William Penn was outstanding. His 'political influence was equal to that of any man outside Parliament',[45] and he used it to the full to promote the interests of his fellow Quakers.

By 1689 he had been the foremost champion in England of religious liberty for about twenty years, and one of the most eminent of Quaker leaders. He was the son of Admiral Sir William Penn, who stood high in favour at court, and his father was at first exceedingly angry when his son declared his intention of identifying with the Friends. The young William was a learned man with courtly accomplishments and fit to be an ambassador or one of the king's ministers, and here he was consorting with Quakers. For a time, when he began to preach and to do itinerant work, his father expelled him from his house; and his father's indignation must have been heightened when his son suffered imprisonment, mainly as a consequence of his publication in 1668 of *The Sandy Foundation Shaken*, with its attack on the orthodox doctrines of the trinity and atonement and the Calvinistic account of justification. Although his father was later reconciled to him it was a painful estrangement.

During the 1670s he became increasingly preoccupied with his ambition to found a colony in America which would assure liberty of conscience for Quakers and others. In 1682 he obtained grants by letters patent of East New Jersey and Pennsylvania; and he drew up a constitution for the colony which permitted any form of worship compatible with monotheism and religious liberty.

Penn was friendly with James II, and publicly thanked him for liberties he granted to Quakers. This brought odium upon Friends who had no Jacobite leanings, and it 'seemed intolerable to many in the Society that their most prominent member, by station and capacity, should be branded as a dangerous Jacobite'.[46] In the thirty remaining years of his life after the Revolution he was imprisoned for High Treason, deprived of his Governorship of Pennsylvania, and harassed by colonial difficulties and financial embarrassments. But he remained actively involved in the affairs of the colony, resumed his practice of itinerant preaching, and in periods of enforced leisure again turned to writing, the most notable result being his *Primitive Christianity* in 1696, in which he identified Quaker principles with those of the early church.

These were the supreme Quaker triumvirate in 1689, but mention should also be made of George Whitehead, one of the most earnest of preachers and probably the most accomplished of all the Quaker literary controversialists, who was in the prime of life and fullness of activity in these years at the turn of the century. With such leaders, and with a penchant for the extensive and effective use of the press, the Quakers were quite successful in spreading their distinctive beliefs in the post-Toleration Act era. Between 1688 and 1690 licenses were taken out for 131 new temporary, and 108 new permanent Quaker places of worship.

The Quakers were strongest in three main areas: the counties of Cumberland and Westmorland and the Furness district of Lancashire, the scene of their early life with its focal point at Swarthmoor Hall; the city of Bristol, a place of importance for all the main Dissenting denominations, and soon to be second only to London as a centre of early Methodism; and London, together with the counties immediately to the north – Bedfordshire, Hertfordshire, Huntingdonshire and Essex. Although they were less numerous than the Presbyterians and the Congregationalists, they had more meeting-houses, and they were more evenly distributed over the country than any of the other Dissenting denominations. 'Of the five major groups of Dissenters only the Quakers had meetings in every English county, a tribute both to the missionary enthusiasm and to the organizational ability of the first Friends.'[47] With 39,510 members and 672 congregations, they had a smaller average size of congregation than the Presbyterians, the Congregationalists or any of the Baptist groups. Perhaps this was one of their attractive features; especially in urban situations. Certainly the close fellowship of the Methodist societies, classes and bands was to prove an immeasurable asset.

The Roman Catholics

In the eyes of the law, the English Catholics in the first quarter of the eighteenth century were 'gagged, and bound by a multiplicity of restraints and penalties'.[48] A large number of penal statutes dating from the Elizabethan era and later remained in force, as did a list of civil disqualifications which had been extended in 1689 and in the following years. In times of crisis, or when the fear of popery was in the ascendent, proclamations repeatedly threatened their enforcement. Ever since the sixteenth century, as the country had become more protestantized, the Roman Catholics had increasingly been treated as an alien and potentially dangerous group whose loyalty to the English Crown and Parliament was constantly in doubt. Whenever the cry of 'the church in danger' had been raised it had not infrequently been the Roman Catholics who had been targeted as the group which posed the greatest threat. Then, against this background, came the Revolution.

The Roman Catholics were deeply shocked by the events of 1688–9.

James II had been a friend to them and, despite the undiplomatic manner in which he tried to assist them, they had at least realized that he was pro-Catholic, and had their interests at heart.[49] They feared the worse when their champion fled the country. Popular hostility towards Catholics was running as high as it had ten years before – or so it appeared during the destructive outburst of mob violence against Catholics and Catholic property in December 1688. The prospect of war against Catholic France only heightened the tension and increased the animosity. After the passing of the Bill of Rights there could be no expectation of another Catholic king, unless he braved the perils of invasion and armed insurrection. The Toleration Act explicitly ruled out 'any ease, benefit or advantage to any papist or popish recusant whatsoever'. The Revolution also had a devastating effect on the Catholic peerage. 'Half its members were exiles, and often attainted and so financially ruined. The rest were living under suspicion of treason and deprived of all government office. Of the thirty-eight Catholic peerages of 1688 only twenty-three survived 1714.'[50]

New acts prohibited Catholic possession of arms or cavalry-size horses, and residence within the bounds of London or Westminster. It was also made more difficult for Catholics to own land or to take up careers in the professions. The double land tax imposed on recusants in every Land Tax Act after 1692 was a particularly heavy burden for a community which contained, and which so much relied upon, a disproportionate number of landed gentry. It continued to be burdensome for perhaps twenty-five years, after which declining assessments, administrative inertia, and devolution to tenants deprived it of its bite.

'The Protestant Establishment was now at least as virulently anti-Catholic in its pronouncements as it had been in the days of the Spanish Armada. In its propaganda Anglicanism was equated with political liberty, lay control of the clergy, plain truth-telling and all the other virtues of "Englishry". Catholicism was equated with political despotism, priestcraft, moral double-talk and all the other foreign vices.'[51] This is the period to which Linda Colley traces the origin of that drawing together of the English, the Welsh and the Scots, when they were 'made to feel separate from much of the rest of Europe – by their common commitment to Protestantism'.[52] From the Act of Union of 1707 to the Battle of Waterloo in 1815, Great Britain was engaged in successive, very dangerous wars with Catholic France. At the same time it was in the early stages of carving out a massive and worldwide empire. And in all of this 'Protestantism was able to become a unifying and distinguishing bond as never before.'[53] The common religious 'Other' which opposed the British Protestant crusade was Roman Catholicism. It had reared its ugly head at many crisis times in the post-Reformation history of England, and it was now seen as inextricably involved in French and other forms of resistance to the fulfilment of Britain's destiny.

This virulent anti-Catholicism fed on a flood of popular literature. *Old Moore's Almanac*, the contemporary equivalent of the modern tabloid press, perpetrated that interpretation of English history which depicted Roman Catholicism as the enemy of the people. In the half million copies of different kinds of almanac sold in Great Britain each year, in rural as well as in urban areas, the same message was repeated with almost monotonous regularity. 'The majority were crude and intolerant productions, offering a jumble of useful and sensational information, combined with "an endlessly popular diet of jingoism, abuse of Catholics, and predictions of the downfall of the Pope and the French".'[54] But together with sermons these almanacs were the only history lessons the majority of English people received.

And then there was the matter of Jacobitism – 'the idea and the expression of support for the exiled Stuarts'.[55] Whatever the extent and content of Jacobitism, and this has been a matter of considerable debate among historians, its enemies were prone to identify the support of the Stuarts with the evils of absolutism and Roman Catholicism, which for them were virtually interchangeable. After each real or imagined plot and rebellion, as with those in 1696, 1700, 1706, 1715 and 1722, new measures imposing ever greater restraints on Catholics were introduced, or the enforcement of old ones was threatened. At the time of the various Jacobite scares searches were made for arms and horses. It was all part of a policy to keep Catholics well under control. Colin Haydon gives considerable importance to the fear of Jacobitism in his assertion that anti-Catholicism did not decline throughout the eighteenth century. 'It is true', he says, 'that, from mid-century onwards, elite political and intellectual culture ceased to fear Catholicism as a political force, and more than ever questioned the social utility and morality of religious persecution. Yet among the populace at large, and in particular within religious circles, the old hatred of Popery continued unabated.'[56] Haydon questions the longstanding view that Hanoverian England was a state that was particularly tolerant of religious pluralism. He believes that the evidence 'shows that religious animosities were ubiquitous and strong for much of that period. Fraught with confessional tensions, English society under the first two Georges appears in this, as in other respects, the natural continuation of society under the Stuarts.'[57] The hatred of Catholics, which was rooted in post-Reformation history, and the anti-Catholic panics in 1745 were carbon-copies of the *peurs* of 1641–42 and 1688. The papists were subject to hostile stereotyping. In particular, 'the events of 1642–60 laid the foundations of bitter folk memories'.[58]

The Catholic community was harassed and hamstrung, and it wilted under the oppression. Historians have mostly concurred in their judgment of the depressed and depressing state of the Catholics in this post-Revolutionary era. E.I.Watkin concludes that the Revolution had 'inaugurated for English Catholics the most dispiriting period of their history, of persecution without the heroism and glory of martyrdom, of exclusion from the government, administration, and military service of their country, a period of defections and diminishing numbers when their religion was generally despised as the finally discredited superstition of the past'.[59] David Matthew concurred. 'For the Catholics', he writes, 'this was a period of dispirited discouragement. A definite proportion of that generation of the surviving landed gentry which had grown to manhood in the reign of Queen Anne and in the first years of her successor had abandoned the old religion. The outlook seemed hopeless; lacking even the stimulus of severe persecution. The vicars apostolic were for the most part elderly and there was a need for new blood among both clergy and laity. It was perhaps at this time that the hopes of the Catholics were at their lowest.'[60] John Bossy argued 'that English Catholics during the century after 1688 were not on any reasonable judgment an oppressed minority', and 'that their history had gone rather satisfactorily'; but he later reviewed his assessment, and wondered if he had been too patriotic and too Whiggish.[61]

Nonetheless, even if post-Revolution Catholicism was pressed on all sides and was not experiencing one of its most buoyant periods, it showed some signs of health and vigour. There is evidence that Catholic missioners emerged from their hiding places after the immediate Protestant post-Revolution fury had largely spent itself, and resumed their work. Town and country chapels, whether they had been wrecked or not, were quite rapidly re-established, although usually in less conspicuous premises. The old, small Catholic schools, together with a few that had begun in 1686–8, restarted in quieter places. Most significantly the Chapters and the assemblies of missioners took place as usual in 1689. In fact, in the period 1680–1720 the number of Catholic missioners soared to over 750; and if priests retained on the continent are included this inflates the figure to possibly between 1,000 and 1,100 – far in excess of mission requirements. They declined steeply after 1720, to 500 by 1760 and 380 by 1773. But this only helps to emphasize that the Catholic community in the half century after the Revolution had some life and sense of mission; an impression which is enhanced by the realization that lay adherence to the English Catholic mission actually increased after 1700, at a rate of around 0.5% per annum.[62] Such signs of spiritual life and missionary enterprise should make us hesitate to condemn the post-Revolution Catholic Church as being in a state of torpor and almost irreversible decline.

Part 2

Revival

3

The Churches in England,
*c.*1735 to *c.*1791

Generalizations about the health of the eighteenth-century churches in England can be most misleading; but they can be made with caution, and with reservations. Our knowledge is still slight and patchy, but it has greatly increased in the last fifty years. There have recently been some very useful local studies, and studies of particular aspects of the churches in the period I am about to describe and analyse. 'We are still very far from possessing a complete picture of any of the issues that have been used as indexes of the vitality of the Georgian Church. Much material still lies unexplored in diocesan and county record offices and much work remains to be done. But the broad outlines are clear, and, even when we have a more complete picture, it is still unlikely that it will be any easier to interpret.'[1] Such a conclusion applies, if not equally at least in large measure, to the Dissenting denominations and to Roman Catholicism as well as to the Church of England.

The work of historians in the last third of the twentieth century has also helped to create a new agenda for the study of the churches in the eighteenth century. There has been a significant shift from the blanket condemnations of the nineteenth and early twentieth centuries, when sweeping general charges of corruption, stagnation, inertia, worldliness and time-serving were employed, and also away from the protracted, and to some extent sterile, debate between the 'pessimists' who assumed the mantle of their judgmental forebears, but with modifications, and the 'optimists' who took a more rosy view of the eighteenth-century church scene. There has been concern in recent years to understand the role of the churches within eighteenth-century society as a whole, and to appreciate more fully some of the key elements in its corporate life. The attention of historians has therefore been focussed on the unquanti-fiable as well as the quantifiable aspects of church life: on pastoralia, the quality and nature of the work of the clergy, the characteristics of worship, differences in churchmanship, and the work and witness of the laity. Many of the studies emphasize local and regional variations. And they quite often reveal a north-south divide; but with very distinct, and sometimes startling, contrasts from one area to another within regions, and also between the towns and the countryside. Such studies are at a very early stage, but they are beginning to open up new vistas, and to refine or replace previous generalizations.

But perhaps a word of caution is in order. However extensive the data may one day be, and however comprehensive our knowledge or sophisticated our analysis of this or any other period, on the one hand there will still be the outstanding, untypical individual who defies any easy categorization, and on the other hand there will always be the silent majority whose way of life and whose beliefs are ever in danger of being undervalued because they are so elusive and so undramatic. Both place an embargo on the full reliability of generalizations in any historical study, but most especially in the history of the churches. And to these barriers to full knowledge must be added the sometimes warped perspective we adopt. Perhaps our indices of 'success' or 'failure' may often be misconceived if we are concerned to assess whether the churches have been true to their calling. Gordon Rupp well summarizes these limitations, and the need for hesitation in making generalizations. The 'saint and cynic, moralist and sceptic turn to one side of the picture, one part of the evidence. The historian has to allow for the immense silences of the unassuming and unpublicized, the multitude of the inarticulate, the unremembered acts of kindness, the cup of cold water. The records and the registers, the diaries and sermons, satirists and publicists may add up to something impressive in the way of evidence, but may miss altogether those authentic standards by which, according to the New Testament, the Christian quality of life is to be judged.'[2] All studies, especially those which most commonly and reasonably rely on primary or secondary written sources, will describe what was, as it were, the 'public face' of the church. Such works, like the history of the churches in general, are bound 'to fail to do justice to the spiritual experience of ordinary church members and adherents, concerning which clear evidence is difficult to come by. Similarly, the reasons for church growth most commonly given by participants – a combination of their own labours in the Gospel and divine grace mediated through "special providences" and outpourings of the Holy Spirit – tend from the external perspective available to the historian to be seen at best "as through a glass darkly". There is a tendency, therefore, to undervalue those elements in the situation which contemporaries felt were the most important, not out of any conscious reductionism, but because of the nature of the evidence; because, as Owen Chadwick has noted in another context, "measuring tithe is easier for the historian than measuring the inside of John Stuart Mill".[3]

The Church of England

The Church of England in the second quarter of the eighteenth century suffered a severe mauling at the hands of its own contemporaries. Writing in 1736, that intelligent and astute observer of the contemporary scene, Bishop Butler, bemoaned a general decay and disregard of religion:

> It is come, I know not how, to be taken for granted, by many persons, that Christianity is not so much a subject of enquiry; but that it is, now at length, discovered to be fictitious. And accordingly they treat it as if, in the present age, this were an agreed point among all people of discernment; and nothing remained, but to set it up as a principal subject of mirth and ridicule, as it were by way of reprisal for its having so long interrupted the pleasure of the world.[4]

Two years later George Berkeley, Bishop of Cloyne, declared that morality and religion in Britain had collapsed 'to a degree that has never been known in any Christian country'. 'Our prospect', he wrote, 'is very terrible and the symptoms grow worse from day to day.'[5] In the same year Thomas Secker, Bishop of Oxford, in an episcopal charge, added his lamentation:

> In this we cannot be mistaken, that an open and professed disregard of religion is become, through a variety of unhappy causes, the distinguishing character of the age. Such are the dissoluteness and contempt of principle in the world, and the profligacy, intemperance, and fearlessness of committing crimes in the lower part, as must, if the torrent of impiety stop not, become absolutely fatal. Christianity is ridiculed and railed at with very little reserve; and the teachers of it without any at all.[6]

The hostility to the clergy was particularly vicious, as this last quotation indicates, with attacks on their motives and morals, often in coarse and pungent language, and quite frequently in comments tinged with savage ridicule:

First, as a rule I'll lay it down
That in this giddy, busy town
The clergy least religion have
Of all the folks this side the grave.
For now the black-coat greedy dons
Are almost like old Eli's sons,
Keep up the priesthood for a cloak
Though most believe it all a joke.[7]

Of course all of these adverse appraisals can be dismissed out of hand or given little credence on the grounds that the authors were biased, and had their own particular reasons for discovering, and perhaps exaggerating, evidence of deterioration which they could then attribute to the neglect of principles which they held dear, or, as in the latter commentary, and ones similar to it, because of innate antagonism to organized religion in whatever form it appeared. It can also be said that each generation is prone to decry its contemporaries, and to view the current religious and moral situation as dire, and more deplorable than in former times. Likewise, the comment of Montesquieu that in England there was 'no religion and the subject, if mentioned, excites nothing but laughter',[8] can be ridiculed as a reflection of the prevailing opinion of the circle in which he moved, and reckoned as not applying to the population as a whole. Far more importantly, if we consider the wider European and transatlantic religious setting, attention can be drawn to the fact 'that in the contemporary perception of the early eighteenth-century Protestant world the Church of England enjoyed a chorus of admiration which, if not quite unanimous, far exceeded anything which has since come her way, and her divines, so suspect at home in the nineteenth century, enjoyed a European hearing such as has been denied them, on the whole justly, for two centuries or more'.[9] But even taking into account all these qualifications, the severe criticism, of which samples have been given, cannot be ignored. At the very least they predispose the historian to think that all was far from well with the church.

And the limited statistics available point in the same direction. In a study of patterns of church growth Currie, Gilbert and Horsley have indicated from a sample of parishes where relevant data was available that throughout the period from 1738 to 1811 the number of communicants was consistently low at about 5% of the total population. In the selected parishes the number of communicants also fell by a quarter between 1738 and 1802 and rose in 1811 to no more than 83% of the 1738 total. They conclude that if 'total church-membership rose during the eighteenth century, the increment must be largely or wholly attributable to churches other than the established churches, that is to say to the Nonconformists and the Catholics'.[10] There were deep-seated and long-term causes for this malaise.

For one thing, as I have previously observed, the church structure was not conducive to effective nationwide evangelism or adequate pastoral oversight. 'The very shape of the Church was antiquated: at one end the cumbrous sees of York and Lincoln, at the other a parochial system with its roots in the Heptarchy, unable to adjust itself easily to a shifting and rapidly growing population.'[11] There were great disparities in wealth between dioceses such as Durham and Winchester at one extreme and Bristol at the other, and between beneficed clergy and perpetual curates. A serious mismatch was developing between the demographic and social structure of the country and both the pattern of distribution of the Church of England manpower and the rewards offered to those employed in parochial, deanery and diocesan ministries. And this was compounded by the pluralism which we have already seen as an important factor in the late seventeenth and early eighteenth centuries. We are witnessing the early stages of a process which was to become a central feature in the history of the Church of England in particular, but also the churches in England in general. The fact that religious pluralism, which had been developing for almost two hundred years, assumed a central importance in the religious history of the nation at a time when the coherence of the pre-industrial social order was disintegrating under demographic, economic and political pressures was of crucial significance for the long-term history of religion, and also for the way the English adjusted to industrialization and political transformation in the century after the conclusion of the Napoleonic Wars.[12]

In effect the Church of England in the 1730s was confronted with a situation of emerging *de facto* voluntarism. A new tolerance of a variety of religious traditions and, by implication if not in explicit terms in the statute book, of irreligion, combined with fairly widespread, long-standing pastoral problems, meant that the Church of England had to cope with a serious loss of status and influence. Its religious monopoly was no longer enshrined in the law of the land. The pressure upon people to conform was social and religious rather than legal. There is no firm evidence about the number of people who managed to evade or ignore the provisions of the Uniformity Laws in the time before

1689, but the position was undoubtedly worsened by the Toleration Act and general trends in society in the post-Revolution decades. The 'Church of England was beginning to experience, on a significant scale, the problem of being a religious Establishment in a society no longer constrained to accept its leadership'.[13]

But this loss of status and power should not be over-stated. Political authority and social control were highly localized in eighteenth-century England, and the clergyman was able to dictate religious norms in countless parishes where he was in alliance with local ruling elites. Where the incumbent was resident and enjoyed the wholehearted support of the local land-owners and the magistracy, he could guarantee a high level of religious practice and uniformity, and make religious Dissent virtually untenable. Of course this 'dependency system' had its grave disadvantages. In an age of increasingly rapid change the local clergy may have been able to respond more effectively to social, political and religious pressures if they had not relied on the patronage and support of a class whose position was tied to a certain order of society which itself was to become one of the casualties of the impending political, industrial, agricultural and social revolutions. But in the meantime the force of traditional parochial, and especially rural, life should not be underestimated. The Church of England had become firmly embedded as an integral part of the corporate life of the local community in countless villages and small towns. In such situations it was largely protected from some of those forces which have most readily caught the eye of the historian, and have resulted in a pessimistic view of the eighteenth-century Church of England's state and prospects.

> The bitter-sweet music of its jangling bells hovered over the fields and towns as though expressing a sway over the very elements. Within the walls of its parish churches the greater part of the nation was baptized, married, and laid to rest. Through all the changing scenes of life, in trouble and in joy, thither the tribes came up in national crisis or in private need, to reckon with their Maker. Whether the priest were faithful or unfaithful, the liturgy went on, Holy Scriptures, prayers, the Word and the Sacraments. And if most of it was as unexciting and unspectacular as daily bread, it was as vital to the continuing life of a Church with its roots going back a thousand years.[14]

At the national level, the bishops of the land were faced with a new and problematic relationship between the church and the state. 'The essential difference between the post-Revolutionary position of the Church of England and that which obtained earlier was not one of increased erastianism, so much as change in the nature of the political power to which the church was subject. Prior to the accession of William and Mary authority was prescriptive, being seen to repose in a divinely appointed ruler. With the rejection of the Stuart dynasty in the bloodless coup of 1688, control of ecclesiastical as well as secular affairs passed in some measure to the will of Parliament. Royal fiat was replaced, especially after the reign of Queen Anne, by the corporate decision-making of the Lords and Commons. '[15] The proroguing of Convocation in 1717 was an ominous portent of things to come. The House of Lords became the only official medium for the expression of ecclesiastical opinion, and 'matters affecting religion vied with other issues for the attention of government'.[16] As the eighteenth century progressed the pressure was placed more firmly on the bench of bishops to become a special group of political functionaries. Such a new situation, and a modified role for the episcopate, may have had a deleterious effect on spiritual leadership within the Church of England and, combined with the prevailing patronage system, may, in some cases, have resulted in an unseemly scramble for translation to wealthy sees, and a diversion of attention from the administrative and spiritual responsibilities of bishops in their own dioceses. But the harmful consequences of the revised church-state relations can be exaggerated.

For a great number of the bishops and clergy of the eighteenth century the maintenance of Prayer Book worship and of pastoral oversight, without any extremes of theological stance, either High or Low, Latitudinarian or Evangelical, was the accepted duty. Perhaps the bulk of Hanoverian churchmen regarded the Church of England as the Aristotelian mean between ecclesiastical extremes; and with the experiences of the seventeenth-century conflicts between High Churchmen and Puritans ever before them as a warning against any form of ecclesiastical or theological excess, they studiously avoided any semblance of 'enthusiasm'. In the age of Enlightenment, when great value was placed on the ideals of equilibrium, proportion and harmony, it is not surprising that many churchmen stressed 'moderation'; and rejoiced in the Church of England as the *via media* between the infallibilist authoritarianism of Rome and excessive individualism of radical Protestants.

This emphasis on a balanced avoidance of extremes is epitomized in some of the leading bishops of the Hanoverian era. There were many who were eminent in learning, wisdom and pastoral care. The worthy roll of honour includes the saintly Thomas Wilson, Bishop of Sodor and Man, who, in an episcopate of fifty-seven years, from 1698 to his death in 1755, was instrumental in raising the standards of spiritual life and pastoral efficiency in the island, and was active as a church-builder, farmer and founder of public libraries. He was assiduous in his administration of church discipline, and was fearless in using his Ecclesiastical Constitutions of 1704 to inflict penalties for slander, perjury, immorality and other offenses. He left behind him what almost amounted to a legend of episcopal excellence. Of a different kind of excellence was Joseph Butler, whom we have already met as the distinguished author of *Analogy of Religion* (1736), and an outstanding philosopher, much admired by John Wesley despite some of his criticisms of Methodism. A fellow philosopher-bishop, George Berkeley, in addition to his important philosophical works, showed a remarkable and perspicacious missionary interest and concern for a man of his day and generation, as demonstrated by his energetic attempts to found a missionary college in Bermuda. In certain respects he was in advance of his time in his missionary thinking, as was Archbishop William Wake in the matter of ecumenism. Wake's efforts to implement a plan for the reunion of the Church of England and the French church place him among a select band of such enthusiasts of all ages. Among the foremost theologians of the century we must include Bishop William Warburton, whose works in defence of the church were of considerable importance. And, lastly, there were the two distinguished Bishops of London, Edmund Gibson and Robert Lowth, and the outstanding High Church bishop of the century, Samuel Horsley.

Bishops of this calibre would have adorned any century in the history of the church. They were exceptional, but there were others who deserve commendation. There were such pastors as Keppel, Ross, Blackhall, Fisher, Trelawny, Clagget, Lavington of Exeter, Horn of Norwich, Bagot of Bristol, Hinchcliffe of Peterborough, Benson of Gloucester and Hurd of Worcester. 'Despite all their secular preoccupations, it is evident that many good and conscientious bishops took seriously their duties and laboured hard and earnestly to ordain, confirm, and conduct their visitations, and to impress a sense of pastoral responsibility on the Church in charges and in sermons.' [17] Indeed, in the course of the eighteenth century some episcopal progress was made. Improvements in pastoral supervision were achieved by the increasing use of articles of inquiry directed to the clergy at visitations, which we have already considered, and by the reintroduction of rural deans into some dioceses.[18] Such reform depended on the energy and initiative of individuals, and it was therefore piecemeal. The kind of overall fundamental reform which had been advocated by Bishop Gibson in the 1720s, and was later proposed by Bishop Richard Watson in the 1780s, never took place. The notorious, scandalous, or simply lazy or inefficient exceptions clearly existed on the bench of bishops throughout the long eighteenth century, but they should not be used to characterize and castigate the bishops as a whole. It has been argued, and it may be true, that after the influence of Edmund Gibson there was a loss of strong leadership and a dilution of churchmanship at the highest levels of the church. Some of the leaders were not especially dynamic. It has been said of Thomas Herring, the Archbishop of York from 1743 to 1747, and Archbishop of Canterbury from 1747 to 1757, that he 'was by no means as colourless a person as he was made out to be, but he was conservative and suspicious of any proposals that might endanger existing arrangements, and excite either clergy or laity'.[19] And this is the kind of criticism which is commonly levelled at so many Hanoverian churchmen. But in general, and on balance, it seems that the 'eighteenth century episcopate deserves a juster measure of appreciation than has been their lot at the hands of many historians . . . They strove, on the whole, with diligence, and not without a good measure of success, to discharge the spiritual administration of their office.' [20]

The same applied to the clergy; but in their case, to the uninspired, uninspiring and lethargic were added the immoral, the drunkards and the bigots. The hard-drinking, hunting 'squarson' undoubtedly existed, as did those who were known more for their skill at card-playing than for their ability to preach. There were also those like James Woodforde who, despite his obvious delight in the meat which perisheth, his uneven temper, and his eye for an elegant woman, nevertheless showed great kindness and generosity to his parishioners, concern for their well-being, and faithfulness in the performance of his duties. And there is no reason to think that Samuel Wesley, the father of John and Charles, was unique; he was most likely fairly typical of resident parish incumbents. For forty years he was locked away in his parish of Epworth, quietly and unostentatiously undertaking his parochial tasks. 'My father's method', wrote John Wesley after his death, 'was to visit all his parishioners, sick or well, from house to house, to talk with each of them on the things of God and observe severally the state of their souls.

What he observed he minuted down in a book kept for that purpose and in this manner he went through his parish (which was near three miles long) three times. He was visiting it the fourth time round when he fell into his last sickness.'[21] Like so many country clergymen of the Hanoverian years, his daily round may not have been very arduous, and the demands made upon him may not have been very great. In addition, he had a propensity to fall into debt, and he suffered from a short temper. He was clearly subject to the failings of the flesh, but he went about his duties with diligence.

It is John Wesley who provides us with one of the most salutary correctives to an unqualified condemnation of the parish clergy of the eighteenth century. He probably knew them as well as any person in his time, and he had suffered greatly at the hands of some of their less tolerant members, as had other Methodist leaders and a countless number of ordinary Methodist believers. Yet he surprisingly paid his tribute to them. 'It must be allowed', he wrote, 'that ever since the Reformation, and particularly in the present century, the behaviour of the clergy in general is greatly altered for the better . . . Most of the Protestant clergy are different from what they were. They have not only more learning of the most valuable kind, but abundantly more religion. Insomuch that the English and Irish clergy are generally allowed to be not inferior to any in Europe, for piety as well as for knowledge.'[22]

It is clear from a number of studies that, whatever the quality of individual clergy may have been, there was, throughout the long eighteenth century, a high level of non-residence and pluralism.[23] The situation which I have described for the late seventeenth century and the early part of the eighteenth century continued until well into the nineteenth century. 'Curates, both fully priested and at the preliminary stage of deacon's orders, were in a permanent and impecunious state of over-supply. As a consequence aspiring candidates competed for the doubt-ful privilege of serving country parishes at a level of remuneration which made it necessary to unite the work with the cure of one or more neigh-bouring livings.'[24] And, from this base level, the practice permeated through the whole parochial system, especially in the countryside, which in any case represented the bulk of the deployed manpower of the church. The fundamental cause was poverty, and it had not been greatly mitigated by the beginning of the eighteenth century. The vitality of the established church was sapped by economic malaise. Queen Anne's Bounty was a step in the right direction, 'but the ad hoc nature of the distribution system, with its reliance upon the lot, and the inadequacy of the sums available meant that little impression was made upon the overall problem'.[25]

Some at least of the blame for the dire situation must be laid at the door of the bishops and others in authority at all levels within the church. One commentator, after providing statistical evidence to illustrate the extent of these twin problems besetting the church in the diocese of Ely in the eighteenth century, points in that direction. 'What these figures make clear', he writes, 'is that the bishop of Ely did little in the use of his patronage to strengthen the weak places in the economic structure of the church', and he adds that 'there is no reason to suppose he was unrepresentative in this'.[26] Another historian, covering the Archdeaconry of Durham in the last quarter of the eighteenth century and the first half of the nineteenth century, is likewise and even more fully and forcefully condemnatory:

> Evidence indicates that in the light of the unusually large number of advowsons held by the Durham ecclesiastical establishment, a substantial proportion of the blame for the perpetuation of a high level of non-residence and pluralism during the latter Hanoverian period within the diocese and archdeaconry lay with the bishop and chapter of Durham. By the mid century it appeared clear to certain contemporaries that the weakness of the Church in Durham, in the face of rapidly expanding dissent, was a result of successive failures by bishops, deans and chapters, and the parochial clergy of Durham, to take measures against what John Bird Sumner referred to as the 'culpable indifference of those who lived before them'. Considering the resources of Durham's church establishment, such criticism appears well placed.[27]

But again, as with most matters to do with the eighteenth century, the temptation is to make somewhat one-sided judgments. There were certainly disastrous shortcomings, inadequacies, financial restrictions and failings at parochial level and among those in authority which adversely affected the national parochial ministry. Nonetheless, visitation returns show clearly that many of the clergy, even if technically non-resident, undertook their parish duties conscientiously and with a sense of responsibility. In most parishes there was normally at least one service every Sunday, and in the more populous parishes there was typically morning and afternoon worship. In 'the vast majority of country parishes clerical influence, if only in a restraining form, remained an important feature of social life'.[28]

The attitude, style of life and ministry of bishops and clergy was in part determined in a large number of cases by their churchmanship. As we consider church 'party' allegiances we also find that individual and corporate religious and theological partisanship was inextricably bound up with social and political factors. Theological beliefs cannot be taken in complete isolation. 'A broad cultural definition of religious identity, encompassing theology, social and economic values, family and community networks and political predispositions is both more useful and more accurate.'[29] A cultural understanding of religious identity allows for the primacy of theological awareness, but recognizes that this is intermingled with non-theological orientations.

First of all the Latitudinarians. For Latitudinarianism did not die in the second quarter of the eighteenth century; but it did change its form. Although recent historical revision has stressed that Latitudinarianism was not as cohesive and distinctive as formerly portrayed by historians, the term can be applied to an identifiable group of clergymen and bishops. The Hanoverian system of ecclesiastical preferment produced a bench of bishops who were not renowned for their reforming zeal. But there were a small 'but very vocal body of Whig clergy who tirelessly asserted that the activities of their Tory clerical counterparts endangered the Revolutionary Settlement in Church and State and that Whig principles and Anglican doctrine, if correctly viewed, could exist in peaceful amity'.[30] A number of them became so committed to the reforming 'Commonwealth' tradition of Whig ideology that they developed views about the nature of church and state which could not easily be accommodated within the confines of the unreformed constitution. Their criticism of the defects of the church, and their concern for ecclesiastical reform gradually extended to a wider critique of the constitution in general. It was a transition from theological to political radicalism; or at least the politicization of theological radicalism, for the theological element remained as a central concern of these clerical Whigs. They were the latter-day Latitudinarians. And they shared with the former Latitudinarians a broadly common theological, philosophical and political outlook. 'They were not prepared to allow philosophical differences to outweigh their commitment to moderation and, in their different contexts, to the *via media*. Many still hoped for a comprehensive establishment.'[31]

This whole theological and political orientation of such churchmen received its most public expression in the subscription controversy. As we have already seen, subscription was a vital issue in the post-

Revolution era; and although the furore died down it cast a shadow over the lives of many Anglicans who maintained an uneasy loyalty to their preferred church. Occasionally the matter came to the fore, as when the Reverend John Jones published his *Free and Candid Disquisition Relating to the Church of England* (1749), in which he argued for reform on a wide range of church issues and for a modified form of subscription. It was, however, Francis Blackburne who brought the subject fully out into the open. While he had been an undergraduate at Cambridge he had become strongly attached to the principles of ecclesiastical and civil liberty through the study of Locke and Hoadly. He published a pamphlet in 1758 in which he maintained that the arguments used by many Anglican clergymen to defend their subscription to the Articles were casuistical. He was prepared to suffer the consequences of his principles, and refused any further promotion as this would have required further subscription. He launched his full-scale attack on subscription in a work which brought the subject into the public arena and rocked the ecclesiastical establishment: *The Confessional: Or a Full and Free Inquiry into the Right, Utility, Edification, and Success, of Establishing Systematical Confessions of Faith and Doctrine in Protestant Churches*, published in 1766.

Echoing Chillingworth's dictum that 'the bible is the religion of Protestants', Blackburne argued that it was sufficient for intending Anglican clergymen to profess a belief in the scriptures as the word of God. No church has the right to require assent to its own interpretation of the sense of scripture, exclusive of other interpretations, without violating the cardinal tenet of the Reformation, the right of private judgment. The church should be entirely independent of the state; and it should become sufficiently comprehensive to embrace heterodox as well as orthodox Protestants. Such a programme of total separation of the church from the state, complete liberty of conscience and universal toleration provided an agenda for religious radicals in the late eighteenth century.

The book stirred up an immediate and furious debate. The controversy came to a head at a meeting in July 1771 at the Feathers Tavern in London, and a petition, drafted by Blackburne, requesting that subscription to the Articles for clergy and graduates should be abolished, was signed by about 250 people and sent to the House of Commons. It was defeated by 217 votes to 71. The petition did, however, lead to Cambridge University abolishing in 1772 the requirement that BAs should subscribe to the Articles, though they still had to declare that

they were *bona fide* members of the Church of England as by law established.

In response to the defeat a small group of the signatories left the
Church of England. Much to the chagrin of Blackburne, one of these
was his son-in-law, Theophilus Lindsey, the most notable among the
seceders. And well may Blackburne have been concerned, for Lindsey
openly espoused Unitarianism, and he founded the first Unitarian
chapel, in Essex Street, London. The liturgy adopted was a modified
version of that drafted by Samuel Clarke in the early part of the
century, but never used. The law forbidding anti-Trinitarianism was
never enforced against the chapel. It was allowed to continue and
became a focus in the capital for many who had radical religious and
political views. Among those who attended its services were Benjamin
Franklin, Sir George Savile and the Duke of Grafton. Lindsey was later
joined by another of Blackburne's sons-in-law, John Disney. Only about
ten Anglican clergy left the church at this time, and only four, including
Disney, became Unitarian ministers. But what they lacked in numbers
they made up for in zeal, and especially in the energetic promotion of
public causes. Their impact was enhanced by the labours of a small
band of Dissenters, including Joseph Priestley, who had adopted similar
religious and political views, although the bonds of common education
and even intermarriage meant that the former Anglicans remained a
distinct Unitarian group. Perhaps the most effective and prominent pub-
licist among these early Unitarians was John Jebb, a man of considerable and varied ability who left a tutorship at Peterhouse, Cambridge,
in 1775 and was subsequently as active in the cause of parliamentary
reform as in the promotion of Unitarianism.

It was at this time, during the 1770s, that remarkable and dramatic
changes took place which compelled people to take sides on a variety of
religious and political issues.[32] The campaign to abolish subscription
and the emergence of organized Unitarianism coincided with the failure
in 1773 of the first of many petitions to relieve Dissenters. And
this rebuff forced the Dissenting interest into a greater degree of detach-
ment and disaffection. The American Declaration of Independence
encouraged 'patriots' and 'friends of liberty'. The Gordon riots stirred
up, and gave a focus to anti-Catholic sentiment. Various publications
such as Adam Smith's *Wealth of Nations*, Jeremy Bentham's *Fragment
on Government* and Thomas Paine's *Common Sense*, all three published
in 1776, inaugurated a fundamentally new way of looking at human
society and its ills. It was in the same year that there appeared the first

volume of Edward Gibbon's *Decline and Fall of the Roman Empire*, marking the beginning of a frontal assault on Christianity; with David Hume's *Dialogues concerning Natural Religion* being printed, posthumously, three years later. All events, writings and trends such as these fed on an ever more pronounced and explicit philosophical and attitudinal shift, not only in academic circles but among the more literate and informed sectors of the general public. 'Modern labels such as "conservative", "radical" or "progressive", hopelessly anachronistic before the 1770s, gradually became more applicable . . . to a generation living through an increasing polarization of belief and opinion.'[33] J. C. D. Clark, A. M. C. Waterman and others have argued that there was a 'high correlation between theological and political "radicalism" in the last three decades of the century: for Socinian theology "*entailed*" a credo of political revolution.'[34]

Latitudinarianism[35] within the established church helped to trigger off, or at least encourage, some of these movements.[36] But other forms of churchmanship also had important consequences for the immediate and long-term life of the Church of England, even if they did not have the same religiously schismatic, politically radical implications.[37] I will be considering the Church of England Evangelicals in chapter 5.[38] At the moment I focus attention on the High Churchmen.[39]

It was the prominence given to mystery and sacramentalism which, perhaps, distinguished those High Churchmen of the eighteenth century who were most true to their tradition; and among these the Hutchinsonians deserve a place which has been denied them until recently.[40] John Hutchinson was born in 1675. He was the son of a yeoman of Wensley Dale in the North Riding, and he spent many years as steward of the Earl of Scarborough and the Duke of Somerset, with responsibility for work in collieries. His interest in natural science was stimulated by his observations of rock formations and other subterranean phenomena. At the same time he studied the Hebrew language, and he claimed to have found meanings in some of the words which neither the Jewish rabbis nor Christian scholars had detected. He founded a school of philosophy and theology which taught that God had revealed to mankind from the beginning a means of understanding the created world, and this was embodied in the writings of Moses. In his main work, *Moses's Principia* (1724) he predicated that Hebrew was the primitive language of mankind, which, if correctly interpreted, gave the key to all knowledge whether secular or religious.

Some elements of the teaching of Hutchinson, and of his followers for some decades after his death in 1737, were slightly bizarre. But for 'most of the group, philosophical "Hutchinsonianism" was somewhat peripheral to the High Church ecclesiastical, political and sacramental principles which they upheld'.[41] They were closely connected with the University of Oxford, and they included some men of distinction, such as Nathaniel Wetherell, Master of University College, and George Horne of the same college and later President of Magdalen College; and to these must be added William Jones of Nyland, William Stevens and George Berkeley junior. 'Hutchinson's original admirers included many Dissenters hostile to the constitution of the Church of England, and it was only later that . . . George Horne and William Jones . . . imparted to the movement a strongly High Church and anti-Dissenting tone.'[42] By then, the Hutchinsonians were the leading exponents in the Church of England of a revival of the Orthodox political theology associated with the Caroline divines. They established themselves as 'the nearest thing to a coherent body on the High Church side of the eighteenth-century Church of England'.[43] Although their loyalty to the state and their churchmanship did not derive from Hutchinson's writings *per se*, it was to be found in them, and it was consonant with biblical principles for which Hutchinson had taught them to give pre-eminence.

Hutchinsonianism never completely lost its original obscurantist cosmogony, but increasingly the apostles of the movement found a more credible task in defending the traditional church order against continuing erosion. Their central goal was Christian godliness combined with Christian order. As an historian has recently said: 'the dominating characteristic of Hutchinson's thought was its God-centredness . . . Fallen man could recognize spiritual truth only because God chose to reveal it . . . the human intellect was created to enable mankind to contemplate the self-revelation of God . . . [The Hutchinsonians] condemned Natural Religion from their conviction that salvation depended wholly on acceptance of God's revealed will. Hutchinsonians had no patience with the Enlightenment's Pelagianizing concern for "undogmatic moralism" . . . Obedience to God was the one necessary virtue.'[44]

The spirituality of the Hutchinsonians assumed a devotional warmth, an intensity and a zeal which was unusual in their age except among the Methodists and Anglican Evangelicals, and yet they were sacramental High Churchmen. Many of them felt an affinity with the Church of England Evangelicals, and this continued until the late 1790s, when

Charles Daubeny's attack on William Wilberforce's *Practical View* sparked off two decades of controversy. But by then the next major phase in the history of Church of England High Churchmanship, the era of the Hackney Phalanx, was about to dawn.

The Hutchinsonians were mainly ordained men. The time was approaching when laymen would take the leading parts in the life of both the High Church and the Evangelical wings of the church. Nonetheless, even in the earlier and middle Hanoverian years two lay-men warrant mention: William Law and Samuel Johnson. The influence of Law was immense and wide-ranging. It was achieved largely through two works on the Christian life: *On Christian Perfection* (1726), and, more especially, *A Serious Call to a Devout and Holy Life* (1728). The latter was inspired by the teaching of Johann Tauler, Jan van Ruys-broeck, Thomas à Kempis, and other orthodox spiritual writers. It was an urgent call to embrace the Christian life in all its moral and ascetical fullness. The teaching was simple, and the style vigorous, and it was soon established as a classic. It has probably had more influence than any other post-Reformation book other than *The Pilgrims Progress*. Law later came under the influence of Jakob Boehme, and began to emphasize the indwelling of Christ in the soul to such an extent that he verged on the Quaker conception of the 'Inner Light'. This estranged him from some of his admirers, such as John Wesley, but he had already carved out an honourable place for himself in the history of the churches in England in the eighteenth century.

The other outstanding lay churchman of the century was Samuel Johnson, the author, lexicographer and controversialist. He ascribed his conversion as a young man to his reading of Law's *Serious Call*. He has been regarded as a strong High Churchman, regular and sincere in his religious duties, and very generous to his friends and to the poor; and it is because of his perceived brand of churchmanship that he is mentioned at this point, despite the fact that he was not very regular in churchgoing by his own confession. The character and content of his faith are some-what obscure despite the close scrutiny of his life and beliefs by James Boswell, and subsequently by a host of others. 'More than most of his contemporaries, he stressed the darker side of Christ's teaching. An easy assurance of salvation by faith was, for him, precluded by his under-standing of the parable of the talents. God was never a jolly chum to Johnson, but rather a Father (think how authoritarian and distant an eighteenth-century father was) and a Creator, the Omnipresent and Omnipotent. In many of his meditations, Johnson seems to fear God more than he loves Him; there is a constant sense of guilt, failure and unworthiness.'[45]

He stressed works rather than faith; one of the characteristics of his age, and a feature to which he contributed. 'Theoretical questions concerning man's inward nature, the role of God and Christ in his regeneration, and the motives to repentance were of importance to Johnson primarily as they either promoted or hindered the individual's feeling of responsibility for his own salvation through a moral life. With not too much qualification, we can say that Johnson believed in justification by works.'[46] And, again typical of the time in which he lived, he emphasized the importance of future rewards or punishments in the afterlife. 'His major argument was that men were under no obligation to be virtuous unless the happiness promised by virtue out-balanced the temptations to vice. Since virtue, however understood, was not always the greatest happiness of this life, men depended absolutely on the prospect of a future existence.'[47]

Perhaps it was partially because of his greater interest in morality than in dogma that he had a remarkable tolerance of Roman Catholics; although this does not help to explain his accompanying dislike of Presbyterianism and Nonconformity as a whole. Such unfathomed traits were consistent with his great but enigmatic character.

The High Church tradition was kept alive not only by the comparatively small band of Hutchinsonians and a few prominent individuals. There were parishes scattered throughout the country where High Churchmen quietly and unostentatiously ministered and perpetuated their brand of ecclesiology. To important centres like St Andrew's, Holborn, St Clement Dane's, St Giles, Cripplegate and St Mary-le-Bow, must be added the parochial ministries of clergy represented by the Frewens and the Revd Samuel Wesley, and some of the members of the Oxford Holy Club who remained loyal High Churchmen.

All of this is not to imply that there was a nationwide surge of vibrant High Anglicanism. The Oxford Holy Club, the Hutchinsonians and William Law represented an ascetic ideal at one wing of the High Church tradition. The other wing was epitomized by Joseph Trapp, who set forth an ideal of spiritual life which, with its reasonableness, its utilitarian overtones, and its avoidance of excess, recalled the teaching of John Tillotson and William Warburton and the spiritual tone of Latitudinarianism. This spiritual temper, described contemporaneously by some as 'Warburtonian', 'embodied an aversion to extravagant devotional austerities as "useless" and anti-social, if not "popish". The objection was not so much a Protestant repudiation of any implied doctrine of merit, but a dislike of the "irrational", "fanatical" or "enthusiastical" '.[48] A perhaps unintended consequence of anti-ascetical strain was to encourage a 'two-bottle' type of High Churchmanship, which persisted throughout much of the century, and was more widely practised than the ascetic form. And it was this form which gave the High Churchmanship of the period the reputation of worldliness, self-indulgence and spiritual deadness.

Eighteenth-century High Churchmanship, as with the life of the Church of England in general, was probably more animated than has often been assumed, although that which was alive and vital was mixed with much that was dead, decaying or humdrum.

> There was undoubtedly more sacramentalism, more mystery and less moralism than has hitherto been recognized. At the very least, the evidence for a religious establishment dominated by rationalism and moralism has been overstated because the sources are misleading: the frequency of celebrations of communion in a parish church cannot prove much about the sacramental views of the parson, nor can 'rationalistic' sermons prove the obliteration of the presence of mystery in the religious sensibility of the preacher or hearer. The likelihood is that the majority of parochial clergymen in early Georgian England were . . . traditionalists trying to keep their religious foundations secure amidst the shifting sands of government and society.[49]

And it is also likely that such an outlook continued to characterize the bulk of the clergy throughout most of the century.

The Dissenters

Historians are largely agreed that Dissent taken as a whole was in a sorry state in the 1730s. Watts concludes that there is ample evidence to show 'the decay of the Dissenting interest'.[50] A. D. Gilbert expresses the almost unqualified judgment that 'Dissent was in an advanced state of atrophy in 1740' in which its numerical decline 'had been accompanied by a serious expurgation of its Puritan religious culture'.[51] G. I. T. Machin believes that it 'may be stated with fair certainty that for most of the eighteenth century Dissent was no numerical threat to the Establishment'.[52] E. D. Bebb detected a growth of Dissent during the last forty years of the seventeenth century, but decided that in 'the early eighteenth century Nonconformity was ebbing'.[53] John T. Wilkinson joins the chorus of gloom. He also speaks of the decay of the Dissenting interest, in which 'wealthy dissenting families forsook the meeting-house; sons of eminent Nonconformists who had suffered for their Nonconformity passed over to the church; congregations in many cases showed decline, and sometimes became extinct'.[54] He discovered at least fifty Dissenting ministers who entered the Church between 1714 and 1731, and he discerned a serious and growing disquiet among Dissenters, indicated by the large number of pamphlets issued about that time. And L. E. Elliott-Binns alleges that when the evangelical revival began, 'dissent in England was at a very low ebb, and was steadily declining'.[55]

It appears that the decline continued until the middle of the century at least.[56] Then the situation became somewhat more complex, with different sections of Dissent beginning to develop in very different ways. Taking the number of buildings registered as meeting-houses for the purpose of Dissenting worship as a measure of the size and growth or decline of Dissent, it appears that after 1740 some denominations experienced a major recovery which continued at an accelerating rate until well into the nineteenth century, while others experienced stagnation or continuing decline. The evidence for these trends is corroborated by other data on the number of congregations, as distinct from places of worship, and information about membership. The pattern that emerges is of the Congregationalists and Baptists under-going decline between 1710 and the middle of the century, with gradual renewal thereafter, and more rapid increase from the closing years of the century; with a very different pattern for the Presbyterians and Quakers, where the evidence shows a continuous decline right through the eighteenth century and into the nineteenth century.[57]

The rather different picture painted by James E. Bradley stresses that there was an overall decline in Dissent as a proportion of the total, growing, population; and this was greatly affected by the dispropor-tionate statistical influence of Presbyterianism.

The Presbyterians rarely experienced any growth, and since they were the most numerous of the three denominations [Presbyterians, Congregationalists and Baptists] in 1715, the so-called decline among Nonconformists was in fact most often Presbyterian decline. Altogether, the three denominations dropped from about five percent of the population in 1715 to four percent or slightly less in 1773.

Throughout the century, the Quakers numbered less than one percent of the population, but they experienced the same decline as the other denominations.[58]

In fact Bradley reckons that in the period 1715 to 1773 only four counties registered any increase relative to the population, four remained stable, and the remaining thirty-two showed a decrease. And of course there were regional differences, with the Presbyterians traditionally being strong in the north and northwest, the Congregationalists in the South Midlands and East Anglia, and the Baptists in the Southeast and South Midlands.

The period I am at present reviewing also saw within Dissent as a whole and even within individual denominations 'a break-up of the old dissenting tradition and the emergence of various new movements, widely divergent in matters of theology, polity, and conversionist zeal'.[59] The fundamental division which was forged in the eighteenth century was between those sections of Dissent which were reinvigorated, and in various degrees transformed, by the evangelical revival, and those which were not.

Initially there was mutual suspicion, and even disdain or dislike between the emerging Methodists and the Dissenters in general. 'Calvinist Dissenters distrusted the Wesleys' Arminianism, liberal Dissenters suspected the Methodists of Antinomianism, and Dissenters of all shades of opinion disliked Methodist "enthusiasm".'[60] In its early phases the revival was far from transforming Dissent as a whole although it did not entirely pass it by. The picture was patchy and changes were piecemeal. 'There was some impact on Dissent from the first if only at a scattered and individual level.'[61] A number of Presbyterian ministers, including orthodox Calvinists, denounced Whitefield and his followers as 'false prophets', and there were Congregational and Baptist churches which refused membership and communion to people who attended Methodist meetings.[62] In some places, such as Dudley and Devizes, it was said that Dissenters stirred up the mob against the Methodists, and John Bennett was probably not the only Methodist to complain that the Dissenters tried to press-gang Methodists into the army.[63] There was widespread concern among Dissenters, and especially Dissenting ministers, that the Methodists thinned their congregations, disturbed the order of their churches, and infected numbers of their hearers 'with a frenzical kind of zeal that has raised them above sentiment and instruction'.[64] But there may have been a divide in some cases between the Dissenting leaders and their congregations. 'If Dissenting ministers were usually hostile to the revivalists, the rank and file were sometimes more receptive.'[65]

It did not take many years for the most prejudiced Dissenter to see that the potential gain from partaking in the revival was greater than the possible loss. There was an undoubted infusion of new life into all the Dissenting bodies, and especially into the Congregationalists and the Baptists. This can be exaggerated. They were not in such a forlorn state that they would most probably have perished but for the injection of blood from the evangelical revival; but many congregations were rescued from a quite serious condition of atrophy and apathy.

Presbyterianism

Perhaps the Presbyterians gained less than any of the other Dissenting denominations from the revival. 'Presbyterians, like Anglicans in the 1740s, were very distrustful of teachers of justification by faith for fear that this would mean devaluing good works, and the risk of antinomian breaches of the moral law.'[66] Then, to this underlying concern and implied if not explicitly expressed, anti-revival predisposition, there was added the escalating influence of those who stressed rationality rather than faith and religious experience. The liberalizing process among Presbyterians, which I have already considered for the first three decades of the century, continued, and in certain respects gained momentum. The anti-subscription Presbyterian divines of the middle part of the century were keen to champion the principle of entire ministerial freedom for religious inquiry and profession. They were not necessarily heterodox in their beliefs, 'but changes at length inevitably began to appear, according as the practical habit of acting on the easy and non-restrictive method led to a speculative recognition of its pleasantness, and then to an undue over-estimate of its importance or its intrinsic value'.[67] Under their increasingly powerful influence it began to seem that the faith they were promoting had few fixed points, and presented boundless opportunities for inquiry and conjecture. Christian doctrine ceased to be held as a living faith or conviction.

The middle years of the century were thus a sort of intermediate stage for Presbyterianism between the earlier Arianism and the later Unitarianism. A high proportion of the Presbyterian leaders in the Academies presented the Christian faith as 'opinion', and resisted acceptance of restrictive Christian doctrine. It was an approach which is graphically portrayed in the teaching of John Taylor. A man of considerable erudition, his chief contribution to scholarship was his *Hebrew Concordance*, published in instalments between 1754 and 1757, in which he made an important advance in the study of Hebrew roots. But it was his polemical, thoroughly Pelagian, book *The Scripture Doctrine of Original Sin* (1740), in which he propounded his Arian view of the person of Christ and denied original sin, which opened up fresh heterodox speculation and discussion. It had a wide circulation in England, Scotland and America, and did much to undermine the foundations of the Calvinistic system, and to prepare the way for the Unitarian movement in American Congregationalism, as well as Unitarianism in England.

As the century progressed Presbyterianism became not merely influenced by rational Dissent but positively invaded and transmuted by it. An appreciation of the tensions which racked the denomination and individuals within it as they wrestled with the ever-more pressing, and to some minds attractive, claims of the theological radicals, can, perhaps, best be gained from a consideration of the life of Joseph Priestley.

Priestley (1733–1804) was born into a West Yorkshire family, his father being a cloth-worker. When his mother died he was only seven years old. He was subsequently brought up by an aunt, who was a Calvinistic Congregationalist but allowed her home to be the resort of Dissenting ministers from the neighbourhood, irrespective of their theological opinions. He was especially influenced by two of them who held Baxterian views. He was already an Arminian, and he was refused admission to membership of the Heckmondwike church because he 'appeared not to be quite orthodox, not thinking that all the human race (suppose them not to have any sin of their own) were liable to the wrath of God'.[68] He entered Daventry Academy in 1752 in order to train for the Presbyterian ministry. It seems that it was at this time that he became an Arian. After ministries at Needham Market and Nantwich, where he opened a school, he spent six years as languages tutor at the newly-founded Warrington Academy. Soon after becoming pastor of the Presbyterian meeting at Mill Hill, Leeds, he became a Socinian. He aroused considerable hostility by publishing the *Theological Repository*, a critical periodical that appeared irregularly. It advocated the autonomy of the individual congregation and an increase in the number of sects, as well as complete toleration for Roman Catholics; and it was a vehicle for attacks on the idea of a national church. In 1773 he accepted a post as Librarian to the Earl of Shelburne. This gave him sufficient leisure to pursue his scientific studies, which had already gained him a considerable reputation.

By now he had adopted an aggressive creed which regarded Jesus as an ordinary man, 'though honoured and distinguished by God above all other men'. He rejected the worship of Christ as idolatrous, and he saw no necessity for any doctrine of atonement. He incorporated his heterodox views in an number of books, and perhaps most provocatively in his *History of Early Opinions concerning Jesus Christ* (1786). Among the rational Dissenters of the late eighteenth century Priestley's forthright Socinianism had greater appeal than the more cautious Arianism propounded by Richard Price. Samuel Horsley, himself a most able scientist and theologian, was the leading champion of orthodoxy in opposition to this latter-day heresy.

In 1791 Priestley became one of the founders of the Unitarian Society for Promoting Christian Knowledge, which was established on a narrowly Socinian basis.

In 1794 he went to America, having experienced much verbal and physical abuse at the hands of both the sophisticated and literate and the unruly mob. During the remainder of his life he adopted the doctrine of universal restitution and of moral progress in life after death.

The strife between the orthodox and the Arian members in a fairly large number of Presbyterian churches was ferocious and bitter. It sometimes resulted in schism, with the heterodox members seceding and forming their own congregation. It sometimes contributed to the extinction of a church, with some or all of the congregation joining the established church. It sometimes led to members of a local church transferring their allegiance to another Nonconformist body, most commonly a Congregational chapel, or the entire church changing its denominational affiliation, again, most frequently to Congregationalism. 'The paradoxical consequence of the liberalization of Presbyterianism, as of the growth of English Calvinistic Methodism, was thus a considerable strengthening of Congregationalism, not least in those parts of the country, such as Lancashire, Yorkshire, the north Midlands, and the West Country, where Independency had hitherto been weak.'[69]

Congregationalism

The Congregational denomination, itself, however, was not entirely free from the taint of heresy; it would have been surprising if it had escaped such a prolific, powerful and pervasive influence as Unitarianism, which, after all, was able to claim considerable inroads not only into Presbyterianism, but into the strongholds of the established church. Although the problem was not of the same magnitude as with Presbyterianism, at least half a dozen Independent churches ultimately became Unitarian. By the 1740s the shaking of the theological foundations was felt widely among Congregationalists. The retreat from orthodoxy was especially grave in the West Country. Splits and secessions began to sap the vitality of the churches.

There were some vigorous efforts to maintain the traditional Congregational theology. In 1730 the King's Head Society was formed to strengthen evangelical belief and practice. It organized special lectures and sponsored candidates for the ministry. The founding of the Northern Education Society in 1756 was likewise motivated by a desire to turn the tide of heterodoxy, in this case in the North of England; and it adopted as its primary aim the provision of ministers who were sound in the faith. It established Heckmondwike Academy for the students it supported.

In this protracted debate between the orthodox and the heterodox, Congregationalists were greatly influenced by the standpoint of Philip Doddridge. He adopted the kind of theology and catholicity which had characterized Richard Baxter. He was profoundly interested in Christian doctrine, and he adhered to an orthodox but moderate Calvinistic position, but wedded this to 'a gracious tolerance which was based on his own rich experience of religion as personal contact with Jesus Christ. Certainly, he held "that religion consists more in an intelligent, rational and determinate choice of the will than in any ardent transport of the affections," but that was still part of his conviction that religion is "an *inward* Thing".[70] He claimed that the scriptures allowed, and, indeed, recommended, a latitude of expression, and he resolutely refused to subscribe to any man-made confession of faith, or to be a party to any attempt to impose creeds on others. He combined this with an insistence on the value of Christian unity and amity. By taking such a determined and clear stand he found himself in bad odour with the vociferous orthodox, but his broad outlook attracted students to his Academy at Northampton from Independent, Presbyterian, Baptist and Calvinistic Methodist churches. Above all else he was a pastor and evangelist, and he displayed these qualities in his most influential work *The Rise and Progress of Religion in the Soul* (1745), and in his hymns, which helped in the process of transition from

Puritanism to evangelicalism. Doddridge stood at the frontier of two religious ages represented by Puritanism and evangelicalism, and it is a measure of his greatness that he understood that the latter grew out of the former. In such a crucial time for the Christian faith in England, he did as much as any other person to unite eighteenth-century Nonconformists on a common religious ground.

Doddridge caused consternation to Isaac Watts by his readiness to co-operate with George Whitefield. He entertained the leader of the new revival movement in 1739, in the early stages of the revival when the revivalist preacher was causing widespread sensation and arousing much opposition. He also encouraged his Academy students to work in harmony with the Methodists. Whitefield had numerous and close connections with the Congregationalists. At the time when he began his open-air work, the Congregational minister Thomas Cole became the acknowledged leader of the revival in Whitefield's home town of Gloucester, and in the vicinity. Then, later on in Whitefield's career, the 'Connexion' which he organized under the patronage of the Countess of Huntingdon became a considerable source of recruitment to the Congregational ministry. In less than a century the whole Connexion was to become officially linked with the Congregational denomination.

It is impossible to quantify the impact of the revival on Congregationalism. How can we measure, or adequately describe, the personal drama as Congregational ministers in a multitude of places and circumstances encountered the revival message, and in many cases found themselves, their ministry and their churches turned upside down? Existing churches were revivified, and new churches were established; and it all took place in a quiet, untrumpeted, way over a period of half a century or more. This infusing of new life into Congregationalism by the revival was most keenly experienced from the middle fifties onwards. There had been much piety and prayer, disciplined pursuit of Christian ideals and evangelistic concern among the Congregationalists when the revival dawned; and the Congregational churches did not have the machinery which the Church of England had for ejecting unruly Methodists from their midst. Each congregation was free to respond to the new, and for some heady and exciting, revival influence as it felt most appropriate.They were therefore much more open to the impact of the revival than the parishes of the established church where the local congregation was influenced by the attitude of its bishop and the pronouncements of those in the religious hierarchy who were hostile to the revival. Among the Congregationalists there was a sense of new-found liberty, spiritual enlightenment and freedom of the Spirit as people heard the gospel preached in a novel and powerful way, repented and believed. Ministries were changed out of all recognition as the carefully prepared and copiously sub-headed, coolly and somewhat impersonally presented sermon of the early part of the century gave way to the daring extempore preaching by the imitators of Whitefield, in which emotional appeals were often accompanied by groans and sobs. The charismatic elements in public worship attracted more interest, and were given more prominence. The emotional effect was heightened by hymns; and no less than ten hymn-books were published by Congregationalists between 1769 and 1813. Even where some congregations had been nursed into existence under the patronage of the Anglican Countess of Huntingdon and had adopted the Prayer Book liturgy, it was associated with warm evangelical emotionalism. It all added up to a remarkable transformation. Here was a new, exciting, romantic age for some Congregationalists, and it was intoxicating for the many who experienced it.

To these new and more dynamic centres of worship came a number of members of the working classes, and this led to a deep philanthropic and evangelistic desire to provide the poorer children of the community with at least the rudiments of education. From such concern arose the Sunday Schools of the late eighteenth century. It has been questioned whether Robert Raikes was their originator, but he was unquestionably their most successful propagandist. The Congregationalists were among the pioneers. Initially the teachers were paid to teach the children to read and to write; and some of the schools also taught arithmetic. Although the middle of the nineteenth century was the golden age of the Sunday School for Congregationalists, the foundations were well and truly laid in the period 1780 to 1830. Able laymen, and lay women, were mobilized in a movement of immense and long-term consequence, in which socially disadvantaged boys and girls were sufficiently educated to enable them to move from one social class to another, and the Congregationalists, as with the other denominations, were provided with a most efficient and effective means of recruitment.

Of course, not all Congregationalists were happy with these various direct and indirect consequences of the revival. There were ministers and congregations that resisted any revival influence. The Yarmouth church in the late 1760s showed clearly how the older and stricter standards of Congregational discipline persisted, and were at variance with the perceived and unacceptable enthusiasm of the Methodists. In

1767 a local Methodist preacher, John Simpson, and a majority of the members of his Methodist society sought membership in the Congregational Church. The application was carefully considered, but rejected unless Simpson agreed to 'lay aside his character of preacher among the Methodists'. The Congregational leaders 'could not approve of preaching which was not subject to the discipline of the church and which "tended to great irregularity in gathering separate societies out of formed churches". In any case, they had no wish to compromise the reputation of the Protestant Dissenters by becoming connected with the Methodists "who are at best disorderly Churchmen".[71]

The Morley church of Yorkshire under Thomas Morgan from 1763 to 1795 was equally critical of Methodism. In 1765 Morgan wrote of the 'unhappy *Divisions* almost in all the Congregations in the Kingdom chiefly occasion'd by *Methodistical Delusions*.' He vividly summed up the position as he saw it in Yorkshire in 1769: 'Religion at Low Ebb crucified between Enthusiasm and Infidelity'. The poignancy of such remarks is increased by the fact that Morgan was himself a convert of Howel Harris', and during his student days was avid in his hearing of Methodist preachers.[72]

Nonetheless, taken as a whole, the impact of the revival on the Congregationalists was considerable. The same cannot be said of the Baptists, at least until very near the end of the century.

The Baptists

The General Baptists were divided more severely than the Congregationalists over the revival and all it stood for. By 1740 they had become quite seriously infected with Socinianism, and there were only a few of them who had retained the theological principles of their forefathers. As a denomination they were lacking in those qualities of energetic outreach, lively and intense fellowship and an evident sense of purpose and powerfulness which characterized the revival, and yet most Baptists viewed the Methodists with suspicion and shunned any co-operation with them.

Nonetheless, in the middle years of the century the original General Baptist emphasis upon the universality of the redemption provided in Christ was revived, and a new vigour of spiritual life was introduced into the denomination, largely as a result of the work of two men. David Taylor was converted, probably through the ministry of the Moravians, in 1741.[73] He was a servant of the Countess of Huntingdon at

Donnington Park, and she encouraged him to go out to preach, first to the farmers and labourers of the neighbouring Leicestershire villages, and then into Derbyshire, Cheshire, Lancashire and Yorkshire. He joined the Moravians, but he left behind him in Leicestershire a group of converts who organized themselves into a religious society, and in 1745 built a meeting-house at Barton-in-Fabis near Market Bosworth which they registered as 'Independent'. It was led by a blacksmith, a farm labourer, a wool-comber and a schoolmaster. They came to the conclusion that infant baptism was unscriptural, and they proceeded to baptize each other. Energetic evangelism in the neighbouring towns and villages resulted in greatly increased numbers, and by 1760 it became necessary to divide into five separate churches with centres at Barton, Melbourne, Kegworth, Loughborough and Kirkby Woodhouse.

Daniel Taylor was a man of able intellect and great energy, a collier and a Wesleyan preacher from Northowram near Halifax. He had broken with the Methodists, and in 1762 he settled as the minister of a small group of seceders from Methodism who worshipped together at Wadsworth, near Hebden Bridge. He became convinced that there was no justification for infant baptism, and in 1763 he was baptized by a Baptist minister. He won others over to his views, and the Wadsworth fellowship became the first General Baptist church in Yorkshire. However, Taylor soon became disillusioned with the General Baptists, and especially with the disputes between the orthodox and the unorthodox, their tenacious adherence to old customs and their doctrinal laxity. He had a far greater sense of affinity with the Barton Baptists, and he resolved to unite the evangelical churches of the existing General Baptist denomination with the Barton Baptists and their associated churches. The result was the founding in June 1770 of the New Connexion of General Baptists. In six articles of faith the New Connexion eschewed Calvinism on the one hand and Unitarianism on the other, and all ministers who joined the Connexion were required to subscribe to the articles and to give an account of their religious experience. The New Connexion was well organized, with an annual meeting of delegates, called an Association, and with district conferences. It prospered, and it was joined by some of the old General Baptist churches which retained their evangelical tone. The Association of the New Connexion was much more alive to the needs of the time than the old Assembly, and it planted churches in some of the expanding towns, especially in the lace and hosiery centres of the Midlands and the woollen and cotton centres of Yorkshire and Lancashire.

Like the General Baptists, the Particular Baptists were at first little touched by the revival. The Arminianism of Wesley set a barrier between him and the Calvinistic Particular Baptist ministers. And in any case by the mid-century the Particular Baptists were riven by internal doctrinal controversy. They were agitated by what became known as the 'Modern Question'. Three Baptists in particular were involved. There was the High Calvinist, Joseph Hussey, who took his Calvinism to the extreme of denying that God's grace should be offered to the non-elect. Such a view was adopted by John Gill, who ministered to the Horselydown Baptist church in Southwark for more than half a century, from 1719 to 1771, and became one of the most influential men in the denomination. The controversy started to take shape when Matthias Maurice published a pamphlet in 1737 entitled *A Modern Question Modestly Answer'd*. In effect he questioned the hyper-Calvinism of Hussey; and in this he was supported posthumously, for he died in 1738, by what Dr Abraham Taylor, minister of the Deptford Congregational church, had taught, and by the charismatic Philip Doddridge.

Despite much opposition, High Calvinism exercised a dominant influence among the Particular Baptists, froze their evangelistic ardour, and shielded them to a great extent from the influence of the revival until quite late in the century. There were even complaints about the 'Arminian dialect' and 'semi-Pelagian addresses' of the Calvinistic Whitefield. Andrew Clifford alone among the Particular Baptists stood as a loyal friend and supporter of the revival leader: he was the only representative of the denomination at the stone-laying for Whitefield's Tabernacle in Tottenham Court Road, preached in the Tabernacle, and edited a memorial volume of Whitefield's sermons. It became apparent that 'new leaders had to arise before the evangelical revival could cut for itself channels of influence among the Particular Baptists'.[74]

The first stirring of a new approach came in the Midlands. The Northamptonshire Association, which embraced several counties, put out a Circular Letter in 1770 which said:

> Every soul that comes to Christ to be saved from hell and sin by him, is to be encouraged . . . The coming soul need not fear that he is not elected, for none but such would be willing to come and submit to Christ.[75]

It was at this stage that the writings of the Massachusetts divine and American revival leader Jonathan Edwards started to exercise a particular influence. Robert Hall, the pastor of the Arnesby Particular Baptist church in Leicestershire read Edwards' *Inquiry into the Freedom of the Will*, and was convinced that the Particular Baptist Calvinism could be reconciled with the evangelistic commands of the New Testament. In 1781 a sermon of his was published with the title *Help to Zion's Travellers*. 'The way to Jesus', said Hall, 'is graciously open to everyone who chooses to come to him.'[76]

The outstanding man in this thawing of the evangelistic zeal of Particular Baptists was Andrew Fuller. 'The son of a Cambridgeshire farmer, Fuller was a big, broad-shouldered man with heavy eyebrows and deep-set eyes, a man who later reminded William Wilberforce of a village blacksmith, though Wilberforce at the same time paid tribute to his "considerable powers of mind".'[77] He reached the same conclusion as Robert Hall, and also through reading the same book by Jonathan Edwards. In 1785 he published *The Gospel Worthy of All Acceptation*. His contention that there was no contradiction between Calvinism and the universal obligation on those who hear the gospel to respond and believe, did not satisfy Arminian critics such as Daniel Taylor, but it was accepted by the majority of Particular Baptists, and 'Fullerism' became the new orthodoxy of the denomination.

In the meantime it was the Northamptonshire Association and, once more, the influential writings of Jonathan Edwards which were responsible for a major initiative in promoting evangelism. For it was in 1784 that John Sutcliff, the Congregational pastor of Olney church in Buckinghamshire, read Edwards's *Humble Attempt to Promote Explicit Agreement and Visible Union of God's People in Extraordinary Prayer*. He was so impressed that he initiated a programme of prayer for the local Association, whereby the churches set aside the first Monday of each month to pray for the revival of religion not among their own denomination only, or within the bounds of their own locality or nation, but throughout the world by spreading the gospel to the most distant parts of the habitable globe. And the prayer circle expanded to incorporate the Particular Baptist churches of Warwickshire, Yorkshire and the West Country. Their prayers were answered in a remarkable way and in a short time. Eight years later, in 1792, the Particular Baptist Society for the Propagation of the Gospel among the Heathen was founded, and with it the modern era of missionary work by all churches in England was inaugurated. It was symptomatic of the effect of the revival on this previously hidebound denomination.

The Quakers

The Quakers were affected by the revival, but later than the Congregationalists, and even after the Baptists. When the revival appeared like a thunderbolt on the English religious scene in the 1730s the Quakers were in no mood to take advantage of it. They were not open to its potentially transforming touch. Although Whitefield received kindness from individual Quakers, and Wesley had great esteem for them as a body, 'there is no evidence that, taken as a whole the Quakers were deflected from their normal course'.[78] They continued to be preoccupied with their own distinctive beliefs and practices, and were little concerned about other sects, denominations, churches or religious movements, even one as powerful as the revival. Any positive response by the Quakers to Methodism was left to a few scattered individuals.

There were three main hindrances to the Quakers benefitting from the revival, which acted as barriers to those influences which might have restored to them something of the vibrancy of their earlier years: their preoccupation with organization in the years before the onset of the revival, the lack of inspirational leaders, and the very nature of Quakerism, which in certain respects was alien to the core values and life-style of the Methodists.

The historian of Quakerism captures the essence of the first danger which asserted itself in the pre-revival years:

> It must be confessed that the tendency of Friends to combat worldliness by a legalism that laid stress on outward rules was turning the Church aside from its mission and from the deeper way of inward discipline which the First Publishers of Truth had known. The inward way of taking up the cross was dynamic, and could not have failed to be progressive and adventurous, in spite of any temporary limitations of outlook; the outward was a rule which held in bondage the free activities of the soul.[79]

The passion for organization especially manifested itself in the drive for Quaker education, and the development of structures for Quakerism as a whole. By the 1730s there was a very comprehensive provision of Quaker day and boarding schools. The London Yearly Meeting constantly reiterated its advice to Quaker parents not to allow their children to be trained in the world's ways. The children should be educated either in Quaker schools or at home. In either case the advice extended to a fairly detailed regime for the nurture of children. They were to be hedged about with restrictions. It all smacked of excessive regulation, with little vision of the higher meaning of true education. It was the same with the structural changes which were introduced or reinforced. What with Yearly, General and Quarterly Meetings, the Meeting for Sufferings and the Six Weeks' Meeting, and the over-abundance of stipulations and rules, it seems that much of the original sense of spontaneity had drained away. Moreover the charismatic leaders of the pioneer days were not replaced, so that a bureaucratic cast of mind was not challenged by the questioning and probing of out-standing personalities.

The other barrier to Quaker renewal and revitalization through contact with the revival was the inbuilt character of the denomination; its whole disposition and ethos. The emotional excitement sometimes associated with the revival hardly commended it to a people whose principle aim was to follow 'the Inner Light'. In many ways the Quakers of the early decades of the eighteenth century lived attractive lives, and displayed an undemonstrative, calm and firm spirituality in a time of dryness and discouragement; but it was not compatible with the more outgoing style of spirituality and life of the Methodists, and for some time kept them at a distance from the revival.

> They . . . were sure of God and lived in a world of rather sordid aims and increasing scepticism, with their sensitive souls open inward toward eternal realities. They saw no way to remake the world or to establish the Kingdom of God in the earth on any great scale, but they went quietly on bearing their testimony to the fact that they had a direct way of approach to the living God, and were constantly refreshed and fortified by inward resources which the world could neither give nor take away.[80]

During the years of the mid- and later eighteenth century Quakerism was not to any great extent affected by Arianism, Socinianism or Unitarianism. It was, however, dominated by quietism. This spiritual phenomenon had its roots not only in the kind of religious life just described, but in the whole European mystical tradition. Faced with the total depravity and bankruptcy of fallen man, generation after generation of mystics, stretching back through the centuries, had demonstrated an intense and glowing faith in the direct invasion of God into the sphere of human personality. As with those who may be deemed forerunners of the eighteenth-century Quietists – such as Thomas à Kempis, Thomas Aquinas, St Ignatius Loyola, St Teresa,

St John of the Cross, St Francis de Sales, St Jeanne Francoise de Chantal, St Vincent de Paul and Miguel de Molinos – such a spirituality sprang from a conviction that all thoughts and strivings which originate in mere man, and are a product of unaided human consciousness, and all aims, designed, arranged, and planned by reason and the will of man, are tainted with all the imperfections of creatureliness, and come below the sphere of the spiritual. Worthy and valid as some would consider this, it was inimical to almost all the revival stood for. Indeed, we will see how it caused a major rupture within the ranks of the revival itself. And not only so, but, with its great emphasis on silent meetings, spoken ministry became the exception rather than the rule, and, as with the High Calvinism of the Particular Baptists, quietism made Quakerism introspective and helped to stifle the original evangelistic zeal of the movement. Nevertheless, because it was not severely rocked off course by the impact of rationalism, it retained a spiritual spark which was to be kindled at various times during the following two hundred years.

The Roman Catholics

The last fifty years have witnessed intensive study, and a consequent major shift in the perception, of eighteenth-century English Roman Catholicism. In that time scholars have 'lifted the history of the Catholic community out of the confessional and apologetic mould in which it had been traditionally cast, and placed it firmly within the mainstream of the religious and social history of England'.[81] During the nineteenth century and the first half of the twentieth century it was customary for historians to view the first half of the eighteenth century as an unhappy time for English Roman Catholics; and the second half as not much better. The debacle of 1688 was long believed to have inaugurated a century of 'depression, of lost hopes and discouragement' when 'numbers steadily, if slowly, dwindled away'.[82] Such a gloomy assessment was 'reiterated with wearisome concurrence by later writers and enshrined in Newman's "Second spring" sermon, with its lugubrious portrayal of a beleaguered, shrinking remnant (shrinking in a social as in a statistical sense) "dimly seen, as if through a mist or in twilight, as ghosts flitting to and fro".'[83] It has been replaced by an understanding which emphasizes the 'vigour and distinctive character of Catholicism before the transformation wrought by Irish immigration and Italian missionaries in the 19th Century'.[84]

There were undoubtedly severe problems for Roman Catholics, and signs of decline and distress in the period of the first two Hanoverian kings. The Stuart Catholic monarchs, on whom many Catholics had pinned their hopes of better times to come, were in exile, and there was no realistic possibility of them returning. The attempted coups of 1715 and 1745 were rather pathetic affairs, and almost inevitably failed to achieve their objective. But while the Pretenders lived they kept hopes alive, and they were an unconscionable time in dying out. James II died in 1701, although his body was laid in the English Benedictine monastic chapel of St Edmund in Paris, as a visible reminder for pious Catholics of a reign which had promised so much for them, until the revolutionaries of 1789 disposed of it. His son, James III, lived to an extraordinarily old age, not dying until 1765. And his sons, Charles III and Henry IX perpetuated the family's titles and claims into the following century. Roman Catholic Jacobitism and attachment to the family lingered on tenaciously down to the 1770s; the lurking threat which such allegiance represented only helped to maintain a deep-rooted English anti-Catholicism.

Again we are up against some disagreement among historians. Some have asserted that Georgian society was markedly more tolerant than the eras that preceded and succeeded it.[85] Thus, for instance, when R. J. White could not explain the Gordon riots within such a framework, he dismissed them as 'an incident, something that came and went with the short, sharp violence of a dog's solitary bark in the silence of the night'.[86] Likewise, E. R. Norman describes the spirit of the eighteenth century as hostile to persecution, and the riots of 1780 as 'a sort of national purging of anti-Catholic hostility'.[87] These views are too sanguine. In the first half of the century in particular the anti-Catholicism which had persistently been a part of a developing protestantization process was still very much in evidence. It may be somewhat overstating the extent of this to declare it to be 'the prime ideological commitment of most Englishmen',[88] but it was an essential, and indeed arguably the most important, element in that rapidly developing sense of nationhood which Linda Colley has so ably charted.[89] It was 'propagated by the government and the Anglican and Dissenting clergy, and endorsed by the nation at large'.[90]

The governing elite were determined to confine the Catholics within a cage of legislation which had been constructed since the Reformation largely in order 'to protect a nervously Protestant state against what was assumed to be a fifth column in its midst'.[91] In the second half of the century, when Jacobitism had largely been extinguished, and when the influence of the Enlightenment and Latitudinarianism were burgeoning, anti-Catholicism started to be dispelled in the higher ranks of society. Nonetheless, in the wider society the old prejudices persisted, as seen in the Gordon riots. It was in June 1780 that the eccentric and fanatical anti-Catholic Lord George Gordon led a march to Parliament with a petition for the repeal of the Catholic Relief Act of 1778. The huge procession pillaged the houses of Catholics, and then the rioters became completely unmanageable and held the City until they were dispersed by the military. It is reckoned that 210 people were killed on the streets and another 75 died of wounds. It was clear that the population at large were not ready for the granting of concessions to a group which was still feared as a threat.

Of equal concern for Catholics alongside these political and attitudinal problems was the number of aristocratic and gentry families who discarded their Catholicism. In every generation since the Reformation the Catholics in these upper echelons of society had been of immense importance to the health, and even the survival, of Catholicism in England. 'By 1791 there were only seven Catholic peers left: the Earls of Shrewsbury and Derwentwater-Newburgh, and Lords Arundell, Clifford, Dormer, Petre and Stourton. To Catholic legend the nine apostasies and eight natural extinctions since 1714 seemed abnormal and horrific.'[92] In a high proportion of cases when there was a deliberate decision to abandon the faith of their fathers, the apostates repented, though this was usually too late to prevent their heirs being brought up as Protestants; and in an abnormally large number of families the Catholic peers suffered from childlessness. The apostasies among the gentry were of three types, all long familiar to Catholics. There was the long-draw-out slither from Catholic practice as a consequence of bankruptcy and descent into genteel poverty or even further down the social ladder, with the splitting up of the family and a loss of its cohesion and heirlooms. There were apostasies for economic or other benefits, such as trade advantages, access to posts otherwise not attainable or the possibility of honours being bestowed. Then thirdly, and most commonly, there was the genuine conversion, often from a fairly open form of Catholicism, to a Broad Anglicanism.

But the picture of eighteenth-century Roman Catholic loss, oppression and gloom must not be painted in entirely dark colours; there was much of a lighter and brighter hue. 'A great deal of nonsense has been talked about the "catacomb" existence of Catholics in this period, and the London Catholic community is the clearest refutation of any such notion. Accounts of early-morning masses in locked garrets, guarded by burly Irishmen, or the overworked anecdote of Challoner's preaching at the Ship Inn to a congregation disguised as beer-drinkers, have combined to give a quite false impression of a persecuted and underground Church.'[93] Because of their beliefs, their history, the collective antagonism in society, and their chosen, in many ways quite distinctive, way of life, they did experience special problems, and they did have to make sacrifices. Life for many of them entailed disadvantages, sometimes quite severe, which were unknown to most of the Protestant majority of the population. Nonetheless, there are distinct signs of positive change, as well as some decay, in eighteenth-century English Catholicism. Although the apostasies among the gentry were considerable, they made deeper inroads in the ranks of the old Catholic gentry in the period 1660 to 1714 than after 1714. Overall there is in fact evidence of modest Roman Catholic growth, with a particularly encouraging increase in the number of middle-class Catholics. Some of this large Catholic middle class had been Catholic tradesmen, doctors or lawyers in towns for generations past; a considerable number were drawn from Catholic country immigrants, families of tenant farmers on gentry estates. There were some areas like Lancashire where there is evidence of especially impressive numerical growth and a healthy Catholic community. It appears that there were about 4,000 Catholics in Preston, Wigan and Liverpool in 1767, which was something over twice as many as there had been forty or fifty years before; and the Irish constituent was negligible.[94] It also seems that they were accepted by the majority of non-Catholic members of society, with little sign of friction. This provided a firm foundation for the even greater growth in the Catholic community in these towns at the end of the eighteenth century and the beginning of the nineteenth century, when the English Catholics were outnumbered by the new arrivals.

In the course of the eighteenth century there were also a substantial number of converts. These included a few individuals of distinction: Johann Christian Bach, Thomas Arne, Samuel Wesley, Susannah Cibber, Edward Gibbon, James Boswell, Thomas Atkinson, Thomas Hearne and Richard Challoner being among them. Others came under Catholic influence, mostly by marrying practising Catholics. Among these were David Garrick, Fanny Burney, Mrs Thrale, Christopher Smart, Edmund Burke and Henry Fielding.

Richard Challoner made a particular and notable contribution to Catholicism in this period, as Bishop (*in partibus*) of Debra and coadjutor to the Vicar Apostolic, Dr Petre, from 1741 onwards, and then as the successor to Dr Petre from 1758. He does not have the same glamour or heroic stature associated with some of the founders of the English Catholic Mission in the sixteenth century and the martyrs of English Catholic history. He held no high office like Thomas More, and he had no outstanding literary talents. Nevertheless, he played an indispensable part in the evolution of Catholicism in the land of his birth.

> He was above all a pastor concerned to provide for the spiritual needs of a growing people. He was a preacher, a teacher, a man of prayer, concerned with the education and reform of clergy and laity alike. No-one was more aware than he of the power and importance of the martyr tradition, but no-one knew more clearly that a living church needs more than a glorious past. He set himself to formulate pastoral strategies and a tradition of spirituality which would build on the past. If his life offered little scope for heroism, he provided instead a living embodiment of values less spectacular but perhaps in the long run more important.[95]

He was 'the representative of a distinctive English Catholic tradition, which came to maturity in him'.[96] In this ministry, and through his widely read and appreciated prayer-book for the laity, *The Garden of the Soul* (1740), he helped in the development of what can be regarded as a further gain for eighteenth-century English Catholicism: a greater sense of community.

'Popular religion'

One of the characteristics of religion in England at particular times from at least the eighteenth century up to about the First World War and then almost continuously to the present day has been a low level of participation in organized worship and commitment to one of the recognized churches of the land accompanied by evidence of widespread 'religiosity'. My concern here is not with the 'privatization of religion', for I will consider that later, but with the role played by the churches in society. Even when the churches have not attracted the allegiance and active participation of the population at large, they have been acknowledged as legitimated institutions catering for the recognized 'religious' aspects of life. The Church of England in particular has been seen in this light.

It is clear, for example, that the eighteenth-century Church enjoyed a high level of conformity, a low level of attendance, an even lower participation in communion and yet was widely, almost universally, used for baptism, confirmation, marriage and burials. It is equally clear that religion, however that is to be defined, played an important part in the celebratory rhythms of the State and of local customs associated with the agricultural calendar.[97]

Throughout the century there were many areas where the church throve, or at least continued to play a central and crucial part in the lives of individuals and of the local community as a whole, and this was more typical and common than was once thought. Even in places where the church cut little ice the local church continued to be of symbolic importance and, especially in rural areas, the clergyman continued to play an important part in immemorially hallowed festivities. It seems that the strictly religious content of certain rituals and ceremonies, such as Rogation week perambulations of the parish, was less accepted in the latter part of the century, but however much such events were treated with impiety they retained their function in helping to give a 'religious' content to community-based activities. By its involvement in them the church helped to reinforce for the labouring poor 'the geographical basis of the community as a ceremonial unit' and 'reaffirmed an older economic and social structure'.[98]

Anglicanism was remarkably well suited to cater for a wide range of religious needs. It provided conventional, familiar and ordered services, orthodox doctrine, religious continuity with the past, Christian fellowship, and all the comforts of an established religious institution to the devout conformist. For the less religiously committed and pious members of society it provided much valued rites of passage and the all-important festivals and celebrations. For those, and in most communities it may have been the majority, who had little or no theological convictions, it offered a focal point for their corporate loyalties, however vaguely these may have been understood or expressed; and, through the churchyard and other means, it also provided continuity with the past. 'It was both a building to be cared for and a holy place to venerate; it was a place to ring bells and practise music; it was a place where the whole village could "meet together with their best faces, and in their cleanliest habits"; it was a place where some detected the ancient soul of England itself and expressed their affection in the most Freudian of terms.'[99] Because of its permanence, its constant presence at the centre of the village, and its association with such a variety of pivotal and key events in the life of individuals and of the community as a whole, it was possible to combine anticlericalism with devotion to the church. 'Indeed corporate opposition to clerical shortcomings is itself one of the most cohesive and durable features of the Anglican tradition. Popular Anglicanism, as with its more elite versions, was shot through with paradoxes, ambiguities and inconsistencies.'[100]

This 'popular Anglicanism' merged with a more diffuse and even more ill-defined 'popular religion'. In most eighteenth-century communities, and especially in the countless hamlets, villages and small rural towns of the land in which most of the population lived, there was an inextricable intertwining of 'religion', both orthodox and heterodox, magic, superstition, 'folk' religion, and mere social tradition. All these elements played their part in what constituted a powerful and pervasive aspect of the daily life of many, indeed perhaps most, of the inhabitants of England. And of course this religious and quasi-religious culture was as relevant to the Dissenters as to the Church of England. 'Popular religion' continued to exercise its undoubtedly powerful influence right up to the present day; and because this is so it is a topic to which I will be returning later.

4

The Evangelical Revival:
The Methodists

The eighteenth-century evangelical revival was not an isolated phenomenon. It had an international and intercontinental dimension. On the continent of Europe, in America, in Wales, Scotland and England there were revivals of remarkable similarity, and we need briefly to examine these in order to give the necessary wider context for the ensuing full description and analysis of the English revival.

As a preliminary to this, a definition of revivalism will assist in identifying what distinctive features will especially attract our attention and interest, and how revivals differ from certain similar religious phenomena. Revivalism represents a sudden, largely spontaneous, marked and sustained increase in the extent and intensity of the commitment of a number of individuals within a religious tradition in a particular geographical area to the beliefs and practices of their faith; a sudden increase in the concern of such members of a religious tradition for the conversion to a similar faith of those at the time either outside the tradition, or only nominal members of it; and an accompanying increase in the fervour and intensity of the corporate religious life of the believers concerned. A further characteristic feature is a sudden and marked increase in the number of new commitments (conversions) to the same religious faith experienced by those within the revival from among those previously outside it, or only nominal members of the wider religious tradition within which the revival occurs. A revival often entails certain features coming into prominence in the individual and corporate life of those involved, which are normally minimally present, or totally absent in the religious tradition concerned; features which are associated with the original emergence of the religious tradition, and with its nascent individual and corporate life. In the Christian tradition (for revivals, as defined here, have taken place in other, non-Christian religious traditions) these include glossolalia (speaking in tongues), and certain bodily manifestations of intense mental and spiritual experience, such as falling down and crying out. In many respects a revival involves a discarding of much of the accumulated human tradition and formulations of the faith to be found in the broader Christian tradition in which the revival takes place, and a return to the pristine character of the religious tradition; or at least a reaching out after such an ideal. It is an attempt to return to basics.

Revivals occur within a religious tradition. They need to be distinguished from all forms of religious movement, cults, sects and oppositional groups which take as their *raison d'être* the reversal of one or more of the dominant beliefs or norms of an existing religious tradition. Norman Cohn emphasizes that between the eleventh century and the first half of the sixteenth century in Europe, the various millennial sects which arose all stood in opposition to the mediaeval church. Indeed, many of them identified the church of the day as Antichrist, and the church attacked and suppressed such movements as heresies, subverting its authority.[1] The somewhat similar cults in Melanesia and other areas which have arisen in the twentieth century, although they incorporate many elements from traditional Christianity, and from the teaching of the Bible, have invariably been outside the framework of the church. They characteristically have included Christian missionaries among those who will be driven into the sea at the imminent end of the world, when either the ancestors will return, or the reign of eternal bliss will be ushered in with the appearance of God or some other liberating power bringing all the goods people desire.[2]

Revivalism must also be distinguished from three other phenomena which take place within a religious tradition, and more especially the Christian tradition: reform movements, 'enthusiasm', and evangelism.

Reform movements tend to be consciously initiated by an individual or group for specific, usually clearly defined and delimited, objectives, which do not normally include, and even less frequently are restricted to, the features enumerated in the definition just given of revivalism. Among such have been the movement for the abolition of slavery, and various other reforms which motivated the Clapham Sect and the Hackney Phalanx, and Christian Socialism. In the case of such a wide-ranging and revolutionary movement as the sixteenth-century Reformation in Europe, revivalism occurred in certain restricted areas, but the entire movement was too capacious and variegated in character to be defined as a revival.

'Enthusiasm' is a term which was derisively applied as a description of the eighteenth-century revival by those at the time who were not in sympathy with it. They had especially in mind certain groups and movements which had come into prominence at various times throughout the previous two centuries, such as the Anabaptists, Millennarians or Fifth Monarchy Men, Seekers, Ranters, Diggers, Levellers, and, more recently, the French Prophets who appeared in London just prior to the beginning of the revival. Ronald Knox has embraced within such a category many movements from the Montanists onwards; and he includes within the scope of the term any movement in the history of Christianity which was characterized by a high degree of religious emotionalism.[3] This categorization is so comprehensive that it allows for the inclusion of revivals as I have defined them; but it is far too wide to indicate the special and peculiar nature of revivalism as a separate phenomenon apart from other 'enthusiastic' movements.

Lastly, revivalism must not be confused with Christian evangelism. The two have frequently, and mistakenly, been used synonymously, especially by American writers.[4] Evangelism represents an organized attempt, through planned meetings and other means, to present the claims and demands of the faith to those who are not committed to it, in order to produce conversions. Again, as with enthusiasm, there are certain elements in common with revivalism, and revivals often include a considerable amount of evangelism, but there is a spontaneity, and inbuilt momentum in revivals which is not to be found, at least to anywhere near the same extent, in evangelism. Revivals, typically, are not organized, and not absolutely dependent on a figure equivalent to the evangelist, although we will, of course, find that George Whitefield and John and Charles Wesley loomed large in the eighteenth-century revival, and John Wesley was a superlative organizer; but these three may be viewed as catalysts and focal points in a movement which had its own momentum. We will, indeed, find an interplay between their distinctive contributions, especially as evangelists, and the sense of innate dynamism which characterized the movement. It is generally true that there are circumstances which help prepare the way for revivals, and these might include organized evangelism. It is perhaps a matter of balance; in evangelism the pre-arrangement is paramount; with revivalism, there is an unorganized upsurge of spiritual energy, new life, vitality and renewal. It is arguable that the eighteenth-century revival and early nineteenth-century Primitive Methodism, which followed hard on the heels of the eighteenth-century revival, were the last large-scale examples of revivalism as I have characterized it, and that revivalism merges into evangelism as the element of spontaneity gives way to what might be described as organized revivalism. But the purer form of revivalism was also evident in those revivals which ran in parallel with the English revival, or preceded it.

Revivals in America

The first widespread revival in eighteenth-century America was the Great Awakening between 1740 and 1743. But this was preceded by intermittent local revivals in the third decade, of which the most influential, as in many ways the most interesting, occurred in 1734–5 in the New England town of Northampton. It was associated with the work of Jonathan Edwards, who gives a full and graphic description of its chief features, in an account which was rapidly and widely distributed in America and Europe.[5]

Northampton was a small town of approximately two hundred families which had been established in about 1654. In many ways it was a typical pioneer settlement. In the first eighty years of its existence it had only two ministers, both of whom were zealous Christian pastors and evangelists; so that when Jonathan Edwards became its third minister he entered into an evangelical inheritance, and served a people who basically accepted the tenets of the Christian faith. Nevertheless, in the exercise of his duties, he first observed 'a time of extraordinary dullness in religion'.[6] After two or three years this started to change, and the young people in particular showed a greater receptivity to religious matters. A sudden increased religious concern was manifested among the inhabitants of a neighbouring village about three miles away, accompanied by some conversions. A series of events, including two deaths in the area, helped to focus attention on religious issues. Five or six persons were converted in a short space of time, including one woman with a somewhat tarnished reputation. The rapid developments which then took place are best described by Edwards as an eye witness. Even though allowance needs to be made for his possible over-enthusiasm, he conveys an impression of the total effect and course of events, and captures the mood of the times:

> . . . a great and earnest concern about the great things of religion, and the eternal world, became universal in all parts of the town, and among persons of all degrees and ages. The noise among the dry bones waxed louder and louder; all other talk but about spiritual and eternal things, was soon thrown by; all the conversation in all

companies, and upon all occasions, was upon these things only, unless so much as was necessary for people carrying on their ordinary secular business. Other discourse than of the things of religion, would scarcely be tolerated in any company. The minds of people were wonderfully taken off from the world; it was treated amongst us as a thing of very little consequence . . .

. . . The only thing in their view was to get to the kingdom of heaven, and every one appeared pressing in to it; the engagedness of their hearts in this great concern could not be hid, it appeared in their very countenances. It was then a dreadful thing amongst us to lie out of Christ, in danger every day of dropping into hell; and what persons' minds were intent upon was, to escape for their lives and to 'fly from the wrath to come'. All would eagerly lay hold of opportunities for their souls; and were wont very often to meet together in private houses for religious purposes; and such meetings, when appointed, were wont greatly to be thronged.

There was scarcely a single person in the town, either old or young, left unconcerned about the great things of the eternal world . . . and the work of conversion was carried on in a most astonishing manner, and increased more and more; souls did, as it were, come by flocks to Jesus Christ. From day to day, for many months together, might be seen evident instances of sinners brought 'out of darkness into marvellous light' . . .

This work of God, as it was carried on, and the number of true saints multiplied, soon made a glorious alteration in the town; so that in the spring and summer following, in the year 1735, the town seemed full of the presence of God . . . It was a time of joy in families, on account of salvation being brought to them. Our public assemblies were then beautiful; the congregation was alive in God's service, every one earnestly intent on the public worship, every hearer eager to drink in the words of the minister as they came from his mouth; the assembly in general were, from time to time, in tears while the word was preached; some weeping with sorrow and distress, others with joy and love, others with pity and concern for the souls of their neighbours.

. . . Those amongst us who had been formerly converted, were greatly enlivened and renewed with fresh and extraordinary visitation of the Spirit of God; though some much more than others, according to the measure of the gift of Christ: many that before had laboured under difficulties about their own state, had now their doubts removed by more satisfying experience, and more clear discoveries of God's love.[7]

There were probably only about just over three hundred people converted in the town and the immediate surrounding area, but they represented a high proportion of the total population, they were all converted in the space of about six months, and the religious life of the town and region was transformed. Edwards estimated that a large majority of the people in the town over sixteen years of age had a knowledge of salvation, and that this was true of all other places affected by the revival. But its significance was not just local. The stimulating news of it reached the British Isles just at a time when a revival had begun in Wales, and when the first glow of revival was discernable in London and Bristol, which was soon to spread as a fire throughout the length and breadth of the land. It was also the immediate herald of the Great Awakening in New England.

George Whitefield landed at Newport, Rhode Island, on 14 September 1740. On the two succeeding days he read prayers and preached in the morning and afternoon to very large congregations, more than a thousand following him to his lodgings after the afternoon service on the second day, according to a contemporary account. On 18 September he arrived in Boston, where he proceeded to conduct a powerful preaching ministry. Typical of these days are the events recorded in his Journal for Saturday 20 September:

Preached in the morning, to about six thousand hearers, in the Rev Dr Sewell's meeting-house; and afterwards, on the common, to about eight thousand; and again, at eight, to a thronged company at my lodgings.[8]

Repeatedly during the ensuing few weeks, the preaching was attended by great crowds, and there was a fervent response from among the people present. The preacher himself was aware of the great impact of his preaching, as his Journal entry for Saturday 27 September indicates:

In the morning, preached at the Rev Mr Welstead's meeting-house; in the afternoon, on the common, to about 15,000 people. Oh, how did the Word run ! I could scarce abstain from crying out, 'This is no other than the house of God and the gate of heaven.[9]

Throughout his first month in America Whitefield was instrumental in inaugurating a widespread revival; but its continuance did not depend upon his presence. Others were also on hand. In Boston, Gilbert Tennent preached with immense effectiveness for about four months, commencing two months after Whitefield left, and this helped to ensure that the impetus given by Whitefield was not diminished, but rather increased. An observer wrote:

> And now . . . was such a time as we never knew. The Rev Mr Cooper was wont to say, that more came to him, in one week, in deep concern about their souls, than had come in the whole twenty-four years of his preceding ministry. I can also say the same as to the numbers who repaired to me. Mr Cooper had about six hundred persons in three months; and Mr Webb had, in the same space, above a thousand. There repaired to us boys and girls, young men and women, Indians and negroes, heads of families and aged persons; some in great distress for fear of being unconverted; others lest they had all along been building on a righteousness of their own, and were still in the gall of bitterness and bond of iniquity; some fearing lest the Holy Spirit should withdraw Himself; others in great anxiety lest He should leave them for ever. Nor were the same persons satisfied with coming once or twice, as formerly; but they came again and again, I know not how often, complaining of their evil and accursed hearts; of their past and present unbelief; of their pride, hypocrisy, and perfidiousness; of their love and captivity to sin; and of their utter impotence to help themselves, or even to believe in Christ.[10]

The Great Awakening lasted about three years, and was most fruitful in the Puritan, Southern and Middle colonies. Outside New England its main centres were New York, New Jersey, Pennsylvania, Maryland and Virginia. 'By what I can understand,' wrote Edwards in January 1742, 'the work of God is greater at this day in the land than it has been at any time.'[11] It was a landmark in the spiritual history of the country, and again, as with the Northampton revival, news of what was happening across the Atlantic influenced the course of events in England, although by then the English revival was well under way.

Influences from the continent of Europe

'The morale of the Protestant world was at a low ebb in the half century before the awakening of the 1730s and 1740s. Catholic expansion had shorn Continental Protestantism of much of its strength, a fact brought home to the Anglophone world by the successive waves of refugees who poured into it: the Huguenots, Palatines, Salzburgers, and Moravians.'[12] Within the Protestant fold itself there was a crisis in those Protestant territories not established and protected by the Westphalia treaties.[13] The epicentre was Silesia and its neighbours, and the source of the spiritual earthquake was Pietism. In 1675 Philipp Jakob Spener set out a programme of church renewal. He castigated all classes for the poor state of the church, and made proposals for improved clerical training and preaching. The crux of what he had to say was, however, not to do with such procedural matters, but with the very spring of spiritual vitality, the new birth. This doctrine became the hallmark of Pietism 'not because it was peculiar to them but because of the prominence they gave it. The essence of the matter was how best to realize the priesthood of all believers.'[14] In his book *Pia desideria* (1675) he stressed the need for the church to re-emphasize the study of scripture and to ensure the active involvement of the laity; for greater importance to be given to evangelism, and to practical living rather than to intellectual acumen; for preaching to be aimed at the salvation of the listener, rather than simply giving instruction and correction; and for ministerial training to emphasize the development of moral and spiritual qualities in the life of the pastor. Spener advocated *collegia pietatis* or class-meetings, in which the faithful ministered to each other by teaching, warning, converting and edifying one another. Christianity was a way of life; and it was learnt in the process of doing. Although he started his class-meeting at Frankfurt as an elite group, he soon found that artisans and servants of both sexes who attended had remarkable knowledge. They helped to make the classes a further distinguishing characteristic of Pietism and an ideal way of supplementing the regular devotions of the church.

The organizing genius of Pietism was August Francke. At the University of Halle he skilfully combined the proclamation of the distinctive Pietist teaching with the promotion of the educational aims of his institution. True to the Pietist concern about action, and what struck the ordinary observer, was not the theory, nor even the work of the theological faculty, but the charitable bodies which Francke created outside the walls of the town: the Orphan House, the dispensary, the schools, the teacher-training institutions and the Bible Institute. Although he followed Dutch models, the scale of his enterprise was staggering for his day, and unparalleled. It 'gave a shape to charitable activity all over the Protestant world'.[15] His Orphan House was one of the largest buildings in Europe, and provided accommodation, and a base for the life and work of 3,000 people. 'The dispensary was the first producer of standardized branded medicaments on a commercial scale, able and anxious to sell a complete public health kit for a city or a province, and marketing its wares by brochures in Latin, French, English, Dutch and Greek.'[16] The priorities of Halle were clear: the supply of medicaments and of Bibles and other religious literature. The press soon became one of the leading ones in Germany, and its publications were widely distributed in a range of languages.

One of Francke's pupils was Count Nicholas von Zinzendorf. Under Francke's influence he decided to dedicate his life to religion. An opportunity to further the Pietist cause presented itself when a representative group of the persecuted remnant of the Unitas Fratrum visited his estate at Berthelsdorf in Saxony in 1722. Refugees of this ancient Protestant church of Bohemia and Moravia sought asylum, and he allowed them to establish the settlement which became known as Herrnhut. In 1727 Zinzendorf asserted his authority over the community and insisted that it should abide by the Pietist principle of 'ecclesiola in ecclesia' – a church within the church. The task of the 'Moravians' was, he asserted, not to establish a new denomination, but to help revitalize existing churches. He transformed them from a band of quarrelling nomads into a body of dedicated evangelists; and soon missionaries from Herrnhut were going to the West Indies (1732), Greenland (1733), to the Indians of Surinam (1734), to the Hottentots of South Africa (1737), and to the Gold Coast and Ceylon (1737).

A further influence emanating from the continent was the great emigration of Protestants from Salzburg in the winter of 1731–2. It was part of a series of migrations which had repercussions throughout Protestant Europe and America. They 'not only increased the efficiency of the Protestant intelligence system as expatriates reported back to their mother churches; they were also to have important effects in cross-fertilizing Anglo-Saxon Protestantism. What would the history of Methodism have been if John Wesley, High Church Anglican, had not met Peter Bohler, a Moravian ? '[17]

The revival in Wales

The eighteenth-century Welsh revival is interesting because it pre-dated, and was for some years independent of the English revival, and because its origins and progress were connected with the concurrent but almost separate labourers of three different men, Howell Harris, the Revd Daniel Rowland, and the Revd Howell Davies. But mention must first be made of the work of the Revd Griffith Jones.

Griffith Jones has been referred to by some as 'the Apostle of Wales', and by others as 'the morning Star of the Revival'. In 1710, at the age of twenty-seven, he began his curacy in the Vale of Taf, where he remained for the rest of his ministry. By his powerful preaching, mainly in and around his parish of Llandowrer, he attracted large congregations, both in churches and in the open air, for he was a pioneer of field preaching. He also initiated the Circulating Welsh Charity Schools as a supplement to the Charity School Movement, and this helped further to increase his influence. Finally, he was instrumental in the conversion of Harris, Rowland and Davies.

Howell Harris was born in 1714 in Trevecca, near Hay-on-Wye, and converted in 1735. He went to Oxford University, but being immediately disgusted with the prevailing immorality and godlessness, he returned at the end of the first term. Soon afterwards he began to go from house to house throughout his home area, warning and exhorting his neighbours, and proclaiming to them the way of salvation which he had recently experienced. He opened a day-school in Trevecca. Crowds gathered at the houses he visited, and they soon became so great that there was not a place in the vicinity sufficiently large to contain them. Many underwent spiritual crises in their lives as a consequence of his preaching, and from 1736 onwards he established religious societies in order that such seekers and converts might be assisted, and the spiritual effect of his ministry enhanced. Family worship was begun, or re-introduced into many homes, and the church services were generally crowded. In the words of the Revd William Williams, 'Thus began the mighty preaching that raised Wales from the sleep of ages, and thus commenced the great Welsh Methodist revival.'[18]

Simultaneously, but apparently independent of this local revival, in the neighbouring county of Cardigan, another work of spiritual renewal took place. About forty miles from Telgarth where Harris ministered, but separated from it by ranges of wild, trackless mountains, was the little village of Llangeitho, where the Revd Daniel Rowland was curate to his elder brother. About this time he experienced conversion, and went about preaching in his own and other parishes. His fame increased and spread, and he accepted invitations to preach in other counties. As he travelled through the country, large crowds flocked to hear him. The preaching had a powerful effect both upon the unbelievers and within the fellowship of believers. Numbers of people were converted, there was an increase in the spiritual vitality within the congregations, and at the parish church of Llangeitho those 'rejoicings' began which were to be characteristic of some subsequent Welsh revivals.

A further strand in the revival was the response evoked by the Revd Howell Davies. He was ordained to the curacy of Llysyfran in Pembrokeshire, where his ministry was so effective that many people came together to hear him. There were, however, influential parishioners who could not tolerate what he proclaimed, and as a result of their opposition he was dismissed. He thereupon proceeded to travel throughout the country preaching in churches and in the open air; and he, like the other two, witnessed a great number of conversions.

Revival in Scotland

The revival in Cambuslang and Kilsyth in Scotland was, like the one in Wales, apparently independent of the English revival, although it took place in 1742, when the English revival had been in full flood for about three years.[19] The parish of Cambuslang was small at the time of the revival, with most of the people living within one mile of the church. The sudden increase in the tempo and intensity of religious life arose out of the ordinary work and life of the parish. A more than normal concern about religion appeared among the people, and in January 1742 a number of them presented a petition to the minister requesting a weekly lecture to help them in spiritual matters. In February 1742, for three days prior to the first lecture, there were fervent meetings for prayer. The call for spiritual instruction became so persistent and strong that the minister instituted a daily sermon, with a few days excepted; and he usually spent some time afterwards in exhortation, prayers and the singing of psalms. About three hundred people were awakened to a deep concern about salvation at this time; and there was also a noticeable effect on the lifestyles of the people touched by the revival. The Revd James Robe witnessed some of these consequences of the revival in Cambuslang and elsewhere. Although, as with other such accounts, we must treat the hyperbole with a measure of caution, what lies behind the rhetoric can be reasonably inferred. He tells of

> . . . a visible reformation of people who were formerly notorious sinners; particularly, the laying aside of cursing and swearing and

drinking to excess, among those who were addicted to these practices; remorse for acts of injustice, and for violation of relative duties, confessed to the persons wronged, joined with new endeavours after a conscientious discharge of such duties; restitution, which has more than once been distinctly and particularly inculcated in public since this work began; forgiving of injuries; all desirable evidences of fervent love to one another, to all men, and even to those who speak evil of them . . .[20]

At the nearby parish of Kilsyth, with its population of about eleven hundred, a similar phenomenon took place; although in this case there were more bodily reactions to intense spiritual experiences. The preaching was accompanied by bitter cries of anguish, groans and weeping. About two hundred of the parish found relief and were awakened. Nor was this localized revival confined to these two parishes. The minister of Kilsyth refers to other parishes experiencing its effect:

In the parish of Kirkintilloch there are known to the minister about a hundred and twenty under a more than ordinary concern about their salvation . . . In the parish of St Ninians, the number of the awakened must be considerable . . . In the parish of Gargunnock, lying west from the parish of St Ninians, there are, as I am well informed, nearly a hundred persons awakened . . . In the parish of Calder, according to the information I have from their minister, there are above a hundred awakened. There are about the same number in the parish of Campsie.[21]

Some of those involved in the English revival witnessed these events at first hand and spread the news of what was happening, and there were also written accounts which were circulated quite widely.

An international communication network

All these influences, from America, the continent, Wales and Scotland, impinged upon England, largely because of the opening up of communication which had taken place by the fourth decade of the eighteenth century. There was by then a massive exchange of correspondence between America, continental Europe and England. Gotthilf August Francke, the son of the great August Hermann, received news of the revival in New England from English sources via the German community in Pennsylvania, as well as from friends of his late father in the

Rhineland. There was much more European migration, and travel generally between countries and continents than in former times. There was a great expansion in the press, and literature crossed national borders to an extent not previously known. There is evidence of the development of an international Protestant frame of mind. In such a situation, there was a sense of defensiveness; an awareness of loss of morale, of the inroads of secularism and of a loss of numerical strength. As a countervailing force, news spread of the remarkable transforming effect of revival when it came to a region or to a country.

The extent and importance of this wider context of the English revival has not, until quite recently, received the attention it deserves. Studies of revivals in the first half of the eighteenth century have tended to concentrate on particular areas and countries and to ignore or underplay the relevance of this international frame of reference. This is rapidly changing.

The events of the 1730s and 1740s in England were perceived by many of the participants as part of a single, transatlantic, God-inspired phenomenon.

On November 8, 1742, several hundred men and women packed into the London Spa Fields Tabernacle to celebrate the latest news of religious revival. The high point of the meeting came when letters from all over the revival world were read out aloud, after which the congregation joined in a hymn specially written for the occasion:

> Great things in England, Wales and Scotland wrought,
> And in America to pass are brought,
> Awaken'd souls, warn'd of the wrath to come
> In Numbers flee to Jesus as their Home . . .
> What is this News, that flies throughout our Land?[22]

And this sense of international divine activity was nurtured throughout the succeeding decades.

Evidence suggests that Calvinist evangelicals on both sides of the Atlantic were highly conscious of one another's activities. This transatlantic evangelical consciousness grew out of the isolated correspondence of individual ministers. Ministers and lay promoters extended the correspondence into a reliable, nonpersonal system of contacts, which they developed into a number of procedures for spreading the news from individuals to groups of committed laity and beyond to a wider lay audience. Because revival news was of great importance to Calvinist evangelicals, they had a strong motivation to create a relatively durable chain of correspondence . . . It is not too much to say that through that exchange of ideas and materials Calvinist revivalists of the mid-eighteenth century built a 'community of saints' that cut across physical barriers and, on occasion, theological divisions.[23]

Correspondence was supplemented by other means for promoting an awareness of identity of purpose in what was increasingly regarded as a single enterprise. 'Through itineracy, advance publicity, publication of their sermons and journals, and the printing of new evangelical magazines, the leading revivalists created and reinforced expectations, taught people appropriate behaviour during a revival, informed pastors of successful combinations of revivalist techniques, and forged a transatlantic movement.'[24] Public readings of foreign and domestic news became institutionalized as Letter Days; and even prayer took the form of coordinated prayer days, organized as the united Concert of Prayer for revival.

The unity of contemporary revival history was axiomatic to many early evangelicals, and they would have been surprised at any attempt to fragment it and to present it as a number of separate revivals. Despite their controversies, they 'were usually agreed that the outpourings of the Spirit witnessed by their age were generically the same. "Evidently one work with what we have here" was Wesley's comment on the American awakening.'[25] Of particular importance in raising consciousness of this international, transatlantic identity of experience was the ministry of George Whitefield. He, far more than any other person, helped to promote this sense of a transatlantic revival community. By his frequent visits to Scotland, Wales and America; by his charisma; and by his brilliant and innovative use of publicity techniques, he raised the awareness in the various revival areas of similar phenomena near at hand and far afield. Indeed, it has been claimed that he did more than this.

Frank Lambert and Harry S. Stout have portray Whitefield, and more widely the revival itself, in the context of an expanding and increasingly entrepreneurial Anglo-American consumer society.[26]

In the course of his extemporaneous, open-air preaching to mass audiences, he transformed the traditional sermon into something different: a dramatic event capable of competing for public attention outside the arena of the churches – in fact, in the marketplace. Whitefield showed that preaching could be both edifying and entertaining. Others had preached out-of-doors before him, to be sure, but none had ranged so far in ever-expanding itinerant circuits, nor had any enjoyed Whitefield's personal, transatlantic appeal. It was left to Whitefield to become Anglo-America's first religious celebrity, the symbol for a dawning modern age.[27]

It was not just the preaching and the forceful personality which cast him in this role and gave him such an important part in the religious, and more general cultural, history of the countries where he concentrated his vibrant ministry. He perhaps largely or entirely united some of the religious and the commercial norms of countries undergoing radical economic change. Prior to Whitefield public religion was restricted to the tradition of churches and meetinghouses; and the governing procedures, practices and language of both were distinctive and discrete.

George Whitefield's greatness lay in integrating religious discourse into this emerging language of consumption. Before him there had been only established 'churches' and tolerated 'sects'. Aspiring religious leaders and reformers could think of nothing grander than reviving their own denominations and convincing those in other denominations of the errors of their ways. Only Whitefield thought to transcend denominational lines entirely and, in effect, ply a religious trade in the open air of the marketplace. His 'product' he offered to all who would voluntarily enter under its canopy and participate.[28]

It does not lessen the integrity or religious authenticity of Whitefield if what he did was unconsciously part of a social or religious process of which he and his contemporaries were not aware. Throughout history there have always been unintended consequences of intended human action; and this applies in the religious sphere as much as in any other realm of human activity.

The Methodist revival in England – the early phase

The eighteenth-century revival in England began suddenly and dramatically, and soon gained considerable momentum.

In August 1736 George Whitefield[29] arrived in London by invitation in order to fulfil the duties of the Revd Thomas Broughton at the Chapel of the Tower of London while he was away. He immediately aroused curiosity:

The effect was immediate and visible to all; for as I went up the stairs almost all seemed to sneer at me on account of my youth; but they soon grew serious and and exceedingly attentive, and after I came down showed me great token of respect, blessed me as I passed along, and made great enquiry who I was. The question no one could answer, for I was quite a stranger. I speedily slipped through the crowd.[30]

His ministry at the Tower lasted two months, and people from different parts of the city went to hear him preach on the new birth, probably coming mainly from the religious societies. Some titled persons who were later numbered among his followers, first became aware of him at this time.

About six months later, in March 1737, Whitefield re-visited London in order to meet James Oglethorpe and the other Trustees of the colonial territory of Georgia, as he was about to offer his services as a chaplain in America. On this occasion he preached more frequently than before. His preaching attracted large congregations, as it did when he left London and preached at Bristol, Gloucester and Bath. He returned to London again in June 1737, and accepted invitations to preach at Cripplegate, St Ann's and Froster Lane churches, and to administer the Holy Communion. Of these services Whitefield reports that:

. . . so many came, that sometimes we were obliged to consecrate fresh elements two or three times; and stewards found it somewhat difficult to carry the offerings to the communion table.[31]

As he preached in more and more London churches, some where weekly lectures were held, his fame increased, and the numbers of those present became even greater. It is apparent that many of the services were sponsored by the religious societies, and not supported by the churches as such. On Sundays he would usually preach four times, as well as reading prayers two or three times.

By the middle of September his activities had come to the attention of the newspapers. One of these reported:

. . . that there was a young gentleman going volunteer to Georgia; that he had preached at St.Swithin's, and collected £8 instead of ten shillings, £3 of which were in half pence; and that he was to preach next Wednesday before the Societies at their general quarterly meeting.[32]

Whitefield protested to a printer about this type of publicity, but he acknowledged that 'by this means people's curiosity was stirred up more and more.'[33]

During the following three months or so he generally preached about nine times a week, and the crowds coming to hear him massively increased. Often many people had to be turned away even from the most spacious churches. Despite some possible exaggeration, and Whitefield was later to express regret at the terminology and ego-centricity of some of his early Journal entries, his vivid accounts convey a good impression of the impact of his preaching in these first few months of what was to be an outstanding evangelistic ministry:

> On Sunday mornings, long before day you might see streets filled with people going to church, with their lanterns in their hands, and hear them conversing about the things of God . . . People gave so liberally to the charity schools, that this season near £1,000 sterling was collected at the several churches besides many private contributions sent in afterwards.[34]

With the departure of Whitefield, the revival he had initiated was not only sustained, it became even more widespread and established. This was partly achieved by the publication of some of his sermons and other works, which, in the early months of 1738, were produced in abundance, but of particular importance were the religious societies. The sudden presence of so many people earnestly wanting spiritual help gave new life, energy and zest to both the old, established societies and to those which had been recently founded. Moreover, whereas the societies had previously been separate bodies with little awareness of any mutual relationship, their newly acquired zeal and common strong allegiance to the evangelical doctrines proclaimed by Whitefield resulted in new and strong bonds of fellowship; and their quarterly meetings demonstrated this spiritual vigour and sense of unity. Some members of the societies now declared that they would only submit to clerical oversight if the clergyman in question was one of the few thoroughly evangelical men at this time ministering in London. Whitefield ensured his continuing influence with the societies by sending reports of his activities in Georgia to James Hutton, to be read at their meetings; and these were subsequently published.

The society which met at the Bible and Sun, the home and book-seller's shop of James Hutton in Little Wild Street, greatly increased in membership, and moved as a consequence to a chapel in Fetter Lane.

The Earl and Countess of Huntingdon frequently attended its services, as did several moderately prosperous business families. John Wesley exercised a considerable influence in this gathering, but it was predominantly a Moravian fellowship. The Moravian visits to England in the period 1728 to 1737 were not undertaken in order to provide a foundation for the building of a Moravian Church in England. At no stage was the motive evangelistic. The main intention was to establish ecumenical relationships, and secondly to promote the settlement in the new American colony of Georgia.[35] The formation of the Fetter Lane Society was unplanned, but 'it was both initially and increasingly Moravian in style. Although John Wesley played an important part in events, his role has been exaggerated.'[36] It was by chance that he attended the inaugural meeting, and he afterwards spent five of the first eight months of its early life away from London. Many developments took place which he opposed or at best supported unenthusiastically. He reluctantly accepted the decision to have a separate women's meeting, which their husbands but no other men might attend, before the weekly general meeting. He was uncomfortable about the provision for a continual fast by three members of the Society each day, making fasting only meaningful as part of communal worship, as he placed considerable store on the value of individual fasting as a means of promoting personal holiness. He was also unhappy with the introduction of the Moravian office of 'monitor', whereby two members of the Society, chosen by lot, would be responsible for telling everyone what faults were observed in them, while concealing the informers, as he thought that such a practice would undermine the responsibility of band-leaders to reprove their fellows. Such an arrangement was also unnecessary as God had provided priests and deacons for the very monitoring ministry in question. Most seriously, Wesley was alarmed at the teaching about 'stillness'. It was a standard Moravian tenet and had been part of the Moravian corpus of teaching in London before Molther arrived. I will be considering it in detail in a few pages time, and at this stage it need only be noted that it was soon to become the ostensible main ground for the departure from the Fetter Lane Society of a significant number of the fellowship under the leadership of Wesley.

Although the Moravian church very largely refrained from proselytizing, and even later, when the revival was in full spate, was 'much more a refuge for the awakened than an agent of awakening',[37] it unintentionally helped to give birth to Methodism.

In May 1738, first Charles Wesley, and then his brother John, were converted in London, and immediately began to declare 'salvation by faith' to individuals and groups in homes, in the religious societies, and in the few churches which had not closed their doors to such preaching and preachers. On his return to London in December 1738, Whitefield could write in response to what he saw:

> Here seems to be a great pouring out of the Spirit, and many who were awakened by my preaching a year ago, are now grown strong men in Christ, by the ministrations of my dear friends and fellow-labourers, John and Charles Wesley.[38]

As the revival developed in London during the Christmas period of 1738 and the early days of 1739, so the antagonism of some of the Church of England clergy grew. This is well illustrated, as is the central issue at stake as seen by the revival leaders, in an incident in which Whitefield and John Wesley discussed at length with two Anglican clergymen and some others who opposed the revival preaching, what was the core concern in the rift which was emerging. After describing the main drift of the debate, Whitefield continued:

> God enabled me, with great simplicity, to declare what he had done for my soul, which made them look upon me as a madman . . . Now, therefore, I am fully convinced there is a fundamental difference between us and them. They believe only an outward Christ, we further believe that He must be inwardly formed in our hearts also. But the natural man receiveth not the things of the Spirit of God, for they are foolishness unto him, neither can he know them, because they are spiritually discerned.[39]

At that stage the revival received a new impulse which increased its effectiveness and immensely enlarged its outreach; for it was then that Whitefield and the Wesleys began their open air preaching. The activities of the revival leaders had spread to Bristol, but both there and in London it was confined to churches and religious societies. When first of all Whitefield and then the Wesleys ventured out into open spaces beyond the confines of buildings they inaugurated a new phase in the revival and gave it one of its distinguishing marks. In London, at Upper Moorfields and Kennington Common, and in Bristol, most especially among the miners of Kingswood, they now addressed thousands of people, including vast numbers who were untouched by the regular ministry of the churches. The actual size of the crowds was variously calculated by both the preachers and contemporary witnesses. Even allowing for considerable over-estimation (and it has been suggested that a realistic figure would be obtained if the numbers given by Whitefield and the Wesleys were halved), there is little doubt that there were often a few thousand present, and not infrequently as many as ten to twenty thousand. Such gatherings also remained consistently large after the novelty had gone and open air preaching had become a regular feature of the revival, despite the fact that they often began at five or seven o'clock in the morning. Of course this all helped to heighten public awareness of what was happening. It also entailed a noticeable intensification in the commitment of the supporters of the revival, as they saw it expanding and applied themselves more fully to its extension; and a perceptible and marked addition to the number of converts. The field preaching was on the principle of preach and return, with a continuous return to the same location. Also, as many of those who attended the outdoors preaching were from the religious societies, there was a close relationship between the development and effectiveness of both. There was no clear distinction between the open air meetings as being evangelistic, and the society meetings as being gatherings of believers met for Christian edification. Indeed, many converts had their final, culminating experience of conversion in the smaller society, class or band meeting; for, by now, there were three such groupings.

One of the great needs resulting from the revival was for those whose interest and concern had been awakened to meet together in order to seek and find the salvation for which they longed, and then to be established in the faith once it had been received. John Wesley was quick to recognize this, and he provided for it. In 'The Nature, Design, and General Rules of the United Societies, in London, Bristol, Kingswood, Newcastle-upon-Tyne, etc.' he relates:

> In the latter end of the year 1739, eight or ten persons came to me in London, who appeared to be deeply convinced of sin, and earnestly groaning for redemption. They desired (as did two or three the next day) that I would spend some time with them in prayer, and advise them how to flee from the wrath to come; which they saw continually hanging over their heads. That we might have more time for this great work, I appointed a day when all might come together, which from thence forward they did every week, namely, on Thursday, in the evening.[40]

On the first Thursday twelve were present, at the second meeting those attending rose to forty, and soon after to one hundred. The only requirement for any person wishing to go was that they should have a genuine desire to 'flee from the wrath to come'. The Society was defined as:

> . . . a company of men, having the form, and seeking the power of godliness; united in order to pray together, to receive the word of exhortation, and to watch over one another in love, that they may help each other to work out their salvation.[41]

It met at the Foundry in Moorfields; a place which rapidly became one of the main centres of the revival in the country.

After a time, some of the members abandoned their initial resolve to seek 'the power of godliness'. There were those who gave way to what was considered by the leaders as unworthy behaviour. John Wesley viewed this as a grave problem. He recalled his concern:

> We groaned under these inconveniences long, before a remedy could be found. The people were scattered so wide in all parts of the town, from Wapping to Westminster, that I could not easily see what the behaviour of each person in his own neighbourhood was: so that several disorderly walkers did much hurt before I was apprized of it.[42]

The kind of difficulties to which Wesley alludes were to a substantial extent met by the system of bands and classes, which, from the time of their introduction, became an integral and vital element in Methodism. The bands were small groups of five to ten persons who voluntarily joined together 'for intense spiritual nurture and support. Their primary activities were confession and prayer; their goal was spiritual growth.'[43] The Moravian pattern was adopted. Each band was homogeneous. There were bands for women, for men, and even for boys; and in addition to gender distinction they were segregated by marital status – single men, single women, married men and married women meeting in different groups; and there were later even select bands for those who were leading an exemplary life. It was reckoned that such an arrangement allowed for the maximum degree of openness and candour. Wesley himself was clarifying in his own thinking and experience the relationship between justification, as the forgiveness of sins which God accomplishes for us, and sanctification, as holiness of life, and what God does in us, and the bands were intended as aids to the growth in holiness. 'The Wesleyan bands, therefore, were not so much spiritual elitist groups in which the leader monitored the perseverance of the saints, as they were more collegial groups that stressed nurture by means of mutual accountability, confession, and growth in grace through Christian fellowship and religious conference.'⁴⁴

To provide for those who were not members of a band, and initially in order to systematize the means of mobilizing financial support for the local society from all its members, the society was divided into classes, which became the basic unit in the organizational framework of the revival, not only for the Methodists, but in some of the Church of England Evangelical parishes, as we will see in the next chapter. They were neighbourhood subdivisions, each composed of about twelve members with an assigned leader. This proved to be an excellent method of exercising pastoral oversight, and of training lay leaders. In their weekly round in which they contacted every member of the society, the leaders discovered problems of domestic dispute, drunkenness and other sorts of unacceptable behaviour which was incompatible with the pursuit of holiness, or personal difficulties experienced by members which might not otherwise have been apparent. The system had the added advantage of allowing Wesley himself to keep in touch with an ever increasing membership as he met with the leaders weekly when possible. It also facilitated the imposition of disciplinary measures when these were considered necessary.

Some indication of the intimacy and intensity of the corporate life of these groups is given in the rules of the bands in their more developed form, as stated in John Wesley's *Plain Account of the People called Methodists*. He writes:

> In order to 'confess our faults one to another', and pray for one another that we be healed, we intend, (1) to meet once a week, at the least. (2) To come punctually at the hour appointed. (3) To begin with singing or prayer. (4) To speak each of us in order, freely and plainly, the true state of our soul, with the faults we have committed in thought, word or deed, and the temptations we have felt since our last meeting. (5) To desire some person among us (thence called a Leader) to speak his own state first, and then to ask the rest, in order, as many and as searching questions as may be, concerning their state, sins, and temptations.⁴⁵

In surveying the system in 1748, he further comments:

> Great and many are the advantages which have ever since flowed from this closer union of the believers with each other. They prayed for one another, that they might be healed of the faults they had

confessed; and it was so. The chains were broken, the bands were burst in sunder, and sin had no more dominion over them. Many were delivered from the temptations out of which, till then, they found no way to escape. They were built up in our most holy faith. They rejoiced in the Lord more abundantly. They were strengthened in love, and more effectually provoked to abound in every good work.[46]

The intensity of social interaction and deep commitment to God, to the revival, and to one another was further reinforced by the institution of a monthly watch-night service and a love-feast, where the time was employed mainly in relating personal and corporate Christian experiences.

In the societies, classes and bands, in pastoral oversight and in evangelism, Methodism from its early days depended very much upon lay leadership. The leaders of the classes and bands, and the majority of those involved in the management and control of the societies were laymen. This gave opportunities to those with the appropriate talents to exercise their gifts in a way which would probably not have been possible in any other sphere of their lives. One aspect of this was the scope given to women. Wesley was a warm admirer of women, but it took many years before his expectation of them as evangelists was raised. He was surprised by their enthusiasm for his teaching, and their success as proselytizers, so that he gradually revised his initially conservative views. By the 1760s he was encouraging the most talented among his female followers to relate their spiritual experiences and to read in public from his sermons or other devotional writings. Soon after this they were not only allowed to testify but to exhort at prayer-meetings, class-meetings, band-meetings and love-feasts, and their share in these fellowships was impressive. Later still they were able to preach, as Wesley 'eventually acknowledged them as fulfilling the function of the deaconess in primitive Christianity'.[47] Such a progression of expanded opportunities for women Methodists may have been a consequence of exceptional circumstances rather than of conscious egalitarian impulses, but it was important both in itself, as a feature of Methodism, and as a contribution to the general, and more specifically religious, emancipation and liberation of women.

It was in 1739 that lay preachers were first employed. By then there was an urgent need for responsible lay leadership. The Wesleys and Whitefield were moving from one part of the country to another, and they were not long enough resident in one place to exercise the kind of high quality, sustained local leadership which was required. They were called upon to preach in an ever-widening area of the country; they were engaged in establishing new societies nationwide; and, in the case of Whitefield, there was the pressing demands of ministry in the American colonies. Although the appointed local lay leaders were generally competent, and exercised very considerable influence, their authority, powers and responsibilities were clearly defined and limited, and their appointment and dismissal was almost entirely dependent in these early days of the revival on the opinion and decisions of the ordained leadership.

The dominance of the Wesleys and Whitefield was especially pronounced, and more particularly the prominent part played by John Wesley. This exercise of authority extended to the individual members of the classes and bands throughout the land. When he was in one of the larger towns, and especially on his visits to London, John Wesley fixed an hour every day for speaking with each of the bands, in order to discover any 'disorderly walker', or 'any of a careless or contentious spirit'. In London, for example, he was available from 10 a.m. to 2 p.m. on every day but Saturday. On occasions he also read over the names of the society members, noting those who were of a doubtful character, so that a full enquiry might be made concerning them; and he subsequently spoke to those concerned, placing on trial any who did not show sufficient proof that they were 'seeking Christ in sincerity'. It not infrequently happened that when he returned from a period away from one particular centre, he found divisions, or contention, or spiritual decline which had caused havoc in the local society; and it was then only by his personal intervention and counsel that order was restored, and the society regained a fuller measure of spiritual health and vitality.

The revival leaders encouraged the societies to express their faith in action; and they led by example. John and Charles Wesley visited the inmates of Newgate, the Marshalsea and other prisons, and ministered to them; and in particular they showed compassion for those condemned to execution, whom they often accompanied in the death cart to the gallows at Tyburn and elsewhere. Ordinary lay members tried to imitate this example, as with Silas Told in London, of whom John Wesley could say:

For many years he attended the malefactors in Newgate, without fee or reward; and I suppose no man for this hundred years has been so successful in that melancholy office. God had given him peculiar talents for it; and he had amazing success therein. The greatest part of those whom he attended died in peace, and many of them in the triumph of faith.[48]

It was in this same spirit that efforts were made to provide assistance and relief to the sick and the poor. Through the class system, and by assigning special responsibilities to specially designated individuals, there was a thorough and regular visitation of the sick. In addition John Wesley decided in 1746 to administer physic to the poor. About three hundred sought this help in the first three weeks, and the facility was continued for several years. Financial assistance for the poor was provided by the systematic giving of the society members, and by periodic collections organized by John Wesley.

As the revival attracted ever more people, new and larger meeting places were acquired. In London, there was a building in Moorfields to which Wesley and a number of his followers transferred after they broke away from the Fetter Lane Society over the question of Moravian 'stillness'. There was also a chapel in West Street, near the Seven Dials, which was obtained in May 1743, and which thereafter acted as a strategic base for outreach into the more recently built areas of West London. Then, three months later a further chapel, at Spitalfields, was acquired, which served the society formed in Long Lane, and provided a centre for evangelistic work in parts of the capital south of the river. Such expansion was typical, but on a smaller scale, in a number of provincial towns.

The numerical growth of Methodism in these halcyon, pioneer days of the revival was impressive. Take the London society as an indicator. From the original twelve at its initiation in the latter part of 1739, the numbers increased dramatically. By 17 April 1742, there were 426 members, and 201 on trial; by August 1742, 523 members and 219 on trial; by 1743, there were a total of 1,950; and by December 1743, a total of 2,250 members.[49] As a result of the strict standards required, or because more fell away than were added, the total number fluctuated at around two thousand for the next few years. Taking a broader, extended, view, by the time of Wesley's death in 1791, there were 72,000 Arminian Methodists in the British Isles, and a further 60,000 in North America.

Towards a national crusade

The intervening period of some fifty years, from the exhilarating early years of the revival to the new era heralded by the death of John Wesley, was an unfolding saga of relentless effort, enormous and persistent courage and determination in the face of physical and verbal abuse, ridicule, and rejection by the Church of England, the parent church of many of the converts, the trauma, distress, and bitterness of internal divisions and secessions, and a gradual drift towards denominational separation.

The unrelenting effort was typified by John Wesley's fifty-three years of tireless ministry in the service of the Methodist revival. From the moment on the evening of 24 May 1738, in the religious society in Aldersgate Street, when he felt his 'heart strangely warmed', and he 'did trust in Christ, Christ alone, for salvation', to his peaceful death at the age of eighty-seven, surrounded by some of his dearest fellow-Methodists, his strenuous efforts for the promotion of the gospel were quite staggering. In 1770 he calculated that he had ridden 'above a hundred thousand miles' on horseback',[50] and he still had twenty years of travelling before him, although for these latter years he was compelled to leave the horse for the coach. He regularly rose at four, preached at five, and spend his days in a full round of preaching, counselling, exhorting, correcting, organizing and encouraging. He went round England annually, paid twenty visits to Scotland, and the same number to Ireland; and even while he travelled he spent his time usefully, reading history, poetry and philosophy on horseback. He suffered at the hands of the mob, was reviled and insulted, and yet he won through, and at the time of his death was widely honoured and respected. Throughout all of this he had the burdens of a work of God, and the spiritual responsibility for an ever growing body of believers which only those who bear them can fully appreciate. It was an heroic life, and one which bears comparison with any other Christian leader in English history.

Of course there were, in the first half-century of the revival, countless unsung and unrecognized Methodists who exerted themselves in exemplary ways, and suffered indignity, deprivation and all that is entailed in a life dedicated to the promotion of an unpopular cause. We can but catch a glimpse of these quite remarkable men and women, and it tells us little of the daily toil, and the faithful service which they offered.[51] When we read about the aggression of the mob in various parts of the country, and the opposition of those in authority, it shows us but the most dramatic and public aspects of what it meant to be despised and rejected, and to be counted by most of their fellow men and women as at the best odd, and at the worse public enemies. The systematic ransacking of Methodist homes in Wednesbury in 1744, with windows being broken, possessions looted, and furniture removed and broken up; the assault upon John Nelson's pregnant wife, with the consequent loss of her unborn child; the attack on the Methodist meeting place in Exeter in 1745, in which the rioters tore the clothes off the backs of the women, with one woman having to jump from the gallery to avoid being raped; the press-ganging of Methodist men on account of their religion; the depriving of Methodist men of their work because of their faith; the eviction from their holdings of Methodist farmers; the dragging through the common sewer of the Methodist preacher in Pateley Bridge in Yorkshire in 1752; the felling to the ground of another Methodist man at Hepworth Moor in Yorkshire in 1747 by a blow from a brick on the back of his head; or the striking on the head of William Seward in 1742, which proved to be fatal, and gave Methodism its first martyr; all of these were but indicative of a public venom which must have made the life of many Methodists a not easy pilgrimage.

It must be acknowledged that much of the opposition arose out of genuine and deeply felt fears and aversions. The fear of Jacobitism was aroused by a movement which, quite understandably given the tense emotional atmosphere of the time, was regarded by some as a cover for Jacobite intrigue. Then there were the manifestations of 'enthusiasm', with the spectre they aroused of Commonwealth sects and French Prophets. The convulsions, strange sighs, cries and groans which accompanied some of the preaching, the visions, claims of demon-possession and healing were perplexing to the revival leaders, and a cause of alarm and scandal to many outside the circle of the revival. The revival leaders moved in a highly-charged charismatic atmosphere, and they found it hard to decide what was a marvellous re-enactment of the scenes of the Acts of the Apostles and a reproduction of all the gifts of the apostolic age, and what was simply the weakness of human flesh, or worse, the activity of the devil. The quite frequent appearance of such phenomena is another indication that the revival was touching the lives of ordinary people in a quite remarkable way.

It is noteworthy that there were pockets of revival throughout the country in the late thirties and early forties, in which preaching was accompanied by unusual signs of powerful forces at work in the lives of individuals and groups, before Whitefield or the Wesleys appeared on the scene. The initial igniting of revival throughout the land was not the work of Whitefield and the Wesleys alone, or indeed of them together with their army of lay leaders. There is evidence that the national revival network which was built up owed much to freelance evangelicals, Anglican Evangelical clergy and Moravians, and that John Wesley established his connexion simply because he combined his own itinerant evangelism with opportunistic organization and supervision. 'It could be argued that the Wesleys' role was really to weld parts of hetero-genous local revival groups and small local or regional networks into a coherent national "connexion".'[52] The Yorkshire societies of Benjamin Ingram provide a good example of this nationwide process. Benjamin Ingham had been converted in Georgia in 1737, and on returning to England in the same year had started evangelistic work in Yorkshire. He established a group of societies, and in 1742 he invited the Moravians to take them over. By then there were, according to Ingham, 2,000 'constant hearers' in about 60 places, with about 300 considered as true converts. He systematically preached once a month at each of the places where these seekers and converts were to be found, and he had a monthly 'general meeting', which was a miniature 'connexion'. His itineracy included Leeds, Dewsbury, Wakefield, Halifax and Birstall, and many of the places he visited had organized societies. It was in some of these centres that there was the greatest response to the Methodist preaching; the ground seems to have been prepared.

In addition to London and the North, the Methodist advance appears to have been most noticeable in the Midlands and the South-west; and in some of these areas, such as Cornwall, it was substantially starting from scratch. Early Methodism grew fastest in areas of Anglican parochial weakness, and especially where the supervision of squires and parsons was at its most rudimentary. It appealed also to particular occu-pational groups in closely knit communities such as small industrial, mining and fishing villages. So, taking the nation as a whole, there was a mixture of pioneer, ground-breaking evangelism, and a building on foundations which others had laid. In total it amounted to an impres-sive start to a movement which was still only in its infancy.

The organizational structure of Methodism was essentially complete by the end of the 1740s. The large number of societies, both great and small, were grouped together in circuits of varying sizes to which one or more travelling preachers would be appointed for a period of one to four years, and would travel round the societies. Circuit officials would gather together to administer its temporal and spiritual affairs at quarterly meetings, under the supervision of the senior travelling preacher (the 'assistant'). There was a yearly Conference at which Wesley and his travelling preachers and a few carefully chosen others would settle the doctrine and discipline of the whole connexion.

By 1743 a large proportion of the societies had become distinctly 'Weslyan'; under the control of Wesley, and separate from the Moravians and from the followers of Whitefield. In that year, in 'Rules' drawn up for the purpose of defining objectives and reinforcing a sense of corporate identity, he termed them 'The United Societies'. Meanwhile, Whitefield was heading in a somewhat different direction.

The Wesleys and Whitefield were clearly, and, from 1740 onwards, publicly, divided on the doctrine of predestination, and other issues that flowed from that fundamental conflict of belief.[53] The Wesleys on one side, and Whitefield on the other, believed that what they preached was seriously at variance with what the other proclaimed. Late in March 1741 John Wesley met in private with Whitefield, and in that critical interview the two evangelists agreed to go their separate ways. It was a tragic parting of friends. Although the coolness between them did not last long, with the agreement to differ even to some extent helping to define boundaries, and although there was a measure of truce between them which held until Whitefield's death in 1770, there were henceforth two identifiable wings to the revival. The Wesleys and Whitefield had their own congregations and their own meeting places. On the surface there was little evidence of hostility. All three had great respect for each other. Each recognized that the others sincerely sought to promote God's work, and there was continual intercourse between the two parties. Whitefield often preached for Wesley, and scrupulously avoided commending predestination or disparaging Wesley's much cherished and highly contentious doctrine of perfection, which I will consider in detail in a moment. Wesley was welcomed at Whitefield's tabernacles, and from 1768 onwards also preached at the Countess of Huntingdon's chapels. But, despite these signs of amity, one senses that the division went deeper than was permitted to appear. Perhaps it is no coincidence of timing that the eruption came in the year or so after the death of Whitefield. This bears out the contention of Ronald Knox that 'the inevitable separation was only staved off by the immense respect which the rival controversialists had for one another'. It was, Knox added, 'against their own better judgment' that 'they persisted in trying to persuade themselves that their differences were of minor importance.

Never were theologians so resolved to make a molehill out of a mountain.'[54] I will consider the predestinarian controversy in the next section, but in the meanwhile it is well to recall the genuine Christian affection which bound Wesley and Whitefield together, even amidst all the noise of party strife. 'Whitefield's attitude to Wesley is perhaps best reflected in his reply to the enquiry of a censorious Calvinist who asked whether he thought they might see John Wesley in heaven. "I fear not", replied Whitefield, "he will be so near the throne, and we shall be at such a distance, that we shall hardly get a sight of him." '[55] Wesley was the one chosen to speak at Whitefield's funeral, and he spoke movingly of the great evangelist's tender friendship. 'Charles Wesley did well to rejoice, as he looked upon these two comrades in arms, that "friends at first" were "friends again at last".'[56]

Nonetheless, there were the two groups within the revival. Numerically, the Calvinist part in England was far inferior to the Arminian part. In the capital Whitefield established the Moorfields Tabernacle in 1741 and the Tottenham Court Chapel in 1756; and by 1747 there were thirty-one Whitfieldian societies and twenty-seven preaching stations throughout the country.[57] Among the most important of these were Kingswood and Penn Street Tabernacles in Bristol, and the Rodborough Connexion in Gloucestershire and Wiltshire.[58] But Whitefield did not excel in organizational ability, or at least he chose not to apply his energies to establishing his own 'connexion'. He had a full evangelistic programme, including frequent visits to America, where, as we have indicated, he was the central figure in the New England revival; and he had a burdensome responsibility for his orphanage in America. He burnt himself out as an evangelist, and evangelism was his consuming passion. It left him no time for other matters. In the estimation of J. C. Ryle, he was 'the greatest preacher of the gospel England has ever seen',[59] and he spent his entire ministry from 1736 to his death in 1770 in an uninterrupted proclamation of the good news as he understood it. In these thirty-four years it has been calculated that he preached publicly eighteen thousand times, and always with immense, and frequently startling, effect. In one single Whitsuntide week, after preaching in Moorfields, he received about one thousand letters from people with various concerns. As we have seen, he was the one who first startled the somewhat moribund Hanoverian churches, and ushered in the revival, and throughout his life he was a power in both America and Britain.

Whitefield found a patron, ardent supporter, and an organizer in the distinguished, and somewhat daunting Countess of Huntingdon. She was born on 24 August 1707, the second daughter of Washington, Earl Ferrers. From early childhood she had a deep seriousness of mind and concern about religious matters. She met Whitefield in 1736, and attended the Moorfields Tabernacle; but it was largely through the influence of her sister-in-law, Lady Margaret Hastings, that she was converted, probably sometime in 1738. From 1738 onwards she and her husband attended the Fetter Lane meetings, as did some other persons of rank. Lord Huntingdon died in 1746; and soon after that the Calvinist doctrines started to appeal to her. It was in 1748 that she made Whitefield her chaplain and gave him unique opportunities for preaching to members of high society. Whitefield soon appreciated the boon of having her as a friend and supporter. In 1749, he wrote to her with evident relief and expectation: 'A leader is wanting. This honour hath been put upon your Ladyship by the Great Head of the Church.'[60]

The Countess believed that she was a strict churchwomen, and she did in fact use her influence to keep her followers true to the Church of England. But at the same time she was anxious to assist in the spreading of the revival, and was pleased to have a revival structure built around her, with a band of clerical and lay people who looked to her for inspiration, a charismatic focus, and financial help. She was delighted to have Church of England Evangelical clergy as her chaplains to provide an evangelical ministry in her many scattered chapels which were located largely in fashionable resorts such as Brighton (1760), Bath (1765) and Tunbridge Wells (1765). She watched over these carefully selected clergymen, as a mother in Israel, and sought ways for their advancement, so that they might have fuller opportunities of service. Thus William Romaine, who was her senior chaplain, owed his appointment to St Anne's, Blackfriars, to her, and she personally chose John William Fletcher to be the first superintendent of her college at Trevecca for the training of men for the ministry. By the time of her death in 1791, there were between fifty-five and eighty active ministers of congregations who had been trained at the college.[61]

Despite all her efforts, in 1782 she reluctantly had to secede from the Church of England, and to register her chapels as Dissenting places of worship. It was the signal for all of her chaplains to resign; and her tenuous connections with Anglican Evangelicalism practically came to an end. The final link with her erstwhile spiritual companions in the Church of England was broken with the ordination of ministers for her Connexion at the Spa Fields Chapel in 1783. It anticipated by one year the same move by Wesley; and it is significant that one of the two officiating clergymen, Thomas Wills, justified the action by use of the same argument Wesley was to adopt, claiming that in apostolic times 'it is evident that Presbyters are Bishops . . . that Presbyters, therefore, might and did ordain'.[62]

The Countess had gone her own way. But she did leave a legacy. The seven remaining chapels of her denomination were united in a Connexion which persisted to the present day, and there were also between about fifty-five and eighty other chapels which, although independent, were more or less identified with her Connexion. An evangelistic work had been accomplished among the aristocracy, with results which are not easily measured but which may have been significant. By the time of her death, the Connexion had 'established a commanding and distinctive presence on the Calvinistic wing of the Revival, offering a home (in close proximity to the Church of England) for Evangelicals drawn to a Calvinist theology whose needs, for whatever reason, were not met by the Church in the locality in which they lived.' There were 'few areas of the country in which the Connexion had not left a continuing work'. Her preachers 'were a catalyst for revival amongst churchmen and dissenters in many places where the Connexion itself left no continuing presence'. She provided, 'like Wesley, a model for ordered church growth that was to have a significant impact on Dissent in the last years of the century. Most significantly of all, her college established the model of an evangelical seminary that was to be widely copied, as well as providing ministers for a large number of Anglican, Dissenting and Calvinistic Methodist congregations. The best of her former students were to play a major part in the evangelistic and missionary enterprise of the last years of the century, and the Connexion itself was poised to play a corporate role, through its mission to Sierra Leone, in the early proselytization of Africa.'[63] The 'elect Lady' has her place in the history of the eighteenth-century evangelical revival.

The ordinations by Wesley, to which I have just made reference, were symbolically and actually perhaps the single most decisive step taken in the lifetime of Wesley in bringing about the transformation of the movement into a denomination, and in the severance of the movement from the Church of England. When he authorized such a move he still held an episcopal view of succession, but not as traditionally understood. He believed that 'presbyters discharging their function as *episcopi* had the right to ordain'.[64] The American Methodists needed ministers. The

American break with Great Britain had entailed the severance of any ties with the established church; and Wesley reckoned that this gave him freedom to manoeuvre without disloyalty. It seems that the initiative to set apart Thomas Coke, already a presbyter of the Church of England, as 'superintendent', on 2 September 1784, was Wesley's alone. Richard Whatcoat and Thomas Vasey had been ordained deacons the previous day, and they were now ordained presbyters by Wesley, Coke and James Creighton. Later Wesley was to rebuke Francis Asbury and Coke for calling themselves 'bishops' rather than 'superintendents'. The ordinations may have been 'a link in the chain of actions leading to final separation',[65] but Wesley wanted to avoid schism, and to minimize the fallout effect of his questionable actions.

Internal theological conflicts and problems

For the Methodists as a whole, and for the leaders in particular, there was, in addition to the opposition from without, the stress of internal division, and all the tensions which were, perhaps inevitably, the lot of a newly-emergent group which laid such store on the guarding of what they treasured as true, saving, doctrines. Cynics and critics can dismiss these various internal strifes as self-inflicted wounds, but it needs to be borne in mind that the issues over which they fought were reckoned as fundamental to the very spiritual life of the converts; they were seen as matters of spiritual life and death. After two centuries and more, and with a very much changed spiritual and ideological perspective, it is not easy to us to enter into the passionate convictions and commitments of these erstwhile revivalists; but unless we do so, what were to them beliefs for which they were willing to suffer and die will appear as unnecessary and rather petty squabbles.

The first of these unhappy contentions, and the one which was to be most long-lasting and damaging to the 'fellowship in the gospel' was over the doctrine of predestination; and, related to it, John Wesley's beliefs concerning perfection. As early as the 1720s Wesley had made his opposition to the doctrine of predestination clear. It was the instinctive reaction of a man nurtured in a High Church tradition. Behind his aversion to the dogma was a belief that as salvation came by faith, so perfection could likewise be attained in this life by a disciplined life, and by faith. The belief in predestination not only dishonoured God, it also undermined all moral effort, and thus the priceless striving after perfection. On the other hand, the Calvinists, led by George Whitefield, were suspicious of what they regarded as an over-optimistic view of human nature and of the human capacity for achieving high moral standards. To them, man could do nothing either to achieve his own salvation or to grow morally; it all depended on the working of God in the lives of individuals; and, what is more, the effectual working of the grace of God in the life of any one particular person was pre-ordained by God. The debate was widespread among the Methodists, and lasted for decades, but it was focussed on the increasingly acrimonious exchange of views between Whitefield and John Wesley which we have already encountered, but which we will now examine in more depth.

At first their opposing views were declared in a firm but moderate way, with an evident concern to maintain unity despite diversity. They both expressed their positions clearly: Wesley in his sermon on 'Free Grace' in 1740 and Whitefield in his 'Letter' in response to the sermon.

> Wesley argued in terms which did not really vary throughout his numerous subsequent controversies on the issue. All versions of pre-destination (he claimed) teach that by an unchangeable decree of God, one part of mankind is infallibly saved, one part infallibly damned. Preaching is therefore vain; nothing we can do makes any difference to our fate, hence all motive for pursuing holiness is removed. Predestination tends to poison relationships between people; it destroys the happiness of Christians. The doctrine contra-dicts scripture and, worst of all, it implies blasphemy, making Christ's 'come unto me all ye that are weary and heavy-laden' a mockery and destroying God's attributes of justice, mercy and truth, making him worse than the devil.[66]

Whitefield replied in a well-reasoned 'Letter' in which he presented the traditional Calvinist arguments. He upheld the doctrine of an elect, chosen by God from before the foundation of the world, but said that this did not invalidate evangelism, for we do not know who the elect are, and we must therefore preach to all as an appointed means to salvation. In his exposition, and in this support for evangelism, he was taking his stance on the milder form of the predestinarian doctrine: the stricter hyper-Calvinists spoke of a double-predestination, in which the damned are predestined as well as the elect, and evangelistic appeals were condemned as derogating from the divine initiative. Whitefield also asserted that by evangelism even the non-elect may be restrained from sin. The elect perform works of holiness, not for the reward they bring, but because it is a sign of election. The elect need the assurance of election and of final perseverance in order that they should not despair. It was no denigration of God's character to say that sinners are justly condemned to satisfy the law and justice; and how can it be claimed that Christ died for all when, as Wesley admitted, not all are saved? In summary, the Calvinists, as represented in this response by Whitefield, felt that the Arminians, as represented by Wesley, made salvation depend not on God's 'free grace' but on human free will; and thus denied the basic premise of the revival message. The Arminians claimed that the Calvinists so stressed the divine initiative, that they virtually negated human free will.

Wesley and Whitefield, the Arminians and the Calvinists, never came to an agreement on these matters. A crucial point in the controversy was the issuing of the Minutes of the Methodist Conference of 1770. These appeared to the Calvinists to be a blatant denial of their cherished beliefs and, what is more, a challenge to them in a quasi-public document. Because they were so pivotal in the debate, I will quote them.

We said in 1744, 'We have leaned too much toward Calvinism.' Wherein ?

(1) With regard to *man's faithfulness*. Our Lord Himself taught to use the expression. And we ought never to be ashamed of it. We ought steadily to assert, on His authority, that if a man is not 'faithful in the unrighteous mammon,' God will not give him the true riches.

(2) With regard to *working for life*. This also our Lord has expressly commanded us. 'Labour' – literally, 'work' – 'for the meat that endureth to everlasting life.' And, in fact, every believer, till he comes to glory, works *for* as well as *from* life.

(3) We have received it as a maxim that 'a man is to do nothing in order to justification.' Nothing can be more false. Whoever desires to find favour with God should 'cease from evil, and learn to do well.' Whoever repents should do 'works meet for repentance.' And if this is not in order to find favour, what does he do them for? Review the whole affair.

(1) Who of us is *now* accepted of God? He who now believes in Christ, with a loving, obedient heart.

(2) But who among those that never heard of Christ? He that feareth God, and worketh righteousness, according to the light he has.

(3) Is this the same with 'he that is sincere'? Nearly, if not quite.

(4) Is this not 'salvation by works'? Not by the *merit* of works, but

by works as a *condition*.

(5) What have we, then, been disputing about these thirty years? I am afraid, about words.

(6) As to *merit* itself, of which we have been so dreadfully afraid: we are rewarded 'according *to our works*,' yea, '*because of our works*.' How does this differ from *for the sake of our works*? And how differs this from *secundum merita operum* – as our works deserve? Can you split this hair? I doubt I cannot.[67]

The Revd John William Fletcher, the Vicar of Madeley, and an intimate friend of Wesley, as well as someone who was highly regarded by the Countess of Huntingdon, tried to act as a mediator between Wesley and the Countess, and, through her, to the Calvinists in general, but to no avail. Part of the problem was that the Minutes did not clearly express the Arminian position, or how that position could be reconciled with the Calvinist doctrines. But, more fundamentally, attitudes had become too much entrenched, and even institutionalized, as with the teaching of the college at Trevecca.

A second and, in the early years of the revival, an equally serious split was over the outbreak of 'stillness' in the Fetter Lane Society and elsewhere, which emanated largely from the teaching and practice of the Moravians. Some of the Moravian brethren, led by Philip Molther, claimed that those in the Fetter Lane Society who did not have true faith, and this was indicated by their sighings and groanings in the meetings, should be 'still', abstaining from the means of grace, especially the Lord's Supper, until they found faith. The ordinances, they asserted, were not means of grace at all for such people, there being no other means but Christ. But John Wesley argued that there were degrees of faith, and the ordinances strengthened such faith as a person had. It was an issue which split the Fetter Lane fellowship, for, on 20 July 1740, Wesley confronted the members with an ultimatum, 'gave them up to God' and invited those who agreed with him to follow him. He then withdrew; and he was followed by eighteen or nineteen of the society. The dissidents started meeting at the old King's Foundery which Wesley had acquired and fitted up for preaching during the previous November. This was a decisive move, in that it freed Wesley from the constraints of the Moravians, the Fetter Lane Society, and even of Whitefield, and firmly placed in his hands, and under his control, not only the New Room at Bristol, but the society in London: it was the beginning of an independent organization which grew into his 'connexion'.

But the most serious controversy for the young movement concerned neither predestination nor 'stillness', but antinomianism. For many years Wesley fought with tenacity and courage in a fierce battle 'against those who maintained that once a man was justified by faith he was exempt from keeping God's Commandments; he was above such elementary things, he was on the verge of perfection or actually in the enjoyment of it'.[68] Wesley was an enemy to antinomianism, but his doctrine of Christian perfection did not help him in the struggle against the antinomians. He taught that there was a second stage in the Christian life beyond justification when a believer 'experiences a total death to sin, and an entire renewal in the love, and image of God, so as to rejoice evermore, to pray without ceasing, and in everything to give thanks'.[69] The perfect Christian, Wesley held, not only does not commit sinful acts, but is freed from evil thoughts and tempers. The mistakes he makes are involuntary, and therefore not properly sins, and for these Christ's atoning work is necessary. For Wesley, the only type of action that can reasonably be classified as sin is 'a voluntary transgression of a known law'.[70] Such a definition made it plausible for some Methodists, though not Wesley himself, to claim a state of Christian perfection or, as they usually preferred to call it, 'perfect love'. Wesley believed that it was received by faith, and instantaneously, although progress in holiness usually preceded and followed it.

The doctrine of perfection was not a late addition to the total theological armoury of Wesley; it was central to his thinking from an early stage. For him 'the true goal of the Christian life is sanctification, holiness, even to the point of perfection'.[71] His enthusiasm for justification by faith from 1738 onwards did not entail the abandonment of his stress on holiness; he simply believed that after many years of weary frustration he had found the way to obtain it. The Conferences of 1744 to 1747 explored various aspects of sanctification and perfection, and somewhat qualified previous views. It was said that to be a 'perfect' Christian was to love God with one's whole heart, mind, soul and strength; but it was acknowledged that there is no sure way of knowing who had attained to such a status, for only 'sensible proofs' from conduct could indicate that such a state had been reached. Indeed, Wesley tended later in his life to suggest that justification was a door into a process of increasing holiness which is only likely to be completed just before death. He chastened his brother Charles for some of his hymns which expressed more extreme views, and he corrected those which he thought were erroneous in their teaching.

The perfectionist movement of the 1760s was a salutary experience for Wesley. It appears that some lay preachers were calling Wesley a 'child of the devil, who dislikes the doctrine of sinless perfection'; and that 'he is no true Christian who has not attained to it'.[72] The climax, which came in 1762, was a scandal for Methodism, and a great blow to Wesley's favourite doctrine. After some cases of perfectionist claims in London, Wesley issued warnings against pride. But after he had departed for a preaching tour, 'enthusiasm' broke out. At the centre of the turmoil were Thomas Maxfield and George Bell. Maxfield owed his career to Wesley, who had given him leave to preach, obtained ordination for him, used him as an assistant and defended him when he was in trouble; yet it seems that he encouraged perfectionists who claimed that they had visions and were superior to others. Bell had only been converted for four years, but already he claimed sanctification, to have had a vision of Christ, and to have effected a physical cure by means of prayer. All of these were not unusual for Methodism at that time. But he went further. He gained a following, held his own meetings, and declared that God had dispensed with sacraments and was only to be found in his assemblies. His followers considered that they had been restored to the purity of Adam and Eve and were incapable of falling. They professed gifts of healing, including the ability to raise the dead; and they believed that they were exempt from death themselves.

Wesley was hesitant what to do. He was fearful that if he hindered the perfectionist revival he might be fighting against God. But at last Bell went too far, and prophesied that the world would come to an end on 28 February 1763. Wesley was forced to disown him and to deny that the Methodists believed in the prophecy. Bell and his friends were imprisoned, and it was said that he later moved from enthusiasm to infidelity, and became a radical reformer.

The more formidable figure of Maxfield had, it appears, been behind Bell in all his actions. And now he came out into the open; he asserted that Wesley did not teach perfection, accused him of hypocrisy and double-dealing over Bell, and seceded. He gained a large congregation, but later seems to have resumed friendly relations with the Methodists.

This manifestation of perfectionism and enthusiasm did great damage to the Methodist cause. It made some cautious; apprehensive that the revival could so readily produce the excesses associated with the mid-seventeenth century Ranters. It discredited Wesley's doctrine of perfection, and alienated him even more from Lady Huntingdon and the

Calvinists; and it aggravated the rift between Wesley and the Church of England Evangelicals.

Postscript: *the revival as a social and religious phenomenon*

The eighteenth-century revivals in America, continental Europe and Great Britain were forerunners of other revivals in the following two hundred years in various parts of the world; and all of them shared certain social and religious characteristics. In the United States of America there were revivals in the late eighteenth century and early nineteenth century, and at intervals during the nineteenth and early twentieth centuries, and especially in the period 1857–60.[73] Revivals occurred in Wales, Ireland, Scotland and England in the years 1857–60, and in Wales in 1904–5. They have also taken place in the Scottish islands of Lewis and Harris in 1949, in Korea, starting in the early years of the twentieth century and continuing until the present time, and in Rwanda and Burundi in Central Africa from the late nineteen-twenties onwards for many decades, as well as other parts of the world.[74] I will therefore briefly consider the eighteenth-century English revival as a social and religious phenomenon, bearing in mind these other manifestations of a similar phenomenon, and draw attention to features in the eighteenth-century English revival which also characterized the later revivals.

The eighteenth-century English revival, like almost all the others I have just mentioned, largely occurred in small communities where there was a high degree of social interaction within a social unit which allowed for intense, community-wide, experiences. Even when it manifested itself in places as large as London, this was not an exception to this generalization, because eighteenth-century London consisted to a great extent of a number of fairly well defined sub-communities, and this social structure helped in both the igniting and the spreading and consolidating of the revival. The open air preaching was conducted regularly in these local areas; the meeting places were situated strategically in conformity to broad social divisions; and the class meetings were organized on a geographical basis, as we have seen, thus benefitting from districts with a large measure of community awareness. Deborah Valenze shows in several descriptive studies how popular evangelicalism re-created the world of cottage industry, village familiarity and household unity in what was becoming an increasingly urban and factory dominated environment. Repeated waves of rural migrants into rapidly growing manufacturing towns eschewed employer-sponsored Anglican churches and Nonconformist chapels which tended to be associated with the new authority structure of the emerging towns. They favoured the more intimate and informal religious atmosphere of the Methodist societies in which they could share experiences with their peers, unencumbered by the link with their employers, and in which the professional preachers had no part.[75] Of course, the provincial towns were small by modern standards, and allowed for this same sense of community identity. Such social structures also enabled the knowledge of activities like open air preaching to be widely disseminated in a short space of time, and for the core content of the preaching to be made known to a large proportion of the population. This process was additionally enhanced by the quite recent advent of daily and weekly newspapers and magazines, and by the increasing use of pamphlets, which were readily produced and distributed by the revival leaders. When all of these features were combined to provide a supporting environment for a body of local converts determined to propagate their faith, it ensured that the local community felt the full impact of the revival.

Much play has been made by sociologists in recent years of the significance of rapid social change as a factor in 'explaining' revivals, and more especially the eighteenth-century English revival.[76] The traumatic effect upon individuals and communities of such accelerated social change may have had a part in the origin and effectiveness of the revival, but from the evidence available it seems at the very least that the sociological case has, in some instances, been very much over-stated. The sense of individual and corporate alienation as a result of sudden and unmanageable population growth, and as a consequence of the dislocation caused by an overwhelming influx of hordes of alien workers, was more typical of the period from the late eighteenth century to the mid-nineteenth century than for the middle two quarters of the eighteenth century when the revival originated and took root. There were some problems of alienation and disorientation as a result of rapid social and industrial change, and the Kingswood miners of Bristol may be cited as an example of this, but the overall effect of the demographic, social and industrial developments during the formative years of the revival was not such as to create a large, unskilled, uprooted industrial proletariat, lacking a sense of community identity and wide-open to revival influences. Very acute social problems existed, as they have in every age, but they were not fundamentally of the type or magnitude to make them a key to unlocking the mystery of the birth and growth of the revival.

The social composition of the revival groups is also revealing. From the survey of 'London Inhabitants Within the Walls, 1695' a socio-economic scale can be constructed, and this can then be applied to the known membership of sixteen Church of England religious societies in London and Westminster in 1694, giving the following social structure:

Category 1	Gentry etc.	6	3.5%
Category 2	Occupations paying surtax in 1692	5	3.5%
Category 3	Occupations with the majority paying surtax	26	15.0%
Category 4	Occupations with less than half paying surtax	74	42.5%
Category 5	Occupations paying 1s. tax only	64	35.5%

This shows that the groups consisted in the main of what may be designated the lower-middle and working classes. It is instructive to then apply the same scale to the lists of the Fetter Lane revival group from 1742 to 1750. Allowance must be made for a certain degree of change in the socio-economic status attached to particular occupations since 1695, but the occupational structure had in fact been fairly stable in the intervening years. The application of the five categories to the members for whom the occupational information is available, produces the following picture:

Category 1	0	
Category 2	4	18.0%
Category 3	0	
Category 4	7	32.0%
Category 5	11	50.0%

This slender evidence hints at no great departure from the previous pattern, but with some improved penetration into the lower social strata. There is no reason to think that there had been a sudden, and extensive turning to the Christian faith by masses of religiously alienated members of society. This, and other research, appear to show that although there was a noticeable outreach to those previously unconnected with organized religion, the most prominent evangelistic feature of the revival was the impact of a religion which offered vital personal faith to nominal members of the existing church. This is substantiated by contemporary observations. At the time of the settlement of the Moravian London Congregation in 1742, William Holland states that members of the group '. . . were almost all of the Church of England and about half of them had been members of Religious Societies'.[77]

It is also relevant to note that the constant return to the same locations for preaching ensured that the same people were often quite regular attenders. Indeed, John Wesley claimed that despite the huge numbers involved, he knew most of those present at any one of the massive meetings. This again indicates that there were several thousands of people who were intensely influenced by the revival, rather than, or perhaps as well as, a much greater number of individuals who were more superficially influenced.

Once individuals were incorporated within the Methodist fellowship, the society, class and band system could hardly have been more effective as an aid to commitment and conformity. The ordinary members were made aware of their value and significance as part of the total body of believers; they found a warmth and a ready acceptance which was most attractive; and they discovered that they could make an acceptable contribution to the life of the society they had joined. The groups provided a defined social context for men and women who may have experienced some disorientation in their own social situation, or who may not hitherto have had any opportunity to participate in such an egalitarian company of like-minded people. The groups gave a reassuring sense of cohesion, and of a common concern and objective; and the members endorsed each other's resolve to achieve their common goals. Such determination to remain loyal to strongly-held beliefs was reinforced by the sense of being strangers and pilgrims in a hostile world. The opposition and aggression which was experienced both corporately and individually tended to enhance the awareness among the converts that they were exiles, bound together in a fellowship of suffering. In their personal spiritual journey, the sharing of uncertainties and hindrances to faith helped initially to point the way to a climacteric conversion experience, and the articulation of doubts and perplexities was then a potent factor in the ability of the converts to cope with personal spiritual difficulties. In summary, these groups were a vital factor in making the revival a continuous, living reality in the lives of those involved; and although the mechanisms varied from one revival to another, these same characteristics are to be found in all subsequent revivals.

Then there was the opportunity for lay leadership. This has been accorded great importance by various historians as a contributory factor in the emergence of the working classes as a force in the political and social life of the nation, in the development of radicalism and trade unionism, and in the general emergence of 'democracy'.[78] Whatever part the revival may have played in these nationwide political, industrial and social developments, there is no doubt that at the local and personal level the scope for lay leadership was of very considerable significance. This often included unusual opportunities for women. And the women who came to the fore in eighteenth-century Methodism did not conform to the type of idealized domestic angels depicted in Victorian fiction. They were far different in character and lifestyle. Typically they were acquainted with grief and hardship from their youth; they were hardy and dedicated, with an independence which was reinforced by geographical mobility and late marriage; and they were frequently young when they began their preaching careers – around eighteen years of age. They were resolute and not easily controlled by any authority. They epitomized a 'world turned upside down' which repudiated the constraints which the formalism of churches and chapels would place upon them, and the disciplines of economic and social control.[79]

Men and women who in their secular employment and social situation may have been in subordinate positions, and who may have lacked status and authority, were assigned tasks of leadership, albeit, perhaps, at a fairly low level, which drew upon their talents, gave them some authority, and demonstrated that they were valued and needed. Despite the overriding control exercised by Whitefield and the Wesleys, lay people like George Clerk had a vital role to play:

> He was soon made a class-leader at the Foundry, and his success attracted so many members that he had to form a second, and then a third class, and conduct them all himself.[80]

The lay leaders were often outstanding in personality and in the service they rendered, but there were not many of them, so the onus for spreading the revival message rested heavily on all the ordinary members, who were constantly reminded of the responsibility of all true believers to be evangelists in their daily lives; and this gave a great sense of value and involvement to the Methodist membership as a whole.

Charles Wesley himself was helped very considerably in the crucial days before his conversion by a Mr Bray, whom he succinctly describes as: '. . . a poor ignorant mechanic, who knows nothing but Christ; yet by knowing him, knows and discerns all things'.[81]

The converts were anxious to pass on the gospel news to their families. One of them, Sarah Middleton, writing to Charles Wesley, states:

> I find I gather strength daily for I usd to be afraid to speak to my carnal relations what God had done for my soul but now I find I am constrained to speak tho I know they will cast me out as a byword and a proverb of reproach.[82]

The place of work was also a primary sphere of witness, as was evident in the case of William Barber. He also wrote to Charles Wesley, in 1741, to recount his indebtedness to such a testimony:

> The first instrument under God of bringing my soull out of darkness into the marvellous light was our Brother Cooper for he happyly coming to work where I was and having opportunity he began and to tell me whatt the Lord had done for his soull . . . he (invited?) me to go along with him to Fetter Lane Society where you was expounding . . .[83]

But, important as this lay evangelism was, the main, ordained leaders did reign supreme; and they displayed a magnetism, and aroused a degree of awe among their followers in general which was attested by many. To take a few examples. John Nelson, who later contributed substantially to the progress of the revival, and himself exhibited remarkable powers of leadership, recalled how he had attended John Wesley's first open air sermon at Moorfields on Sunday 17 June 1739:

> Oh that was a blessed morning to my soul! As soon as he got upon the stand, he stroked back his hair, and turned his face towards where I stood, and I thought fixed his eyes upon me. His countenance struck such an awful dread upon me, before I heard him speak, that it made my heart beat like the pendulum of a clock; and, when he did speak, I thought his whole discourse was aimed at me. When he had done, I said, 'This man can tell the secrets of my heart . . .'[84]

Nathaniel Hurst, an early convert, relates a similar experience:

> . . . then the Lord was pleased to let me hear Mr John Wesley one

night at Fetter Lane he expounded on the eleventh Chapter of John of Lazarus come forth. I found myself that Lazarus whom he spake of. I was all of a tremble for my bones shook as if they would part from my flesh but before Mr Wesley had done his discourse the Lord spake peace to my soul . . .[85]

Another of the converts, Elizabeth Hinson, recalled, in May 1740, what effect the preaching of John Wesley had on her, in a letter to Charles Wesley:

. . . it pleased God to send your dear brother . . . I wondered at him he told me my heart. I thought he spak to me an when I look at him I thought he spak to me only . . .[86]

Likewise, Samuel Webb speaks of the impression made upon him by the preaching of Charles Wesley. He writes:

. . . your zealous looks and forsable words caused me to think you spake as never man spake . . .[87]

This charismatic influence over those involved in the revival continued after the initial conversion experience, within the circle of the believers. The converts largely accepted the pastoral role of the ordained leaders, and looked to them as a source of inspiration. Samuel Webb testifies:

. . . I never had ye expectation of being blest so much under any ones ministry as your[s] and ungrateful as we are I believe many are like minded and pray God to make us all faithfull hearers as you are teachers that you that sow and we that reap may rejoyce together.[88]

The dependence of some of the Methodists on the ordained leaders is reflected in the words of Martha Sones, at a time when John Wesley had left London for an extended period:

. . . you and your brother gone we were left as sheep without a shepherd . . . I was brought into great confusion . . . I continued in great perplexities and had almost given up my hope when God sent you to us again and on Easter Sunday I heard you preach and the Lord strengthened and confirmed my faith my doubts and fears vanished and the Lord made his way plain before my face . . .[89]

These quotations give some taste of perhaps the foremost religious characteristic of revivals, and certainly of the English eighteenth-century revival, the intensity of the individual and group experiences. Here, it was believed by the Methodists, was God powerfully at work in a personal way. They were encountering God in experiences which involved the mind, will and emotions. The experiences were not derived at second hand, or as the result of any required, formal or stylized conformity to a religiously orientated situation; they were immediate, spontaneous and genuine; they were most vividly real and relevant to actual felt needs; and what was perceived and received was acknowledged as of God and from God. Examples which may be cited to illustrate this are legion; two must suffice. William Holland recounts how he obtained a copy of Luther's *Commentary on Paul's Epistle to the Galatians*, and returned with it to the home of Mr Bray, where Charles Wesley was ill in bed. The three of them considered it together. He continues:

> . . . and Mr Westley began reading Luther's preface to his Comment and at the reading of these words, 'What have we then nothing to do? No, no nothing, but only to accept of him who is made unto us of God Wisdom Righteousness Holiness and Redemption' there came such a power over me I cannot well describe. My great burden fell off in an instant, my heart was so filled with peace and love that I burst into tears and thought I saw our Saviour at some distance. Mr Westly and Bray perceiving me so affected fell on their knees and prayed. When I went afterwards into the street I scarce could feel the ground I trod upon, my body seeming so very light and I found that I was dead to ye noise of the world.[90]

Mrs Clagget recalls the climax at the end of a protracted period of spiritual conflict in her life, when finally, as a result of many and varied influences, she entered into the revival experience. The impression left upon her was indelible:

> My heart overflow'd with the love of God, the Spirit also bearing witness that I was a child of God, and [I] cou'd not help joining the immortal choir in their Halleluahs.[91]

These experiences contrasted with the form of religion which was prevalent in many of the churches, and the contrast tended to add force to the effect upon the people concerned. Sarah Middleton is representative of many others:

> . . . indeed I went to church and said my prayers and (had?) a form

of profession but new nothing of the power I had no oyl in my lamp no inward principal of holiness in my heart . . .[92]

Then:

. . . I heard a voice say unto me daughter be of good cheer thy sins be forgiven thee at the same time I felt so much love in my heart that I could hardly contain myself for I wanted the whole world to feel what I did . . .[93]

Even more revealing is the contrast repeatedly dwelt upon in the testimonies of the converts between their own former state of alienation from God, and the new spiritual status and sense of liberty into which they had entered as a result of their climacteric encounter. There was, most typically, an initial sense of need, as expressed by John West, one of the early English Moravians. He writes:

. . . I had long been wishing to feel the reality of faith in the heart, and experimentally to be able to say what it means, longing to know Jesus, when he was pleased to reveal Himself to me . . .[94]

The converts found it difficult to convey the wonder of the actual conversion experience. Maria Price tried to do so in a letter to Charles Wesley:

. . . Dear Sir i came to you as a blind man from his birth that never had no thought of sight . . . i was like a person that was born blind and that moment received light . . . i received such light as i never had before i as plainly felt a burden taken of my heart as i could feel one took of my back it was done in a moment it was such a work so plainly felt and so wonderfully wrought that i almost lose my senses to explane it and can not do it . . .[95]

One more example will reinforce the sense of awe and wonder which the conversion experience evoked. This time it is a certain Mr Bristow who is writing to Charles Wesley in April 1740:

. . . the Lord . . . hath taken the scales off my eyes: I was lame he hath made me walk: I was bound with chains of darkness: but he hath broken my bonds asunder. He hath pluckt me as a fire brand out of hell: and shall I dare to hide this: shall I not declare what the Lord hath done for me . . . O behold a miracle indeed a greater one than if a dead body had been raised: out of the earth: I was dead in trespasses and sin: and Jesus raised me: he brought me from the pitt of hell: into the Kingdom of light . . .[96]

Many of them had long histories of religious concern. Few of them speak of their conversions as having arisen out of a very suddenly awakened interest in religious matters. Often there was a long prelude of spiritual searching. There is frequently in their testimonies a looking back on past preoccupations with moral and religious questions, and not infrequently a recollection of prior numinous experiences. Indeed, the testimonies provide a good illustration of what Rudolf Otto delineates in *The Idea of the Holy*,[97] and perhaps especially the element of the 'mysterium' in man's idea and response to the numinous:

> . . . the *mysterium* is experienced in its essential, positive, and specific character, as something that bestows upon man a beatitude beyond compare, but one whose real nature he can neither proclaim in speech nor conceive in thought, but may know only by a direct and living experience. It is a bliss which embraces all those blessings that are indicated or suggested in positive fashion by any 'doctrine of salvation', and it quickens all of them through and through; but these do not exhaust it. Rather by its all-pervading, penetrating glow it makes of these very blessings more than the intellect can conceive in them or affirm of them. It gives the peace that passes understanding, and of which the tongue can only stammer brokenly. Only from afar, by metaphors and analogies, do we come to apprehend what it is in itself, and even so our notion is but inadequate and confused.[98]

The conversion experience was a climax, and the beginning of a new life, but it did not herald a time of uninterrupted peace and tranquillity; rather the reverse. The converts were conscious that they had entered upon a spiritual battle; they tell of being constantly assailed by the force of evil, which sought to undermine their faith, deprive them of their salvation, and mar the fruits which they were convinced should have been evident in their lives as a consequence of the transformation which had taken place. They frequently depicted this as a spiritual warfare, with the armies of God opposing the hosts of Satan on the battlefield of their souls. Although often cast down by such inner conflicts, they were confident of victory. One of the Methodists, Martha Sones, is typical of many in what she experienced:

> . . . I was distressed on every side. It would be endless to recount every temptation that beset me and conflict which I endured by which my soul was brought nigh unto hell and I almost despaired of seeing this

great salvation. Yet I was enabled to say unto the Lord though thou slay me yet will I trust in thee. Though I much doubted of my justification because I did not always feel it so strongly as at the first . . . I could not but believe . . . I continued in great perplexities and had almost given up my hope when God . . .'[99]

From the very beginning of the Methodist movement Wesley had stressed the importance of personal faith and personal experience. His 'search for personal certainty of salvation led him to emphasize experiential religion to an extent that made many people uncomfortable, but it was experiential religion that had brought him spiritual peace . . . In Wesley's mind, to be extremely sensitive to the sentiments of those who opposed experiential religion would have meant that he was less sensitive to God's providential direction for Methodism.'[100]

In all of this there was a built-in and ever-present tension between the norms of the relatively unstructured revival, with its sense of spiritual freedom, excitement and adventure, and institutionalized Christianity, especially in the form of the established church. The Church of England had all the advantages, but also all the constraints, inherent in its history and status as a church 'by law established'. 'Among the Methodists experiential religion took precedence over ecclesiastical protocol and canon law.'[101] The Church of England laid stress upon the authority of a hierarchical body of ordained clergy, whereas the revival increasingly emphasized the importance of charismatic gifts, and the priesthood of all believers, with the right and duty of all members of the body to fulfil their appointed roles and functions in the life of the whole. The Church of England was concerned to inculcate in its members a loyalty and conformity to institutional practices, and for them to regard the way of salvation as being found, in part at least, within the means of grace and the ministry which the church provided. This was in contrast to the revival which proclaimed a way of salvation open to all by simple faith, obtainable anywhere, at any time, and without the aid of any human or institutional mediator. The Church of England, by virtue of its heritage, historical development, and unique position in relation to the whole establishment, consistently and constantly promoted order and regularity in its services and in its life in general, and required such behaviour of its members. The revival permitted a high degree and variety of individual non-conformity, together with a widespread acceptance of irregularity in its public preaching, worship and other forms of corporate life. The concern was to allow a considerable measure of flexibility in order not to restrict in any way what the revival members viewed as the freedom of the Spirit.

In all these ways, the established church and the revival were but demonstrating the characteristic differences between a church and a sect which sociologists such as Max Weber, Ernst Troeltsch, Richard Niebuhr, Peter Berger, Y. M. Yinger, Bryan Wilson and others have analysed.[102] Even by the time of the death of John Wesley in 1791, a more formal and rigid structure was in the process of being formed, regulations and rules were assuming greater importance than in the pioneer days, there was less emphasis upon individual charisma, and more on conformity to a set of established norms; and in every way the trend was in the direction of changing from a sect to a denomination – a transition fully recognized by the sociologists to whom we have just referred. It was to prove a not easy development. It was not only resisted by those who did not want to loose the sect-like qualities of former times, but led to secessions, as we will see in chapter 7.

In the meantime, revival was taking place within the Church of England itself, among those who had no intention of departing from the church of their birth.

5

The Evangelical Revival:
The Church of England

Whitefield and the Wesleys in particular, but also a countless host of Methodists in the first fifty years of the revival, remained convinced, and they would have said true and loyal, members of the Church of England. They would have claimed to have lived as faithful sons and daughters of the established church, and to have come to the point of their deaths firm and secure in its fellowship. Such an attitude may be treated with cynicism, and even be regarded as gross hypocrisy, in view of the steps which were taken before the end of the century which effectively severed the connections with the Church of England, but it was genuine for all that. There remained the hope that one day the Anglican Church would acknowledge them and the work they had done, and would allow them and the movement of which they were a part to enrich its own life, worship and witness. But this was not to be. Almost two hundred years of Methodist history were to pass before such a prospect was fully explored; and then without success.

By the time of Wesley's impending death there was an ever widening gulf between the Methodists and the Church of England; and this also extended, albeit not to quite the same extent, to the relationship between the Methodists and the Church of England Evangelicals. Before I trace the emergence, consolidation, growth and increasing influence of the Evangelicals in the Church of England, the identification of five points of gradually more pronounced difference between them and the Methodists, with whom they had much in common, will help to make the unfolding drama more comprehensible.[1]

First, there was the clericalism of the Evangelical movement.[2] In contrast, Methodism, as I have shown, almost from its inception and increasingly as the century wore on, was heavily dependent on lay involvement, with lay leaders at every level, and with lay preachers as its chief agents. John Wesley rued this cause of division, and, as a former High Churchman who retained much of his inherited ecclesiastical attitudes, he sympathized with the Evangelical Anglican point of view, but considered the promotion of the revival was paramount and required the extensive use of lay assistants. He tried to organize an association of Evangelical clergy who would be loosely linked with the Methodists and work together with them in a gesture of evangelical ecumenicalism, but, as we will see, he failed dismally.

Secondly, Evangelicals were strict churchmen. In general they adopted what had been a common trait of their Anglican forebears, and were chary of any co-operation with Dissenters. Wesley shared this intense loyalty to the Church of England. But the position of Methodism, even before actions in the 1770s and 1780s quite clearly placed them in the category of Dissenters despite protests to the contrary, was equivocal. It was most unfortunate that the movement did not evolve as an integral part of the Church of England, accepted, even if reluctantly, by the hierarchy of the established church; but in the event it was generally opposed by the Church of England at every level. Arguably it was forced to forge its own structures and identity, with these becoming more firmly consolidated as it grew in size, strength and influence. There was a certain internal dynamic which drove it along this path, but it was also regrettable that more effort was not made to work within the framework of the Church of England, and to renew that church from within.

Thirdly, the Evangelicals were unhappy about some aspects of the theology and the general ethos of Methodism. The Evangelicals were not uniformly Calvinist, for the Calvinist-Arminian divide cut across the Evangelical-Methodist grouping; but a large number of them were moderate Calvinists. The resolute Arminian stance of Wesley, which was imparted to the movement as a whole, was a barrier to full co-operation between the Evangelicals and the Methodists. And this was aggravated by the Evangelical opposition, and in some instances positive hostility, to Methodist teaching on such matters as Christian perfection, and to what was perceived as an over-reliance on the emotions.

Fourthly, it seems that Wesley had a particular regard for the primitive church, and viewed it as a model for present doctrines and practice. He based many of his innovations on what he considered to be primitive practice, whereas the Evangelicals, especially in their formative years in the middle two quarters of the century, looked more to the Reformation and to the Puritan tradition for their inspiration and pattern of belief and conduct. Of course, the Methodists valued the

Puritans and what they stood for, but not perhaps to the same extent as the Evangelicals.

Finally, and most crucially, there was the problem of church order. This was at the root of the divergence between the two movements. It was an attitude which flowed from the Evangelical ecclesiology, and the loyalty of Evangelicals to the Church of England. With varying degrees of emphasis, the Evangelicals sought to carry on the revival strictly within the established ecclesiastical structures, and in accordance with the accepted practices of the Church of England. They saw themselves as firmly set within what they regarded as a God-given church order, subject to its constraints, and under the episcopal authority which was an essential part of their inheritance. They were reluctant to do anything which breached what they accepted as legitimate limitations on their actions. The Methodists broke through such restraints, often with impunity and no sense of impropriety; at first in a cautious and tentative way, but later more boldly and blatantly.

Evangelicals were suspicious of some of the practices adopted by the Methodists, not necessarily because they were innovations or objectionable in themselves, but because they endangered church order. This was so with prayer meetings, where lay leadership, without what was considered sufficient regulation and control, was considered a source of potential dissatisfaction with the church and the role of the clergy. Indeed, it was the general prominence of lay leadership, and more particularly of itinerant preaching by lay as well as ordained men, which was seen as the greatest threat to church order, and which most alarmed and alienated a number of the Evangelicals. Some of the most ardent and influential Evangelical clergy resisted lay leadership in anything but a very clerically controlled form. There was a similar and related resistance to preaching by ordained men beyond the borders of their own parishes. A few Evangelicals undertook itinerant preaching, but it was stringently avoided by others such as Samuel Walker of Truro and Thomas Adam of Wintringham.

As the century advanced, both the Methodists and the Evangelicals became more clearly delineated, in the one case as a body separate from the Church of England, and in the other case as a group within the established church. But as they developed their own identity and character, so they tended to distance themselves from each other. Many Methodists continued to attend church, but increasingly two different structures emerged. The Methodists moved, apparently inexorably, towards the status of a fully-fledged denomination, while the

Evangelicals gained in confidence as a group with a distinctive theology, but very much a party within a church in which they felt secure, and which commanded their ungrudging allegiance. I will now trace the development of those Evangelicals as they underwent this metamorphosis.

From humble origins to a full-blown party

The eighteenth-century Evangelical movement in the Church of England did not begin in the same dramatic, and sudden, way as with Methodism. Rather, it started in a silent, tentative manner, in widely scattered and unconnected parts of the land, and was inaugurated in the often obscure ministries of a few devout and energetic clergymen. It continued for much of the century to consist of little more than a small, but growing, number of local individuals who were distinguished by sacrificial, dedicated lives, in which pastoral and evangelistic service was mostly confined to narrow geographical areas. It was a movement of such small and apparently insignificant proportions that it attracted little public attention, and Wesley could refer to the people involved as constituting 'a rope of sand'. There were no commanding national figures like Whitefield and the Wesleys, and no structure equivalent to the Methodist classes, bands, societies, regional bodies and national connexion. Only as they corresponded, as personal contacts increased, and as they united in clerical societies, which were mostly confined to fairly circumscribed regions, did dispersed Church of England Evangelicals become aware of a common bond. And only by the end of the century did they multiply sufficiently, and co-ordinate their activities enough, to become a reasonably cohesive fraternity which was almost unanimous on major questions of faith, order and practice. It has rightly been said that 'the history of the Evangelical Revival is essentially a history of personalities rather than of opinions',[3] and this applies especially to the Evangelicals in the Church of England.

North Cornwall can rightly claim to have witnessed the first stirrings of revival in the Church of England.[4] Even before the preaching of Whitefield produced such startling effects in London, in the remote, windswept village of St Gennys, on the summit of the cliffs overlooking the Atlantic, in the year 1733 or 1734, the incumbent, George Thomson, came to accept the doctrine of salvation through faith alone, and was 'awakened'. A few miles away, the Revd John Bennett, the incumbent of three small parishes, North Tamerton, Laneast and

Tresmere, was also 'awakened', but late in life. In 1743 George Whitefield described him as 'about eighty years of age, but not above one year old in the school of Christ'.[5] A third, more renowned, figure, who we will encounter later as the incumbent of Weston Flavell, James Hervey, had been an early member of the 'Holy Club' at Oxford. His evangelical views led to his dismissal by his rector in 1743 from his curacy of Bideford. But he left behind him a religious society which Thomson visited. Both Thomson and Bennett preached outside their parishes and, understandably, caused indignation among the neighbouring clergy. They increased this hostility by welcoming Wesley in 1745 and Whitefield in 1750, and by assisting at Dissenting places of worship. It is of little surprise that they were severely reprimanded for their behaviour by Bishop Lavington.

In 1747 the Cornish Evangelicals were augmented by a clergyman who soon became their leader and a man of such stature that he stands comparison with the other leading Evangelicals of the time: Samuel Walker.

Walker was born at Exeter in 1714, was converted in 1749, and died in 1761.[6] He entered the ministry in 1737, and became curate of Truro in 1746. After his conversion his new zeal, and the change in his preaching, aroused the interest of the town, and attracted large congregations. Indeed, so great were the numbers that the town seemed to be deserted during the times of services; and it was said that you might fire a cannon down every street in Truro during a church service without a chance of killing a single human being. But there was much and fierce opposition, and more than one attempt was made to get him discharged from his curacy, but to no avail.

The effectiveness of his ministry is attested by Wesley. He considered the lack of conversions to be more condemnatory of both the clergy of the Church of England and the parochial system than any other failing; and in this criticism he included the Evangelicals. 'We know Mr Piers, Perronet, Manning, and several regular clergymen who do preach the genuine gospel,' he wrote, 'but to no effect at all. There is one exception in England – Mr Walker of Truro.'[7] Others, by extra-parochial means, were effective evangelists, but only Walker, in Wesley's opinion, out of all the clergy in England, fulfilled this essential evangelistic task working through the normal channels of the parochial system.

Walker was, in fact, an enthusiast for the Church of England, and for church order. He objected to the system of itinerant lay preachers adopted by Wesley, and he told him so. Those who were fit for, and could procure ordination, should, he asserted, be ordained. Others who had the requisite gifts should be set as inspectors over societies, and assistants to them, and should concentrate upon the moral standards of members. They should remain in one place, watching over those committed to their charge.

Although he experimented with private meetings for the members of his own congregation, similar in intent and organization to the Weslyan class system, it was not a very happy experience. The groups were segregated into two divisions, with one composed entirely of men, and the other of married men, their wives, and unmarried women. Each group was small, with only between five and eight members, and they were governed by detailed rules. Unfortunately there was considerable discord because some of the lay leaders fought hard to assert their authority and independence in the face of Walker's resolute and unrelenting insistence on the need for clerical control.

Walker had a wide view of church affairs, and looked beyond the confines of his parish. In his immediate locality he was the prime mover in the establishment of a club for Cornish clergy, which met regularly probably from 1750 onwards. Its purpose was to increase the efficiency and usefulness of each of the members within their own parishes as a consequence of the exchange of ideas and opinions, and the help and encouragement received from gathering together. Beyond Cornwall he had a countrywide influence on other Evangelicals, as they sought his advice and assistance. He represented that strain in Evangelicalism which was concerned to fulfil the potential of the Church of England as a God-given structure within which to stimulate devotion and evangelism.

It was an approach which was also exemplified in the life and teaching of Thomas Adam, for fifty-eight years the incumbent of Wintringham in Lincolnshire; although in his case a long ministry seems to have been bereft of much fruitfulness.[8] Despite attracting large congregations from his own parish and the surrounding area, the majority of the parishioners appear to have retained their rough ways, and his message went largely unheeded. He firmly, and unwaveringly, resisted the irregularities of the Methodists. In a letter to Walker in 1756 he makes this abundantly clear: 'Methodism, as to its external form, is such a deviation from the rule and constitution of the Church of England, that all attempts to render them consistent must be in vain.'[9]

Wesley himself was aware of his dilemma, and perhaps of his inconsistency in this respect. He was, as we have seen, a strong churchman, and yet his movement clearly had tendencies which were not compatible with loyalty to the established church, and which alienated otherwise sympathetic Evangelicals. Tyerman's epithet that he 'lived and died a hearty but inconsistent churchman' very succinctly and accurately expressed Wesley's personal stance.[10] Something of the tension experienced by Wesley and other Methodists, and of the causes of apprehension for some Evangelicals, is reflected in the Methodist Conference of 1766:

Q. Are we dissenters? We are irregular.
1. By calling sinners to repentance in all places of God's dominion.
2. By frequently using extempore prayer. Yet are not Dissenters in the only sense which our laws acknowledge: namely persons who believe that it is sinful to attend the service of the church, for we do attend it at all opportunities. We will not, dare not, separate from the church for the reasons given several years ago. We are not seceders, nor do we bear any resemblance to them.[11]

Other Evangelical clergy in this first phase of modern Evangelicalism were also loyal churchmen, determined, in the face of much opposition, ridicule, neglect and abuse to remain within the Anglican fold. One such was William Romaine.[12] He was born in 1714, ordained deacon in 1736 and priest in 1738. His ministerial life covered nearly sixty years, and he experienced considerable hardship. He was a man of some erudition, particularly known for his criticism of Bishop Warburton's *Divine Legation of Moses*, and his new edition of the *Hebrew Concordance and Lexicon* of di Calasio.

Romaine was a pioneer Evangelical in London. For a long time the Evangelicals did not have a single church in the capital, and there were only a few unbeneficed clergy. During this lean period, Romaine was their leader. For sixteen years he was not offered a living. His first appointment in 1748 was as lecturer of St Botolph's, Billingsgate. In the following year he was chosen lecturer of St Dunstan's in the West, the famous old church in Fleet Street. The rector disputed his right to the pulpit; and after a hearing at the Court of King's Bench, Romaine was deprived of one of the two lectureships involved, but confirmed in the other. Nevertheless, resistance continued. The churchwardens kept the church closed until the exact hour of the lecture, and refused to provide light when it was needed. Romaine frequently read prayers and preached by the light of a single candle held in his own hand. The crowds attending the lectures had to wait outside. On one occasion the

Bishop of London personally observed what was happening and promptly arranged for an earlier lecture, and for the church to be opened and lit well in time. From then to the end of his life Romaine continued in the quiet exercise of this ministry, without disturbance. The lectureship was only worth eighteen pounds a year, but he persisted in it for forty-six years.

Romaine held the quite minor posts of assistant morning preacher at the fashionable St George's, Hanover Square, and curate at St Olave's, Southwark, before he was finally offered a parish: St Andrew-by-the-Wardrobe with St Anne, Blackfriars. During these intervening years he was sorely tempted in his insecurity and neglect to abandon all hope of satisfactory employment in the Church of England. Some of his admirers offered to build a chapel where he might minister as an independent preacher, but he declined, encouraged by Walker to remain loyal to the established church, and not to secede. Even with his new appointment, he was once more dogged by opposition. There was an appeal to the Court of Chancery against his election which took over a year to be decided in his favour. He was instituted to the incumbency in February 1766, held it until his death in 1795, and made the church an Evangelical rallying-point in London.

Far away from London, and living in a rectory which was to be made famous by the Bronte family, William Grimshaw took a very different line in his ministry to that adopted by Walker, Adam and Romaine.[13] His style of life, his approach to his evangelistic and pastoral responsibilities, his attitude to the Methodists and his policy on the question of church order singled him out from all the other early Evangelicals. He was born in 1708, ordained in 1731, and served two curacies before he went as an Evangelical to Haworth in 1742, having had a conversion experience perhaps only a few months before. For twenty-one years he ministered in the isolated, straggling grey village set in the midst of the desolate moors of northern Yorkshire. The parishioners were mostly sullen, rough, superstitious people, unsympathetic to the Christian message and suspicious of strangers. The situation demanded a man with courage, who would be forthright and declare a simple message in plain and unambiguous language, with a demonstrable concern for the local residents which would be expressed in an unsentimental but compassionate manner. Grimshaw provided these qualities and this approach, with the addition of an earnestness and persistence which demanded attention.

He began as he intended to continue. He preached fervently and took drastic steps to remedy what he thought to be unacceptable social and personal behaviour. His dramatic and unconventional approach appealed to the people, and produced results. John Newton, the converted ex-slave trader, whom I will consider more fully later in this chapter, tells us, for example, that it was frequently Grimshaw's custom to leave the church at Haworth while the psalm before the sermon was being sung, to see if any were absent from worship and idling their time away in the churchyard, the street, or the ale-house; and many of those whom he found he would drive before him into church. Newton tells of a friend of his who was passing a public house in Haworth on a Sunday morning and saw several people making their escape out of it, some jumping out of the lower windows, and some over a low wall. The observer feared that the house was on fire, but on enquiring he was told that the fleeing occupants had seen the parson coming. They were more afraid of him than of a justice of the peace. On one occasion he disguised himself as an old woman in order to surprise a group of antisocial young people in their horse-play, and on revealing himself he reprimanded them, and so dealt with them that it was said that he never had to repeat his censure. Another well-authenticated anecdote tells of him praying earnestly that some prominent local races, which were accompanied by drunkenness and wild behaviour, might be rained off; and it happened.

Most controversially, as far as Evangelicals like Walker, Adam and Romaine were concerned, Grimshaw undertook itinerant preaching in other parts of Yorkshire, in Lancashire, Cheshire and north Derbyshire. He seldom preached less than twenty, and not infrequently thirty times a week. Not long before his death, he stood on a hill near Haworth, and declared that when he first came to the area he might have gone half a day's journey on horseback toward the east, west, north or south without meeting one person whom he described as 'truly serious', or indeed even hearing of one. But by the time he spoke, he could tell of several hundred people who attended his ministry and were devout communicants.[14] He justified his itinerancy as a response to pluralism and non-residence, and the inadequate evangelistic ministry of the church in hundreds of parishes in the north of England.

Grimshaw not only itinerated, but he worked fully and willingly with the Methodists. Indeed, he acted as an 'assistant' to John Wesley, who spoke of Mr Grimshaw's circuit.[15] He visited Methodist classes, gave out tickets and held love-feasts. He made his parsonage a centre for Methodist preachers, training and encouraging them. He finally built a meeting-house in Haworth in order to help safeguard the future of evangelical Christianity in the village. Nonetheless, he was a strong churchman, believing the Church of England 'to be the soundest, purest most apostolic Christian Church in the world'.[16] In another age and another place he may have restricted himself to a parochial ministry. He judged that the state of the country needed exceptional action. Regularity, he considered, was of secondary importance to the demands of the hour.

Such dedicated service, and forthright preaching in other parishes of a message which often attracted considerable crowds, and resulted in many people experiencing a vital, life-transforming conversion, understandably provoked opposition, especially from the incumbents of the parishes concerned. The most violent reaction came from the Revd George White, the perpetual curate of Colne and Marsden in Lancashire. In a published sermon in 1748 he attacked Grimshaw and all his fellow labourers. He additionally proceeded to stir up a mob to oppose the preaching by force. He issued a proclamation:

> If any men be mindful to enlist under the command of the Revd George White . . . for the defence of the Church of England . . . let them now repair to the cross, when each man shall have a pint of ale in advance, and other proper encouragements.

When Grimshaw and John Wesley went to Colne to preach on 24 August 1748, they were assaulted by the drunken mob which was armed with clubs. They were dragged before White like criminals and as soon as they left him and went outside the unruly crowd closed in on them, tossed them about with great violence and covered them with mud. The people who were assembled to hear them preach had to run for their lives amid showers of dirt and stones. Some were trampled in the mud, others dragged by the hair, and many unmercifully beaten with clubs.[17]

On at least two occasions complaint was made to the Archbishop about this extra-parochial preaching, but to little avail. 'How many communicants had you when you first came to Haworth?', the Archbishop enquired of Grimshaw on receiving the first complaint. He answered, 'Twelve, my lord.' 'How many have you now?' was the next question. To which the reply was, 'In the winter, from three to four hundred; and in the summer, near twelve hundred.' On hearing this the Archbishop said, 'We cannot find fault with Mr. Grimshaw when he is instrumental in bringing so many persons to the Lord's Table.'[18] On the second occasion the Archbishop visited Haworth church for a confirmation service, and Grimshaw was required to preach a sermon at very short notice. After the service, in the midst of all the assembled clergy, the Archbishop took Grimshaw by the hand and said, 'I would to God that all the clergy in my diocese were like this good man.'[19]

The pattern of loyalty to the Church of England combined with active co-operation with the Methodists was adopted by another Evangelical, John William Fletcher, and carried on by him almost to the end of Wesley's life.[20] Fletcher was born at Nyon in France in 1729. He had been intended for the Calvinist ministry, but he was revolted by the doctrine of election, and withdrew. On coming to England he took up various teaching posts. He was ordained deacon on 8 March 1757, and on the same day assisted Wesley in one of his services. He refused the offer of the valuable living of Dunham in Cheshire, on the grounds that there was too much money and too little work and, in 1760, he was inducted as vicar of Madeley in Shropshire. It was an industrial town whose inhabitants were mainly colliers or iron-workers, and they were seemingly somewhat brutal and ignorant. No other clergyman in the county sympathized with Fletcher's evangelical views, and the surroundings were utterly uncongenial to his sensitive, delicate nature: it was a tough assignment. The first two years were hard and discouraging, with much opposition, and little signs of any progress. There then followed comparative calm; and for twenty-five years Fletcher did the work of an evangelist and pastor, mainly in his own parish, although he undertook some itinerant preaching. He died in 1785 from a fever caught when visiting a parishioner.

Fletcher thought it was 'shameful that no clergyman should join John Wesley to keep in the Church the work which God had enabled him to carry on therein'.[21] He therefore determined to translate his concern into practical help. Not only did he minister in Methodist services, but his kitchen was in regular use by Methodist preachers and he vigorously and ably defended John Wesley's doctrinal views, primarily in a series of published *Checks to Antinomianism*. Wesley thought that Fletcher was more qualified than Whitefield to 'sound an alarm through all the nation' and expressed the hope that he would succeed him as leader of the Methodist movement. But Fletcher utterly refused to accept such a plan, though he promised that if he outlived Wesley he would co-operate with Charles Wesley in keeping the Methodists together. In the event Wesley outlived his younger friend. The high regard of Wesley for his designated successor is evident in the funeral sermon he delivered.

'In four-score years,' he said, ' I have known many exemplary men, holy in heart and life, but one equal to him I have not known, one so inwardly and outwardly devoted to God.'[22]

The Countess of Huntingdon also held Fletcher in great esteem, and about 1765 he was appointed President of her new college at Trevecca. He terminated his association with the college in 1771, possibly because the theological controversy between the Calvinists and the Arminians was at a climax then, because he found it difficult to retain two spheres of activity, and because parochial work always had priority with him. Wesley considered that he was hiding his light under a bushel by restricting his ministry largely to one small area of the country, but he remained a fine model for those Evangelicals who gloried in the Church of England, and in the parochial system, and were fully content to channel their evangelistic and pastoral ministry mainly, if not entirely, through the established structure while being prepared to advance the Methodist cause.

Another variant on the Evangelical approach to church order is to be found in the ministry of Henry Venn.[23] The task which he faced when he went as vicar of Huddersfield in 1759 was similar to that which confronted Fletcher almost at the same time. It was only the previous year that he had been 'brought to believe for himself'. The parish was large by eighteenth-century standards, covering a wide area, and having a population of about 5,000. The inhabitants were not unlike those at Madeley. 'A wilder people I never saw in England,' wrote the much-travelled Wesley in 1757. They were largely hardened weavers and farmers living in the remote and somewhat barren environment of the Yorkshire dales.

Like other Evangelicals I have considered, Venn soon drew congregations which exceeded the capacity of the church. He also made preaching excursions to various parts of England. He was often at Lady Huntingdon's chapel at Oathall near Brighton, and at Bath; he preached at Trevecca college, at Bristol, Cheltenham, Gloucester, Worcester and London. Whitefield and Wesley preached at his church, but he experienced a somewhat taut relationship with the Methodists, despite his willingness to work in harmony with them. The main problem was that there was an active Methodist society in Huddersfield when he arrived, and Wesley refused to arrange for it to be discontinued. A compromise was reached whereby the visit of Methodist preachers was limited to one a month.

Venn was not parochial in outlook: he was concerned about the

Church of England as a whole. He was closely associated with the Elland Society which provided funds for Evangelical candidates to go to Oxford and Cambridge. He was also delighted that during his incumbency there were twenty-two candidates from his parish who offered themselves for ordination, all from working-class backgrounds; although he was disappointed that none of them were able to gain admittance to university, so they went to Dissenting academies, and were lost to the Church of England.

By 1771 Venn was exhausted with his parochial and other duties, and he accepted the less-demanding incumbency of Yelling, near Cambridge. The most fruitful and rewarding aspect of his new ministry was the beneficial influence he was able to exert upon Cambridge students, among whom were William Farish, Thomas Robinson, John Flavel, Charles Jerram and, most significantly, Charles Simeon. In his Evangelical isolation during the early years of his Cambridge ministry Simeon, who was to be the leading Evangelical clergyman of the next generation, depended greatly on Venn: when he had time to spare he eagerly rode the twelve miles to Yelling over the open countryside to meet with his spiritual counsellor. 'In this aged minister,' he said, 'I found a father, an instructor and a most bright example.'

Fletcher and Venn were zealous Evangelicals, but they were more or less conventional in their preaching, and it did not produce the kind of bodily manifestations or intense emotional reactions which characterized some of the Methodist preaching. Such preaching with such consequences was rare among the Evangelicals. But it was not uncommon in the ministry of my final example of these early Evangelicals, John Berridge.[24] He did not become committed to Evangelicalism until after his ordination, and after having served one curacy and some time as incumbent of Everton with Tetworth. While at Everton, he undertook a close study of the scriptures and became convinced that the doctrine of justification by faith, which he had formerly considered foolish and harmful, was true. At once he destroyed all his old sermons and began preaching in a totally new manner, often extempore. The effect was startling. The church became crowded and many people came to an evangelical faith.

In 1758 he began to preach outside his own parish, and in the following year commenced preaching out of doors. In his extra-parochial preaching he covered most of Bedfordshire, Cambridgeshire and Huntingdonshire, and many parts of Hertfordshire, Essex and Suffolk. He would not infrequently preach twelve times and ride a hundred miles a week. In order to care for those who were aroused by his sermons, he arranged for lay evangelists to look after the converts or seekers when he left the area. Some of the evangelists appear to have been humble labouring men, for whose maintenance Berridge provided out of his own pocket. John Thornton, the rich Evangelical London merchant, also gave financial assistance.

Berridge was both effective in his evangelism, and bizarre. He even outdid Grimshaw in the extremity of some of his behaviour and the results it produced. He was continually saying odd things, and he employed strange illustrations to convey his meaning. He acknowledged that he was born with a fool's cap on, and said that a fool's cap was not so easily put off as a night-cap. But he was no buffoon. His outline sermons, and the extant examples of his preaching, show no signs of the absurd. They are not very deep or profound, but with all their simplicity they are based on the Bible and true to the Evangelical gospel. Some of those hearing him did, however, react emotionally: they cried out loudly and hysterically, they were thrown into convulsions and, in some cases, fell into a kind of trance or catalepsy which often lasted a long time. Berridge never encouraged such demonstrations, and did not regard them as a necessary mark of conversion. He was at times perplexed by them, and initially may have attached more value to them than they deserved. Nonetheless, the whole subject of ecstatic response, like demon possession, is a deep and mysterious one, and too much emphasis should not be placed on such a phenomenon. Perhaps dramatic responses were part of the initial impact of the revival message: they certainly became less common among the Wesleyan Methodists after the pioneer decades, and when they did appear were reckoned as aberrant behaviour, and they were almost non-existent in Evangelicalism at the end of the eighteenth century.[25] In any case, even with the ministry of Berridge, they were essentially peripheral to what he accomplished. He was a gifted man of real humility, constant self-denial and self-discipline, always showing abundant kindness, and utterly devoted to his calling.

Grimshaw, Fletcher, Venn and Berridge, like the early Cornish Evangelicals, and Walker, Adam, and Romaine were fired by a passionate desire to make the gospel known. Others included James Hervey, in his quiet, unobtrusive country ministry at Weston Flavell in Northamptonshire;[26] Martin Madan, the barrister turned priest; Joseph Jane, who made St Mary Magdalene the focus of Evangelicalism in Oxford; Richard Symes, who provided a centre for Evangelicalism in

Bristol; John Baddiley, who championed Evangelicalism in Derbyshire; James Stillingfleet at Hotham; William Richardson, for fifteen years vicar of the largest church in York; Henry Crooke, who made Leeds a nodal point of Evangelical activity; Richard Conyers at Helmsley in the North Riding; John Crosse, the blind vicar of Bradford; Miles Atkinson at Leeds, who received great help from William Hey, the famous surgeon; and a succession of Evangelical clergy at Slaithwaite. They all made their contributions to a movement which was to blossom into a worldwide fellowship.[27] And there were countless undiscovered and untrumpeted clergy and lay people bearing their witness.

David Bebbington has helpfully analysed the qualities which were the special marks of Evangelical religion in those far-off, heroic, days, and which have continued to distinguish the Evangelicals in succeeding generations: '*conversionism*, the belief that lives need to be changed; *activism*, the expression of the gospel in effort; *biblicism*, a particular regard for the Bible; and what may be called *crucicentrism*, a stress on the sacrifice of Christ on the cross'.[28] The pioneer Evangelicals of the eighteenth century shared with all their fellow evangelicals a belief in original sin, justification by faith and the new birth, which was not merely a cerebral acknowledgment of a set of doctrines, but was a deep-seated, and indeed passionate, part of the very fabric of their personalities, because it was born out of experience. They *knew* that the doctrines were true, because they had found them to be so in their own lives. And such knowledge was like a fire burning within them. They had to share the good news; they could do no other. The message which had transformed their lives was contained in the Bible; and the Bible, therefore, was precious to them. It was their meat and drink; their authority; and the basis for all their faith and practice. And at the very centre of the biblical message was the cross. They proclaimed a person; a saviour and redeemer. As we have seen with the experiences of the early Methodists, it was all to do with relationships: man alienated from God because of sin; man restored to God because of the life, death and resurrection of Christ; new birth; a new and living relationship with God arising out of the conversion experience; a new life in Christ and with the Holy Spirit. With such experiences, and with such an evangel to declare, they could not remain silent.

The Evangelicals were at their best when they were expounding those doctrines which were to do with conversion, and the spiritual life of individuals. They were not so strong when it came to the doctrine of the church, the sacraments, or the social and communal aspects of the faith.

This is not to say that these topics were totally ignored; far from it. As we have seen, Evangelicals were firm and convinced churchmen, and it does not need to be re-emphasized that they had a clear, unequivocal view of the importance in the economy of God of the corporate life of Christians, and of the church as a God-given body.

Evangelicals also laid considerable stress on the sacrament of holy communion; it was not regarded with indifference, or as a mere appendage to an essentially individual walk of faith. It was crucial; it was a part of the total Christian life, and it mattered. It was also not regarded as solely a commemorative feast, as is clearly stated by Romaine: 'What is their attendance upon the Lord's supper? Is it not the communion of the blood of Christ, and the communion of the body of Christ, a real partaking by faith of His broken body, and of His precious bloodshedding, and of all the benefits of His passion?'[29] Likewise Walker, in his *Short Instruction for the Lord's Supper* said: 'what is signified, received, and assured in and by the sacraments, is Christ in all his benefits'. He proceeded to explain that the 'feeding upon Christ's body' is spiritual and not corporeal, the latter being 'an absurd popish invention, not less unprofitable than it is abominable and superstitious'.[30] These early Evangelicals as a whole believed, like Walker, that as the body and blood are received by faith, only those who have real, saving, faith, and are joined to the Lord, may partake in the sacrament. They did not believe in any automatic, mechanical, effect of the sacrament; and even believers had to be cautious, and not attend holy communion until they were ready to receive it.

The later Evangelicals

As the age of revolution approached, there was a significant increase in the cohesion, momentum and comprehensiveness of the Evangelical movement. The Evangelical network was strengthened in the first instance by an almost unintended consequence of personal correspondence and interaction. Samuel Walker and Robert Adam in the way they consulted each other, and freely offered mutual help and advice, were typical of what was developing. William Romaine took counsel with Walker, and Henry Venn sought advice from Adam. These were but the small beginnings of what was to become a much fuller intercourse in the latter part of the century. The diaries, journals and voluminous correspondence of such later Evangelicals as John Newton indicate that the value of such exchanges was more and more appreciated. Personal correspondence was later supplemented by published evangelistic and devotional literature. This introduces into my unfolding narrative some outstanding figures who came into prominence in the last third of the century, and helped to take Evangelicalism into a new phase of influence and maturity.

John Newton was not only one of the most remarkable of the eighteenth-century Evangelical leaders, but arguably one of the most remarkable men in the whole history of the Church of England.[31] It was his personal history prior to his ordination which was so unusual, for it reads like an adventure story from the pages of fiction. He was born in 1725. His mother died in 1732, and at the age of eleven he went to sea with his father. He was away from England five times in the next six years. In 1742 he met Mary Catlett, and the love he felt for her never abated from that moment to the end of his long life. Soon after this he was seized by a naval press-gang and endured great hardship for a while, until his father arranged for him to be posted as a midshipman on the quarter-deck. In 1744 he deserted, was caught and returned in irons, stripped and publicly flogged, degraded from office and boycotted by command.

There followed three years of fluctuating fortune. He was placed on a ship engaged in the West Africa slave trade, and then put under a master on an island known as the Plantanes, where he was reduced almost to the level of a slave; he was insulted and harshly treated by his master's negro mistress, chained by his master to the deck of his ship, and almost starved to death. He was driven to a state of abject misery and depression. It was only with a change of master that his lot improved, and he was able to return to England.

He continued to be involved in the slave trade and in the sea voyages of slave traders. He gave himself up to extremes of blasphemy, including parodies of the cross and the passion, and was becoming hardened in a tough, demanding and often cruel life. But a personal spiritual crisis was near at hand. A casual reading of Thomas à Kempis; fear of eternity engendered by a violent storm and the real possibility of death; and thoughts of God aroused by a serious fever in West Africa, all made him resolve to serve God.

In 1750 he married Mary Catlett. He rejoined slave ships, first as mate, then as captain, for as yet he saw no objection to a trade which he was later vehemently to condemn. A series of further wild adventures ensued, among natives on the African coastline, among mutinous crews, and in quelling or preventing slave revolts. In 1754 he met a Captain

Clunie in the West Indies and through him came to an Evangelical understanding of his faith. He continued to consider his calling lawful and reasonable, but he was tired of a life which ever had to do with bolts and chains and shackles, and he now had a Christian message which he could commend to others with all his heart. He led his crew in Prayer Book worship on a deck beneath which all the horrors inseparable from a slaver were to be found.

Illness prevented further voyages, and Newton was given the lucrative and not very onerous post of Surveyor of Tides for the Port of Liverpool. He came to know Whitefield, Wesley and Grimshaw. By intense exertions he learnt not only to read the New Testament in the original Greek, but also acquired some knowledge of Hebrew. He sought ordination unsuccessfully among the Dissenters. He applied to the Archbishop of York, and was refused. Finally, on 29 April 1764, through the influence of Lord Dartmouth, he was ordained by the Bishop of Lincoln as the curate of Olney.

Newton served for fifteen years as the substitute for an absentee vicar at the lowly remuneration of £60 per annum, although Lord Dartmouth, and the rich banker and member of the Clapham Sect, John Thornton, gave funds to relieve the poor; and Thornton also gave upwards of £3,000 as a supplement to his salary. The bluff former sea captain soon became well known to the 2,000 poor and ragged inhabitants of the town, as he diligently and devotedly visited every quarter of his parish, dressed in his blue sea jacket rather than his clerical attire. People came to him in great numbers for counsel, and his own experiences gave him a profound appreciation of other people's problems.

Two of Newton's friendships were of special significance for the Evangelical movement as a whole. One was with the self-confessed Socinian Thomas Scott, who was in charge of two neighbouring parishes, Weston Underwood and Stoke Goldington. By his steady, unforced companionship, example and help, Newton played an important part in the progress of Scott towards an Evangelical view. Scott succeeded Newton as curate of Olney. He had great influence through his writings, especially his autobiographical work, *The Force of Truth* (1778) and his *Commentary on the Bible*; and he was the first Secretary of the Church Missionary Society.

Newton's published works also exercised a wide and considerable influence. Most notable among these were his autobiography, *An Authentic Narrative* (1764), and a volume of his letters under the title,

Cardiphonia (1780). The first was used by William Wordsworth in an early draft of *The Excursion*, and it also gave ideas to Samuel Taylor Coleridge for *The Rime of the Ancient Mariner*. But his most lasting literary product was the collection of 348 *Olney Hymns*.

This was the joint work of Newton and his close friend in Olney, William Cowper. Cowper contributed such masterpieces of poetry and devotion as 'Hark, my soul, it is the Lord'; 'O for a closer walk with God'; 'God moves in a mysterious way'; 'There is a fountain filled with blood'; and 'Jesus, where'er Thy people meet'. Newton exquisitely expressed his faith in 'Amazing grace'; 'How sweet the name of Jesus sounds'; 'Approach my soul the Mercy Seat'; 'Come my soul, thy suit prepare'; 'Great Shepherd of Thy people here'; 'Glorious things of Thee are spoken'; and 'Begone unbelief, my Saviour is near'. Hymns were still a new thing in the worship of the Church of England, and the greatest change the Evangelicals made in the church services in the eighteenth century was the introduction of congregational singing. The Olney hymns were important in this development.

Viewed within the context of the revival as a whole Newton was also important for the part he played in widening the horizons of Anglican Evangelicalism. He was a strong churchman, but his personal experiences led him to have broad evangelical sympathies. From the beginning of his adult Christian life his 'understanding of evangelicalism was rooted in a religious landscape of acceptable diversity'.[32] He sought a balanced pan-evangelicalism in which there were clear principles of evangelical cooperation. He saw that some cherished denominational beliefs had to be put aside if evangelical cross-denominational activity or nondenominational evangelical work was to flourish. He recognized 'that evangelicalism could be transdenominational only in so far as it subordinated denominational distinctiveness on matters of church-state constitutionality, church order, and sacramental discipline to the over-riding concern of the gospel'.[33] Likewise, in his theology Newton reached out after a wide understanding, and a healing of the rifts between evangelicals of different theological convictions. Between Wesley's Arminianism and High Calvinism 'Newton's own evangelical theology strove to steer a middle course, maintaining an even equipoise between predestinarian grace and responsible voluntarism.'[34]

William Cowper was also important in imparting a broader, more embracing and less restrictive, character to Evangelicalism. He was one of the foremost poets of the day, and his poetry carried the Evangelical ethos into quarters which the movement had hitherto not reached, and which Wesleyanism was never to reach.[35] Evangelicalism was portrayed by him as a philosophy of life which could appeal to the educated and sophisticated, as well as to the less intellectual, less literary, members of society. But he had a mental and religious history of such extreme vicissitudes and anguish that it is surprising that he ever managed to create so much sensitive, high quality verse.

He was born in 1731 to a respectable middle-class family. His father was an Anglican clergyman, and for the first six years of his life he appears to have been happy and secure. Then his mother died. It was a shattering blow to him. He was miserable at his first school. He became despondent and convinced that he was under a curse. He was happier during his years at Westminster School, but he still lacked self-confidence. During his post-school training in law he experienced intense depression. He fell in love with a woman named Theodora, but his father, for reasons which are not clear, forbade marriage. After the death of his father in 1756, and the severing of the last link with his happy early childhood, he became morbidly introspective. Faced with an examination for a possible new post, he had a mounting sense of tension fear and despair, and finally, in an extremity of torment, he made an unsuccessful attempt to hang himself. He was admitted to Dr Cotton's House for Madmen at St. Albans.

Dr Cotton was an Evangelical, and helped draw Cowper towards Evangelicalism. He went to stay with the Unwin family in Huntingdon, in 1765, and there his Evangelicalism was bolstered. Mr Unwin was a clergyman, but it was Mrs Unwin who especially influenced Cowper, perhaps by supplying something which had been missing since the death of his mother and the loss of Theodora. In 1767 Mr Unwin died after a riding accident. Neither Mrs Unwin nor Cowper considered that they were in love, but they longed to remain together and to live in the neighbourhood of an Evangelical incumbent. At this juncture they met John Newton, and he arranged for them to move to Olney.

In Olney, Cowper lived a life which was composed of helping Newton in his ministry, writing poetry and hymns, going for walks, and coping with intermittent bouts of severe depression. In 1786, seven years after Newton had left Olney to take up a new post in London, Cowper and Mrs Unwin moved to the nearby delightful village of Weston Underwood. But he still had to fight against a most troubled mind, and great self-questionings about his faith. In all this Mary Unwin was at his side, tenderly caring for him. Then, to his utter horror, Mary had a stroke and was seriously ill. The final devastating blow came when she died. His final years were an almost ceaseless battle against mental illness, and the strife did not end until he finally died in 1800.

Cowper was the only one of the first two generations of Evangelicals to make any significant contribution to general literature, but by 1791 Hannah More had launched out on her quite remarkable literary career, in which she provided a somewhat less sophisticated offering, but one which had a remarkable contemporary impact.

Hannah More was one of five very pious, intelligent and highly competent sisters.[36] She was born in 1745 at Staplleton in Avon, and from about 1757 she attended a school which had been established by her sisters in Bristol. In the early 1770s she went to London and was fortunate to gain entry into a circle of elderly and middle-aged literati which included Samuel Johnson, Soame Jenyns, David Garrick, Joshua Reynolds, and such Blue Stocking ladies as Mrs Montagu, Mrs Vesey, Mrs Carter and Mrs Chapone, all of whom were many years the seniors of the young women from Bristol. Samuel Johnson in particular encouraged her to publish plays and poems, and by the 1780s she had achieved very considerable fame. After the death of Garrick in 1779, she devoted herself more to religious activities. She was able to combine wit and charm with religious orthodoxy and genuine piety in a way which was unique for her day, and outstanding for a woman of her generation. She had a most significant impact through her personal friendships with a host of distinguished men and women, including Horace Walpole, and also through her literature.

At this stage in her life and career a major change took place as her interest in 'secular' literature and the theatre was replaced by a passionate interest in philanthropy, and an absorption in the world of evangelical activity. Of special importance was her friendship with William Wilberforce. She remained an orthodox churchwoman throughout her life, and 'regarded the Establishment with a reverence not commonly expressed in her day'.[37] She was drawn into the campaign against the slave trade and other issues which were of central concern to those Evangelicals of the time who have subsequently been dubbed The Clapham Sect and The Saints. Her main early contributions to religious literature consisted of a series of Sacred Dramas, published in 1782 for the instruction of young people and, more importantly, writings in support of the movement for the 'reform of manners'. In her concern to address the rich, and to confront them with faults which were generally overlooked, she produced a slim but widely circulated and influential anonymous volume in 1788 entitled *Thoughts on the*

Importance of the Manners of the Great to General Society. She courageously challenged those in the higher echelons of society for their abuse or neglect of Sunday, for their careless conversation in the presence of the younger generation, and for other reprehensible conduct unbecoming in those who should set an example of uprightness and righteousness. She expected to be shunned by the people she had castigated, but instead her forthright and pointed booklet enhanced her reputation and gained her even more friends among the elite of society. Two years later, when alarm caused by the French Revolution was at its height, she issued an even more trenchant attack on the irreligion of the privileged members of society in her *Estimate of the Religion of the Fashionable World.* The content and style revealed a growing 'enthusiasm', and showed her to be more dogmatic than in the former work. It was the same religious zeal which was also the driving force behind her bold initiative in founding schools in the Cheddar area, and the motivation for writing religious tracts which she was soon to produce in great quantities, as we will see in the following chapter.

Hannah More was part of a robust Evangelical movement which was noted for its evangelistic and devotional works. Printed sermons abounded. They were characterized, as was all Evangelical literature at this time, by language which was scriptural, by constant appeal to the Bible, and by an emphasis upon the application of biblical teaching to the lives of individuals. Perhaps the most popular collection, and one which demonstrated Evangelical preaching at its best, was entitled *The Christian: being a Course of Practical Sermons,* which had a preface by Adam. Of a similar genre were the fuller expositions of scripture and teaching on various aspects of the Christian life. Together with the sermons, such publications were the staple diet of Evangelical reading other than the Bible itself. Of particular note were Scott's *Commentary on the Bible,* Romaine's series *The Life of Faith* (1763), *The Walk of Faith* (1771) and *The Triumph of Faith* (1795), James Hervey's *Meditations among the Tombs* (1746) and *Theron and Apasio* (1755) and Henry Venn's *The Complete Duty of Man* (1761). The latter was an attempt to replace *The Whole Duty of Man,* which had been printed anonymously in 1657, and had gained such a vogue after the Restoration that it ranked next after the Bible and the Prayer Book in the estimation of many churchmen. Evangelicals were not happy with this, as they considered that the seventeenth-century book made eternal life dependent on works and duty. Venn's book became popular with

Evangelicals, but it failed to displace the earlier work, probably because of its prosaic style and lack of literary grace.

Some of the works of Evangelicals in this period were addressed to wider matters of church life, as with Adam's *Lectures on the Church Catechism* (1753) and the work by Walker, which appeared in 1763, two years after his death, *Fifty-two Sermons on the Baptismal Covenant. the Creed, and the Ten Commandments*. There was a paucity of Evangelical works of a more scholarly nature. Three only are worthy of mention: Romaine's *Hebrew Concordance and Lexicon* of Marius de Calasio, which was possibly written at a time when Romaine may have been influenced by Hutchinsonianism, Erasmus Middleton's *Biographia Evangelica* (1779–1786), and Joseph Milner's *History of the Church of Christ*.

Evangelical literature helped to foster the growth and unity of Evangelicalism. So also did the establishment of clerical associations. Some of the earlier Evangelicals lacked much sense of corporate Evangelical identity, and had a desperate feeling of isolation from official Anglicanism. The Evangelical societies provided mutual encouragement and exchange of views, and allowed the participants to share suggestions about pastoral duties and how to cope with parochial problems. Other than Walker's in Truro, the most renowned were the Elland Society in Yorkshire, the Eclectic Society in London, and the societies in Bristol, Creaton and Rauceby.

The Eclectic Society was especially significant. It was destined to play a prominent part in the life of Evangelicalism, not only in London, but nationwide, as a forum for much constructive Evangelical debate. It was established in 1783, and almost all the London Evangelical clergy were members, together with a few Evangelical laymen. It met fortnightly in the vestry of St John's Church, Bedford Row. It was there that some of the most important initiatives in the history of Evangelicalism originated; and most notably it was in the debates of this little society that the ideas which came to fruition in the founding of the Church Missionary Society (1799) germinated, and out of its discussions on the whole issue of Christian communication that plans were devised which culminated in the founding of the *Christian Observer* (1802).

Another device for advancing Evangelicalism was the practice of selective patronage. Aristocratic patrons were important. Lord Dartmouth moved Henry Venn to Huddersfield, Matthew Powley to Dewsbury and James Stillingfleet to Hotham; Lord Smythe provided Henry Venn with Yelling; and Lady Huntingdon, in addition to employing Evangelical chaplains, placed Walter Sellon at Ledsham, probably much to her regret as he became a decided Arminian. Other humbler patrons included Richard Richardson, who supported Erasmus Middleton; William Wilberforce, whose political popularity helped him to secure Hull vicarage for Joseph Milner, and St Crux, York, for John Overton; and John Thornton, who bought the advowson of St Mary's Hull, and inaugurated the Evangelical patronage trusts.

To mention such names as Wilberforce and Thornton is to touch on the fringes of a new and expansive era for Evangelicalism: the age of the Clapham Sect, of the Saints in Parliament and such campaigns as that for the abolition of slavery. It brings us up with quite a jolt, for it reminds us just how far Evangelicalism had travelled in less than sixty years since its somewhat inauspicious origins in remote parts of Cornwall and Yorkshire.

A sociological footnote to chapters 4 and 5

A sociological perspective, and especially the sociological analysis of church, denomination and sect, can assist us in understanding the eighteenth-century revival. It can cast light on the emergence and development of Methodism and of Church of England Evangelicalism, as well as on the relationship of the Methodists to the Evangelicals.

In his delineation of the characteristics of a church, as compared and contrasted with a sect, Max Weber particularly highlighted four features.[38] First, the existence of a professional priesthood removed from the 'world', with salaries, promotions, professional duties and a distinctive way of life. Secondly, claims to universal domination which transcends familial, sectional, and ultimately national boundaries. Members are born into the church rather than having to join it. Thirdly, dogma and rites which, although based on scripture, have become part of a systematic education. Fourthly, the incorporation of these features into some kind of compulsory organization; the distinctive factor being the separation of charisma from the person and its attachment to the institution and to the office.

Because of its claim to charisma of office, and with it the claim to be the custodian of all things sacred, the church is able to make demands on political power. In fact its jurisdiction extends in principle to all areas of conduct; no area is seen to be outside the limits of its authority. The church is able to deploy sanctions in the furtherance of its monopoly. And because of its claims to charisma of office the church is irrevocably opposed to all forms of personal charisma. In the church charisma is routinized and incorporated into the regular organization, so that, for instance, the priest alone administers the sacraments, and does so only because he is qualified as a priest and has undergone a period of training.

The sect, by contrast, opposes charisma of office. Within the sect the individual can partake of the sacred only by virtue of his own personal charisma, that is by experiencing the sacred directly. Thus he or she can only become a member by virtue of a publicly established qualification, such as an articulated conversion experience. Because the emphasis is on personal charisma as opposed to charisma of office there is, in the pure sect situation, no separate stratum of specialists whose task is to mediate the sacred to the rank and file. The emphasis is upon the priesthood of all believers.

Weber's pupil Ernst Troeltsch[39] also saw the church as overwhelmingly conservative, in a large measure accepting the secular order and dominating, or striving to dominate, the masses. The church is universal in that it claims to control the beliefs of all who come within its political jurisdiction, and even beyond that limit. It therefore claims to have a monopoly of the truth, a claim which is supported by traditional myths of divine origin. The individual does not choose to join but is born into the church or joins involuntarily, as exemplified in infant baptism.

The sect, on the other hand, is a voluntary community whose members join of their own free will. Those who join sects seek personal inward perfection and fellowship between members. The attitude of the sect to the outside world may be one of tolerance, indifference or hostility.

Paradoxically the sect too believes that it possesses absolute truth but it does not, according to Troeltsch, seek to universalize this truth because it is believed to be beyond the spiritual grasp of the masses. If the truth is ever to permeate the mass of mankind this will only be during the 'last days'. Furthermore, since scripture forbids sectarians to use force, authority or the law they must renounce imposing their opinions on others. Sects thus tend, both Troeltsch and Weber argue, to extend the principle of tolerance to other bodies like themselves and to demand the religious neutrality of the state.

While churches utilize the state and the ruling classes and become part of the existing order, sects are connected with the lower classes and the disaffected. Likewise Richard Niebuhr claimed that in Protestant history the sect has always been the child of an outcast minority, which has characteristically arisen in the context of the religious revolts of the poor, of those who were without effective representation in church and state.

The sociological character of sectarianism is such that it is always modified in the course of time by the natural processes of birth and death. By its very nature the sectarian type of organization is fully valid, and partakes of a pure sect-type character, only for one generation. It is imperative that arrangements are made to educate the second generation and inculcate them with the mores of the sect. Rarely does the second generation hold the convictions which it has inherited with the same fervour as that of its fathers for whom these beliefs were a protest against persecution and possibly martyrdom.

As generation succeeds generation isolation from the community becomes more difficult. Furthermore, wealth frequently increases when the sect subjects itself to the discipline of asceticism. The connection between asceticism and the acquisition of wealth and the problems this poses for a religious movement was appreciated by John Wesley:

> Wherever riches have increased the essence of religion has decreased in the same proportion. Therefore I do not see how it is possible in the nature of things for any revival of religion to continue long. For religion must necessarily produce industry and frugality and these cannot but produce riches. But as riches increase so will pride, anger and love of the world in all its branches. How then is it possible that Methodism, that is a religion of the heart, though it flourish now as a green bay tree, should continue in this state? For the Methodists in every place grow diligent and frugal; consequently they increase in goods. Hence they proportionately increase in pride, anger, the desire of the eyes and the pride of life. So although the form of religion remains the spirit is swiftly vanished away. Is there no way to prevent this – this continual decay of pure religion? We ought not to prevent people from being diligent and frugal; we must exhort all Christians to gain all they can and to save all they can; that is in effect to grow rich. What way then can we take that our money may not sink us into the nether most hell? There is one way and there is no other under heaven. If those who gain all they can, and save all they can, will like-wise *give all they can*, then the more they gain the more they will grow in grace, and the more treasure they will lay up in heaven.[40]

Niebuhr depicted denominations as sects in an advanced stage of development and adjustment to each other and to the secular world. Howard Becker elaborated on how the early zeal of the self-conscious sects has generally disappeared by the second or third generation, and how the problem of training the children of believers almost invariably causes some compromise to be made in the rigid requirements for membership which are characteristic of earlier phases.[41]

Liston Pope challenged Niebuhr's contention that the evolution of sects into denominations was predominantly a response to their changing class composition. In his study of a textile area in North Carolina Pope found that it was more a matter of an increase in size which moves the organization in the direction of greater compromise towards the 'world': 'A sect, as it gains adherents and the promise of success, begins to reach out towards greater influence in society . . . In the process of doing this it gradually becomes accommodated to the surrounding culture and thus loses influence over those who are relatively estranged from society; at the same time it begins to attract a more privileged clientele.'

Although he did not altogether reject the argument that the practice of frugality and industry cause members to become more wealthy, Pope found that sectarian teaching seemed to operate so as to maintain the previous socio-economic position of the workers: 'Emphasis on personal virtues produces more efficient workers; it does not necessarily produce owners and managers . . . '

In recent discussions of the sociological concepts of church, denomination and sect two British sociologists have played a leading part: David Martin[42] and Bryan Wilson.[43]

In addition to the characteristics of the sect identified by earlier sociologists, Wilson emphasizes exclusiveness. Expulsion is exercised against those who contravene doctrinal, moral or organizational precepts. A sect's self-conception is of an *elect* – a group of individuals possessing special enlightenment; and personal perfection is the expected standard of aspiration.

Wilson stresses the fact that although sects differ among themselves in terms of internal characteristics the commitment of the sectarian is always more total and more defined than that of the member of other religious organizations. The ideology of the sect is much more clearly crystallized than that of the denomination or church and the sectarian is much more distinctly characterized than is the member of one of the other types of organization. The behavioural correlates of his ideological commitment set him apart from the world. Sects have a totalitarian rather than a segmental hold over their members, that is they tend to regulate the totality of their lives. Ideological conformity may be achieved by compulsory participation but the method of control varies from sect to sect.

A denomination by contrast exhibits other features. These include its acceptance of adherents without the imposition of prerequisites of entry and its employment of purely formalized procedures of admission; its emphasis on breadth and tolerance; the absence of tight control over membership, and a reluctance to expel members who are apathetic or wayward; a lack of any clear self-conception or of any concern to impose doctrinal standards; a readiness to be considered one movement among others, all of which are thought to be acceptable in the sight of God; an acceptance of the standards and values of the prevailing culture and of conventional morality; a restriction of lay participation to particular areas of activity; the formalization of services, and the absence in them of spontaneity; a greater concern for the education of the young than for the evangelization of the outsiders; and the fact that activities additional to its regular services are largely non-religious in character. Members are drawn from any section of the community, but within one local congregation or one region, membership will tend to limit itself to those who are socially compatible.

Part 3

The Churches
in an Age of
Revolution and War

6

The Church of England:
From One Revival to Another

The period on which we are about to embark saw the inauguration in all its essentials of the modern phase of English history. In these years the foundations were laid for those political, constitutional, economic, social and religious developments which were to constitute the main characteristics of modern English society. Clearly, this is not to say that such monumental achievements were confined to a short span of just over forty years: there was a long pre-history during which forces were at work. But so much of what went before reached its apogee in this 'age of revolution', and so much of what came after can be seen in retrospect as being rooted in the events and movements of these remarkable years.

For the causes of the epoch-making, interconnected, series of 'revolutions' during this period one needs, initially, to look beyond the shores of the country itself. The American revolution did not only entail a loss of territory and sovereignty, it was traumatic as a rebellion against the exercise of authority, and an assertion of the rights of the people. The political philosophy of rule for the people, by the people, and its attempted implementation, albeit three thousand miles away, was potentially destructive of some traditional beliefs and values. Ideas could not be imprisoned within the confines of one country. The concept of 'democracy' was in the air; and it was bound to spread. The *ancien regimes* of Europe could not be insulated from such questioning ideals, and from the implications of their enactment. A new dimension had been added to the whole outlook of the radicals and potential radicals; and a new hope of success in achieving change had been given to them.

Then, of course, there was the French Revolution, nearer at hand and following on the heels of the American assertion of independence. As we have seen, some revisionists have questioned the suitability of 'revolution' when applied to the industrial, agricultural, and even social, changes which took place in the eighteenth and early nineteenth centuries. However, none would question that the events in France between 1789 and 1830 deserve the appellation. Nor would any deny that the repercussions in other countries, including England, were of major importance. 'On the Continent, above all in France, the Middle Ages themselves can almost be said to have endured to the end of the eighteenth century. With the French Revolution the last remains of the old world were broken up. The three watchwords, Liberty, Equality and Fraternity, were screamed aloud in the ears of an astonished world, and the Grand Monarchy, supreme example of magnificence and privilege, was dissolved as in a night.'[1]

In England, the early reactions to the events in France were overwhelmingly favourable. For the Whigs it was a time of euphoria. 'How much the greatest event that has ever happened in the world,' declared Fox, with perhaps pardonable exaggeration, when he heard of the fall of the Bastille in 1789, 'and how much the best!' How telling for them that it was the time of the centenary celebrations of that comparatively bloodless coup d'etat of 1688, which had made the great Whig families for a time the governors of England, and which they regarded as representative of all that they held dear. For idealists, like the young William Wordsworth,[2] or his young friend Samuel Taylor Coleridge, it was the dawn of a new age. For some Nonconformists, like the Baptist Robert Hall, or the Unitarian, Dr Joseph Priestley, it harboured hopes of better days to come. For the radicals like Thomas Paine it was clearly a cause of great rejoicing. For many in the population as a whole, who were neither radicals nor revolutionaries, the collapse of French absolutism, the limitations placed on the privileges of the Catholic Church, and the declaration of civil and political equality without regard to religious affiliations, was good news. It was only as the escalating acts of violence in France, and the aggression against other countries, plunged Europe into a generation of war and conflict, that the rapidly mounting hopes of many were dashed, and transformed into despair, disillusionment and anger. Nevertheless, whatever the changing emotions at the time may have been, the unfolding drama of the revolution, the reign of terror, the coming to power of Napoleon, and the subsequent protracted wars, changed the politics and the values of England for ever. When it was all over, it was found that England was a different society from when it had all begun; and radically different.

One of the main changes was the bringing into prominence of reform movements which were to press relentlessly for political and religious 'rights'. Such movements had, of course, existed before, but they now assumed a strength and persistence which would not rest content with empty promises. Whatever the interpretation of the post-Napoleonic War situation, and it has been a matter of some discussion among historians as to whether, and if so to what extent, there was a real danger of revolution in Britain during the ten years after the war, the situation was serious.[3] The Spa Fields Riot, the March of the Blanketeers, the Pentridge Rising, the Peterloo Massacre and the Luddite riots were real enough, and alarming. And, what is more, those involved were ordinary working men and women. It was the same with the emerging radical societies. Artisans such as Christopher Wyvill, John Horne Tooke or Earl Grey were beginning to organize things for themselves, without relying on leaders from outside their ranks. In London, it was a shoemaker, Thomas Hardy, who was prominent in setting up the London Corresponding Society, which demanded universal male suffrage, the abolition of the property qualification for Members of Parliament, equal electoral districts, the payment of Members of Parliament, annual parliaments and the secret ballot. The pressures generated by such stirrings, such events and such active propaganda were instrumental in bringing about reform.

The churches could not remain untouched or unchanged amid such international and national trends and developments. This was an age of activity and transmutation. It was a melting pot for philosophies of all kinds. It was a time when long-accepted beliefs and norms were questioned, perhaps as never before in English society. It was an era in which people were required to identify themselves with one side or another on issue after issue. 'It was the best of times, and the worst of times . . .'[4] And it was as epoch-making for religion as it was in matters political. 'The generation overshadowed by the French Revolution was the most important generation in the modern history not only of English religion, but of most of the Christian world.'[5]

The Church of England

Turning the spotlight on the Church of England, we are to an extent faced with an enigma, and it is not easy to come to a general conclusion about its progress or decline as an institution. There is certainly ample evidence of some deterioration in its overall status, standing and situation. A. D. Gilbert has claimed unconditionally that the period 1740–1830 was 'an era of disaster, for whereas the Church of England had controlled something approaching a monopoly of English religious practice only ninety years earlier, in 1830 it was on the point of becoming a minority religious Establishment. There may', he continues, 'even have been an *absolute* decline of conformist practice during this period, despite the rapid expansion of English society.'[6] There was, he says, a massive drop in religious practice both in relation to the size of the society as a whole, and in relation to the rapidly growing extra-Establishment religious movements. There may have been more practising Anglicans in England in 1830 than ninety years before, and there is evidence of a gradual increase in the quarter-century before 1830 – but the number of non-Anglicans was vastly greater than in 1740. Gilbert sees nothing in his statistical analysis to divert him from the view that little was done in terms of additional personnel or in terms of accommodation for worship to compare with the increase in population from about 5,500,000 in 1740 to over 13,200,000 in 1831. The church was 'a static institution, characterised by inertia if not always by complacency'.[7] The growth in Anglicanism, he asserts, came after 1830, and was sustained until the First World War, but it was negligible before 1830.

The Church of England certainly continued to suffer from some of the shortcomings which had been only too evident during the whole of the eighteenth century, and it was in certain respects ill-prepared to meet the needs of the hour as it entered the nineteenth century. It is an exaggeration to say that it 'had stood still: aristocratic at the top, pauperized at the bottom, worm-eaten with patronage and pluralism, angry and astonished at the collapse of the Catholic Church in France',[8] as such an unqualified condemnation is not justified, but it was confronted with an enormous need for adjustment, vigorous evangelism and dedicated pastoral oversight in view of the rapid and radical economic, social, demographic changes which were taking place, and it found the challenge hard to meet. It soon found that it was losing out to Methodism, and to a rejuvenated Nonconformity.

There was a serious mismatch between where, geographically, the Church of England was strongest and where there was especially pronounced population growth. 'If a line be drawn around the southern and central counties of England so as to exclude Devon and Cornwall, Wales and Monmouthshire, Shropshire, Staffordshire, Leicestershire, Rutland and Lincolnshire, and all English counties to the north, and Scotland, the region thus enclosed very largely represents the traditional heartland of English (and Anglican) power and prosperity. Early industrialization saw a shift of population away from this area, which fell between 1781 and 1841 from 44 to 41 per cent of the total British population."[9]

Some local studies highlight the struggle to adapt to changing circumstances, the success achieved by the church in doing so in some areas, but the move towards Dissent which also characterized the late eighteenth century and early nineteenth century. P. Rycroft, in his examination of the church, the chapel and the community in Craven in the period 1764 to 1851, showed a major shift in the denominational orientation of the Deanery.[10] At the beginning the Church of England was the main provider of religious service in most parishes; whereas at the end of the period the Nonconformists attracted nearly three times as many worshippers as the Anglicans. This study also endorses Gilbert's findings about the recovery of lost ground after 1830; for the established church in Craven did in fact show signs of revival.

Mark Smith, in a most helpful study of Oldham and Saddleworth between 1740 and 1865, portrays a church which was vigorous in its evangelistic and pastoral life over an extended period of time, with remarkable results. He cogently summarizes his conclusions:

> The leading characteristic of the churches in Oldham and Saddleworth between 1740 and 1865 was their commitment to growth. They built and prayed for growth, and they mobilized an increasing proportion of their membership within a wide variety of social milieux to go out into the urban mission field and work for growth. Some of their commitment derived from denominational competitiveness, and some from a concern about the moral health and general stability of the new industrial society. Its compulsive force, however, derived mainly from the evangelical concern of many individuals and church fellowships to share with their neighbours the felt benefits, both moral and spiritual, of a personal relationship with God, and thus to secure their eternal destiny.[11]

The evangelicals in Oldham and Saddleworth developed and exploited a variety of points of contact with the population at large, which Smith thinks were the means and measure of their success. The most evident and the most important of these were the church buildings, mission rooms, and converted cottages, which provided accommodation for Sunday worship and a variety of activities during the rest of the week. By the time of the 1851 census, the Anglican church had lost its monopolistic position, but it was still by far the largest church in Oldham, with well over twice as many attending its services as its nearest rival, the Wesleyans. Attendance at services in the town was divided into roughly three equal parts, one-third Anglican, one-third Methodist, and one-third other Dissenting denominations, mainly Congregationalists and Baptists. Although the Church of England had not done quite so well in Saddleworth, it, the Wesleyans and the Congregationalists each accounted for roughly a quarter of the attendances, with smaller churches and undenominational preaching rooms making up the remainder.

The resurgence of the Church of England in Craven was largely due to the efforts of the local Anglicans. By 1851 sixteen new churches had been built, endowments had been found for fourteen extra clergymen, and over thirty National schools were in operation. There was a marked improvement in clerical standards, with non-residence all but eliminated, as Evangelicals and Tractarians led the way to renewed clerical zeal.

The opportunity for evangelistic outreach was there, if only the churches would grasp it, although there were social factors which impeded, and even negated, evangelistic efforts:

The place of each denomination within the overall pattern of religious practice in Craven was determined largely by its responsiveness to the opportunities for organized religion in the communities of the Deanery. The Established Church was reduced to the choice of a minority by its failure to expand from the old parish centres. Neglect, rather than protest against the Establishment, opened the way to the nonconformist denominations. Methodist, Baptist and Congregationalist appealed alike to a social constituency which mirrored the occupational structure of the wider society. The relatively greater strength of Methodism appears to have been due, not to an ability to reach social groups neglected by the other denominations, but to the adaptability of Methodist structures to the possibilities for evangelisation in Craven communities.[12]

Where the Anglicans showed signs of reasserting themselves they were partly successful, although severe limits were placed on the extent of such success by the strong Nonconformist culture which had developed, and by the shortcomings within the church itself:

The campaign of Church extension was motivated in part by a desire to reestablish the Church as the predominant provider of religious service. The Church had retained the loyalty of some of the communities where it had been long established, and it was able to strike roots in some of the places where new churches were built, attracting up to one fifth of the adult population of Craven to its services. But the success of the campaign of Church extension was limited. The demands of Establishment – the need to endow a clergyman in each new area of outreach and the clergy-centred ecclesiology – ill suited the Church for the missionary role it faced in the nonconformist dominated communities of Craven.[13]

I conclude, that the Church of England in the period 1740 to 1830 had to struggle hard to cope with major shifts in population, and disturbances of long-established social patterns as a consequence of urbanization and agricultural and industrial changes of a magnitude which can, with some justification, be construed as revolutionary. In trying to adapt to hitherto unknown situations it, perhaps inevitably, experienced many defeats, and it often failed to respond adequately to massive social, economic and demographic realignments. But the local studies of Rycroft, Smith, Urdank, Virgin, Warne and others indicate that the Church of England, as well, in many cases, as the old Dissent and the Methodists, had a considerable degree of success in meeting such radically altered circumstances. Although it is not possible to extrapolate from these findings to any generalized, 'optimistic', conclusion for the country as a whole, they do not support any conclusion of a long term, general decline in the effectiveness of the church's ministry.

Population increase and social and economic change were especially dramatic in the period 1791 to 1833, and the disruption of social mores was greatly increased by the devastating effects of a prolonged condition of war and the traumatic post-war readjustments; and this presented the Church of England, as well as the other churches, with grave problems. The building of churches does not seem to have kept pace with the rate of population growth and, in addition to the difficulties of urban ministry, the 'real tragedy for the Church in this period, it may be argued, was not that industrialization concentrated people where her endowments, manpower and accommodation were thinly spread, but that things went so badly where her resources were concentrated'.[14] Nonetheless, it needs to be remembered that in addition to evidence of lively local church life revealed by local studies, these years also witnessed the remarkable work of the Sunday Schools, and the outstanding achievements of the Clapham Sect, the Saints in Parliament, and the Hackney Phalanx, all of which will be considered in detail in this chapter.

This is not to imply that the Church of England enjoyed the support of the population as a whole during these traumatic decades. It remained as a central feature in the lives of countless people, and it was especially a focus for social as well as religious life in numberless hamlets, villages and country towns; but it attracted considerable venom, even in some rural areas. The hostility against the established church was clear. The radicalism which the American and French Revolutions, with their attendant literature and propaganda, helped to stir up encouraged the critics of the church to be more voluble than in former times. They were now less inhibited. And they had many issues ready to hand with which to beat the established church about the head. The more the Church of England became alienated from the majority of the population in the growing towns, the more the working-class population became discontented with it, and viewed it as fair game for abuse or indifference. There were two matters in particular which were inflammable, and guaranteed to arouse indignation in the population generally: church rates, and reform. 'The outcry over church rates served to stoke the fires of anti-clericalism in the towns.'[15]

In the countryside the tithe system aroused a frenzy of resentment against the clergy in certain quarters. This had been so for a long time, but now local protesters were bolstered by a new climate of opinion. The nationwide increase in radicalism meant that there were sympathizers outside the local scene who were only too willing to give their support to those who struggled to bring about change in their locality, so that the resistance was stronger and more vocal. And the enclosure movement, which was at its height in the latter part of the eighteenth century, was hardly less damaging. Enclosures 'made many clerics into prosperous farmers or absentee landlords to the certain detriment of their ministry. In addition, as its benefits were unequally distributed among the clergy, the movement served to widen the already scandalous gap between rich and poor in the church, and so offered useful ammunition for the developing radical attacks on the establishment.'[16] And these problems persisted into the nineteenth century. W. R. Ward suggests that it was a factor in the great religious displacement of the time. 'When large sums were being invested in agricultural improvement, tithe not upon profit but upon gross output fell savagely upon the marginal increases which were the most expensive to produce.

And, secondly, the regressive nature of tithe was particularly burden-some at a time of depressed agricultural incomes.'[17]

The late eighteenth and early nineteenth-century animosity towards the church was further encouraged in the countryside by a change in the status of some rural clergymen: for it was at that time that the clerical magistrate or 'squarson' became more common, and more prominent in local and national life. By the influence they exercised they strengthened the alliance between church and state; but the price paid for such a development was a quite frequent weakening of the ties between the local incumbent and the village community.

Another fundamental cause of heightened anti-clericalism in these years was the church's inflexible attitude to the question of reform. This, above all else, helped to cause the flames of anti-clerical feeling to leap high, and to be expressed in a public way. As *The Extraordinary Black Book* put it just before the passing of the Reform Act: 'Whenever a loyal address is to be obtained, a popular petition opposed or a hard measure carried against the poor, it is almost certain that some reverend rector, very reverend dean or venerable archdeacon will make himself conspicuous.'[18] The church at all levels was identified with reaction. Radicals especially, but others of a more moderate and conservative dis-position, never forgot that it was a clergyman who read the Riot Act at Peterloo, and that two of the members of the bench which called the troops were Anglican clerics.[19] Feeling ran highest, however, in the wake of the rejection of the second Reform Bill by the Lords in October 1831. 'The press remarked that if the twenty-one bishops had voted in the opposite sense the bill would have passed. At crowded meetings on 10 October the mention of bishops was greeted with groans and yells and hisses. In Regent's Park the chairman, Joseph Hume, was handed a large placard inscribed "Englishmen – remember it was the bishops, and the bishops only, whose vote decided the fate of the Reform Bill".'[20] Whig and radical newspapers railed at them as enemies of liberty and oppo-nents of the rights of the people. For weeks on end reforming orators denounced them, made comparisons between their wealth and style of life and the biblical picture of apostolic simplicity, asserted that they had no right to meddle in politics but should be about their pastoral duties, and demanded that they should be excluded from the House of Lords. They were charged with allowing self-interest to override justice and concern for others, as they owed their income to corruption and had therefore to defend corruption. They delighted in luxury, and knew nothing of the lot of the poor. In some cases the fury of the critics was levelled against individual incumbents and bishops: the 'vicar of Huddersfield was groaned at and hissed in his own vicarage, the vicar of Sherborne had his windows broken and cellar sacked . . . a mob of 8,000 paraded through Carlisle and burnt the effigy of their bishop at the market cross. Bishop Ryder of Lichfield and Coventry received a threat that if he passed through Coventry he would be thrown in the pond.'[21] There were riots in Bristol, Nottingham and Derby. It was one of the lowest points for the Church of England in its entire history.

It was also a time when new political, social and religious alignments were forged. Politically, Utilitarianism was born, radicalism as a unified and organized force made its appearance, the foundations were laid for the modern Conservative party, and the legislation of 1828 to 1832 set in motion the modern phase in the evolution of English constitutional monarchy. Socially, there was an acceleration of the process whereby the industrial working class was created as a clearly identifiable and forceful entity; and changes were taking place in commerce, industry and the professions which were to produce the new and dominant middle classes of the Victorian age and the twentieth century. And in the sphere of religion, the 'new Dissent' was finding its identity, as were the various branches of Methodism; religious groups such as the Brethren and the Catholic Apostolic Church first saw the light of day; and the Unitarians emerged to give corporate expression and coherence to religious beliefs which had existed in a somewhat ill-defined, incoherent and unorganized way for a century and more. Within the established church, it was a time when previous, not too well-defined groupings coalesced into 'parties', and when changes took place which were to set the general pattern of its life for the long term future.

The study of the Church of England in the forty-two years after 1791 can therefore be usefully illuminated by a consideration of the three main groups which assumed a clear identity at that time: the High Churchmen, the Evangelicals and the Liberals.

High Churchmanship

Pre-Tractarian High Churchmen, or the 'Orthodox' as they preferred to be called, continued to operate, like their fathers and grandfathers, within a basic pre-supposition that religion and politics were inescapably and inevitably intertwined. 'For the Orthodox prior to 1828, political concerns were a necessary ingredient of churchmanship and were perceived as a legitimate sphere for the application of principles which were essentially theological.'[22] They were but continuing a long tradition, encapsulated in the teaching of Richard Hooker, that in a Christian country the national state and the national church were identical; they were but 'two aspects of the same thing'. The era of the French Revolution, with its rampant Jacobinism, helped to clarify and give focus to this association of the religious with the political. Loyalty to the state was equated by late eighteenth and early nineteenth-century High Churchmen with theological orthodoxy, and disloyalty with theological heterodoxy. It was a view that tended to be shared by Evangelicals, but it contained within it an almost mystical, sacral theory of monarchy, which was a distinctive mark of pre-Tractarian High Churchmanship.

Turning from this political theology to more doctrinal and ecclesiastical matters, four features seem to characterize the High Churchmen of the half century or so before the Oxford movement: belief in the divine origin of the ministerial commission, and in the fact that episcopacy was the means chosen by the apostles for transmitting spiritual authority to the clergy down the ages to the present time; a distinctive view of the eucharist; an emphasis on the mysterious quality of the Christian religion; and the important position assigned to tradition as an arbiter in matters of church doctrine and practice.[23] Although in general these had been the marks of High Churchmanship in the earlier part of the century, they assumed a somewhat different form as the century came to an end, and as the new century got under way.

Belief in apostolic succession had characterized High Churchmen for generations. The Hutchinsonians were in the front line in proclaiming it; and it was upheld in a number of High Church publications, which included: William Stevens' *Nature and Constitution of the Christian Church* (1773), William Jones of Nayland's *Essay on the Church* (1780), Charles Daubeny's *Guide to the Church* (1798) and *Appendix to the Guide* (1804), Thomas Sikes' *Discourse on Parochial Communion* (1812), John James Watson's *Divine Commission and Perpetuity of the Christian Priesthood* (1816), Thomas Burgess' *Primary Principles of Christianity* (1829) and the Bampton Lectures of Thomas Le Mesurier (1807), John Hume Spry (1816) and Godfrey Faussett (1820).[24] In practice, the doctrine was valued as an aid to devotion and a claim to respect for the clergy in contrast to the Nonconformist minister. This was especially important in a period which was to witness a surge of demand for the disabilities of Nonconformists to be removed by changes in the law of the land. The

High Churchmen were the foremost champions of the status of the Church of England as the established church; part of the universal Catholic Church. The Tractarians were not the first High Churchmen to uphold this Catholic interpretation; they entered into a High Church inheritance in which considerations of the standing of the church were intimately bound up with an elevated view of the dignity, and divine authority of its clergy and bishops.

Alongside this preoccupation with the catholicity of the Church of England, and the sacred nature of its ministry, was a stress on the centrality of the eucharist in the life of the divine community. There was no great debate on the nature of that rite in these years, as there was almost a consensus between Orthodox and Evangelical churchmen regarding eucharistic doctrine. The divergence was to come after the earlier phase of the Oxford movement. Although the Orthodox tended to adopt a virtualist rather than a receptionist doctrine, whereas the Evangelicals somewhat favoured the latter over the former, this was not a cause of severe division either within the High Church ranks, or between them and the Evangelicals. In virtualism the bread and wine were considered not to be changed physically into the body and blood of Christ as a result of being set apart, but became so in virtue, power and effect. In the receptionist interpretation, the real presence was subject to the worthiness of the recipient of the eucharist.

Likewise, although High Churchmen of the time, as throughout the eighteenth century, differed from Evangelicals in admitting to a preference for the communion service in the first Prayer Book of King Edward VI, over the amended version of 1552 which removed those features which were most strongly suggestive of the sacrifice of the mass and the real presence of Christ in the sacrament, this did not become a 'hot' issue until it became associated with what were seen as Romeward trends among the Tractarians.

The High Church emphasis on mystery was possibly a reaction to the element of 'plainness' in Low Church circles. It was a natural corollary to their exalted view of the church, its ministry, its sacraments and its liturgy. Samuel Horsley, one of the most eminent High Church bishops of the time, was critical of the Methodist 'disorderly zeal for the propagation of truth', but admired its spiritual fervour. He sought a deep spirituality which would embrace evangelical doctrine, and yet exercise restraint. He was representative of those High Churchmen whose moderation should not be mistaken for dryness. He charged his clergy to preach justification by grace through faith, for 'that we are justified by faith, is not on account of any merit in our faith, but because faith is the first principle of that communion between the believer's soul and the divine spirit, on which the whole of our spiritual life depends'.[25] Such a sense of the mysterious also found expression in the adornment and decoration of church interiors, and in a reverence for holy places. For most of these High Churchmen 'making the visible into "a type of the invisible" meant a decent chancel, altar-hangings, communion-rails, etc. in the restrained Laudian tradition of 'the beauty of holiness" '.[26]

The last characteristic of pre-Tractarian High Churchmanship was the widespread acceptance of tradition; of the teaching of the primitive church as exemplified in the writings of the early fathers. High Churchmen looked to the Bible as the supreme and unrivalled source of inspiration and teaching. But they also turned back to antiquity, to the whole history and teaching of the church in the first three centuries of the Christian era, for a vindication of scriptural faith.

If one person more than any other in late eighteenth-century England enshrined in his life and ministry all these High Church characteristics, it was Samuel Horsley.[27] He was a trained scientist of some eminence. He was Bishop first of St Davids, then of Rochester, and finally of St Asaph. He was a staunch Church of England man and, especially after about 1790, a fully convinced and forthright High Churchman. He believed that the established church was in danger, and he was the chief opponent of the Protestant Dissenters in their efforts to remove the Test and Corporation Acts. In contrast, and some would say inconsistently, he saw the Roman Catholics as allies against revolution and unbelief, and he was tireless in his efforts to promote their relief. His favour towards them was rooted in a sincere belief in toleration as understood by conservative churchmen of the time. It was additionally based on a sense of shared theological conviction which extended to various parts, though not to the whole, of the Roman system. The endorsement he gave in the House of Lords to the Ultramontane position on canonical obedience, and to John Milner's public recognition from the Roman Catholic side that there were those in the Church of England who were well disposed towards Roman Catholicism, acted as a counterweight to the prevailing 'orthodox' High Church anti-Roman views at that time.

When he died in 1806 there was only a loosely compacted High Church 'party', in the sense that there was a group of churchmen who shared a sense of theological and ecclesiastical identity without there being any close-knit organizational expression of such unity, but he had helped to generate a High Church momentum. His death was an irreparable loss to the group as it deprived the High Church reform movement of its figurehead and statesman. He had achieved much, and he had prepared High Churchmanship for the more advanced phase of renewal into which it was about to enter. Indeed, the High Church influence in the inner councils of both church and state was perhaps at its height during the twenty years or so prior to the Oxford Movement. High Churchmen dominated the episcopate, and many were archdeacons, deans, royal chaplains or Heads of Houses at Oxford and Cambridge. It was a dominance which was exemplified in the fact that, as we will see, under the administration of Lord Liverpool in particular, Henry Handley Norris, a leading member of the Hackney Phalanx, was popularly known as the 'bishop-maker'. High Churchmanship had been kept in a sufficiently good state of health during the period since the 1688 Revolution to allow it to burst out afresh in the form first of the Hackney Phalanx and then of the Oxford movement.

To all the various doctrines of political and ecclesiastical theology which I have surveyed, which were demonstrated in the life of Horsley, and which underpinned the High Churchmanship of the decades before 1833, there was added an essentially practical strain which was to prove essential in what was soon to be accomplished. For this credit must largely go to William Stevens and his circle. They were crucial in establishing the hallmarks of early nineteenth-century High Churchmanship. 'The commitment to charitable giving, with a particular emphasis on the needs of the parochial clergy; the principle of working wherever possible with quasi-official institutions and episcopally governed structures; the deep and passionately felt concern for "sacred learning"; the devotion to Word, Sacrament and Office; and the preference for working in an informal alliance of friends and family bound by close ties of mutual affection, were all later echoed by his younger associates.'[28] These were the distinctive marks of the Hackney Phalanx, which was at the very centre of High Church thinking and action in the first three decades of the nineteenth century.

The Hackney Phalanx and early nineteenth-century High Churchmanship

The reputation of the Hackney Phalanx has suffered at the hands of historians. It has often been denigrated as a dull and inconsequential propagator of mere ecclesiasticism. It has frequently been perceived as a group of unimaginative 'High and Dry' Tories who displayed little warmth or depth of spirituality. It has been eclipsed in historical accounts of the period, almost to the point of being ignored, by the attention given to the Evangelical Clapham Sect, and by a focus upon the Oxford Movement, which has been portrayed as the sole and true reviver of authentic traditional High Churchmanship in the first half of the nineteenth century. But such judgments are unfortunate, inaccurate and inadequate. The Hackney Phalanx fulfilled a vital role in the evolution of Anglican Catholicism, and played an important part in the history of the Church of England as a whole. The members of the Phalanx, and the circle of people around them, had an enthusiasm of their own, which gave them a zeal matched only by the Evangelicals in the era of the French Revolution and Wars, and more especially in the post-War years. For them the *status quo* was no matter of mere utility; it was sacred. What they wrote and said was not animated by a concern for personal piety, although this was of central importance to them, but by a passion for the preservation of existing authority at a time when such authority was under serious threat, in an age of iconoclasm, and with pressures for reform or revolution in all and every aspect of national life. For them, church, state and salvation were all part of a total matrix; and they were engaged in a God-given crusade to uphold the existing state of affairs.

The history of the Phalanx is to a great extent bound up with the personal history of Joshua Watson.[29] He was the son of a wealthy wine merchant and government contractor. In keeping with what his father had taught him, he tried to combine a firm and resolute belief and trust in God with business acumen and diligence. During the Napoleonic era he made a fortune, but in 1814 he decided to abandon his business career in order to devote himself to certain tasks which he considered it his Christian duty to perform. He did not experience any sudden conversion, or climacteric moment of decision. He simply gave sufficient notice to allow a replacement to be found, and retired from the City. During the remainder of his life, but especially during the following twenty years, he made a contribution to the life of the Church of England which places him among a select band of laymen of all time. He was one of a few leaders who were instrumental in shaping and executing the policy of the Church of England and, like his contemporary William Wilberforce, he demonstrated what a wealthy man, dedicated to the service of God, could achieve. Unlike Wilberforce, he was not a charismatic personality, able to arouse the enthusiasm of a crowd. He was more at home on a committee than in the vanguard of a crusade; but it was committees which were needed then. Unfortunately, neither he nor the Phalanx as a whole attracted the young, and this was to prove a major problem when the young enthusiasts of the Oxford Movement were not sympathetic to what they saw as the ponderous old men of Hackney who were lacking in vision. But this was all in the distant future. In the meantime, from the time of the battle of Trafalgar to the passing of the Reform Bill, much of the creative work in the Church was inspired and organized by Watson and his friends.

The Hackney Phalanx, like the Clapham Sect, was a tightly-knit group of friends which combined scope for individuality with brotherhood and corporate action to achieve a common purpose. There were between fifty and one hundred laymen and clergymen who counted themselves part of the Phalanx or worked in close association with its members to achieve its objectives. These included the Revd Thomas Sikes, the 'Pope' of Guilsborough, the Revd Charles Daubeny, the unpaid curate of the church at which the Hackney Phalanx members worshipped, Henry Handley Norris, Edward Churton, Archdeacon of Cleveland, and Archdeacon Watson, Joshua's brother, and the vicar of Hackney. Prominent laymen included Dr Christopher Wordsworth, who became Master of Trinity College, Cambridge, and was the author of an exposition on the doctrine of the Church, *Theophilus Anglicanus* (1843); the Tory propagandist John Gifford, who edited *The Anti-Jacobean Review*; two judges, Sir John Richardson and Sir James Alan Park; the magistrate John Bowler, and the Bowler family, who had supported the last of the Nonjurors; John Reeves, the barrister who organized the Loyal Association; the authoress and pamphleteer Sarah Trimmer; Robert Southey, the Poet Laureate; Sir T. D. Acland, a prominent Tory Member of Parliament; and Professor Baden Powell, although he ultimately abandoned the Hackney standpoint. The Phalanx also received the support of many bishops and other high-ranking churchmen. Of particular importance were Bishops George Horne, William Van Mildert, Samuel Horsley, John Douglas, Herbert Marsh, Charles Manners-Sutton, John Randolph, and Thomas Middleton, the first Bishop of Calcutta. Special mention has been made of Bishop Horsley, but William Van Mildert ought also to be singled out. He was very much aware of the need for the church to be salt and light in the world by its involvement in the affairs of the country locally and nationally. He dreamed of the Church of England 'as the soul of the State, as the servant of every citizen, as the custodian of true learning and wisdom . . .'[30]

The group members shared news and information about family matters in an abundance of letters, they shared holidays, and they found a deep and abiding fellowship in the tasks they undertook together. For there was a complementarity of talents among the fraternity, so that each member was able to make his or her distinctive contribution to the collective work which was undertaken.

Charles Daubeny was the leading writer on theological matters among the Phalanx members. Of particular importance was his celebrated *Guide to the Church* which came out in 1798. It was as rigid in its teaching as any latter-day Anglo-Catholic work. He was dogmatic in his insistence that the true church must have a duly commissioned ministry deriving its authority in direct line from the apostles. The priesthood was a divine institution. Sacraments were the 'seals of the divine covenant'.[31] The sacraments of the Dissenters were mere human ordinances and without effect, because the Dissenters lacked a properly constituted ministry. He reserved a milder censure for the Roman Catholic Church, for he claimed that Canterbury and Rome were agreed on essentials.

Watson had really assumed the mantle of William Stevens, who, until the advent of Watson, had been the leading lay High Churchman. Together with William Jones, vicar of Nayland, Stevens had published a series of pamphlets during the period of the French revolutionary crisis, attacking the English supporters of the Revolution and especially Tom Paine and Dr Priestley. He was Treasurer of Queen Anne's Bounty, a member of several church and charitable societies, and one of the founders of the gathering of friends named Nobodys Club. Established in 1800, this brought together High Churchmen with such common aims as the retention and enhancement of the independence, authority and influence of the established church. The elected members of the Club between 1800 and 1850 fully represented the leadership of the old High Churchmanship, as distinct from those who were to be tagged Tractarians. It had an essentially establishment character, with many of the High Church members being archdeacons, deans and bishops, or, among the laity, lawyers.

The Phalanx had an important vehicle for communication in the influential magazine, *British Critic*. It had been founded by a group of High Churchmen who had been appalled at the spread of revolutionary principles. About 1812 it was acquired by Watson and H. H. Norris, and edited by Van Mildert. In its pages, attacks on the church were vigorously opposed, while actions such as the sending of bishops to

India were applauded. Voluntary organizations and societies, including the Church Missionary Society, which did not have the official sanction of the church leaders and the state, were treated with suspicion. The journal appealed to those who valued serious, well-written theological articles, but it also included consideration of literature, foreign affairs and other topical matters. With this wide range it displayed a breadth of perspective and a degree of animation far removed from the dryness associated with eighteenth-century High Churchmanship.

The Phalanx looked back especially to William Laud and the Caroline Divines, with Jeremy Taylor as a particular source of teaching and inspiration. The Phalanx members focussed on the incarnation rather than the atonement; they exalted the place of the visible church as an essential part of God's scheme of redemption; they believed that there was no salvation outside the true church and that Dissenters were in a state of schism. They were of the view that the efficacy of communion depended on its administration by a properly commissioned clergyman, with the service conducted within a true branch of the Catholic Church, and of course this included the Church of England. They stressed the great importance of the liturgy and the sacraments, rather than preaching, in the life of the church; and they felt that God could accomplish his purposes through the regular services and ordinances of the church, administered by his ordained bishops and clergy, without any special effusion of his Spirit, as in apostolic times. This is not to say that they did not have an intense, profound and rich individual and corporate spiritual life; they did, but it was characterized by constraint and self-discipline, a lack of introspection, and an emphasis on the steady, undemonstrative, unobtrusive, spirituality of people who were secure in their own faith and knew what they were about.

Politically, the Phalanx members were loyal supporters of the cautious new reforming Toryism which was led successively by William Pitt, Spencer Perceval, Lord Liverpool and Robert Peel. They greatly distrusted the radical movement, and were horrified by the 1832 Reform Act, with its extension of the franchise.

The achievements of the Phalanx were impressive, especially in education, in the provision of new churches, in the regeneration of the old church societies, in supplying additional staff for parishes, and in supporting the church overseas.

The Clapton Sect, as they were alternatively known, as the High Church equivalent to the Evangelical Clapham Sect, first addressed itself to educational matters. They were concerned about the many thousands of children in London and the rapidly expanding new industrial towns who were growing up to be ignorant and illiterate. Some attempt to tackle the problem had recently been made by Dr Andrew Bell and Joseph Lancaster, both of whom had founded schools, the former accepting and the latter rejecting Church of England control. There was almost universal recognition that Christianity should be part of the education provided under any scheme, but in practice there was competition between the established church and the Dissenters over the right to supervise any system which was devised. And of course anything on a scale which even remotely measured up to the need would be massively expensive.

An inner group of the Phalanx, headed by Watson, H. H. Norris and John Bowles, set to work on a project which resulted in the inauguration in 1811 of The National Society for Promoting the Education of the Poor in the Principles of the Established Church, more commonly known as The National Society. After four years of vigorous campaigning, every diocese in England was consulting the society, and one hundred thousand children were in its schools – a number which rose to almost one million twenty years later. It was a major achievement: the Phalanx had successfully conducted a mass literacy campaign; they had pioneered popular elementary education, provided an important counterbalance to the secular tendencies of the age, and enabled the national church to control directly at least some of the schools as a prelude to the dual system introduced in 1870. It was not a mean record.

The Phalanx members were acutely aware of the need to strengthen the church, especially in the new industrial towns. It was John Bowler who originated a High Church scheme for church-building. An Incorporated Church Building Society was founded. It fought hard for action to be taken; and all the effort bore fruit. In 1818 the House of Commons voted £1,000,000 for a programme of church-building, to be administered by a Commission on which Watson served; and this was supplemented in 1824 by a further £500,000, to which was added over £200,000 in private subscriptions. Watson was a key figure in the wise management of the Government grants and in raising large voluntary donations during the next twenty years: and it taxed all his abilities. 'The building programme depended upon him more than any other single man.'[32]

It was not until 1837 that there was a tangible outcome of the effort of the Phalanx members to provide extra curates to assist the desperately hard pressed urban clergy; for it was in that year, almost entirely as a result of the sustained work of Watson and a small group of his colleagues, that the Additional Curates Society was launched. It was typical of Phalanx policy that the new society was pledged to work through the bishops, in contrast to the Evangelical Church Pastoral-Aid Society, which had been established two years before.

An account of the Hackney Phalanx would be incomplete without a testimony to their contribution to world mission: but I will delay this until chapter 9, when I will view it in the context of mission at home and abroad throughout the whole of the long eighteenth century.

By 1833 Watson was over sixty and beginning to feel the effect of many years of strenuous labour and responsibility. He continued to exert considerable influence, especially as the close friend and confidant of Bishop Blomfield, but his halcyon days were passed. In the 1830s the Phalanx maintained its work, but at a lower key, and in a less forthright manner. It was particularly concerned to encourage church reform, with three priorities: 'appointments to be made according to merit, translations of bishops to be greatly restricted, and ecclesiastical property to be redistributed'.[33]

The Phalanx and its leaders were not only worn out; they were somewhat fearful about what the future held in store for the Church of England. Despite their remarkable achievements, they had failed to attract many new, and especially young, recruits. They had no theologians who could speak out boldly and authoritatively on behalf of a church which was assailed by liberals and reformers, and was undergoing a crisis of confidence as severe as any in its history. The so-called High Church revival which was about to dawn was clerical and academic, rather than lay and practical; and it was reformist and adventurous rather than conservative and reticent. In brief, the movement centred on Oxford differed in certain fundamental ways from the movement centred on Hackney. Watson was to remain in contact with the new movement as a friendly critic, but it was clear for all with eyes to see, that he and his Hackney friends had been superseded.

The Evangelicals

The strength of Evangelicalism in the closing years of the eighteenth century and the opening decades of the nineteenth century is widely acknowledged. Eugene Stock reckoned that it was 'indisputably the strongest force in the country'.[34] John Stoughton acknowledged the imperfections of the Evangelicals, but concluded that at the beginning of the nineteenth century, and for a long while after that, they 'did what no other band of clergymen were doing at the time'. Few, he said, would deny that they were an 'immense power', and 'that they were the very salt of the Church of England, during a period when influences existed threatening decay and corruption'.[35] Two nineteenth-century High Churchmen gave a similar judgment. H. P. Liddon declared that

> the deepest and most fervid religion in England during the first three decades of this century was that of the Evangelicals. The world to come, with its boundless issues of life and death, the infinite value of the one Atonement, the regenerating, purifying, guiding action of God the Holy Spirit in respect of the Christian soul, were preached to our grandfathers with a force and earnestness which are beyond controversy.[36]

William Gladstone, who had been brought up among Evangelicals, said of the Evangelical clergy:

> Every Christian under their scheme had personal dealings with his God and Saviour. The inner life was again acknowledged as a reality, and substituted for that bare, bald compromise between the seen and the unseen world which reduces the share of the 'far and more exceeding and eternal' to almost nil.[37]

Of the Evangelicals in general, C. S. Carpenter said:

> They did not cover all the ground, because there were not very many of them, and there were some matters which their limited range did not enable them to reach, but they were in deadly earnest, and wherever their influence penetrated at all it penetrated very deep.[38]

The Evangelicals were a despised minority despite their pervasive influence. Some bishops tried to extirpate Evangelicalism from their dioceses; some parishes resisted the appointment of any 'serious clergyman', as they were called; Evangelicals were excluded from pulpits; promotion as a clergyman was hindered by a reputation for being 'serious'; and some people even cast doubt on their loyalty to the government and constitution. But they were a growing part of the established church. In 1789 there were possibly no more than forty or fifty Evangelical clergy, none above the rank of parish incumbent; by 1800 there were about 500.[39] By 1833 they accounted for between one eighth and a quarter of the clergy,[40] and they were more accepted. There were also a number of

Evangelicals in the higher echelons of the Church of England. Henry Ryder, the first of the Evangelicals to be elevated to the episcopate, was Bishop of Lichfield and Coventry, C. R. Sumner was Bishop of Winchester, and J. B. Sumner Bishop of Chester; Henry Raikes was Chancellor of the Diocese of Chester, Henry Law Archdeacon and Canon of Winchester; while Thomas Burgess, the Bishop of Salisbury, was sympathetic to the Evangelicals.

During the Napoleonic era the Evangelicals also appear to have acquired a greater theological comprehensiveness. It remained true that 'the world-view of Evangelicals was primarily theological and it was distinctive',[41] and it was certainly the case that what distinguished them from non-Evangelicals 'was the emphasis they gave to particular doctrines, and the fervour with which they practised "vital religion" ',[42] but to the basic doctrines at the heart of eighteenth-century Evangelicalism, which I have already considered, was added a greater concern for moral and ethical matters, a reaching out after a more reasoned faith, and a search for greater order and decency in faith and practice. In the 'practical' Christianity promoted by William Wilberforce, Hannah More and the Clapham Sect, and in the columns of the Evangelical *Christian Observer*, there was manifested a more moderate, wider and more inclusive Evangelicalism than had characterized the earlier Evangelicals. It was a trend which was to cause severe divisions within Evangelicalism in the third and fourth decades of the nineteenth century, for there were those who thought that such mellowing was treachery.

This deepening and broadening of Evangelical theology and social concern was accompanied by a reinforced attachment to the established church. The hostility of other churchmen towards them, and the lack of opportunity for promotion, did not drive a wedge between the Evangelicals and the institutional church of which they were members. 'By the 1830s it was plain that the evangelicals were tenacious establishment men, despite the hammering they had received from the high-church.'[43] As we will see later, this created a barrier between them and their fellow evangelicals among the Dissenters, and was thus a hindrance when it came to any attempt to promote pan-evangelicalism.

As it became both theologically and socially easier to become an Evangelical, and as they were increasingly perceived as part of the establishment, so the lay social composition of Evangelicalism underwent a change. The middle and upper-middle class convert was no longer asked to be identified with a rather socially confined, predominantly lower-middle class, and somewhat sectarian, party within the established church. The process of social transformation was slow, and even as late as 1810 the list of subscribers to the Church Missionary Society contained no names of peers or bishops, and no members of the universities except Simeon's friends. But within a few years the Grosvenors, the Pelhams, the Ashleys, the Shirleys, the Vansittarts, the houses of Roden and Ducie and even a Prime Minister, Spencer Perceval, were to contribute to the strength of Evangelicalism, and it was represented in Parliament by a formidable body of advocates.

Throughout the period 1791 to 1833 the twin focusses of Evangelicalism in England were Cambridge and London. In Cambridge, the dominant figure was Charles Simeon; in London it was William Wilberforce, ably supported by the other members of the Clapham Sect, and the 'Saints' in Parliament.

Charles Simeon was born in 1759, educated at Eton and King's College, Cambridge, of which he became a Fellow, ordained deacon in 1782 and priest in 1783. He was curate-in-charge of Holy Trinity, Cambridge from 1782, in which capacity he laboured for fifty-four years, until his death in his Cambridge rooms in 1836.[44] Such are the bald facts, but they do not tell the story of the man whose true status and standing is more accurately given by his contemporary, Lord Macaulay. 'If you knew what his authority and influence were,' said Macaulay , 'and how they extended from Cambridge to the most remote corners of England, you would allow that his real sway over the Church was far greater than that of any primate.'[45]

He was converted to an Evangelical faith within a few months of becoming an undergraduate, not as a result of the influence of any other evangelical in Cambridge, but from his own reading and reflection. Indeed, the waves of the eighteenth-century revival appear to have left Cambridge untouched, and for three years Simeon had no fellow Evangelical in the town with whom he could share his faith.

His appointment to Holy Trinity was most unpopular, and life was made difficult for him. On Sunday mornings, for a long time, the church was made as inaccessible as possible to him and his congregation. Most of the pew doors were locked, with the authorized occupants absent, leaving only the aisles for the congregation. On the first Sunday the church was almost empty; but after a few weeks the numbers had grown, so that there was scarcely enough room. Simeon placed benches in the aisles and seats in nooks and corners at his own expense; but the churchwardens removed them and threw them into the churchyard. The belligerents persisted for about ten years in their attacks and in their efforts to frustrate his ministry, but he continued to attract greater numbers and to extend the provisions for evangelism and pastoral care.

During all this time Simeon exerted great and increasing influence over undergraduates in particular, but also over senior members of the colleges. He held three Deanships at King's from 1788 to 1790, 1792 to 1798 and from 1827 to 1830; and he was Vice-Provost from 1790 to 1792. From the start of his ministry at Holy Trinity he attracted many undergraduates, and there were some remarkable conversions. These included the future chaplains to India, Henry Martyn, Thomas Thomason, Daniel Corrie, James Hough and Claudius Buchanan, and distinguished men such as Thomas Sowerby, the Senior Wrangler (the student heading the list of those placed in the first class of Part II of the Mathematical Tripos) of 1796; Henry Kirke White, the protégé of Robert Southey; James Scholefield, subsequently Regius Professor of Greek; Charles Clayton, who often preached at Holy Trinity church; Thomas Rawson Birks, second Wrangler in 1834 and later Professor of Moral Philosophy; and William Carus, who became Fellow and Dean of Trinity College, Simeon's curate, his biographer and his successor. Initially there were few men of influence in the colleges who were in essential agreement with him. Even Isaac Milner, the Senior Wrangler of 1774, who was chosen President of Queens' College in 1788, and an Evangelical, was at first suspicious of the new preacher.The only other person of note who in any way associated with Simeon in his early days at Holy Trinity was William Farish, the Senior Wrangler of 1778, a gentle, courageous man who upheld his Evangelical convictions as Jacksonian Professor.

Simeon's influence upon undergraduates in general, and upon ordination candidates in particular, was his greatest contribution to the life of the Church of England of his day. About half the total undergraduate population had come to college with the sole purpose of qualifying for holy orders. In a situation where there was no special theological training provided by either the church or the university, and where the ordination examination consisted merely of construing a passage from the Greek New Testament on the day of ordination, Simeon's opportunity to be of assistance to those anticipating ordination was very considerable; and he availed himself of every means of providing help. By 1817 half his congregation were undergraduates, and through his sermons, his sermon classes and his conversation parties, he provided a theological education which was unparalleled in the country.

His writings were prolific, and spread his influence nationwide. Of special importance were his 'skeletons', as he called them: well-ordered outlines of expositions arranged according to the books of the Bible.

He made his mark on the development of Evangelical theology by his irenic, mediatorial role in the aftermath of the fierce Arminian-Calvinist controversy, when divisions and hard talking persisted. He propounded a new way in which he said that he oscillated between the two extremes, and by so doing claimed to follow the example of the apostle Paul. Sometimes he was a high Calvinist, at other times a low Arminian, so, he continued 'if extremes will please you, I am your man; but only remember, it is not one extreme that we are to go to, but both extremes'.[46]

In almost all that he did Simeon saw himself as serving his beloved Church of England, for he was a strong churchman. He taught ordinands to keep to their parish boundaries and to value their membership of the Church of England. He was a key figure in ensuring that Evangelicalism continued within the established church, at a time when Methodism was becoming fragmented, and the Countess of Huntingdon's Connexion was dwindling into a small denomination. In order to prosecute this objective he used money inherited through a brother's death to buy the patronage of some livings. Others 'purchased income', he wrote, 'I purchase spheres, wherein the prosperity of the Established Church . . . may be advanced.'[47] Gradually other Evangelicals gave money for the same purpose, or handed over to him livings that were in their gift. In this way the Simeon Trust came to embrace the appointment to more than a hundred parishes, including some of the most important incumbencies in the country. These included churches in strategic centres such as Cheltenham, where he secured the parish church for £3,000; Bradford, where he acquired what is now the cathedral; Colchester, Newcastle-under-Lyme, Drypool, Darlaston, Clifton, Hereford, Northampton, Ipswich and Chichester. He and his colleagues also successfully negotiated for Bath Abbey, Bridlington Priory, Derby Parish Church and Beverley Minster.

As we leave Simeon, at least for the moment, I am aware of his incalculable contribution to the work of the church overseas; but I will leave this to chapter 9, when its significance will be more fully appreciated in the context of worldwide missionary outreach, especially as it developed in the last decade of the eighteenth century and the opening decades of the nineteenth century.

In the other focus of Evangelicalism in these years, London, the pre-eminent figure was William Wilberforce.[48] He was born in the same year as Simeon, 1759, into a family which had been made exceedingly rich by a fortune made in the Baltic trade. After graduating from Cambridge, he entered Parliament in 1780. In the Commons he was the close friend and supporter of the Prime Minister in his battle against the Fox-North coalition. He soon became a powerful orator, with a fine blend of gentleness and range of tone, warmth of feeling and the ability to apply great pathos and sarcasm to devastating effect.

Wilberforce had come under Evangelical influence at school and through relatives, and he went into political life with the values and perspectives of Evangelicalism well and truly implanted in him. The first cause to attract him, the one which was most to occupy him for the rest of his life, and his major opportunity to show the fruit of his Evangelical convictions, was the movement for the abolition of the slave trade. It was Pitt who finally persuaded him to introduce a motion on the subject into the Commons. Wilberforce was not unaware of the implications of such a commitment, and the magnitude of the task confronting him. As he started out on the crusade, he was encouraged to receive what was possibly the last letter written by the octogenarian John Wesley before he died:

My dear Sir,

Unless the Divine Power has raised you up to be an Athanasius *contra mundum* I see not how you can go through your glorious enterprise in opposing that execrable villainy which is the scandal of religion, of England, of human nature. Unless God has raised you up for this very thing, you will be worn out by the opposition of man and devils; but, if God be for you, who can be against you? Are all of them together stronger than God? Oh, be not weary in well doing. Go on, in the name of God and in the power of His might, till even American slavery, the vilest that ever saw the sun, shall vanish away before it. That He who has guided you from your youth up may continue to strengthen you in this and all things is the prayer of, Dear Sir, your affectionate servant –

John Wesley[49]

From 1787 onwards the life of Wilberforce and a small company of fellow Evangelicals was dedicated to this 'glorious enterprise', and to other aims of national and international importance, consistent with, and expressive of their Evangelical faith. An inner band of them lived in the same neighbourhood, and subsequently became known as the 'Clapham Sect'; a few were Members of Parliament, where they were collectively designated 'the Saints'.

The Thornton family had long been connected with Clapham. In 1792, Henry Thornton, the son of the philanthropist John Thornton, arranged for Wilberforce to share his residence, Battersea Rise House; and in the next ten years they were joined in Clapham by Charles Grant, Sir John Shore, the first Baron Teignmouth, Granville Sharp, Zachary Macaulay and James Stephen. All of them were identified with the Evangelical movement, and they had as their rector the Evangelical John Venn. It was an outstanding group, which was about to achieve great things.[50]

Henry Thornton, although very rich, decided early in life that he would only retain for himself sufficient money to allow him to live in reasonable comfort, and he remained faithful to his resolve throughout his life.[51] Before his marriage he gave away nearly six-sevenths of his income, and after marriage one-third. He was a Member of Parliament for more than thirty years.

John Shore could look back on a meteoric career in India, which reached its pinnacle when he was made Governor-General and raised to the peerage.[52] On his return to England, and to Clapham, he sought a second career, and found it as the first President of the British and Foreign Bible Society.

Granville Sharp had occupied humble positions as an apprentice linen-draper and an employee of the Army Ordinance Department, before he came into some prominence as the champion of a number of individual negroes. This culminated in a trial before Lord Mansfield in 1772, and the historic verdict that no man who has put his foot on English soil can be a slave. It was a milestone in the emancipation struggle. Sharp was chosen to be the Chairman of the Abolition Society, which was founded in 1787, and the first Chairman of the British and Foreign Bible Society.

Zachary Macaulay went to Jamaica to seek his fortune, and experienced slavery at first hand.[53] He returned after four years, dis-illusioned and without plans for the future, until he met a friend of Wilberforce, and an ardent abolitionist, Thomas Babington, who arranged for him to visit and assist the newly-founded colony of Sierra Leone. So well did he acquit himself that he was promoted, and soon became Governor. He returned, and after a period as Secretary of the

Sierra Leone Company in London, he devoted almost forty years without stint to the abolitionist movement. In addition, he undertook the editorship of the *Christian Observer*, the newly-launched monthly periodical designed to represent Evangelical opinion in the Church of England.

James Stephen spent eleven years in the West Indies, and returned to England in 1794, burning with indignation at the horrors of the slave system.[54] He immediately joined Wilberforce in the campaign against the slave traffic. He was Master of Chancery, but ungrudgingly gave whatever spare time he could to the cause of the slaves.

Charles Grant went to India as a youth. Early in his career he entered the East India Company and, like John Shore, he soon achieved the highest seniority in its service.[55] During his time in India he joined with two friends in establishing a local church, and he paid the salary of a chaplain sent out from England. The three of them also attempted to start what was named the Bengal Mission. Although it was unsuccessful, it led indirectly to the establishment of the work of the Church Missionary Society in India. He and his friends persisted in their efforts to attract men for service in India, and they succeeded after many years. Grant had much to do with the sending of Henry Martyn to India. He settled in Clapham in 1790, when he was nearing the summit of his career, for in 1805 he was made Chairman of Directors of the East India Company.

Lastly, there was John Venn, who, from 1792 until his death in 1813, was rector of Clapham. He was the son of Henry Venn of Huddersfield, whom we have already met as one of the leading early Evangelicals. He was a man of culture, good judgment and perseverance, who organized his parish on vigorous Evangelical lines. He was one of the first clergymen to introduce parish schools; boldly started a Sunday evening service when this was most uncommon; organized a system of district visiting; published a collection of psalms and hymns for use in the parish; and was active in the work of the Society for Bettering the Condition of the Poor at Clapham. He was a member of the Eclectic Society, and he co-operated with Simeon in drafting a set of initial rules for the Society for Missions in Africa and the East (the future Church Missionary Society). Above all he was the personal friend and spiritual guide of perhaps the most notable congregation in the whole of England in his generation.

Of those who did not reside in Clapham but were closely identified with the thinking and action of the Clapham Sect special mention

should be made of Hannah More. In the previous chapter I have
described the early activities of this remarkable women. In the second
part of her life, when she was a close friend of Wilberforce, she was preoccupied with evangelical concerns, and she was an impassioned
champion of the African slave. Her *Cheap Repository Tracts* during the
nineties contained tales and ballads and Sunday Readings on slavery
'which kept the question before tens of thousands of readers at a time
when the Abolition Committee had abandoned its efforts to distribute
literature'.[56] They were in the tradition of the SPCK publications of the
previous one hundred years and similar works by the Wesleys and
Hannah's friend Sarah Trimmer. The 700,000 copies which had been
sold by July 1795 achieved some success in helping to provide moral
and religious instruction for the poor. In these works, and in her *Village
Politics*, which was intended as an antidote to the poison of Thomas
Paine's *Rights of Man*, Hannah More broke new ground for she
adopted 'not only the lively stories and ballads for community singing
as supplied by chap-book and broad-sheet, but their format also, and by
under-selling the hawkers and pedlars' she 'beat them at their own
game'.[57]

There were others throughout the land who also identified with the
Clapham Sect in its multifarious activities and objectives, but it was the
Clapham fraternity, who were overwhelmingly though not exclusively
Evangelicals, who were the hub of all that was attempted. The members
of the group were committed to each other, and prepared to unite their
efforts in agreed common aims. Their individual talents, which varied
considerably, were combined and harmonized in a remarkable way.
They were good friends as well as colleagues in various crusades. Their
homes were open for casual and informal visits as well as for the more
formal hospitality which they delighted to offer one another. Their
children played together, and the families enjoyed joint holidays. It was
a fraternity with a very deep sense of unity and shared interests.

The term 'Clapham Sect' was never applied during the lifetime of
Wilberforce. The recognized forum of activity of these crusading
Evangelicals was Parliament. And in that arena they were part of a wide
parliamentary coterie of Evangelicals. Political and religious affiliations
during the period from 1791 to 1833 were considerably more complex
than has often been appreciated.[58] It appears that there were 112 or
more Members of Parliament between 1784 and 1832 who can be
reckoned as Evangelicals. This included a small group of somewhat
extreme millenarianists; a large group who, while being Evangelicals in

their religious beliefs, owed political allegiance to one of the two main political parties, and in the case of the majority of them to the Tory party; and the Saints proper, whose most determined and unshakeable maxim was total repudiation of all party alignment and the maintenance of absolute independence. Because of this stress on individual conscience, the Saints did not always vote in the same way. The number of the Saints so defined varied, but there was an average of about thirty during the years under review.

The outstanding achievement of the Saints, and more particularly the Clapham Sect, was the abolition of the slave trade, and then of slavery itself within the British Empire. It was a titanic struggle. It may be that 'abolitionism attracted the support not only of the evangelical middle classes who had an economic as well as a religious interest in abolition, but also appealed to the urban artisans as part of a wider political protest against paternalism and dependency in the early industrial revolution'.[59] It is also true that in the all-important initial impulse of anti-slavery sentiment in Britain the Quakers and some of Wesley's followers made vital contributions; that by the 1820s the anti-slavery movement 'enjoyed the mass support of an increasingly powerful evangelical Nonconformity'; and that 'this support was enlarged still further by a radical libertarian strand of politics among the British working classes'.[60] But Church of England Evangelicals represented the consistent and persistent core of the campaign. They were the storm troopers, and at the very centre of the movement, giving it the inspiration, resolve, determination and organizational efficiency without which what was achieved would not have been possible, at least within the time span in which the task was in fact successfully brought to a conclusion.

Arrayed against the abolitionists was a formidable array of opponents. The slave-owners, the perpetrators of the slave trade, the shipowners, the financiers and all those whose fortune was bound up in slavery, as well as the many whose fear of the consequences of freedom was aggravated by the events in France, joined in an almost impregnable alliance. And the power of vested interests was buttressed by well-marshalled arguments. Slavery had become a long-established and accepted part of the life of the colonies. The slave trade was integral to the whole commercial relationship between the colonies and the mother country. The cry was raised that Liverpool would be ruined, the colonies lost, and that the negroes would rise up and massacre their owners. The abolitionists were viewed by many as ultra-revolutionaries, bent on a measure which would be to the great disadvantage of their country.

Then, perhaps as wounding as any of this to the Evangelical abolitionists, there was the indifference of some other Evangelicals to the cause, their unwillingness to identify themselves with it, and even their tacit or explicit acceptance of slavery. In fact, the anti-slavery campaign brought to light different philosophical and theological presuppositions and perspectives which had not previously found such public expression among Evangelicals. At its most profound level the whole movement was an expression of a wide and deep philosophical, ideological and theological current which had been flowing for some considerable time. It was a fruit of the Enlightenment; of a movement in European, and in this case more specifically English, thinking and the re-ordering of perceptions and values, which had been gaining momentum for a century and more. The Evangelicals of the Clapham Sect added their own insights as Evangelicals, and the determination, energy, dedication and persistence which stemmed from their faith, and made the cause their own, but it sprang from a movement of the human spirit which was more comprehensive than Evangelicalism.

> Anti-slavery was not intrinsic to Evangelicalism: some of the stoutest defenders of slavery in the American South were preachers of the gospel. It was the tide of opinion running against slavery among the philosophical luminaries of the eighteenth century that prepared the way for British abolition of the slave trade in 1807 and the extinction of the institution in the British dominions under an act of 1833. Benevolence, happiness and liberty, three leading principles of the time, all created a presumption in favour of abolition. Unless they had been thoroughly imbued with these values themselves, Evangelicals would not have taken up the cause.[61]

Nonetheless, it was to the eternal credit of the Clapham Sect that they did conduct the campaign. Others who shared the same Enlightenment inheritance lacked any clear resolve to abolish slavery, were apathetic to the cause, or were actively hostile to any change. Roger Anstey points out that most of the influential thinkers of the eighteenth century had specifically condemned slavery.[62] By the end of the century little serious intellectual support was being offered for it. By the 1770s 'the content of received wisdom had so changed that educated men in Britain, including the political nation, were likely to regard slavery as morally and philosophically condemned'.[63] Also, the slave trade had not proved to be a greatly profitable business. The Clapham Sect members accepted many of the prevailing principles, including the emphasis on liberty, benevolence and happiness, but they 'transposed them into a religious key'; they ardently believed that the moral order was sustained by God, and that they were summoned by God 'to mould the world to a righteousness which would avert national catastrophe, relieve the earthly sufferings of men and pave the way for the salvation of men's eternal souls'. 'Finally, in the very warp and woof of Evangelical faith, slavery, of all social evils, stood particularly condemned, and because slavery and freedom represented the externalization of the polar opposites of the Evangelicals' inmost spiritual experience, they were impelled to act in the cause of abolition with a zeal and a perseverance which other men could rarely match.'[64]

Even with all the efforts and the success of the Clapham Sect and the Saints, there remained much to do. After the first milestone in 1807 which outlawed the trade, slavery itself still flourished. And it was another Evangelical, Thomas Fowell Buxton, who subsequently entered the lists, and saw the total cause through to its final and complete success in 1833.[65]

Associated with the whole issue of slavery was the founding of Sierra Leone. As early as 1787 Granville Sharp had been concerned to help London's 'black poor'; the freed slaves and unemployed black people formerly employed as servants. With Treasury help he shipped some of them to form a self-governing community at the abandoned trading stations of the small mountainous peninsula which formed Sierra Leone. It was to be a 'Province of Freedom' in which peaceful commerce replaced the slave trade. First Sharp and then Henry Thornton were Chairmen of the company established to further this venture. Thornton and Wilberforce each contributed large sums of capital. Macaulay served as Governor, and experienced some of the early traumas of the settlement. The little community had to weather many trials. The capital, Granville Town, was burned to the ground by the local chieftain in revenge for an outrage perpetrated by some unruly settlers. The French invaded the colony, burned the houses, destroyed all they could lay hands on, robbed the colonists of their possessions and wrecked the contents of the church; and there were tensions and difficulties among the members of the settlement itself. Nevertheless, the colony survived; one more testimony to the unremitting endeavour of the Clapham Sect.

There are few historians and others, if any, who would not applaud the Clapham Sect for its key role in bringing about the abolition of slavery in the British Empire, and for its efforts to promote the well-being of various overseas communities; but when it comes to the domestic affairs of England, the Evangelicals have been accused of hypocrisy and double standards in their attitudes and actions. Ian Bradley voices such criticism:

> For all their protestations about the cruelties inflicted on the negro slaves and other groups in the far flung corners of the world, the Evangelicals generally and the Saints in particular, seemed to be singularly unconcerned with the sufferings of those at home.[66]

Bradley concedes that there was a strong humanitarian element in the Evangelical creed, but he says that it was essentially spontaneous and individualistic. The Evangelicals did not have a vision of a Christian society with mutual ties and obligations; nor did they either reflect on, or take any action against, the social mores which resulted in misery and want. They did not formulate a plan for reordering social and economic structures as the early Christian Socialists did. The basis of their response, he asserts, was emotional rather than ideological. Such an approach resulted in works of individual, and occasionally corporate, charity and relief rather than curative measures. Political action was restricted to the remedying of specific and acute suffering. They were concerned with the fruit of social injustice without regard for the root causes.

The condemnation goes beyond the philosophy and action, or lack of it, of the Clapham Sect and the Saints, and provides a critique and criticism of Evangelical social action as a whole. Bradley and others are censorious about the ethos and philosophy underlying various expressions of Evangelical philanthropy and social involvement. Hannah More and her sisters laboured tirelessly amid the Mendip Hills, providing schooling for about twenty thousand socially and educationally deprived children over a period of twenty-five years. Some latter-day commentators, including the Hammonds, while commending these charitable efforts and works of mercy, reprimand the Mores for not giving thought to the system which produced such poor conditions. 'It never seems to have crossed the minds of these philanthropists', say the Hammonds, 'that it was desirable that men and women should have decent wages, or decent homes, or that there was something wrong with the arrangements of a society that left the mass of the people in this plight.'[67]

This is a stricture echoed by Ford K. Brown:

The Evangelicals were concerned with no reform but the reform of vice and sin and of infidelity that to their mind was the sole cause of vice and sin. Their only object was to have a nineteenth century peopled by Evangelical Christians leading moral lives of a puritanical kind.[68]

It is evident that the Clapham Sect members, the Saints and the Evangelicals in general did not, in the words of Stephen Neill, challenge the false theories 'that lay behind the industrial evils of the age'. As he says, 'They took it for granted that poverty would always exist, and that all that could be done was to mitigate the sufferings which accompanied it'.[69] But in so doing they were but children of their time. It was generally taken as axiomatic that the hierarchical order of society was providential. Social mobility was possible, but all men should conduct themselves according to their status in life – and it was men in this context who were being talked about in all this discussion, for it was considered self-evident that women had their appointed and very limited and static roles. Those in positions of wealth, power and influence should use their God-given privileges for the good of their fellow members of society who were less well endowed with this world's goods. That was the way to bring about an improvement in the lot of the needy and the underprivileged.

Thus, when Wilberforce introduced the bill to strengthen the laws preventing the combination of workmen against their masters, which became the detested Combination Act of 1799, he did not see this as a repressive measure against 'the workers'. He saw himself as politically on the side of the working men. He regarded the Combination Act as a defence of the realm; he was helping to save the poor from political agitators. Also, the forcing up of wages would increase the cost of living and thus hurt the poor. His action was consistent with his social philosophy: it was fundamentally benevolent, albeit somewhat paternalistic and reactionary. He, and his fellow Evangelicals in this and other actions, cannot be too severely condemned, if at all, for being conditioned by the prevailing thought of the day.

Although they acquiesced in domestic legislation which would now be considered repressive, Bradley admits that 'the Saints were more liberal in their attitudes and activities than most historians have acknowledged'.[70] Not only did nearly every Evangelical Member of Parliament fully participate in the crusades against the slave trade and colonial slavery, when this represented quite advanced liberal thinking, but they 'emerge as a group of highly active and liberally inclined Christian politicians, committed to bringing about reforms on a wide variety of fronts'.[71] They were more questioning, and more willing to introduce change than most of their peers in church and state who were largely paralysed by fear of radicalism and Jacobinism. The Evangelicals did as much as any other group in their generation to meet the promptings of their own consciences. As early as 1786 Wilberforce carried through the Commons a small measure of penal reform, and subsequently supported Romilly in his various attempts to abolish the death penalty for various offenses. The Clapham Sect advocated the abolition of the press gang, improvement in the conditions of asylums and madhouses, the relief of climbing boys and the regulation of factory conditions. Wilberforce united with Sir Robert Peel in introducing the first Factory Act in 1802, but protested that it did not go far enough. In 1805 he took up the cause of the Yorkshire weavers; and in 1818 he supported Peel in a further extension of the Factory Act. The liberal Sir James Mackintosh judged Wilberforce to be a Tory by predilection, but by his actions 'liberal and reforming'.[72]

There were differences of view and emphasis among the Evangelicals, but they were united in their final analysis of cause and effect in matters political, social and economic. To them it was ultimately a question of morality and personal religion. Whatever the issue currently at stake, the most pressing need was for the country to return to the Christian faith and Christian morality. Wilberforce had expressed it well, and at length in his *Practical View of the Prevailing Religious System of Professed Christians* (1797), and such a perspective remained at the centre of all the Evangelical thinking and activity in these troublesome years for the nation and the church. It was so in their literature, such as the many and influential tracts and popular works of Hannah More and Legh Richmond, and in the novels of Mary Sherwood;[73] and it was evident in their newspapers, such as the *Christian Guardian* and the *Record*. As we have seen, and as we will see later, there were serious theological divides within the ranks of the Evangelicals, but they were agreed on the basic content of their faith and morals.

Although the Evangelicals did not have a conscious, articulated, political, economic or social 'policy' and agenda for action, it is possible to discern fixed guidelines in their approach to these matters. The Clapham Sect and the Saints, like other leading evangelicals of their generation and their immediate successors, such as John Bird Sumner and the Scottish divine and church statesman Thomas Chalmers, 'reinforced the evangelical preference for voluntary, face-to-face action', showed 'a distaste for state intervention', and emphasized 'above all the key necessity for preaching the gospel.' They, together with Sumner and Chalmers, were 'important in fixing many nineteenth-century evangelicals into a social policy option based on a rurally-derived, paternalistic model of pre-industrial social relations, a confidence in the rational workings of the market and the power of associational effort. It was not that they failed to move from practice to theory but that they chose a theory which, as the nineteenth century wore on, was less and less able to cope with the dynamic and unstable realities of an industrializing nation. Rural parochialism just would not work in an urban environment.'[74] In the fullness of time it also became apparent that the persistent stress on voluntarism alone would not address those urban problems without an acknowledgment of the possibility of a role for the state. Indeed, Evangelicals had, from the late eighteenth century onwards, appreciated the part played by the state in the implementation or promotion of causes which they championed. The abolition of slavery and the amelioration of harsh factory conditions were dependent on Acts of Parliament.

The extent to which the Evangelicals were responsible for the marked change in the moral tone of the country in the years between 1791 and 1833, and the degree to which they laid the foundation for Victorian morality, is a matter of debate.[75] But whatever the part they may have played in creating a distinctive moral climate it, like so many other aspects of Evangelicalism, has attracted criticism. The outraged Sydney Smith, having listed such Evangelical prohibitions as the theatre, cards, dancing, dancing dogs and blind fiddlers, complained that it was not the abuse of pleasure that Evangelical Christianity attacked, but pleasure itself.[76] And T.B.Macaulay seemingly had an eye to the Evangelicals of the first half of the nineteenth century in his jibe that the Puritans 'hated bearbaiting not because it gave pain to the bear, but because it gave pleasure to the spectators'.[77] There are grounds for such accusations. The Evangelicals certainly stressed the need for seriousness. They were accustomed to vigorous self-examination and a profound sense of the importance of redeeming time. They were sabbatarians, and they forbade indulgence in a wide range of 'pleasures'. They tended to reject secular literature as unnecessary, or at least approached it with great caution.

But Evangelical morality was the fruit of Evangelical faith; it was a consequence of the very features which gave the movement its force and energy. The vital individual discipline and application to 'the one thing that mattered' was a cause of what may be construed as narrowness. Some of the pleasures they resisted were deserving of resistance, as with the theatre, which had reached a low level of artistry and a high level of decadence. Also, some authors, such as Milton, Shakespeare to a limited extent, the eighteenth-century moral essayists with certain reservations, and some poets, notably William Cowper, were approved or were even popular among Evangelicals. Likewise, some music was hesitatingly and cautiously given the seal of approval. But, in spite of these exceptions, it is true that in large tracts of their lives Evangelicals of that generation could only subjugate and not sanctify the senses; and this subjugation frequently took a religious form. As has been cogently observed, the senses which were expelled from mainstream Evangelicalism 'took up residence with a vengeance on the peripheries of the movement, in enthusiastic preaching and the excitement and drama of Irvingism . . .'[78] Nonetheless, it is well to recall that the demanding morality of the Evangelicals went hand in hand with strong personal faith. When the Evangelicals lost some of the dynamism and concentrated purposefulness of this faith and morality, and became more diffuse, mechanical and stereotyped in belief and practice at a later date, they ceased to exercise the influence, and to cut ice in the same way as their forefathers.

Before we leave the Evangelicals, with their zealous beliefs and strict morality, it is appropriate to mention that institution which, perhaps more than any other, was to typify the robust evangelicalism of the Victorian era: Sunday schools. They have been described as 'the major distinctive contribution of evangelicals to popular education'[79] and they were undoubtedly of central importance in the life of the Church of England and of Nonconformity for well over a century.

They emerged in the mid-eighteenth century with a triple purpose: to provide elementary education to poor and deprived children, mainly in the developing new industrial cities; to counter what were seen as the dangers of Sunday idleness, contrasted with the weekday employment of children; and to provide 'that saving ability to read the Bible that many poor parents were failing to provide'.[80] Sunday schools can be traced back at least to the 1760s, when individual clergymen and lay men and women had taken the initiative to start such a work in their churches, but it was after Robert Raikes publicized the success of the Sunday schools in Gloucester in 1783 that the movement rapidly gained momentum and spread throughout the country. As they developed they also expanded their purpose. In the words of one of their Methodist supporters the object 'was not only to teach the children of poor people to read and write, but to instruct, in the most important practical principles of religion, all the children either poor or rich who were sent to them'.[81] In its attempt to use education in this way as a means of evangelism the Sunday school movement was 'in effect a continuation of the charity-school movement, adapted to the changed circumstances of Britain of the industrial revolution'.[82] They flourished because they met obvious and felt needs, there were vast numbers of children and parents who were glad to take advantage of the service they provided, and because their teachers were part-time and unpaid. And their growth was astounding. By 1800 200,000 children were enrolled; and this increased to over 2,000,000 by 1851, representing 13% of the population. By the 1840s half the children in England in the five to fifteen age range were attending Sunday schools, and Thomas Laqueur comments that 'the magnitude of enrolment was such that very few working-class children after 1830 could have escaped at least a few years in Sunday school'.[83]

Sunday schools underwent a distinct change of character as the they developed during their first hundred years. In the initial phase they were intended to occupy the whole of the day and to include compulsory attendance at public worship. In some of the larger towns special buildings were erected, the schools were interdenominational, and the teachers consisted largely of former pupils. In many other places the schools were denominational; and in other situations – usually smaller towns or villages – they were adjuncts to churches or chapels. As the nineteenth century advanced some of the schools, with their unreachable standards of dress for working-class children, and their general move towards a more pronounced middle-class ethos, found that they no longer attracted the very poor and needy. It was one of the factors which led to the establishment in the 1830s of ragged schools. Nonetheless, the Sunday school had not had its day; it continued to be an important part of Church of England life until about the middle of the twentieth century. And even then in much of the country when it disappeared it was replaced by modified versions under new names. Two hundred years is a noteworthy life for any such institution.

Nobody denies the statistical success of Sunday schools. What is more questionable is the measure of their success in providing the rudiments of secular education or in preparing children for future church or chapel membership. Lacqueur, in the most exhaustive study yet of Sunday schools, concludes that they 'were a failure as recruitment agencies for church and chapel'. And he goes further, asserting that in 1851 there was 'a strong negative correlation between church attendance and Sunday school enrolment . . . suggesting that in certain urban areas, particularly in the north, Sunday schools replaced church or chapel as the focus of working-class religious life'.[84] On the other hand R. Carwardine claims that they played an important part in church expansion, and argues that a high proportion of the converts in the revivals of the 1830s and 1840s were drawn from Bible classes and Sunday schools.[85] And both Tudur Jones and D. G. Evans, who are representative of many other historians, claim that the schools were a vital part of a vigorous nineteenth-century Nonconformist evangelicalism.[86] A fair assessment seems to be that the 'Sunday schools may not have assisted the churches in making major inroads into completely irreligious families, but they were an additional factor in predisposing children from religious homes towards Evangelical conversion.'[87]

The 'Liberals'

To call the 'Liberals' a party, in the sense that it is possible to identify the High Churchmen or the Evangelicals as a party, is arguably a misnomer, for, by definition, they shared a belief in freedom of belief and an openness to differences of opinion; they were opposed to dogma, and they made a virtue of variegated views. Indeed, 'it is no uncommon thing for Liberal groups to consist mainly of leaders without followers'.[88] But I must adopt some sort of broad definition if I am to identify those I am seeking to describe. A good starting point is John Henry Newman. Despite his distinctive churchmanship and theological bias, he was a contemporary, highly intelligent and observant critic, with a particular sensitivity to theological nuances. 'Liberalism, then,' he wrote, 'is the mistake of subjecting to human judgment those revealed doctrines which are in their nature beyond and independent of it, and of claiming to determine on intrinsic grounds the truth and value of propositions which rest for their reception simply on the external authority of the Divine Word.'[89] Certainly those I am about to mention were not afraid of applying human reason to dogmatic matters, nor hesitant in questioning received truths; although some would regard them as low church Latitudinarians rather than a new breed of 'Liberals'. In church matters they were typically Erastian, and tended to regard the church itself as a kind of government department; 'and organized religion as chiefly useful for preserving morals and supporting venerable institutions, as in fact the cement of the whole social structure'.[90] However viewed, those who seem to fit the kind of characteristics I have described were few in number, and they were not readily recognizable, at least before the 1830s. It was at that time that opposition from Evangelicals and Tractarians tended to unite them, and to help confer on them a separate identity.

But they had a pre-history of considerable length and distinction. Perhaps the initial decisive 'liberal' impulse was given by the French Catholic mathematician and philosopher René Descartes (1596–1650). He was concerned to discover a means of 'acquiring certainty of knowledge that would be independent of the various systems of thought, still largely inherited from the mediaeval period, which relied heavily on the appeal to tradition and authority'.[91] It was epoch-making to raise the possibility that reason had such independence, with 'its own perceived *a priori* certainties instead of those dictated by external authority', and that it was 'accountable for its conclusions only to the thinking subject himself'.[92] Descartes was not anti-religious. Far from it, for he was seeking after firmer rational grounds for belief in God. But his method entailed radical questioning and doubting in the absence of intrinsically certain propositions; and he opened the way to the Age of Reason in Western society and culture in which there was a steady but sure erosion of the hitherto sovereign and unchallenged place of Christian orthodoxy.

In England Lord Herbert of Cherbury (1583–1648) succinctly asserted a rational religious alternative to traditional Christian dogma. His cosmology consisted of a supreme Being and ruler over all things, the worship of whom comprised the practice of virtue, and who would mete out just rewards and punishments in the hereafter. Such beliefs did not require any divine revelation: they rested on the exercise of unaided reason which was innate in all human beings. It was a philosophy of life which was at the heart of the Deism which I have already considered, and of the Enlightenment which embraced most of the eighteenth century. Two strands in this progressive philosophical and cultural movement were particularly devastating for orthodox Christianity: the rise of historical consciousness and the critical historical method of study; and the collapse of a widely-accepted metaphysical framework for belief.

Christianity had always been acknowledged as grounded in history. There was biblical history; the life, death and resurrection of Christ; the life of the early church and the establishment of the canon of scripture; and the subsequent history of the church, including all the definitions of orthodox dogma. All of this was subject to scrutiny. But scrutiny of what sort, and with what pre-suppositions? For instance H. S. Reimarus (1694–1768) maintained that the Bible could and should be studied as a number of purely human documents, and that the events of the New Testament were capable of an entirely naturalistic, non-miraculous interpretation.

The undermining of the metaphysical outlook was facilitated by the eighteenth-century preoccupation with the problem of knowledge. David Hume (1711–76) reduced all cognition to single perceptions and thereby accepted that all human knowledge was subjective and even meaningless. He brought the British empiricist tradition to the height of scepticism; and his philosophy is reckoned by many philosophers as having eliminated the science of metaphysics. Immanuel Kant (1724–1804) insisted on both the subjectivity of human knowledge and the moral autonomy of man who is responsible, within his own sphere of subjectivity, for his own discernment and acceptance of what is intrinsically true and good. G. W. F. Hegel (1770–1831) took the argument further and maintained that rationality is of supreme and over-riding importance. Ludwig Feuerbach (1804–72) gave a final twist to this philosophical line of development, and suggested that religion could be explained in completely human terms. 'It is not that man is a finite projection of the Infinite Spirit. Rather, the infinite God is man's own projection of himself to form an infinite image of his own higher qualities, which are then worshipped as if they were the attributes of a separate celestial being. Man must reclaim his attributes of creativity, power and goodness, of which he has, as it were, robbed himself and sacrificed to the "God" he has himself created.'[93]

A further strand in the English Enlightenment, the development of science, was not in itself inimical to the Christian faith, but it con-tributed to the transformed philosophical, religious and cultural milieu of the nineteenth century. The church as a whole had never seen science as inherently antagonistic to the Christian faith, despite some notorious examples of resistance to 'scientific discoveries'. Indeed, even those archetypal Protestants, the Puritans, did not see the pursuit of science as incompatible with religious belief and life. 'Puritan devotionalism and Puritan utilitarianism positively encouraged and facilitated the prosecu-tion of scientific researches, and both Puritan and scientist looked forward to an improvement of man's estate as the reward of their respective labours.'[94] The conflict between 'science and religion' did not start to become evident in a serious way until the 1830s, or even the 1840s, when the 'progress of geology had created serious difficulties in the relationship of natural history to its larger implications in natural theology'.[95] But even then the extent and nature of the 'conflict' needs to be carefully examined. It is important to place the whole nineteenth-century debate within the natural theology tradition. Natural theology was concerned with the knowledge of God available from the contemplation of the natural world, as contrasted with revealed theology where doctrines concerning God are derived from God's revelation especially in and through the Bible. It had flourished in the late seventeenth and eighteenth centuries, when it had numbered among its scholarly advocates such scientific practitioners as John Ray, Thomas Burnet and Robert Boyle.[96]

All of these philosophical, cultural and scientific aspects of the European, and more particularly the English, Enlightenment provided the setting for the emergence of a distinctive brand of Church of England liberalism. In the late eighteenth century and early nineteenth century two 'Liberals' stand out: William Paley and the Revd Sydney Smith. Paley was the 'lucid and skilful author of a commonsensical theology',[97] most famously demonstrated in his watchmaker analogy for the argument from design. He represented the apex of the achievement and influence of natural theology, especially as expounded in his *Natural Theology* (1802). He had a utilitarian code of ethics which, at its simplest, affirmed that whatever is most expedient is right. But the most prominent, and the more popular and independent liberal cleric was Sydney Smith, who took his liberalism into politics as an ardent Whig and one of the chief contributors to that organ of the Whigs, the *Edinburgh Review*. He had a low opinion of his sacred calling, regarding it as merely one profession amongst others, and he most typically expressed his liberalism in attacks on the High Church and Evangelical parties in the church. But neither Paley nor Smith were isolated as theological pariahs by the more dogmatic High Churchmen and Evangelicals. For instance, A. M. C. Waterman has shown that Paley was associated at Cambridge with such Orthodox divines as Herbert Marsh and George Pretyman-Tomline in a so-called 'intellectual party', which was regarded as maintaining the cause of orthodoxy at the university.[98]

Liberalism started to assume a corporate form with perceived common characteristics with the assembling of its most distinguished representatives in the Fellowship of the Oriel College Common Room in Oxford in the second and third decades of the century. They were known as the Noetics because of their devotion to knowledge. 'They called everything in question; they appealed to first principles, and disallowed authority as a judge in intellectual matters.'[99] They were a highly intelligent group of academics, but even among that select company some were outstanding. The first place of honour among them must go to Edward Copleston, who was Provost of the College from 1814 to 1828. The years of his provostship 'were the golden age of Oriel, when it made its contribution to the late Georgian "Oxford renaissance" of scholarly study. It was said of the common room that it "stank of Logic" . . .'[100] Copleston was an inspiration to some of the younger men of the group, and he it was above all the others who 'schooled their thought to the chilly clarity which was its distinguishing mark'.[101] But he was 'not at all an original thinker, or in any sense a theological adventurer, and could fairly be classed as a High Churchman'.[102]

Then there was Richard Whately, afterwards Archbishop of Dublin, who stood a little apart in his views from the rest, and taught Newman to think for himself, and to rely upon himself. He was distinguished by his 'hard-headed trust in the all-sufficiency of reason', and as such was 'the very type of a "Noetic" . . . Religion, he was confident, needed a stiff infusion of the critical spirit. Party bias especially was an obstacle to truth.'[103] The others included Renn Dickson Hampden, who was to be the subject of the first pitched battle between the Tractarians and the Evangelicals on the one side, and the Liberals on the other side, when there was an unsuccessful attempt to prevent him being elected as Regius Professor of Divinity; John Davison and Baden Powell; and, most notably for the future of Anglican Liberalism, Thomas Arnold, afterwards Headmaster of Rugby. It is a poignant testimony to the convergence of different church parties in the 1820s, and the non-confrontational nature of different theologies at that time, especially as compared with the period after the mid-1830s, that John Keble and John Henry Newman were also members of this same Common Room and co-existed with the others in considerable harmony, and that a rigid High Churchman such as William Van Mildert had contacts with John Davison and Baden Powell. 'If there was a blurring of theological differences between High church and liberal churchmen in the 1820s, this can partly be explained by recognizing that such *Noetics* as Baden

Powell and Hampden were not then the obvious theological liberals that Tractarian rhetoric depicted them as in the 1830s. Polarization may have taken place in the 1830s, destroying an earlier theological consensus, but this was not a one-sided process. For if the future Tractarians moved in one direction after the cathartic experience of the Peel election in 1829, some *Noetics* moved no less far in the liberal direction.'[104]

Thomas Arnold published one of the clearest expositions of such a more advanced liberal view in the same year, 1833, which witnessed Keble's Assize Sermon and the launching of the Oxford Movement. In his *Principles of Church Reform* he set forth proposals that sent shudders through the Church of England. He declared the times to be critical and the situation dire. He was in despair about the existing condition of the established church; no human power, he considered, could save it. He viewed the church as the state in its religious aspect, in the Hookerian tradition, but not as Hooker had portrayed the relationship. For Arnold the state's officers actually performed a Christian service, and were even in their way Christian ministers, no less than the appointed clergy in the church. In extreme situations they should be empowered to discharge the duties of the accredited church ministers, including the administration of the sacraments. There should not be such a reliance in the church on the rigid and arbitrary distinction between the clergy and the laity. Arnold was not a profound thinker, nor influential theologically. He left his mark because of his forceful personality. He had a noble ideal 'to Christianize the nation, and introduce the principles of Christianity into men's social and civil relations'. He was the embodiment of his own declared conviction that Christianity is primarily a way of life, not a creed or confession or speculative system.

Arnold is of particular importance because he brought a liberal, or Broad Church, perspective out of the somewhat rarefied atmosphere of an Oxford Common Room, and from the circle of academics, poets and men of letters who cherished all that the term stood for, and engaged in endless debate over particular matters involving the application of such principles in the wider public arena. 'The name of Arnold is engraven on the public mind, if not as the first great Broad Churchman – Coleridge, Hampden, and Whately may claim precedence of him there – yet as the first English Churchman who by his aggressive personality, by his moral earnestness, and by his practical embodiment of his views in his conduct, made vivid to Englishmen the strong contrast between the religious views of Newman and Pusey and the broader views suggested by historical criticism and science.'[105] In his essay 'On the Right Interpretation and Understanding of the Scriptures', which was appended to the second volume of his sermons, he clearly, and to some convincingly, expressed the kind of 'liberal' views which were unacceptable to Evangelicals, High Churchmen and a host of others. He claimed for intellectual wisdom a power and right to make judgments about all questions of science, of history, and of criticism according to her own general laws; and he asserted that the decisions reached on these matters through the application of the intellect may not legitimately be disputed by an appeal to the higher power of spiritual wisdom. He therefore logically defined an anti-rationalist as 'one who is afraid to trust himself in the pursuit of truth, and who talks of the danger, perhaps of the profaneness of an enquiry, though its subject be strictly within the province of the intellect'.[106]

Arnold was vehemently attacked in his lifetime for the views he propagated, but even his fierce opponents generally acknowledged the high quality of his character and life. 'When he died at the early age of forty-seven his fellow-countrymen knew that a man of the finest moral grain had passed from their midst.'[107]

Of equal importance to Arnold in the short and long term development of liberal thought were Jeremy Bentham and Samuel Taylor Coleridge. Bentham contributed to it and Coleridge introduced a new dimension to religion and political thought and applied a brake to the possible blatant rationalism inherent in much of the liberal thought of his day. Bentham was the leading philosophical radical of his day, and the founder of Utilitarianism. He championed the view that the supreme end of society was to achieve the greatest happiness of the greatest number. It resulted in the 'permeation of the public mind with a feeling of social responsibility. Men, it was now realized, possess a natural solidarity, of which the body politic, incorporating and articulating the community's reason and conscience, is alike the expression and ultimate safeguard.' Few people who were in any way in touch with the movements of thought of this turbulent age remained unaffected by this Benthamite perspective on life. And this included the religious thought, not only of philosophers and theologians but of a wide circle of people throughout society. 'Such ideas could not but have their effect upon religious opinion. The day of individualism, rationalistic or pietistic, was passing, making possible a recovery of the idea of the Church as a collective entity.'[108] The Benthamite philosophy paved the way for various other philosophical, political and religious systems and trends. It was fundamental to the thinking of F. D. Maurice and the Christian Socialists; it was at the centre of the thinking of John Stuart Mill.

It was Mill who described Coleridge as one of 'the two great seminal minds of England of their age', the other being Jeremy Bentham. He judged that by Bentham 'beyond all others men have been led to ask themselves in regard to any ancient or received opinion, Is it true? and by Coleridge, What is the meaning of it?'[109] Coleridge brought to his thinking the disposition and outlook of a poet, critic and philosopher who was able to atune himself to the essential ideals of a new age of visionary romanticism. He is not renowned for his logical thinking or orderliness of presentation. Indeed his writings are bewilderingly unsystematic, and it is difficult to discern the complex interwoven threads of his philosophy. But what is clear is his stress on the importance of experience rather than argument as a basis of faith. 'The authority of Christianity is to be seen not in logical demonstration, the procedures of which are inapplicable in this realm, but in its power to meet the needs of our humanity. And of this each must judge for himself.'[110] Spiritual truth is distinctive and can only be comprehended through the totality of human experience: the reason and the emotions are involved. He was the forerunner of theories of existentialism, but in his case it was essentially a Christian existentialism, for he was convinced of the reality of God as a Being with whom human beings can hold communion. Such an emphasis was a powerful counterpoise to the rationalistic liberalism of his day, and of the generations which lay ahead.

Local church worship, witness and life

Outwardly, England was still a Christian country in the period 1791 to 1833 and any manifestation of atheism was rare. But there was a growth of indifference and 'secularism'; and while 'no new faiths had yet established themselves in Britain, scholars were beginning to publish serious work on the "foreign" religions of Islam, Buddhism and Hinduism which were being studied through "the science of religion".'[111] England had never been a uniformly and unanimously Christian country, with all, or almost all, the population participating in public worship; but in this era of revolution, rapid industrial and social change, and major political transformations, new ideologies which were antipathetic to the Christian faith were being more openly espoused than probably at any time in the past; and the church was probably more detached from a mass of the people than in any former age.

The single most prominent sector of the population in this cauldron of change was the 'working class'. And here the key factor was variation; no simple generalization does justice to the evidence.

> The whole picture of working-class religion – or irreligion – is confused. It used to be thought that the urban working classes *en masse* were alienated from or at best indifferent to religion, while the country labourer remained a faithful member of church or chapel. However, it is now generally agreed that this is too simplistic a view. Working-class religiousness or lack of it varied widely in different parts of Britain; between town and town, and between one rural area and another, rather than between town and country. Also significant in religious terms were socio-economic differences within the working class itself, particularly in the cities.'[112]

There is also the added complication of defining religiousness, let alone Christian orthodoxy. Throughout much of the working class subculture religious belief consisted of little more than a practical moral code, the essence of which was mutual assistance and 'respectable' behaviour; and it was intermingled with semi-pagan or secular values with no very distinct Christian content.

Even in heavily industrialized, socially deprived, areas it is clear that the church was sometimes effective, as in Oldham and Saddleworth where there were obvious signs of life and vitality in the face of adverse and potentially depressing circumstances. 'Far from being ineffectual or marginalized, the local churches were extremely vigorous institutions, growing steadily in absolute size, commanding the active support of a substantial minority of the population, and exercising considerable influence over most of the remainder.'[113] It is not clear to what extent this success story was due to special elements in the local situation and must be regarded as atypical; but at least 'the experience of the Established Church in these two districts does provide a corrective to the simplistic assumption that the irrationalities of the "unreformed" ecclesiastical system were necessarily damaging to its pastoral effectiveness.'[114] Another example was the Stroud region of Gloucestershire, where, despite the population being composed mainly of poor day labourers employed in the woollen trade, there was a movement to refurbish parish churches, so that 'the Establishment achieved parity with the Dissenters'.[115]

Also, 'religiosity' was not confined to those who attended church or chapel. It 'would be wrong to assume that all those working-class men and women who seldom if ever attended a place of worship were irreligious. Many of them were religious in their own way, but this was not necessarily an orthodox way.'[116] There was also a substratum of popular beliefs which occasionally surfaced in the form of unorthodox or sectarian movements. These operated within society, and more especially among the working class, in a way which was beyond and independent of any activity, successful or otherwise, of the institutional church. 'Common people continued to experience visions, to detect forewarnings and judgments, and to condemn the behaviour of others through interpretations of natural signs. In some instances, as in the cases of the Southcottians and the Primitive Methodists, these beliefs and practices came within the auspices of institutionalized religion. When this occurred prophecy had achieved another goal. United by a distinctive credo, these new groups challenged established religion by providing common people with a mode of self-expression.'[117]

Semi-magical views and impulses were present all the time in society, and contributed to a 'folk religion' which was deeply embedded, especially in the working-class culture. Perhaps they represented a residual element, or redefinition of the former beliefs in astrology, witchcraft, magical healing, divination, ancient prophecies, ghosts and fairies which Keith Thomas so ably depicted and analysed as a constituent part of the English religious scene in the sixteenth and seventeenth centuries.

Popular belief in the supernatural took many forms. In the growing new towns the amalgam of 'religion', 'magic' and varieties of 'superstition', to which I have previously drawn attention, was less evident than in rural communities, which were still the setting for the lives of most of the population. But whether in city, town or village there remained an underlying belief in God, or at least in some, often ill-defined, supernatural power. In its most general and vague guise 'it was a simple, unintellectual type of neo-Platonism: all forms of life are animated by a spirit, and there is an essential oneness of all God's creatures. Further, there is no clear distinction between matter and spirit: the earth is not an inanimate mass but is deemed to be alive, and the universe is peopled by a hierarchy of spirits.'[118] There was an almost universal acceptance that the world is thoroughly subject to invisible spiritual influences and in the quiet of their homes or the solitude of their own personal lives this made the claims of conjurors, magicians and astrologers entirely credible to a great number of people who were not committed to orthodox Christian belief. There is considerable evidence of the persistence of such folk religion. 'Those who are not in daily intercourse with the peasantry', it was reported from Lincolnshire in 1856, 'can hardly be made to believe or comprehend the hold that charms, witchcraft, wise men and other relics of heathendom have upon the people.'[119] It manifested itself in a multitude of ways, for example in astrology, which persisted as a vital component of folk-medicine, with particular parts of the body being thought to be under the rule of different signs of the zodiac, so that treatment was directly linked to the stars.

Much of this folk culture was part of an oral tradition, but there were important exceptions. Almanacs, chapbooks and street ballads were immensely popular, and they reflected the values and the interests of labouring people. 'The almanac was perhaps the most popular book in England for over three and a half centuries, and together with the Bible was the work most likely to be found in a cottage home. Moore's *Almanack*, it was noted in 1810 by an observer in Reading, "may be found not only in every house in the town but also in every one in the neighbourhood and partakes nearly of the same degree of belief in its prognostications as the Bible itself".'[120] Such almanacs contained a calendar, showing the days and weeks of each month and indicating the church festivals; a section giving general astronomical information for the year; a table showing the daily position of the stars; and, lastly, a forecast of events for the coming year.

Alongside almanacs were a vast number and variety of chapbooks, or penny histories, as they were sometimes called. 'They were sold by chapmen (pedlars) at a price of 1d to 6d, and were small, paper-covered booklets, embellished with a crude, and sometimes highly coloured woodcut illustration. The type was of all styles and sizes, the paper was thick and rough, and each production had a vigour and individuality of its own. The contents were seldom original, and as befitted folk art the authorship was anonymous.'[121] They contained a miscellaneous selection of romances, the often somewhat lurid lives and executions of criminals, songs and jests, which were frequently bawdy; comments on fortune-telling, demonology, witchcraft, and the world of spirits; advice on household and personal matters, including sex; articles on the various ramifications of love, such as seduction, elopement and separation, as well as marriage and the family; and printed or reprinted sermons, prophecies, signs and wonders. 'In cities, especially London, street literature included all forms of the chapbook, as well as ballads, broadsheets and handbills. At this point urban and rural folklore were very close together.'[122]

The subterranean, but quite frequently visible, amalgam of beliefs represented by all these forms of 'religion', 'magic' and 'folk religion' also opened a large number of people to the influence of 'popular, largely self-educated, adventist millenarians'. These were dogmatic enthusiasts, condemned by the more opulent and educated classes as 'fanatics and imposters, and by historians as cranks and the lunatic fringe'. Their beliefs 'were derived from a literal, eclectic interpretation of the prophetic scriptures, and a divine revelation vouchsafed to them directly. A simplicity, often crudity, seemed to mark their mentality, for their reliance on the supernatural enabled them to dispense with many of the limitations imposed by logic and reason.'[123]

7

Dissenters and Roman Catholics:
The Road to Emancipation

The period from 1791 to 1833 was a time of immense change and activity for Dissenters and Roman Catholics. We have already noted that by the last quarter of the eighteenth century the revival had started to revitalize certain parts of the Dissenting denominations. In retrospect it can be seen that this was the prelude to renewal and advance in the nineteenth century. It is against the background of the rapid political, constitutional, economic and social changes already outlined in the previous chapter that we must view the stirrings within the ranks of Dissent.

The overall expansion of Dissent was remarkable.

> The chief characteristic of nineteenth-century religion was Evangelicalism, the belief that every man and woman was heir to the sin of Adam and destined to spend eternity in hell unless justified by faith, through the personal experience called conversion, in the sacrifice which Christ had made on his or her behalf on the cross at Calvary. Instead of being damned to suffer eternal torment in the fires of hell, those men and women who experienced conversion believed that they would, after death, enjoy everlasting bliss in heaven. A substantial minority of Anglicans subscribed to the Evangelical version of Christianity in the first half of the nineteenth century, but the influence of Evangelicalism on the lives of the English and Welsh peoples was mediated primarily through the channels of the Baptists, the Congregationalists, and the Methodists: the Dissenters.[1]

For Protestant Dissent 'the late eighteenth century represented the crucial stage in its development; the process of change from contemptible insignificance to the full flower of Victorian Nonconformity'.[2]

This surge forward appears to a large extent to have been at the expense of the established church, not primarily because it entailed poaching members from the Church of England, but because Dissent made advances where the Church of England did not. This is indicated statistically. In comparison with the decline of Anglicanism relative to the increase in the population, which we have already considered, the Dissenting denominations were making progress in the early nineteenth century. Thus, the Methodist churches saw a rise in membership from 143,311 in 1811 to 288,182 in 1831. The Congregational connexion grew from 35,000 members in 1800 to 127,000 in 1837, and in the same period the two main Baptist denominations grew from 27,000 to just under 100,000.[3] Whereas in 1773 a list compiled by the Baptist pastor Josiah Thompson shows 1,685 Nonconformist congregations in England, including Monmouthshire, the 1851 census showed 17,019. This represented not only a massive actual numerical growth but also a significant improvement as a percentage of the total population in a period of population explosion. Taking a wide perspective, it was estimated in the list of Dissenting congregations drawn up by Dr John Evans in 1715–1718 that Nonconformists in England, including Monmouthshire, represented 6.21% of the population. By 1851 this had leapt to 17.02%.[4]

The second half of the eighteenth century had seen the emergence of a new variety of Protestant Dissent, subsequently termed the New Dissent, when the original Dissenting tradition reached a parting of the ways. This comprised the Congregationalists, Particular Baptists and the New Connexion General Baptists. The growth in the number of Dissenters in the late eighteenth century and on into much of the nineteenth century was among these denominations, and not among the Quakers, the majority of General Baptists, the Presbyterians and the Unitarians, who constituted the bulk of the Old Dissent. The denominations of the Old Dissent continued to display many of the somewhat uninspiring trends apparent in the Dissenting tradition before its fragmentation between 1719 and 1770; and they stagnated or actually declined during the late eighteenth and early nineteenth centuries, when the New Dissent was growing rapidly.

The 1851 religious census gave details of the various ways in which Nonconformity had progressed, and this greatly alarmed Church of England members. Out of a total population for England and Wales, disclosed by the census as 17,927,609, those attending churches on 30 March 1851 were stated as: Church of England, 5,292,551; the main Protestant Dissenting Churches (Presbyterian, Methodist, Congregationalist, Baptist), 4,536,264; and Roman Catholics, 383,630. In the East and North Ridings, in Lincolnshire and Bedfordshire the Dissenters had established a long lead over the Church of England, and they were ahead in Huntingdonshire; while they were within striking distance of drawing level in Northamptonshire, Buckinghamshire and Norfolk.[5] With the exception of Norfolk, these were all great enclosure areas, and this supports the assertion made in the last chapter that the Church of England seriously lost influence in the countryside, especially from the 1790s onwards. The areas of Dissenting strength were also great revival territories, and those denominations which showed the most growth were the ones which had responded most readily to the tide of revival.

The geographical distribution of Nonconformity in 1851, which indicated what had taken place in the period 1791 to 1833, was part of a clear socio-economic pattern.

The lowest levels of attendance were recorded in two very different types of area: the poorer parts of large cities, where crowded living conditions and poverty proved to be inimical to religion, and, at the other extreme, sparsely populated mountainous border regions. The correlation between prosperity and religious observance was especially noticeable in London. Four districts in the East End had estimated percentages of worshippers of less than 20% – Shoreditch (15.3), St George-in-the-East (16.1), Bethnal Green (18.7), Poplar (19.5), whereas prosperous low-density areas produced estimates two or three times as great: Hampstead 48.9%, Wandsworth 45.2, Hackney 39.7.[6]

It appears that there was a distinct change in the socio-economic pattern of Dissent in the course of the eighteenth century and the early nineteenth century. In the early eighteenth century Dissent as a whole was proportionately stronger in large towns and cities, which, it must be recalled, were still not 'large' in nineteenth-century terms, than in the countryside. In its initial phase Methodism was also based largely on the expanding towns, and had considerable success in such centres as Bristol and Newcastle. But, when the scale of urban development increased this was reversed. 'If industrialization, in its early stages, facilitated the growth of Dissent, large-scale urbanization frustrated it.'[7] This may well be due to the absence in the new urban industrial areas of those community features previously identified as conducive to revivalism. These were present in the countryside and in the small industrial villages or towns which dominated English social and economic life in the first three-quarters of the eighteenth century, but they did not characterize the larger, more anomic, urban conglomerates of late eighteenth- and early nineteenth-century England. In the former communities there had also been 'a residual attachment to Christianity which the Church of England fostered but could not always exploit to its own advantage, a sense of helplessness that derived from man's reliance on the vagaries of the seasons and his exposure to sudden catastrophes such as mine explosions or cholera epidemics, and the geographical and cultural isolation which meant that both superstitious and Evangelical explanations of human fate were widely accepted and not seriously challenged'.[8] Such social and sociological factors also help to explain why the phenomenal expansion of Nonconformity in the early decades of the nineteenth century 'took place in the countryside, the industrial villages, and the small and medium-sized towns of England and Wales where either language, the absence of landlord influence, the presence of trade and industry, or its own antiquated parochial structure undermined the influence of the Church of England, but where large-scale urbanization had not yet rendered Christianity either psychologically unnecessary or socially irrelevant'.[9]

The exceptional prosperity of Dissent was aided by the adoption of the Methodist practice of itinerant evangelism, and by the Sunday school movement. Although itinerancy had been employed since the seventeenth century, its use had been unmethodical and erratic. For the majority of Dissenting congregations it was not until the era of conflict with Revolutionary France that the age of the field preacher dawned. 'As the practice began to spread during the 1790s the gains resulting from its application were immediate and obvious. Long before the defeat of Napoleon in 1815 it had enabled Dissent to penetrate deeply into the fabric of rural society, especially in areas where Methodism was weak.'[10]

A high proportion of Nonconformists appear to have been converted while they were teenagers, and, despite quite severe questioning of the effectiveness of Sunday schools as recruitment agencies for church or chapel, it does seem that they played a part in at least helping some children of existing chapel-goers to commit themselves to the same faith and chapel membership which their parents so valued.[11]

The outstanding escalation of Nonconformist numbers was achieved in spite of continuing restrictions placed upon individual Nonconformists, and upon them as corporate bodies. The Dissenting denominations as a whole were confined in what they could do by the provisions of the Test and Corporation Acts. The restraints were symbolic as well as actually burdensome, for they marked them out as second-class religious citizens. Towards the end of the eighteenth century three attempts were made to put an end to this disabling legislation; and they all failed. Strong opposition ensured the defeat of the first Bill, introduced in March 1787; and likewise with the second attempt to effect a repeal in 1788, although this time the majority was reduced. In 1790 Charles Fox appeared as a champion of the Dissenting cause, but again the attempt at reform was unsuccessful. By then there was the complication of Dissenters being accused of too strongly favouring the French Revolution. This was probably a view overmuch influenced by the radicalism of Richard Price and Joseph Priestley and the small number of Dissenters who rallied round them or took a similar stance on political issues. In fact many Dissenters were apolitical, and it is noticeable that in the 1790 agitation against the Test Acts the Independents and the Baptists disassociated themselves from Priestley and his followers because of their attacks on the Church of England.

Although Parliament became more tolerant, in that it routinely suspended the operation of the Test and Corporation Acts by annual Toleration Acts, the Dissenters continued to labour under severe restraints. The 'badges of their inferiority were everywhere obvious. They suffered disabilities at the most delicate occasions of life, at birth, marriage, and death.'[12] They had to baptize their children according to the rites of the Church of England if they wished to register their births. The conscientious refused to submit; and the Baptists as a whole, who rejected the practice of infant baptism, could not. Likewise, many of the Dissenters rejected in principle observances which they were obliged to accept if they wished to be married in accordance with the only officially sanctioned procedure; they were often unwilling to bow to the authority of the church in this or any other matter. Even in death they were not permitted to acquire a burying place in the local graveyard unless they complied with the ceremonial of the established church.

Educational limitations were a further cause of constant frustration for all Dissenters, and a severe barrier to career advancement. Only if they were prepared to conform to the Church of England and subscribe to the Thirty-Nine Articles could they enter Oxford; and Cambridge, although it allowed them to matriculate without religious tests, required such subscription before degrees could be taken. As the College of Physicians and Surgeons admitted only university graduates, and the Inns of Court lengthened their bar courses from three to five years for those lacking university degrees, they were handicapped in professional life. It was fortunate for the Dissenters that Scotland did not apply religious tests; and many promising children of Dissenters ended up at a university north of the border.

Perhaps Dissenters resented most strongly those civil disabilities which excluded them from public life. The Test Act of 1673 effectively disqualified them from holding civil and military offices under the crown. Annual Indemnity Acts were passed after 1727 to remove the penalties of occasional conformity, but these were only of benefit to those Dissenters who did not, out of conscience, reject the church sacraments.

Then there was the matter of church rates. To help meet expenditure on the fabric and running costs of the parish church a church rate was levied on all ratepayers. Until the second decade of the nineteenth century this had been regarded as an irritant, but it had rarely been a source of severe conflict. By the 1830s there was a growing protest against the imposition of what was by then seen as an unwarrantable charge when applied to Dissenters. The assault was led by the Quakers, who had opposed the system throughout the eighteenth century and sometimes refused to make payment. In the second quarter of the nineteenth century they were gradually joined by members of the old Dissenting bodies and by many Methodists. As the nineteenth century progressed it was to become a rallying cause for Nonconformity as a whole.

But the passion of Dissenters was aroused far more by the political stance of the established church. 'The outcry over church rates served to stoke the fires of anti-clericalism in the towns; but it was the church's inflexible attitude to the reform question which caused the flames to leap highest.'[13] The bishops were almost unanimously resistant to any concessions to Nonconformity; and the hesitancy with which any relaxation of Dissenting disabilities were conceded caused frustration and annoyance to outweighed any gratitude.

Under pressure from some of the bishops, Lord Sidmouth introduced a bill in the House of Lords in 1811 to restrict itinerant preaching. Although it was intended merely as a means of controlling such preaching, for example by 'those considered too ignorant, too young or too dangerous to be allowed to travel the country peddling their own religious convictions', and was designed simply 'to prevent Dissenting preachers from claiming exemption from civil office and military service, the bill struck at the heart of undenominational itinerant preaching and the entire Methodist connexional system. It was also one of the great attempts to defend the Church of England by legislating against its rivals. Revealingly, Churchmen, not politicians, were the driving force behind the measure.'[14] Although the bill was lost without a division, largely as a consequence of a highly organized Dissenting and Methodist campaign of opposition, on a scale which outdid even the anti-slavery campaign, it helped to reinforce the Nonconformist perception of the Church of England as a resolutely and implacably conservative, and indeed reactionary body.

A certain degree of religious toleration was granted in 1812, when the Toleration Act legalized itinerant preaching and permitted evangelistic work. The new law also allowed twenty people, instead of the previous five, to gather for worship in unregistered meeting-houses. It was greeted with acclaim, although it did little more than legalize what the Dissenters had long practised. In the following year a further concession was made, when a bill was carried granting toleration to the Unitarians.

The Dissenting polemicists published prolifically against the Test Acts in the 1820s. The campaign was directed by the United Committee, under the guidance of the Dissenting Deputies, and its official organ was the *Test Act Reporter*. The Committee effectively mobilized 1,500 ministers to petition against the Test Acts; it won the support of the Corporation of London; and it obtained pledges favouring repeal from thirty Members of Parliament. It supplied Parliament with statistical and legal information; and it appointed a sub-committee of lawyers to draft the repeal bill. It was all reminiscent of the Clapham Sect and the Hackney Phalanx, and showed what organized, concerted action could achieve. It was a moment of triumph when, in 1828, the Acts were repealed, for it was an open abandonment of the principle that membership of the established, state church was a prerequisite for full citizenship under the British constitution.

Although the United Committee, and many individual Dissenters throughout the country enthusiastically celebrated their victory, they were determined to continue to work for religious liberty by seeking relief for Roman Catholics. Since the days of Priestley many Dissenters had been convinced that their own freedom should be sought in conjunction with that of the Jews and the Catholics. They might regard Catholicism as a dangerous superstition, but nevertheless they could not refuse to demand for Catholics what had been granted to them. The Unitarians took the initiative and were in the forefront of a campaign for the emancipation of the Catholics; Dissenters in Manchester demonstrated, and declared their unity on the Catholic question; and Dissenting ministers in London petitioned Parliament in favour of Catholic relief.

With the passing of the Catholic Emancipation Act of 1829, it appeared that even further toleration might be possible. But the limit had been reached for the time being. The whole issue had divided families and broken the warmest friendships. During the debates 'the three royal dukes, Clarence, Cumberland, and Sussex, got up one after another and attacked each other . . . very vehemently,' Greville reported, 'and they used toward each other language that nobody else could have ventured to employ, so it was a very droll scene.'[15] When Robert Grant, a member of the Clapham Sect, introduced a bill in Parliament in 1830 to emancipate the Jews, he was fiercely opposed. Churchmen were resolute in their resistance to any additional concessions. The Tories contended that freedom for the Jews would destroy the Christian constitution; and they carried the House with them. The Jewish relief bill was defeated on its second reading.

Millenarianism, the Catholic Apostolic Church, Brethrenism and Swedenborgianism.

In the meantime, in parallel with all this political activity, the Dissenting denominations were stirred by a widespread upsurge of millenarianism, the appearance of 'pentecostal-type' phenomena, and the teaching of the Irvingites and the Brethren.

Many Christians, and especially evangelicals in both the Church of England and among the Dissenting denominations, moved into the nineteenth century convinced that the latter days were beginning, and that the end of the world was not far off.[16] The French wars and the general high-pitched nature of life in those tense, eventful and traumatic years stimulated prophetic views. Millenarianism was not a novel feature in the churches in general, or among the evangelicals.[17] During the eighteenth century it had been a common preoccupation of intellectuals, and not a fanatical aberration of a few religious enthusiasts, or of social outcasts. In the Enlightenment era belief in a future state of unblemished happiness on earth took the form of postmillennialism – the view that the second coming of Christ would not take place until after the millennium. 'There would therefore be no sharp break from preceding history. Rather, the millennium would be the result of gradual improvement – a belief that shaded into the idea of progress.'[18] Evangelicals were not unanimous on the matter, but the main eschatological thrust among them was in the postmillennial direction. Most of them were persuaded that the future epoch of peace and glory would supersede persistent mission. Such a conviction was shared by William Carey, the founders of the London Missionary Society in 1795, and by John Venn, Thomas Scott, Richard Cecil and other evangelicals around the turn of the century.[19] The novel feature of early nineteenth-century eschatology was the coming into prominence of a premillennial inter-pretation – that Christ will return before the millennium – with its heightened sense of expectation and urgency at the prospect of the imminence of Christ's appearance in splendour and judgment.

James Hatley Frere was the seminal influence in drawing the attention of evangelicals and others to this alternative prophetic interpretation in his work *A Combined View of the Prophecies of Daniel, Esdras, and St John* (1815). But he treated the second coming as a metaphor – 'some extraordinary manifestation of the power of Christ'.[20] This spiritual, and not literal, reading of future events was initially adopted by Edward Irving; but under the influence of the book *The Coming of Messiah in Glory and Majesty*, by the Chilean Jesuit 'Ben-Ezra', which he trans-lated and published in 1827, he concluded that Christ would return in person. It was at that stage that there was a decisive re-emergence of the premillennialist tradition.

Premillennialism both prompted and was also promoted by a grow-ing concern for the conversion of the Jews, with the attendant focus on the prophecies surrounding the destiny of God's chosen people. The interdenominational London Society for Promoting Christianity among the Jews had been founded in 1809, and then reconstituted as an Anglican organization in 1815, and its prime advocate, Lewis Way, had been active in spreading premillennialist views. Most notably, he con-vinced Henry Drummond, a banker and Member of Parliament, of the truth and importance of the doctrine, and he became a Vice-President of the Jews' Society in 1823. During Advent 1826, Drummond assembled about twenty people, including Way and Irving, at his country estate, Albury Park in Surrey, and thus initiated a series of influential annual conferences on prophecy which continued until 1830.

It was in these years that Edward Irving was at the zenith of his great reputation.[21] In 1822 he had been appointed minister of the Caledonian Presbyterian chapel in London. His preaching attracted much attention and drew large congregations. Crowds from the highest classes of society thronged the modest place of worship where previously only a small group of Scots had gathered for worship. 'When he had been in London merely six months success came to him with almost hurricane force and in tidal wave proportions.'[22] The chapel would hold some five hundred people, but there was tumult as twice and thrice that number sought entrance. Almost any Sunday the crush of people included such notables as Zachary Macaulay, Charles Lamb, William Hazlitt, Thomas De Quincey, S. T. Coleridge, and other literary figures who were prominent at the time although little known now. De Quincey declared him to be 'by many degrees the greatest actor of our times', and Thomas Carlyle judged him 'the freest, bravest, brotherliest human soul mine ever came in contact with'.[23]

Irving shared the platforms and gained the confidence of the evangelicals in general, and he took a lead in the prophetic studies which were so dear to so many of them. But he did not share the prevailing postmillenial view. He despised a belief which 'fitted in with liberal utopianism and secular enlightenment rationalism, the hope for the realisation of a world which was happy as well as holy'.[24] He dismissed postmillenialism as the mere optimism of the philosophers, the ultimate ideal of triumphant arminianism, and the fathering upon the scriptures of the optimism of the German and French infidels. 'Where post-millennial Adventism was gradualist and optimistic, in harmony with ideas of *laissez-faire* and of material, mental and moral progress, Irving's premillennialism was catastrophic and pessimistic, seeing both the world and the churches as so lost that only Christ's Second Coming could redeem them. It was not human effort, not societies run by committees of gentlemen who would convert the earth with subscription lists and sermons. The earth would be converted by Christ Himself returning, in the Second Coming. This wicked world would be rendered Christian not by Christians but by Christ, in his Second Coming to an unconverted world.'[25]

Then, to add to the drama, around 1830 there appeared in Irving's congregation what those concerned regarded as manifestations of the Spirit of God: healings, speaking in tongues and the claim of some to be prophets. Irving did not experience any of these charismatic gifts himself, yet he did not discourage them, and was the leader of the Christian community in which they played a central part. The Presbytery became alarmed, and finally dismissed him. He went forth, but not alone, for some eight hundred people went with him. They soon constituted themselves into a new body which eventually became known as The Catholic Apostolic Church. While all this was taking place Irving strayed into heresies regarding the nature of Christ's humanity. He was excommunicated by the Church of Scotland; his popularity evaporated among many of his former admirers; and evangelicals were divided in their attitudes and responses to the whole turn of events.

The Plymouth Brethren also originated, to some extent, as a result of resurgent millenarianism.[26] A small group of evangelicals in Dublin rejected all church order and outward forms and longed for a perfect church, free from such organizational restrictions. In 1827 they united to express the principle that anyone may celebrate the Lord's Supper or preach. The name was appended when the powerful Irish ex-Anglican clergyman, J. N. Darby, a leader of the new movement, went to Plymouth in 1830. Plymouth Brethrenism rapidly exerted a significant influence. It drew away some evangelicals from their various existing denominations, especially the Church of England, largely because of the appealing intensive study of the Bible which was a feature of the new denomination. In particular Brethrenism developed distinctive futurist views of unfulfilled prophecy which caused much questioning in evangelical circles.

Of a very different type were the Swedenborgians. They owed their origin to the Swedish mystic and scientist Emanuel Swedenborg, who claimed to have experienced two visions of Christ in 1744 and 1745 in which it was revealed to him that Christ would return to earth to establish the church of the New Jerusalem in 1757. He attested that 'the Lord manifested himself before me to see the heavens and the hells, and also to converse with angels and spirits, and this now continually for many years.'[27] Under the leadership of John Clowes, the rector of St John's, Deansgate, Manchester, the Swedenborgians argued that the Bible should not be taken literally, but interpreted spiritually; they rejected the doctrine of the Trinity; and they ridiculed orthodox teaching on the atonement. They had limited success, but they did win the support of a few predominantly working-class communities in Lancashire and Yorkshire.

In this period of religious experimentation, somewhat reminiscent of the mid-seventeenth century period of the Interregnum, there were other millennialist prophets and prophetesses who also played their dramatic part on the stage of history and then passed into oblivion to remain objects of curiosity for future historians, sociologists, psychiatrists and those interested in 'fringe' religion. Of such were Richard Brothers, who regarded himself as no ordinary prophet, but rather as the Prince of the Hebrews and nephew of the Almighty, none other than a descendant of King David through James the brother of Jesus; and, more bizarre still, Joanna Southcott, to whom it was revealed in a vision that she was the 'woman clothed with the sun', spoken of in Revelation 12.1. She was the authoress of over sixty-five books of prophecies, and she had a very considerable following. It was also the age of that visionary genius, the poet and artist William Blake.[28] Perhaps, like the disturbed period of the Interregnum, when the whole earth appeared to be moved by world-shattering events, and strange philosophies and religious beliefs abounded, this period of equivalent cosmic upheaval helped to arouse latent spiritual sensitivities, and to fructify those expressions of religious belief which do not so readily emerge and become articulated in more stable times. It was not just a matter of rapid and dramatic political, constitutional, economic and social changes, but rather the cumulative effect of these in producing 'wide-spread feelings of anxiety and insecurity arising out of the stresses and strains of the time. Sudden, unexpected social change (amounting sometimes to a disaster), we may argue, includes personal disorganization and, in some cases, mental upset. The individual's sense of society and his identity in it is destroyed, and old beliefs do not provide a convincing explanation of what is happening to him. Anxiety and feelings of meaninglessness result; and millenarian beliefs provide both an explanation of the present state of things and an indication of how it will be resolved.'[29]

In the meantime the Methodists were rapidly becoming the main Dissenting denomination. But they were not immune from the kind of highly charged forms of religiosity which abounded at that time. Their growth was accompanied by painful secessions and much travail as they experienced the creative yet divisive effects of intense religious experienced in the form of revivals.

The Methodists

In 1791 the Wesleyan Methodist membership was announced in Conference to be 72,476, and this did not include a great number of hearers and helpers or those abroad. By 1800 this had risen to 90,619, and thirty years later it had almost trebled, to 248,592. In contrast to the established church, this represented an increase from 0.85 to 1.53% of the population.

But the two generations after the death of John Wesley in 1791 also witnessed devastating fragmentation. 'With the important exception of doctrines concerning the church and the ministry, Wesleyan divisions were rarely attributed to theological disagreement. The teachings of Wesley were upheld in all quarters and the spiritual pilgrimage from the conviction of sin to entire sanctification possessed the same meaning for each group.'[30] The troubles were largely to do with organizational issues: with dissension over leadership, and the appropriate form of government and oversight for a large, complex and expanding denomination; with differences of opinion over what adjustments were necessary as the new denomination became increasingly independent and separate from the Church of England; and with tension over the place of revivalism, and all it entailed in terms of the freedom of the Spirit, in relation to formalism and ordered structures.

The leadership of John Wesley had been crucial from the first days of Methodism. By his legal 'Deed of Declaration', lodged in the Court of Chancery in 1784, he had provided for the Methodist societies to be placed in the hands of a Methodist Conference consisting of one hundred specified men, and he had made that Conference his successor, with power to fill up its ranks as death diminished them. The body became known as the 'Legal Hundred'. It was a device whereby 'he formed the Methodist Societies into an *ecclesiola in ecclesia*, and gave it a concretely historical existence and constitution'.[31] But this was not a suitable body to exercise the kind of control and supervision which was needed. An assembly which met for not more than three weeks in the year, with a President who was changed annually, was not able to govern a large and growing community. And it was large. It was clear that Methodism by then was of such a size and complexity that it could not continue as a monarchy. But what form should its governance take? The 'Bishops Plan', drawn up by a number of preachers, including Thomas Coke, John Pawson, Henry Moore, S. Bradburn and Adam Clarke, returned to the proposal for grafting on to Methodism a semi-episcopal hierarchy of superintendents who should ordain priests and deacons; but it was rejected by Conference in 1794. When, in 1795, 'Bradburn returned with a further plan for "Travelling Bishops" it was shouted down by a general cry of "down with the bishops!" The Legal Hundred associated themselves firmly with the remainder of Conference in their refusal to concentrate power into the hands of a few of their members.'[32]

An associated issue was the relationship between preachers and the Methodist laity. This came to a head in 1791 at Redruth, in Cornwall, where a group of about fifty leading laymen proposed a more equitable Methodist polity which entailed the end of the Legal Hundred and a greater measure of self-government for circuits and societies.

Then there was the matter of the administration of the sacraments.

There was open disagreement as to whether administration should be limited to those preachers who were ordained by Wesley, or whether it was to 'follow the openings of divine providence', and be permissable for preachers as a whole to fulfil this function. At the Conference of 1792 it was decided by lot, which fell in favour of a more restricted power of administration.

Lastly, in this cluster of related issues, there was the unresolved question of whether services should be allowed at times coincidental with Church of England services. A decision was reached in the form of the 1795 Plan of Pacification, whereby responsibility was thrown on the societies themselves. It was a further step in severing Methodism from the Church of England.

The rumblings of discontent among the Methodists over these various matters found expression in the life, teaching and ministry of Alexander Kilham. He was dissatisfied with the amount of control at all levels which was given to the laity; he was 'the first of a succession of rebel preachers associated with lay demands'.[33] He thought it was unsatisfactory to rely on the oversight of the preachers by the preachers. It gave inadequate protection to the laity. He recommended, some might say demanded, lay representation in all official bodies, including Conference. This was a period of actual or latent Jacobinism, when radical political views were being discussed openly, and when the established church as well as the state felt very much under threat. Leading Methodist preachers were fearful of a radical agitation led by a man of pronounced Dissenting principles. They were nervous about the unwelcome prospect of a mixed Conference; they were also acutely aware of 'a real danger that the public authorities might view widespread unrest as further evidence of patently disruptive social forces within Methodism'.[34] And, to add to the discomfort of the leadership, Kilham combined with his protest against the failure to consult the people, an accusation of financial malpractice. It was a dual charge which was to be repeated in reform meetings a generation later.

Kilham was expelled in 1796. The following year the Conference undertook a fundamental review of connexional law. But in the same year Kilham and his followers, about 5,000 in total, or approximately 5% of the Wesleyan membership, formed the Methodist New Connection. It was the first of a series of secessions which were to fracture Methodism over the following half century. Even within the parent body some judicious concessions were only palliatives. Widespread and deeply-felt grievances remained, and these were forcefully expressed by some two hundred lay delegates who besieged the Leeds Conference of 1797. The outcome was *The Form of Discipline*, which provided Methodism with a new constitution. Nonetheless, Conference maintained its legislative authority and rejected lay representation, both in Conference and in the District Meetings, as incompatible with the essential character of Methodism and inconsistent with the necessary conditions for the preservation of the connexional system. The underlying discontent rumbled on. *The Form of Discipline* lasted, basically unchanged, until 1835, but it was subject to conflicting interpretations. It had not met the demand for greater democratization which had resulted in schism, and the stumbling block persisted in the main body of Methodists. By its conservatism Methodism was storing up trouble for the future. The architect of such changes as were introduced in an effort to transform Wesleyanism from 'a loosely-controlled community of proliferating societies vulnerable to a host of centrifugal forces and capable of constitutional development in various directions'[35] into a body which combined 'democracy' with centralization and effective control, was Jabez Bunting. He was the focus for the animosity which such changes generated.

The son of a radical Manchester tailor, Bunting had early experience of revivalism in his first public ministry in Manchester, where he encountered cottage prayer-meetings which were the spearhead of revival. But as he continued in his Wesleyan ministerial career at Oldham (1799–1801) and Macclesfield (1801–1803) he became ever more cautious, and fearful of the unfortunate divisive effects of revivals. He became increasingly involved in organizational matters and convinced of the need for good administration and control.

It was Bunting's achievement to turn Methodism into a very actively governed community; partly by new central institutions, of which the Methodist Missionary Society (1813) and the Theological Institution (1834) were the most notable; partly by standing and *ad hoc* committees of Conference (on which prominent laymen were invited to serve) to control the raising or expenditure of funds; partly by the exertion of the corporate power of the pastorate in Conference locally, through pressing Superintendents to pursue common policies, or through Presidential deputations or Special District Meetings to enforce discipline or administrative changes. Bunting further shifted the balance from the fringes to the centre by bringing the connexional management into more continuous negotiations with government than it had ever been before, on public order or slavery, foreign missions or education.[36]

Whether his life and labours were eventually a triumph or a tragedy is open to debate. Undoubtedly the success of this conservative, autocratic and Tory man 'in maintaining control over a predominantly poor and working-class Connexion is one of the most remarkable features of Nonconformist history'. His rule lasted long and it coincided with 'the most successful period in the history of English Methodism'.[37] On the other hand there were major and enduring secessions; there was much internal conflict; and 'when he died in 1858, at the age of seventy-nine, the Wesleyans had fewer members per head of the adult population than when he had first been elected secretary of the Conference over forty years before'.[38]

It was not controversy over the character of connexional government, however, but spontaneous local revivals, which led to the secession of the Primitive Methodists, the Bible Christians and the Independent Methodists. Local revivals were a feature of the age of the French Revolution and the Napoleonic Wars. One swept through Yorkshire from 1792 to 1796; there was one of shorter duration in Nottingham from 1798 to 1800 and another in the East Midlands in 1816–17.

In 1801, in the region of the rough, craggy mountain of Mow Cop, on the borders of Staffordshire and Cheshire, there occurred a revival which was to have widespread and lasting effects. As its nodal point was the first of the English 'camp meetings'; and its central figure was the twenty-nine-year-old lay Methodist Hugh Bourne.[39] He describes his experience with obvious enthusiasm. 'New life was imparted to me . . . and Mow Cop was that day consecrated to the Most High . . . The Lord began a new dispensation; He caused a camp-meeting to be held without a name.'[40]

He encapsulates the flavour and dynamic of these events in his graphic account of the most famous of the gatherings at Mow Cop:

The morning proved rainy, and unfavourable . . . but about six o'clock the Lord sent the clouds off, and gave us a very pleasant day.

The meeting was opened by two holy men from Knutsford, Captain Anderson, having previously erected a flag on the mountain to direct strangers, and these three, with some pious people from Macclesfield, carried on and sustained the meeting a considerable time, in a most vigorous and lively manner. They conducted it by preaching, prayer, exhortations, relating experiences, etc. The Lord owned their labours, grace descended, and the people of God were greatly quickened. The congregation rapidly increased and others began to join in holy exercises . . . The wind was cold, but a large grove of fir-trees kept the wind off and made it very comfortable. So many hundreds now covered the ground, that another preaching stand was erected in a distant part of the field, under the cover of a stone-wall. Returning over the field, I met a company at a distance from the first stand, praying for a man in distress. I could not get near, but there found such a measure of the power of God . . . that it was beyond description. I should gladly have stopped there, but other matters called me away. I perceived that the Lord was beginning to work mightily . . .

About noon the congregation was so much increasing that we were obliged to erect a third preaching stand . . . by the side of the fir-tree grove. I got upon this stand after the first preaching, and was extremely surprised at the amazing sight that appeared before me . . . I had not before conceived that such a vast multitude were present; but to see thousands hearing with attention solemn as death, presented a scene of the most sublime and awfully pleasing grandeur my eyes ever beheld. The preachers seemed to be fired with an uncommon zeal . . . numbers were convinced and saints were uncommonly quickened, and the extraordinary steadiness and decorum . . . seemed to make a great impression. Many preachers were now upon the ground, from Knutsford, Congleton, Wheelock, Burslem, Macclesfield, and other places . . . Persuasion dwelt upon their tongues, while the multitude were trembling or rejoicing around.

The congregation increased so rapidly that a fourth preaching stand was called for . . . To see thousands of people all in solemn attention . . . and four preachers dealing out their lives at every stroke – these things made an impression on my mind not soon to be forgotten; this extraordinary scene continued till about four o'clock, when the people began to retire; and before six, they were confined to one stand. About seven o'clock in the evening, a work began among children . . . at about half-past eight the meeting was finally closed. A meeting such as our eyes had never beheld; a meeting for which many will praise God in time and eternity . . . .[41]

Unfortunately, the Burslem Methodist Circuit was resistant to what was happening, and refused to accept the converts into fellowship. Bourne seems to have been genuinely distressed:

I long wished the circuit authorities to take the Harriseadhead, Mow Cop, and Kidsgrove converts into society. And perhaps as they were weary of my applications they at length put a class paper into my hands and told me to take them into society myself. This was rather a knockdown blow; but in the fear of the Lord I undertook it; so I was forced into a kind of headship point blank, against my own inclinations, and the cross was heavy.[42]

This was typical of the reaction in other areas where there was conflict between mainstream and 'primitive' Methodism. As 'established Methodism developed the sociological characteristics of a denomination, rather than a sect, by conforming to social norms, and the exclusion of beliefs and conduct which was considered unbecoming, the contrast with the vibrant new movements became ever more acute. In the case of the North Staffordshire revival this was a serious matter, partly because of the numbers involved, and partly because of the independence and strong personality of Bourne. Within a year more than three hundred persons were added to the Methodist churches in the region, including William Clowes, James Nixon, Thomas Woodnorth and William Morris, all of whom were later to be in the vanguard of that part of the movement which was to assume the name of Primitive Methodism.

The fire of the revival was stoked by the visit in 1805 and 1806 of the American travelling preacher, Lorenzo Dow. In 1808 Bourne was expelled from the Methodist society. The movement of open-air preaching and of camp-meetings expanded. In 1810 the 'Camp Meeting Methodists' were constituted as a fairly ill-defined group. In the same year William Clowes was also expelled from the Methodist church for conducting a similar campaign in Tunstall. In 1811 Bourne and Clowes united their groups to form the Primitive Methodists. By 1836 it has been computed that they had 62,306 members, over 20% of the membership of the Wesleyan Methodists.[43] The parent body could ill afford such a loss of actual and potential members, especially as they represented the revivalist tradition of early Methodism, with all its zeal and commitment.

Another forceful character, William O'Bryan, was instrumental in founding the Bible Christians. Again it was a matter of sudden and unbounded zealousness not being able to be contained within what was fast becoming a somewhat formal and inflexible Methodist regime. After his conversion, O'Bryan 'became an enthusiastic local preacher in the neighbourhood of Newquay, but his zeal did not allow him to be local enough in his activities to satisfy Circuit and Conference regulations'.[44] He was expelled from Methodist membership in 1810. He itinerated as a freelance evangelist, and he formed societies in several areas which the Methodists had to that date not visited. The societies were incorporated in the Methodist Connexion in 1814, after O'Bryan had been readmitted to the Methodist ranks. A repetition of his unacceptable enthusiasm resulted in a second expulsion. He resumed his independent evangelistic work, and then, in 1815, he somewhat reluctantly founded a new community at Shebbear in North Devon, the Bible Christian Society. Organized on Methodist lines, and under O'Bryan as its President, the new movement spread rapidly, despite considerable opposition. By the end of the first year there were 567 members, and by 1836 this had risen to 10,499.[45]

This repeated conflict between, on the one hand, the exuberance of an individual and a group caught up in all the fervour of spontaneous revivalism, and, on the other hand, the concern for orderliness and containment within a body by then rapidly assuming the characteristics of a formalized denomination, was inevitable, especially at this time of heightened activity and feeling because of events on the European continent and at home. Perhaps it is more than coincidental that the late eighteenth and early nineteenth centuries saw a number of organizational and structural changes, all in the direction of consolidating either individual denominations or parties within them. It was a time of particularly rapid political, constitutional, economic, social and religious change, when urbanization was rampant, masses of the population were being uprooted, and there was widespread alienation from institutional expressions of religion. It was also a time when, as we have seen, radical ideology was in the ascendant. In such a cauldron there was an acceleration of that process of religious transformation and re-definition to which I referred in the Introduction, whereby religious groups take on the sociological characteristics of either sects, denominations or churches. The Evangelicals and the High Church party within the Church of England, the Wesleyan Methodists, the Methodist New Connexion, the Primitive Methodists, the Bible Christians and the Independent Methodists, the Congregationalists, the Baptists, the Unitarians, the Brethren and the Catholic Apostolic Church, all came into existence or assumed a more definite form and identity in these years. It was a seedbed for modern English Protestant alignments.

A consideration of the Methodists in the 'Age of Revolution' also inevitably raises the question of the Halévy thesis, and the debate which has surrounded it especially since the 1950s. The essence of the hypothesis is stated succinctly by Halévy in his classic work *England in ... .*

> We shall witness Methodism bring under its influence, first the Dissenting sects, then the Establishment, finally secular opinion. We shall attempt to find here the key to the problem whose solution had hitherto escaped us; for we shall explain by this movement the extraordinary stability which English Society was destined to enjoy throughout a period of revolutions and crises; what we may truly term the miracle of modern England, anarchist but orderly, practical and businesslike, but religious, and even pietist.[46]

Many historians of Halévy's generation, and for about forty years after the publication of the thesis in 1913, found his conclusions persuasive. The hypothesis resonated with the sophisticated and fashionable German historical sociology of Max Weber and Ernst Troeltsch, and had echoes of popular Marxism which saw religion as the 'opiate of the people'.[47] It was, however, a Marxist historian, Eric Hobsbawm, who denied that Methodism 'could have prevented a revolution had other conditions favoured one'. This was partly because the Methodists were too few in number at the time, partly because much of the 'revolutionary unrest of the period' occurred in areas where Methodism was weak, and partly because 'Methodism advanced when Radicalism advanced and not when it grew weaker.'[48] Edward Thompson, another Marxist historian, endorsed Hobsbawm's point that if every Methodist 'shared the Tory principles of their founder' there were not enough of them 'to have stemmed a revolutionary tide'. He concurred with Halévy in the view that Methodism was a stabilizing force among working people, although he thought this was reprehensible; but, in contrast to Hobsbawm, he asserted that Methodism advanced in the downturn of the radical cycle. He postulated the theory 'that religious revivalism took over just at the point where "political" or temporal aspirations met with defeat'. 'Instead of Methodism and radical protest advancing together Thompson suggested that the social process oscillated between the opposing poles of religious revivalism and radical politics.'[49]

It was a shortcoming of those who endorsed the Halévy hypothesis that they were 'writing at a time when the failure to cite hard evidence was not deemed critical, and it was not until the 1950s that this deficiency was effectively noted'.[50] The most thorough study presenting a different interpretation, based on a close study of the appropriate historical data, is that by Bernard Semmel, *The Methodist Revolution* (1973). Semmel claims that most of those who take a hostile stance against the thesis, and indeed most of those who have entered into the debate over the thesis whether they supported or opposed it, have not fully considered eighteenth-century and early nineteenth-century Methodist theology, nor have they undertaken a comprehensive, impartial study of the actual historical situation. He concludes that the revival was a spiritual and social revolution, and that Methodist doctrine, as set forward by the leading spokesmen of the movement, was essentially a liberal and progressive ideology, in the sense that it both confirmed and helped to advance the movement from a traditional to a modern society.

Other late twentieth-century historians have made valuable observations on the thesis. A. D. Gilbert draws attention to the increasing absolute numbers of Methodists, Congregationalists and Baptists and, more importantly, the increase in their proportion as a sub-group of the total population, so that they were, by 1800, of sufficient numerical significance to be able to influence the world-view of their contemporaries. Around the middle of the eighteenth century 'scarcely 2% of the adult population was sufficiently influenced by Methodism or evangelical Dissent to maintain an active association with a chapel community.'[51] Between 1750 and 1800 the combined strength of the Methodists, Congregationalists and Baptists so increased that they represented between 8 and 9% of the total population despite the rapid population growth. By the late 1830s, taking all of those in any way associated with Dissent, the figure had soared to about 20%. Gilbert concludes that because 'the deployment of its resources made religious deviance strong in areas of the country where tendencies towards political disorder actually existed, and granted that it was indeed a politically moderating force, there can be little doubt that the movement had the numbers to make a significant difference in the domestic politics of its contemporary society'. On the 'reading of existing evidence there would appear to be good grounds for conducting discussions of the religion-politics nexus, not in terms of the traditional conservative characterization of Methodism, but in terms of the alternative possibility that religious deviance was a political "safety valve" for the pressures of early industrial politics'.[52]

David Hempton emphasizes that the issues which aroused the most intense passions among the evangelicals as a whole 'were not always to do with class conflict, parliamentary reform and the extension of the suffrage. Whenever chapel communities roused themselves to political action in this period they were as much concerned with protecting itinerant preaching, abolishing slavery, resisting Catholic emancipation, eroding Anglican privileges, establishing elementary education and reforming morals as they were with the "radical" demands of working-class political leaders many of whom treated the religious enthusiasm of the evangelical variety with the utmost contempt.'[53] He goes on to say that the complexity and variety of the eighteenth-century evangelical revival, and of evangelicalism, does not preclude serious attempts to advance a coherent interpretation of its social and political influence, but it does signal a cautious approach, and the firm grounding of theory in a full appreciation of eighteenth-century revival history. And he finds that Halévy in propounding his thesis fails to meet such rigorous demands. He 'exaggerated both the fragility of England's *ancien regime* and the power of evangelicalism to save it from its internal contradictions'.[54] The Halévy hypotheses did, however, usefully draw attention to 'the importance of evangelical religion in forging a rough harmony of values between the pragmatic and moralistic middle class and the skilled and respectable sections of the English working class who were notorious in Europe for their solid virtue and capacity for organization'. Then, secondly, popular evangelicalism, although it 'did not create the free-born Englishman', and likewise 'did not create the capacity for disciplined organization', did 'offer a vibrant religious vehicle for both to operate outside the confines of the Established Church without seriously destabilising the English State'.[55] Hempton also believes that 'the relationship between the growth of Methodism and political radicalism is more complicated than either Thompson's oscillation theory or Hobsbawm's concurrent expansion ideas would permit'.[56]

In summary, recent research, revealing more details of 'what actually happened' and offering a more sophisticated interpretation of the data available, has not resulted in the wholesale rejection of the Halévy thesis, but rather a refinement of it. There is still a reaching out for more satisfactory explanations of the relationship between the history of the churches and other aspects of national life such as politics, social and economic changes, philosophy and popular ideology, and the presence or absence of revolution in a period of traumatic transformation not only in Britain but on the continent of Europe as well. In this academic hunt for clues and insights it seems to be widely agreed that there were fundamental shifts in the values, and in the accepted norms of the various socio-economic segments of society which constituted the population at the time, and that such readjustments may cast light on the central issues at stake in the Halévy thesis. Thus, for example, V. Kiernan comments that 'Evangelicalism brought together the developing sections of the middle classes, gave them an independent outlook, relieved their fears of the more elemental forms of mass unrest, showed how a respectable working-class could be led by a respectable middle-class.' 'In fact', he says, 'it prepared the ground for 19th century English Liberalism.'[57] And another historian, Susan Pedersen, in a study of Hannah More, suggests that the 'real success of More's tracts is to be found less in their conversion of the poor than in their effective recruitment of the upper class to the role of moral arbiters of popular culture'.[58]

Halévy has certainly prompted reactions and academic debate. But no historian has yet provided a satisfactory comprehensive analysis of the relationship between collective values and political, economic and social trends during the first century of Methodism. Such a thorough appraisal is required in order to test the Halévy hypothesis and all the subsequent debate. A valid assessment can only be achieved if the analysis takes account of the total complex interrelationships between ideas and action throughout the period in question. For the thesis addresses but one strand in this total web of interconnected political, economic, social and religious factors. It would be a massive undertaking, and would entail consideration of corporate religious and philosophical trends, folklore and folk religion; and the connection between these and the main concurrent political, economic and social developments; as well as a comparison of this interconnectedness with contrasting situations else-where, and more particularly in certain countries of continental Europe. But only by such a thorough method could the Halévy thesis be replaced after about one hundred years by a better, more research-based and convincing hypothesis.

The Congregationalists

As we have seen earlier, by 1791 the Congregationalists were showing positive signs of having experienced an infusion of new energy and life. The revival was beginning to have beneficial effects. This was evidenced in a number of ways. There was the sheer growth in the number of Congregationalists. Calculated as 15,000 in 1750, they had increased to 26,000 by 1790, and 35,000 by 1800. Thirty-eight years later this had multiplied well over threefold to 127,000.[59] And rapid growth did not produce the problems encountered by the Methodists. Rather, the Congregationalists appear generally to have been avid constitutionalists who dreaded revolutionary talk. There was a streak of radicalism, but it tended to be contained, and it expressed itself in a democratic form. Congregationalists also put a strong emphasis upon schemes for the amelioration of social ills, and not upon ideas of radical change in either society as a whole or their denomination in particular.

Then there was the flourishing of Congregational academies. A new academy was opened at Rotherham in 1795, although it might be reckoned as a continuation of the one at Heckmondwike, and it prospered under able tutors. Others included Newport Pagnell Academy, Trevecca College, and Gosport Academy, which came into prominence as a training school for missionaries. But the most distinguished was that which moved from Mile End to Hoxton in 1791. It established an enviable reputation under the extraordinarily successful tutorship of Robert Simpson. By 1798 there were over twenty students in residence; a number which had risen to forty by 1814. In 1826 it was moved to Highbury, and became known as Highbury College until it amalgamated with Homerton and Coward colleges to form New College in 1850.

A new-found vitality was also manifested in the way Congregationalists involved themselves in helping to establish or perpetuate organizations for a host of social and religious purposes. They were prepared to cooperate with others in founding and supporting non-denominational societies. Thus, the Congregationalist minister John Townsend participated in the formation of the Religious Tract Society in 1802, and in the establishment of the British and Foreign Bible Society and several other evangelical societies, and combined with others to found a Deaf and Dumb Asylum. He was also one of those who, in 1807, helped to start the London Female Penitentiary at Pentonville for the reclamation and rehabilitation of prostitutes. In 1812, Congregationalists were intimately involved in the founding of the London Society for the Encouragement of Female Servants, which offered monetary rewards to faithful servants. And, in 1819, a Congregationalist, Dr W. B. Collyer, was one of the foremost officers in the newly-founded Bible Admonition Society, which prepared posters with suitable scripture texts printed on them, and sold them for public display. The objectives of many of these bodies might appear nauseously paternalistic, but in the early nineteenth century it was indicative of a genuine philanthropy and concern for the well-being of others; and it is evidence that Congregationalists were animated by a sincere social and religious concern to serve the people of their day and generation. A change of attitude was, however, imminent. Congregationalism was about to exhibit further evidence of its renewal, but in a form and spirit which was in contrast to the 'independency' characteristic at the turn of the century.

The practical pietism and voluntary benevolence which were to the fore in early nineteenth-century Congregationalism were viewed by some Congregationalists as a hopelessly fragile dyke against the mounting social distress of the new industrial society. A more robust approach was advocated, and the merits of greater social and political involvement were proclaimed by a new and somewhat disillusioned generation. Between 1815 and 1850 there was an escalation of radicalism among Congregationalists and other Nonconformist leaders. There was a revolution in the attitude of Congregationalists to politics as such. 'It began to attract them. They came to feel that it was part of their Christian business to appear on public platforms.'[60] Of course, they had before them the example of a considerable number of ordinary men and women engaged in 'political' activity, with the accelerated 'democratization' of politics, which we have previously considered. There was also the successful involvement of artisans in what was an important phase in 'the making of the English working class', and the evident effectiveness of the Clapham Sect, the Saints and the Hackney Phalanx in their political activity which provided inspiration, incentive and an example to be imitated. For the Congregationalists it was a slow, less dramatic, process than for the Church of England Evangelicals and High Churchmen; but it was nevertheless real and significant. They participated in the political work of the Dissenting Deputies, and Congregational ministers joined with Baptists and Presbyterians 'in annual and extraordinary meetings to make pronouncements on public policies and to arouse public opinion on questions of civil and religious liberty'.[61] They were especially active in educational matters, with a great concern for the extension of rudimentary education to the mass of the population who did not receive it; in agitation for the reform of Parliament; in the campaign for the abolition of slavery; and in the crusade for the repeal of the Test and Corporation Acts.

In this tentative political engagement the Congregationalists were helping to lay the foundations for a future Nonconformist political influence of considerable magnitude, when 'the Nonconformist conscience' became a feature of national political and social life which could not be ignored. Congregationalists were also paving the way for a time, not long in the future, when they would assume a definite political identity. Already there was a firm alliance with the Whigs, and this was being cemented in these troublesome years. The first tentative steps were cautiously being taken towards an impending greater political commitment. 'Only very gradually did Congregationalists emerge as one of the dominant groups in the many-sided alliance that eventually constituted the Liberal Party. Shy at first, they found themselves drawn irresistibly into the whirlpool of party and national politics.'[62]

Such a political focus did not entail neglect of doctrinal matters. Arianism and Socinianism had so penetrated the old Dissent that by the last quarter of the eighteenth century the majority of Presbyterians had become Unitarians, leaving the Congregationalists and the Calvinistic or Particular Baptists as the sole guardians of orthodox Trinitarian belief among the old Dissenters. Some Congregationalists were not free of the taint of Arian or Socinian heresy, but as a whole they remained true to orthodox doctrines. Two factors in particular may account for the greater conformity to traditional dogma among the Congregationalists as compared with the Presbyterians. In the first place, for a combination of reasons, including the stress placed upon the autonomy of the local congregation and the covenant fellowship in which all members joined, the people rather than their leaders determined the theological direction of the denomination; and the ordinary lay members were noted for their conservatism in the matter of religious belief. In the second place, 'the hymns of Isaac Watts counterbalanced in the Independent congregations the tendency to over-value the rational, apologetic, and argumentative sermons, and served as creeds which the congregations sang. Biblically based, with a strong theological structure, these hymns and the covenants to which every member of an Independent Meeting subscribed on admission to the Church formed the bonds of orthodoxy.'[63]

By the 1830s the Congregationalists were ready for a partial national union. For a body which had stressed the autonomy of the local congregation for over two hundred years this was a breakthrough. But the denomination had reached a point of development at which some measure of coordinated action and national representation was seen as desirable. The union of 1831, which was preceded by county unions with a concern for evangelism, was of a purely advisory nature, not a structure with administrative or disciplinary powers over congregations. It lobbied Parliament, collected statistics and held an annual meeting. It also acted as a point of reference for any other independent chapels which might be attracted to Congregationalism. But a major step had been taken on the road to a more defined corporate identity. The union was more than a clearing house, a provider of information and a means of communication. 'Inevitably, whatever the objectives of the founders of the union, it also gradually became the focus of a denomination.'[64] Once more we are witnessing a stage in that transformation from sect to denomination which is such a marked feature of the history of the churches in England in the long eighteenth century.

The Baptists

Between 1750 and 1838 it appears that the Baptists experienced the same sort of growth as the Congregationalists, and almost at the same rate throughout the period. The membership of the Particular Baptists according to A. D. Gilbert, was 10,000 in 1750, 17,000 in 1790 (an increase of 70%, compared with the 70.33% for the Congregationalists, 70.28% if the General Baptist New Connexion members are included), and 86,000 in 1838 (an increase of 860%, compared with the 846% for the Congregationalists, although 1000% if the General Baptist New Connexion members are included).

The membership of the General Baptist New Connexion, which was founded in 1770, went up from 1,221 in that year, to 13,947 in 1838.[65] Dan Taylor and others attempted to perpetuate the revivalist zeal which had originally motivated the secession from the mainstream of General Baptists. A circular letter of 1793, signed by Taylor, urged the churches of the Connexion to hold frequent conferences for the discussion of spiritual topics, and went on to say that it was a cause of decline among the General Baptists that they had neglected such gatherings and such concern for the maintenance of spiritual alertness and vitality.[66] The New Connexion was carefully organized. It had an annual meeting of delegates, called an Association, with district conferences. There was an attempt to supply periodical literature. The *General Baptist Magazine* (1798–1800) was replaced by the *General Baptist Repository*, which first appeared every six months, but from 1810 began to be published quarterly. Sunday schools were encouraged, and a fund for aged ministers was commenced. In the early years these organizational measures were important, but the dynamic, inspirational leadership of Taylor was perhaps the crucial factor. There was an undoubted sense of freshness and vitality in the new body which was attractive to a number of people. 'Compared with the old Assembly, the Association of the

New Connexion had a new-fashioned air.'[67] It was much more alert and responsive to the needs of the time, and, by accident or design, it planted churches in the towns which were expanding or rising under the influence of industrial growth, particularly the lace and hosiery towns of Yorkshire and Lancashire.

Doctrinal tensions created serious differences between the Assembly of the General Baptists and the New Connexion. The views of Elhanan Winchester, an American preacher who ministered to a London congregation, concerning universal restoration, rapidly gained acceptance among the General Baptists of the Assembly and elsewhere. Unitarian teaching was embraced by some General Baptists, notably the young minister, William Vidler. In 1803 Taylor withdrew from the Assembly. By the middle of the second decade of the century the doctrinal gulf between the General Baptists and the New Connexion was considerable, and growing. In 1813 the New Connexion had become so disturbed by the spread of Socinian 'poison' that it urged its churches not to allow any believers in 'that destructive system' to preach in their pulpits. Unconcerned and unrepentant, an 1815 General Assembly Committee reported on the 'success of Unitarianism, which, with the exception of baptism, may surely be called the cause of the General Baptists'.[68] The outlook of some of the more doctrinally heterodox General Baptists is reflected in the words of one of their number, John Burgess, also in 1815:

> I think the doctrine of the Trinity one of the greatest corruptions in the Christian Church. The doctrine of the pre-existence of Jesus Christ I have entirely given up . . . the doctrine of original sin, of atonement . . . are to me doctrines absurd in the extreme.[69]

It was fortuitous that a changing theological climate within the Particular Baptist churches helped to steer Baptists as a whole in an orthodox direction, and acted as a counter to the heretical trends among the General Baptists. This largely revolved around the increasing acceptance of Andrew Fuller's moderate Calvinism. 'He was the man who dealt the mortal blow to the system which held that it was impossible for any but the elect to embrace the Gospel and that it was therefore useless to invite the unconverted to put their trust in Christ.'[70] Fuller expounded his views in his *Gospel Worthy of all Acceptation*, which was published in 1785, and he supplemented this with a personal expository ministry, which included preaching at Taylor's Whitechapel meeting-house, and making a determined effort to promote theological harmony among all Baptists. 'Fullerism' encouraged evangelism. It opened up the Particular Baptists to other evangelical influences from which they had been cocooned in the period of dominant High Calvinism. The change in theological perspective gave most Particular Baptists a greater sense of denominational identity, and at the same time a greater willingness to join with others in corporate enterprises.

A further very potent influence in binding Baptists together was the common task of worldwide mission. I will be considering this at length in the next chapter, but its powerful effect in helping to unite General and Particular Baptists in the late eighteenth and early nineteenth centuries needs to be noted as an important aspect of Baptist life at that time.

The drawing-together of all Baptists reached a high point with the establishment in 1813 of The General Union of Baptist Ministers and Churches. Its constitution declared that the aim was the promotion of 'the cause of Christ in general, and particularly in our own denomination, and especially to encourage and support our mission'.[71] Although it may have been a somewhat premature venture whose potential was never fully realized, and although it soon came to an end, and was of limited success even when it was re-constituted in 1831, it was a step on the road which ultimately led to the Baptist Union of Great Britain and Ireland, and, indeed, one might claim, to the Baptist World Alliance ninety-two years later.

The Quakers

'The Society of Friends was not, like Presbyterianism, facing virtual extinction at the beginning of the nineteenth century, but neither was it making any contribution to the massive expansion of Dissent. There were about 20,000 Quakers in England and Wales in 1800, only half as many as there had been at the end of the seventeenth century, and a slow decline was continuing.'[72] They had experienced a remarkable birth and early childhood in the middle years of the seventeenth century at a time when various other sects rose, had a brief and often quite dramatic life, and then disappeared, never to be seen again. They had attracted members for an initial period of about half a century, but had then undergone a prolonged numerical slide downwards.

There is evidence of evangelical influence in Quaker circles, but it was largely confined to the efforts of a few zealots. It was mainly exerted by people who had been nurtured outside the Quaker fold, and who came into Quakerism with a slightly non-traditional Quaker perspective. For example, Mary Dudley was an intimate friend of John Wesley in her youth, and he did everything in his power to dissuade her from joining the Friends. She quite remarkably combined a passion for proclaiming the gospel with a thorough appreciation of the more mystical way of approach in worship of the Quakers. Likewise, Thomas Shillitoe united a pronounced quietist element with a thoroughly evangelical dependence for salvation on the mercies of God in Christ. A further example was the prominent Quaker Stephen Grellett.

Nonetheless, the Quakers had drifted from their moorings. They lacked that spiritual dynamic which had characterized them in the seventeenth century. By the nineteenth century Friends 'no longer believed that the distinctive Quaker message offered the only escape from the everlasting torments of hell. In that they were at one with the Unitarians; and in that fact lies the explanation of their common decline.'[73] It is remarkable that despite this rather parlous spiritual state they were infused with a new spirit of social concern which was then and continued to be one of their most outstanding and glorious hallmarks, although some might say that the new focus of concern largely took the place of the former 'spiritual' emphasis. But it was not something completely new. One has only to recall John Bellers (1654–1725) with his great sensitivity to the miseries of the poor and the sufferings of men, to realize that there was a Quaker tradition of social concern. It did, however, become very marked in the period I am at present reviewing, and it made a wider appeal to the membership as a whole than it had, for the most part, in the past.

The first major issue championed by the Friends was the crusade against the slave trade. As early as the mid-eighteenth century Anthony Benezet had been awakened to its iniquity, and to the inhumanity of slavery as a system. From that moment until his death he dedicated himself to the task of awakening Friends and others to the enormity as he saw it. He strove to arouse the Quakers to a united and determined opposition to its continuance. The London Quakers helped in exposing the evils of the system, and in 1774 it was declared that any Friend who had dealings with the slave trade would be expelled. In 1781 the Friends presented a petition to Parliament, and two years later they formed a small group to mobilize public opinion against the trade. This was the vehicle for the Quaker contribution to the anti-slavery campaign during the last years of the eighteenth century and into the nineteenth century. The work it undertook provided the basis for what was then carried on so effectively by the Clapham Sect and others. The leader in the second phase of the crusade, to abolish not only the slave trade but the entire system of slavery in lands under the sway of Britain, was Thomas Fowell Buxton, a man 'so closely allied with Friends by birth and marriage connections and by the spirit of his life that his work seems a vital part of Quakerism'.[74]

Among the leading Quaker social reformers of the age was William Allen, 'one of the most remarkable examples of the expanding power of human goodness in the annals of Quaker history'.[75] It was in 1812 that he called together a group of about forty people to his home to formulate plans for the relief of the poor, suffering, destitute labourers in Spitalfields. A society was formed, as seems to be the wont of the times, and it set about investigating conditions and causes of distress, seeking funds for immediate help, managing centres for the distribution of soup, and devising methods for the permanent improvement of needy families. Allen also started a quarterly journal in 1811, *The Philanthropist*, which had a distinguished career. Then, in 1814, he widened his philanthropic involvement for the bettering of industrial conditions. He formed a partnership with John Walker, Joseph Fox, Joseph Foster, Michael Gibbs and Robert Owen, and they bought cotton mills at New Lanark on the Clyde. In this momentous venture, the work which had been started in a limited way by Owen was expanded into a vast scheme to improve the social and working conditions of factory labourers.

In parallel with this project, Allen worked unremittingly for a more humane criminal procedure, and for the abolition of capital punishment. Lastly, he was associated with the Duke of Kent in the financial reorganization of the Lancasterian Schools. It was an impressive array of efforts to introduce social reform on a number of fronts.

Just as impressive, and more well-known, is the work undertaken by Elizabeth Fry. In an age when the role of women was severely circumscribed, her achievements were remarkable. She was born in 1780, into the Gurney family, the most prominent Quaker family in Norfolk. She was nurtured in a sophisticated and cultured home. She found the local Quaker meetings long and dreary, but she was intensely moved by the message of a visiting American preacher, William Savery, and another itinerant minister, Deborah Darby. She became greatly interested in the condition of the poor, and she frequently visited their homes.

By 1813 she was married with eight children, and reduced to straitened financial circumstances as a result of the financial speculations of her brother-in-law. But it was then that she began her work of reform in Newgate prison. She gathered information about the condition of prisons throughout England. A society was formed by her two brothers-in-law, Samuel Hoare and Sir Thomas Fowell Buxton, and a small group of friends, for dealing with juvenile offenders and for reforming the criminal code and the existing prison methods; and in all of this work Elizabeth Fry made a large and important contribution. In 1827 she published her *Observations on the Visiting, Superintendence and Government of Female Prisoners*, in which she presented well-reasoned conclusions on the problem of crime and correction. This was followed by the even more important and useful *Report addressed to the Marquess Wellesley, Lord Lieutenant of Ireland*, also published in 1827. She extended her work and area of concern to cover the condition of transported criminals. She worked at the same time for the founding of day nurseries; for improvements in the condition of the coast-guards; for the care and oversight of little children both in England and France; for the formation of societies to prevent begging and imposture; and for assistance to discharged prisoners. She also went on preaching in Quaker meetings. She was visited by the most distinguished people of the time, and she was invited to visit royalty throughout Europe. Her fame became almost worldwide, and she greatly influenced men at the head of government in England.

The Quakers were small in number and declining. But when such social work as I have briefly indicated was carried on under the inspiration of that particular religious tradition, and when such love and grace was spread abroad by Friends as a consequence of the same compelling motivation, the tradition and its leading members must surely be accorded a place of honour in the history of this tortuous, fraught, and yet heroic age?

The Presbyterians, the growth of Socinianism and the birth of Unitarianism

The decline of Presbyterianism in the eighteenth century had been rapid; and as compared with the Congregationalists and the Baptists, they did not recover and expand towards the end of the century or in the early part of the nineteenth century. In 1714 they had accounted for about two-thirds of all Dissenting congregations, but by 1808 the total number of congregations was vastly exceeded by those of both Congregationalists and the Baptists.[76] A considerable number of Presbyterian congregations had died out, and the remaining orthodox groups were tending to drift into independency. Presbyterianism in England was

facing extinction. The main problem was the devastating inroads made
by Socinianism. 'Presbyterianism at the beginning of the nineteenth
century was in the process of merging with the new Unitarian movement initiated by Theophilus Lindsey.'[77]

As we have already noted, it was the Presbyterians who were most
adversely affected by the subscription controversy which reached its
height in the 1770s. Those who refused to subscribe were charged with
holding Arian and Socinian ideas. But the same tendency was to be
found within the Church of England. When a petition to Parliament in
1773 for the relaxation of terms of subscription failed, rational Dissent
received an accession of strength from the secession of a number of
liberal Anglicans. This tended to accelerate the Presbyterian slide into
Socinianism; and the more extreme of those inclined to Socinian views
were soon to be offered a new spiritual home. Theophilus Lindsey, who
at the time was an Anglican vicar, resigned his living in 1773, and the
following year, not content to join an existing denomination which
catered for a mixture of Socinian and other doctrinal opinions, he
opened a Unitarian chapel in London; the 'first organized Unitarian
Dissent as a working force in the religious life of England'.[78] Lindsey
attracted a wealthy and distinguished congregation, which included the
Duke of Grafton, the future Duke of Norfolk and several Members of
Parliament.[79]

In 1791 Lindsey combined with Thomas Belsham and Joseph Priestley
to found The Unitarian Society for Promoting Christian Knowledge and
the Practice of Virtue by the Distribution of Books. 'The Rules contained
the first public profession of belief in the proper unity of God, and in the
simple humanity of Jesus in opposition both to trinitarian doctrine and
the ancient Arian formula.'[80] The definite and assertive temper of the
rising Unitarianism may be seen in the *Preamble to the Rules of the
Society of the Unitarian Christians* established in the West of England,
which was circulated in 1794. It declared that though the Christian
religion had its origin 'from the immediate revelation of God', it had
been immensely and perniciously corrupted. Because there had been a
failure to proclaim the truth, a new creed was needed. It was to be a
fundamental principle of the Society, to which all concerned agreed,
'that there is but one God the Creator and Governor of the Universe,
without an equal or vicegerent, the only object of religious worship; and
that Jesus Christ was the most eminent of those messengers which He
has employed to reveal His will to mankind, possessing extraordinary
powers, similar to those received by other prophets, but in a much

higher degree.' They were even more forthright than this in attacking conventional trinitarian doctrine:

> While we thus declare our belief in the strict Unity of God, and cannot but regard every practice as idolatrous which attributes any of the prerogatives of the Deity to another, . . . we would not be understood to assert that we think such practices are attended with the same immoral consequences as the idolatry which prevailed in the heathen world. That they are, however, in *all* cases injurious, and in *some*, highly criminal, we have no doubt.[81]

Throughout this period of Presbyterian decline and degeneration, there was a remnant which adhered to orthodox belief. They were scattered in small numbers in various parts of the country. Outside London they were to be found especially in the northern counties of Northumberland, Cumberland, and areas of Durham in the vicinity of Newcastle-on-Tyne. These congregations looked to Scotland for the majority of their ministers, and many of the Scottish people in their neighbourhood resorted to them. When the Presbyterian Church of England was formed in 1876 it was this 'new Presbyterianism' which had kept the denomination alive. 'During the previous forty years Presbyterianism had grown rapidly in England. From a total of below 10,000 in 1838 the combined membership of the Presbyterians and the Presbyterian Church of England had expanded to about 15,000 in 1851, 27,000 in 1860, 38,000 in 1870, and more than 46,000 when they united in 1876.'[82]

The Roman Catholics

In the years from 1791 to 1833 there were substantial shifts in the numbers, composition and spirit of the Roman Catholic community, in the perception of Roman Catholics by the majority Protestant population of England, and in the standing of Roman Catholicism vis-à-vis the state.

The fortunes and the character of late eighteenth and early nineteenth-century Roman Catholicism were transformed by the influx of Irish Roman Catholics and the increase in clerical control. Between 1800 and 1850 the rapid expansion in the number of Roman Catholics in England and Wales from under 100,000 to approximately 750,000[83] was largely due to Irish immigration. Although most of that was a result of the hungry forties and the great famine the process was well advanced by 1833. The massive exodus from Ireland to England not only helped to swell the numbers of Roman Catholics in England, but contributed to a change in the character of English Catholicism. The dominant spirit of eighteenth-century Roman Catholicism was Cisalpine. That is, its hallmarks were the acceptance of the general tenets of Catholic dogma combined with a concentration on the moral obligations towards the state; a chilly reserve in the attitude towards any pronouncements or actions by the Holy See which were not directly concerned with dogmatic teaching; a pronounced tendency to be very independent and exclusive in views and policies; and a strong resistance to any extension of clergy power.

In contrast to this was the whole theological and attitudinal orientation of the Ultramontanists who were in the ascendancy in the early nineteenth century. They 'stood for an open, loudly proclaimed and selfconscious attachment to the Holy See and, in lesser matters, for a dutiful acceptance of each detail of the papal organization. They received gratefully all the encouragement and guidance which Rome would give to them and throughout gave the Papacy a keen support.'[84] Bishop John Milner, who was dominant in the Catholic minority in the first quarter of the nineteenth century, was an ardent Ultramontanist, and combined his filial devotion to the Holy See with a strong sentiment of loyalty to George III. In his lifelong struggle with his Cisalpine protagonists he had the Catholic middle classes and the people generally on his side. In particular the Irish Catholic immigrants 'were much more willing than the English Catholic gentry to defer to the priest in matters of religion, and so reinforced the rise in English Catholic clericalism'.[85] Opposition to the new Ultramontanism and clerical influence came largely from the wealthy gentry and the peers, a group of lawyers, some writers, both clerical and lay, and in general people of privilege who had been associated with Roman Catholic leadership in the past, but who had seen their influence wane throughout the eighteenth century. Such a trend had largely been a consequence of 'the lightening of persecution and the growth of urban missions outside gentry control'.[86]

This surge of Roman Catholic clericalism became markedly more pronounced during the struggle for emancipation between 1800 and 1829, and also, more generally, as a result of yet further Catholic expansion in urban areas from the 1770s onwards. It was aided by the French Revolution and Napoleonic Wars. These events brought back to England the schools and colleges which had for so long been established abroad; and almost immediately after the passing of the Relief Act of 1791 there was also a great influx of priests to England – over five thousand at one time. The English Catholic clergy had a difficult time establishing their authority, but by 1833 they 'had at least preserved the bare essentials of their existence'.[87] The struggle in which they were engaged was plain for all to see. 'The battle to control the laity filled the air with pamphlets and noisy discussion, but its real course was hidden amongst administrative details and evident only to the few who were well informed. Yet even the wise ordinary priest and parishioner in 1830 could sense this victory; its symptoms were unmistakable. The average missioner had a new sense of assurance and command when he dealt with even his richest parishioners: those parishioners had a novel attitude of deference to their pastors. As for the Vicars-Apostolic, in 1780 they had been worried men, somehow insignificant and on the run. In 1830 they were still deeply worried, but occupied a new, commanding position in the Catholic community.'[88]

The growth and improved health and confidence of the Catholic community in England during the four decades after 1791 did not prevent a noticeably greater tolerance towards Catholics at all levels of society. Within government circles it was not only Edmund Burke and the members of the advanced Whig opposition who supported a relaxation of the penal laws against Catholics. Many conservatives regarded Roman Catholicism as 'a counterpoise to the irreligious and anarchistic influence of France'.[89]

One great solvent which acted powerfully in reducing anti-Catholic prejudices was the bravery and loyalty demonstrated by Catholics on the battlefield. Many of them clearly showed, even to the point of death, that their political and patriotic allegiance was not inhibited by religious loyalty to a foreign authority in the person of the Pope. Such altruistic behaviour persuaded a countless number of Protestants 'that an intolerance forged in the sixteenth century when England was small and vulnerable was inappropriate for the range and power of the British empire three hundred years later'.[90] Yet this trend must not be overemphasized. Among ordinary Englishmen and women, especially in urban working-class areas, there were powerful feelings directed against Catholics. Traditional antagonism actually became sharper in those places which experienced at first hand the flood of Irish immigration.

It was because of this continuance of anti-Catholicism, among the ruling classes as well as in the homes and public houses of industrial England, that the campaign for emancipation was so protracted. And churchmen were as reluctant as any to adopt more enlightened views. Faced with what was evidently a plural society some of the leading literati and churchmen of the early nineteenth century tried to justify the privileges enjoyed by the established church. 'The arguments of the great constitutional writers of the last century were now given a specifically anti-Catholic twist and men of letters such as Southey, Coleridge and Wordsworth, and later churchmen such as Newman, Keble and Blomfield set themselves to restate the theory of the Protestant constitution. The crux of the matter was that the subordination of Catholics was the fundamental law of the constitution.'[91] One of the historical features in forging the unrivalled excellence of the British constitution had been a determined resistance to Roman Catholicism, and eternal vigilance was required in order to guard against any concessions to the long-standing enemy of all that was most precious in the British, Protestant, way of life.

Nonetheless, despite such deep-seated feelings, and resolute resistance, the campaign for Catholic emancipation rolled on towards what, in hindsight, might appear as its inevitable outcome. In 1823 Daniel O'Connell, 'The Liberator' of the Catholics of England and Ireland, established the Catholic Association as a pressure group to challenge English authority at every point. The British government were faced with the mounting tempo of the Irish agrarian crisis, with widespread violence and the threat of civil war. The emancipation campaign was greatly aided by the final disintegration of the Pittite Tory party which had ruled England for so long, and by the ensuing re-alignments and conflicts of leading political leaders. 'By the early 1820s, in fact, the argument that full inclusion of the Catholic population within the body politic was a wiser and more practical strategy than an already modified exclusion had triumphed as far as the House of Commons and an influential sector of the cabinet were concerned.'[92]

The act as passed in 1829 granted Catholics the right to vote and to sit in Parliament, and admitted Catholics to all offices of state except those representing or directly connected with the crown. As concessions to Protestant feeling bishops were forbidden to adopt the titles of sees in use by prelates of the established church, and religious celebrations were confined to churches and private houses. A further clause restricted the freedom of religious orders and their increase, but this provision remained a dead letter. The overall effect of the act was not only to liberate Catholics but to signal very clearly that the country had committed itself yet further to the process of religious toleration and pluralism which was one of the distinguishing features in the religious history of England from the sixteenth century onwards.

Part 4

Overview:
World Mission and Domestic Change

Overseas Mission, 1689–1833

The birth of the modern English Protestant missionary movement

'The discovery of America and the beginning of European colonization let loose in England, as elsewhere, a flood of interest in the primitive peoples who had there been brought to light.'[1] This interest translated itself into expressions of good Christian missionary intent. The American Indians had clearly not previously been evangelized, and there was some contemporary recognition that 'by the late discovery of this new world God was calling his church to new and apostolic venture'. This was acknowledged and enshrined in official documents, as with the charter granted to Sir Humphrey Gilbert in 1583, which referred to the compassion of God 'for poor infidels, it seeming probable that God hath reserved these Gentiles to be introduced into Christian civility by the English nation'. Likewise, when a charter was granted to the colony of Massachusetts by Charles 1, it included the statement that the principal end of the plantation was that the colonists might 'invite the natives of the country to the knowledge of the only true God and Saviour of mankind and the Christian faith'.[2]

On the whole the Church of England did not have a very distinguished record of spreading Christianity among their neighbouring Indian inhabitants of the continent until the early years of the eighteenth century. The Christian faith the Church of England colonists represented was, like that of other European nationals, bound up inextricably with the culture and the political and commercial interests of their country of origin.

The Spanish, French, English, Dutch, and Swedish colonies in North America were outposts of European Christendom, intended to transplant the cultural milieus of the competing national states into a wilderness setting. The churches played an important role in this movement of peoples; in most of the colonies that dotted the edge of the continent in the seventeenth century there were official establishments of religion. Christian beginnings in North America were thus closely related to the efforts of colonization made by the European nations. Much of the drama in the story of the churches lies in the way the initial patterns were altered and transformed through the centuries.'[3]

It was assumed that the patterns of Christendom long familiar in the home countries would be continued abroad, and that the churches would not only be intrinsic parts of the colonial settlements, but would be the accepted vehicle through which the conversion and nurturing of souls would be undertaken. The spreading of the gospel was thus, perhaps inevitably, caught up with the promotional interests of particular churches and particular religious traditions. 'Most colonial leaders hoped that the particular church in which they believed would be established in territories they controlled, and intended that others should submit to it or stay away.'[4]

This institutional focus for the proclamation of the gospel did not preclude valiant individual endeavours. Outstanding among such pioneers were the Presbyterian John Eliot (1604–90) and the friend of Jonathan Edwards, David Brainerd (1718–47). But the missionary task was far greater than a handful of individuals could tackle.

The same was true for that other great scene of British colonialism, India. The East India Company had been formed in 1600. From 1607 efforts were made to provide ministrations for its servants by means of chaplains in India and beyond, but there were far too few of them for the work to be done thoroughly. Although the Company periodically issued regulations requiring chaplains to learn local languages in order to make known to the 'Gentoos' the truths of the Christian faith, such injunctions remained a dead letter, and only one Church of England baptism of an Indian is recorded in the seventeenth century. Again, as with America, an effective missionary work awaited some initiative which would allow a dedicated, corporate and concerted effort. And this brings us back to England, and to the activities of the remarkable Dr Bray.

When Dr Thomas Bray and three of his acquaintances met in the Lincoln's Inn rooms of one of their number, the barrister John Hooke, on 8 March 1699, and formed themselves into the Society for Promoting Christian Knowledge, they were inaugurating the modern era of missionary work at home and overseas, not only for the Church of England, but for English Protestants as a whole.[5] The new society was cast in the image of the good doctor, and of the strong churchmanship to which he had been accustomed. It 'had one central concern: the implementation of a programme of evangelical philanthropy, which would reassert the spiritual and political primacy of the Church of England in the nation'. But in its endeavours, 'the society saw itself as a subordinate auxiliary of the clergy'.[6] Two methods in particular were adopted to attain the society's main aim of promoting Christian know-ledge: the distribution of Christian literature and the use of catechetical education. For the former it took advantage of such recently adopted literary devices as the tract, the newspaper and the pamphlet, and used them as means for disseminating information, knowledge and propa-ganda among large numbers of the population. This was the era of the first provincial presses producing local newspapers; it was the age of magazines such as Addison and Steele's *Spectator*; and it was a time when prints, pamphlets, cartoons and ballads were printed, but never in sufficient quantities to fully satisfy the colossal demand. The SPCK attempted to spread Christian knowledge by distributing 'small useful Tracts' to their Correspondents, which they were to use 'for the Instruction of the Poorer sort in the Knowledge of God and of our Holy Religion, and for their Assistance in a Christian Practice'.[7]

The second SPCK channel for the spreading of Christian knowledge was education. 'The founders of the SPCK with zeal and driving power developed an existing institution.'[8] This was the widespread system of charity schools. Schools for the poor and underprivileged had a long history before the SPCK came on the scene, but the new society gave the movement a massive boost. The schools prior to 1699 were generally financed by subscribers, who were mostly laymen, and run by share-holders on joint-stock principles; while others resulted from bequests. The SPCK provided a co-ordinated approach which had previously been missing. As a consequence of this new stimulus, the number of schools multiplied rapidly, so that the enterprise assumed national proportions and importance. 'Founded to combat the prevalent irreligion and licence, these schools sought to cultivate virtue and religion on the basis of literacy; but their curriculum was strictly utilitarian. Their object was to give the children of the poor sufficient education to earn their living by manual labour and to read the improving religious tracts issued by the SPCK, without raising them above their station and producing an aversion to menial work.'[9]

Bray also had a deep concern for the work of the church overseas, and he decided that the furtherance of his aims in that direction required another society. The original design was for a body incorporated by

Royal Charter which would allow consultation at the highest level in the Church of England about promoting religion in the plantations; which would seek out suitable clergymen to be commissioned by the Bishop of London for work there; which would establish libraries in the plantations; and which would give financial assistance to any person sent out under its sponsorship.[10] The Charter for the Society for the Propagation of the Gospel in Foreign Parts was laid before the SPCK on 23 June 1701.

The SPG began its work with enthusiasm and zest. Archbishop Tenison summoned the members to its inaugural meeting at Lambeth Palace within four days of its Charter, having been requested to do so by the SPCK; and he was supported by Henry Compton, the Bishop of London, together with the Bishops of Bangor, Chichester and Gloucester, and ten other clergymen as well as fifteen laymen, all of whom were men of distinction. The main work of the Society was care for the needs of the Anglicans in America and the West Indies, who for two centuries had been left without immediate episcopal oversight, but high priority was also given to missionary work among non-Christian peoples as is shown by the two resolutions carried by the Society on 20 April 1710:

> 1. That the design of propagating the Gospel in foreign parts does chiefly and principally relate to the conversion of heathens and infidels, and therefore that branch of it ought to be prosecuted preferably to all others.
> 2. That, in consequence thereof, immediate care be taken to send itinerant missionaries to preach the Gospel among the Six Nations of the Indians according to the primary intentions of the late King William of glorious memory.[11]

Bray and his colleagues had always envisaged a work which would embrace concern 'for the conversion of the Negroes whom the colonists employed as slaves, and of the Indian tribes whose land they had entered'.[12] The missionaries were given a wide brief to care for all whom they could reach, and many of them faithfully fulfilled that duty. 'There can have been few whose returns in the *Notitia Parochialis* did not show, fairly frequently, the baptism of Negroes; more rarely, that of Indians.'[13] An early survey of the missionary situation was made. The Revd Samuel Thomas was sent as a missionary to South Carolina, where no work had been officially undertaken by the Anglican Church except at Charlestown. He was prevented from working among the

Indians because of the outbreak of war between them and the Spaniards to the south, but he began to teach the Negro slaves, and he made good headway among the colonists. Other clergymen were sent, and the new society made funds available for their support. It also supplied Christian literature. For eighty years the attention of the Society was directed almost entirely to the American colonies; it was the first organized attempt by the Church of England to exercise a ministry outside the bounds of the homeland.

The missionaries were commendably zealous and conscientious. There was keenness and vision for the task at home and in America, and the members and benefactors of both societies assiduously helped to maintain the work. But the difficulties of evangelism and pastoral care among the Indians were considerable. Each tribe had its own language, all of which were hard to learn, and few of which had been reduced to writing, so that the missionary often had to rely on an interpreter; and nomadic habits prevented continuity of contact and systematic teaching. Most seriously, the colonists, by taking the Indian land and encroaching on their hunting grounds, by their evident disregard for the Indians, by their prolific use of rum in bartering, with all its evil consequences, and by the quite frequent conflicts with them, aroused among the Indians a widespread hostility which placed the missionaries at an immediate disadvantage. And, lastly, for their further discouragement, the missionaries realized that the Indians were a dying race. 'The wonder is, not that little progress was made, but that so much was accomplished.'[14] It is, for example, quite remarkable that in 1735 the officer in command of the garrison of Fort Hunter, New York State, could report:

> I have found the Mohawk Indians very much civilized, which I take to be owing to the industry and pains taken by the Revd Mr John Miln in teaching and instructing them in the Christian religion. The number of communicants increases daily . . . They are very observing of the Sabbath, convening by themselves and singing Psalms on that day, and frequently applying to me that Mr Miln may be oftener among them.[15]

The same obstacles which stood in the way of missionary work among the American Indians did not hinder the ministry of missionaries to Negroes; or, at least, not to the same extent. But even here, indifference or maltreatment by many brutal or coarse masters set up barriers between the missionaries and the Negroes, prevented slaves coming to instruction, or turned them against Christianity.

In India the British authorities had to enlist the help of German missionaries in order even to help meet the pastoral needs of the troops and other British subjects who were increasing in numbers in all parts of the sub-continent. Also, the East India Company was hostile to missionary effort, largely because of its policy of non-interference in the affairs and customs of the country, and its fear that religious propaganda might provoke resentment and be detrimental to the development of commerce. This overall stance was somewhat relaxed in South India in a remarkable ecumenical experiment in which German missionaries were employed as chaplains by the newly founded SPCK. They used the Prayer Book, baptized and celebrated communion according to the Anglican rite; and yet had never received Anglican episcopal ordination. Outstanding among them was Christian Fredrich Schwartz (1724–98), who served in India without a break for forty-eight years. Before his death there were hopeful signs for the generations ahead: William Carey had arrived in Bengal, and the first Protestant mass movement in India had begun. These pioneers in spreading the gospel in India had achieved great things, and had accomplished indispensable preparatory work for the future growth of the church in the sub-continent. Thus, in the Tanjore area, where Schwartz finished his service, there were upwards of 5,000 baptisms between 1795 and 1805, and the foundation had been laid for the Tinnevelly church, out of which in little more than one hundred years there was to come the first Indian bishop of the Anglican Communion.

The outstanding insight, vision and achievement of Bray and his companions was in stark contrast to contemporary Anglicanism which was remarkably insular. Such parochialism compared unfavourably with 'the vigour of the missionary activity of the Counter-Reformation Church', and 'it took a remarkably long time for a missionary culture' to develop within the Church of England, even under Evangelical influence in the early nineteenth century'.[16] Sydney Smith may have displayed his mild eccentricity when he ridiculed missions, and implied that Anglicanism was not for export; but such a view may have been typical of mainstream clerical opinion in the mid-eighteenth century. It may also explain why the SPG, which started with such enthusiasm in the early years of the century at a time which offered great opportunities, when overseas interests were rapidly and widely extending, prosperity was increasing, and there was command of the seas with consequent growth in trade and in wealth, at first 'expanded while the vision lasted, then kept on a fairly steady level, and at the end began to decline'.[17]

But there were others who kept the flame of non-parochialism and mission alive: most notably William Wake, with his persistent efforts to promote ecumenicalism, and the Moravians, albeit with their base and source of inspiration on the continent.

William Wake, the ecumenical impulse and the work of the Moravians

The coming to the English throne of the Calvinist, occasional conformist, William of Orange, to be succeeded by Queen Anne, with a husband who was a Lutheran and an occasional communicant of the Church of England, and the Act of Settlement of 1701, with its provision for the perpetuation of the Protestant succession in the House of Hanover, all combined to provide a basis for union between the Church of England and the Lutheran and Reformed Churches of the continent. This was made the more attractive with the close association of the principal Protestant powers in the coalition against Louis XIV. Daniel Ernst Jablonski was the moving spirit in an irenic project, the object of which was 'the union of the Lutheran and Reformed Churches in the dominions of the King of Prussia on the basis of their acceptance of episcopacy and of a Liturgy modelled closely on the Book of Common Prayer, and thereafter of a union of both with the Church of England'.[18] There was considerable correspondence between ecclesiastical and political leaders, and it held out hope of furnishing a practical programme for action, but the whole enterprise was frustrated by the quarrels amongst the allies in the negotiations leading to the Treaty of Utrecht in 1713.

Avenues of discussion had, however, been opened up, and it was timely in this respect that in 1716 William Wake was nominated to succeed Thomas Tenison as Primate of all England, for he was 'a firm friend and indefatigable champion of the ecumenical movement of his age'.[19] Wake was clear in his distinction between fundamentals and nonfundamentals in matters of faith. He thought that the Creeds of the first four General Councils were the last resort. He was especially concerned to forge some measure of unity between the Church of England and the Gallican church.[20] He was convinced that this was feasible in his life time:

I make no doubt that a plan might be framed to bring the Gallican church to such a state that we might each hold a true catholic unity

and communion with one another, and yet each continue in many
things to differ, as we see the Protestant churches do . . . To frame
a common confession of faith, or liturgy, or discipline for both
churches is a project never to be accomplished. But to settle each so
that the other shall declare it to be a sound part of the catholic church
and communicate with one another as such – this may easily be done
without much difficulty.[21]

Wake also entered into discussions with other continental churches,
and most notably with the Swiss churches. Although his massive volume
of correspondence and his wide-ranging overtures did not result in any
particular scheme of unity, he established lines of communication which
paved the way for others. In the meantime the SPCK maintained a
close link and co-operation with continental Lutheran and Reformed
churches, and with their leading clergy. Arrangements were made for
the translation of some SPCK publications into continental European
languages, and some important foreign books into English. In addition,
the society supported German Lutheran missionaries in South India,
and gave financial assistance to missionaries sent out by the Danish-
Halle Mission to work in the Danish territory of Tranquebar. As we
have previously noted, the international aspect of such mid-eighteenth
century missionary enterprises was brought to the fore with the employment of Lutheran missionaries as salaried chaplains by the East India
Company to minister the word and sacrament to members of English
communities. There was similar international cooperation in a scheme
whereby Lutherans, under the aegis of the SPCK, ministered to scattered
congregations of English people, Indians or Eurasians.

Then there were the Moravians. 'Ecumenical activity was for Zinzendorf a necessary consequence of his faith.'[22] And England experienced
something of the missionary zeal of his enthusiastic followers when
Moravian centres were established in London as part of a network
which included Germany, Holland, North America, Sweden and the
Baltic countries. It was of course the testimony of some of these
missionary-minded Moravians which was so influential in the lives of
John and Charles Wesley, and they helped to give momentum to the
early revival in England.

Nonetheless, despite all these glimmers of hope, the ecumenical
efforts of the eighteenth century came to nothing, and the Church of
England could hardly be described as impelled by a concern to evange-
lize the world or to unite with other churches and traditions in pastoral

and evangelistic tasks. It was almost entirely focussed on domestic matters, and it showed little awareness of any evangelistic responsibility for the many lands beyond the shores of its native country where the gospel had hardly been heard. This absence of concern for overseas mission was even more pronounced among the Dissenters. None of the Dissenting bodies were sufficiently coordinated or freed from pre-occupation with their internal problems to widen their evangelistic vision to embrace other countries. All this was to change in the last decade of the century.

The late eighteenth-century missionary surge

By the end of the eighteenth century the churches in England were still very blinkered in their outlook, despite the noble exceptions just briefly reviewed. In this they partook of the character of Protestantism in Europe as a whole. Notwithstanding over two hundred years of colonial penetration into North and South America and Asia, as well as parts of Africa and other regions of the world, Christianity remained as a predominantly European religion. No European Protestant country had embarked on a systematic programme of overseas mission, or even made much effort to confront non-Christian peoples, lands and cultures with the Christian gospel. 'In 1800 it was still by no means certain that Christianity would be successful in turning itself into a universal religion . . . America, together with the West Indies, had become a white man's world. The dominance of his religion and his civilization in those areas provided no answer to the question whether Christianity could make itself permanently at home in the lands of the great and ancient non-Christian civilizations.'[23]

But considerable progress had taken place in the last few years of the dying century. The 1790s saw a leap forward in the application of the churches in England to the task of global mission. The progress made then proved to be the first stage in a quite amazing saga of world mission. The change wrought in the worldwide Christian scene within little over a century was to be astonishing. By 1910 only a handful of countries, such as Afghanistan, Tibet and Nepal, remained obstinately closed to all missionary endeavour. Some remote regions were still to be reached, and a few, such as northern Nigeria, were to all intents and purposes kept closed by the colonial powers. 'Otherwise, there were hardly any limits to the extent of the missionary enterprise. It stretched from China to Peru, and was at work both beyond the Arctic Circle and in the desolate and hostile wastes of Tierra del Fuego.' Of course there was much superficial Christianity, with vast tracts of countries and continents merely touched by the gospel; but with each year the totally unevangelized territories were becoming fewer; 'the Christian faith was on the way to becoming literally a world-wide religion'.[24]

For the immediate origin of the late eighteenth-century missionary impulse we need to go back to 1781, when a Baptist, Robert Hall, published *Helps to Zion's Travellers*. In spite of its somewhat pietistic title, it was a resolute and unflinching assertion in the face of years of dominant high Calvinism, that the gospel was available to whosoever would come to receive salvation. On many occasions the young William Carey would walk twenty miles in order to be in Hall's congregation; and Carey was deeply moved by his favourite preacher's publication: 'I do not remember ever to have read any book with such raptures.'[25]

In 1784, John Sutcliff, the pastor of Olney, issued his famous 'Prayer Call'. At the Association's meeting he proposed that churches should be encouraged to hold a special meeting on the first Monday evening of every month for united prayer; and in the Association's Circular Letter he urged its readers not to remain parochial in their praying:

. . . let the whole interest of the Redeemer be affectionately remembered, and the spread of the gospel to the distant parts of the habitable globe be the object of your most fervent requests.[26]

The 'Prayer Call' was copied in other lands. By 1814 there were similar monthly prayer meetings in Holland, Switzerland, Germany, America, India and Africa. 'A new sense of urgent missionary concern was gradually spreading through the churches. The effects of Sutcliffe's call were to widen the geographical and spiritual horizons of Christians of all denominations in this land and beyond.'[27] But this is to look ahead a few years; for in the intervening period there had been an astonishing outburst of innovative missionary activity.

The first move was made by the Methodists. Although John Wesley was no enemy of missions, in fact the very reverse, on two occasions he appears to have delayed the efforts of Thomas Coke, his lieutenant, to promote foreign missions in order to concentrate on the harvest at home. Ever persistent, in 1783 Coke issued his *Plan of the Society for the Establishment of Missions among the Heathen*, and from 1786 there were Methodist missionaries working in the West Indies, Newfoundland, Nova Scotia and Quebec. It was also in 1786 that Coke proposed an annual subscription for the support of missionaries, which had the added merit of being a recruiting device in which the preachers were encouraged 'to spend and be spent' in the missionary cause. Even so, it was not until 1813 that the Weslyan Methodist Missionary Society was founded.

It was the Baptists who took early and decisive action. In 1792 William Carey published a work entitled *An Enquiry into the Obligation of Christians to Use Means for the Conversion of the Heathen*. In it he argued that the Great Commission of Christ to go and preach the gospel to all nations was still binding on Christians. Here was an expression of the activism which was one of the characteristics of the new breed of evangelicals. The influential Jonathan Edwards encouraged the belief that human beings can be the appointed agents in bringing the gospel to the unevangelized nations, and he set an example by the support he gave to his friend David Brainerd in a mission to the Indians, as well as by undertaking a similar work himself. Carey was entering in to this rapidly developing tradition. In 1792 he was instrumental in establishing the Baptist Missionary Society, 'the first foreign mission to spring from the revival'.[28] By the following year he was pioneering its operation in India. It was the 'first British missionary society designed exclusively to convert the heathen',[29] and as such it was a significant step forward in world mission.

Carey arrived in India with his family on 11 November 1793. He consciously stood 'in a noble succession, as the heir of many pioneers in the past. Yet his work does represent a turning-point; it marks the entry of the English-speaking world on a large scale into the missionary enterprise – and it has been the English-speaking world which has provided four fifths of the non-Roman missionaries from the days of Carey until the present time.'[30] Although he was the first missionary of the Baptist Missionary Society he was extraordinarily independent and advanced in his missionary strategy. He had a comprehensive and holistic view of missionary work with five components: the wide-ranging presentation of the gospel; support for this by the distribution of the Bible in the language of the people; the early establishment of a church; a profound study and appreciation of the background, culture and thought of the non-Christian people concerned; and the earliest possible training of an indigenous ministry. It was partly his comprehensive grasp of missionary strategy that led to tensions between the Serempore Trio in India, consisting of William Carey, Joshua Marshman and William Ward, and the home committee in England with its more restricted outlook. In addition there were problems over funding policy and various other administrative and strategy issues. To this was added personality clashes among the missionaries themselves, and irritation in the ranks of the younger missionaries at the continuing pre-eminence of the Trio. The early years of missionary endeavour were exciting, heroic and distinguished, but they were not unsullied times of harmony and light.

While Carey was undertaking his seminal missionary work in India, Samuel Marsden was spearheading another missionary thrust in New Zealand. He had arrived in the Antipodes in 1794, and eventually reached New Zealand and the Maoris, among whom he was convinced God wanted him to serve as an evangelist, in 1814. He and Carey were but two better known pioneers in an age of heroic missionary effort which was to continue, with peaks and troughs, for the whole of the nineteenth and twentieth centuries.

Meanwhile, there was a further missionary advance on the home front. In 1793 the Warwickshire association of ministers decided to unite in order to promote Christian mission among non-Christians; they opened a fund, and they set aside the first Monday evening each month for missionary prayer meetings. The following year Carey's first letter from India so inspired David Bogue of Gosport, Robert Steven of the Scots Church, Covent Garden, and John Hey of Castle Green Independent Church, Bristol, that they met in Bristol for prayer and consultation on the best way to arouse support for the missionary enterprise. The interdenominational journal, *The Evangelical Magazine*, had been founded partially in order to promote missions, and first Brogue, then Thomas Haweis, the Evangelical rector of Aldwincle in Northamptonshire, contributed articles to it which challenged Christians to establish a society dedicated to mission. The immediate outcome was a series of fortnightly meetings at the Castle and Falcon in Aldersgate Street, London, followed by an enthusiastic gathering at Spa Fields Chapel which witnessed the inauguration of the new London Missionary Society. It was 'the first interdenominational society and the first to make such a large-scale bid for public support'.[31] It was launched amid scenes of unbounded joy and great expectation. Financial support was immediate and generous.

There were other developments which helped in this fast-growing missionary awareness. The first ship-load of convicts was sent to Australia accompanied by a chaplain; as we have seen previously, the SPCK Lutheran missionary Christian Friedrich Schwartz visited Tinnevelley, and set in motion a series of actions which led over twenty years later to the establishment of the Church Missionary Society

Tinnevelley Mission; and Dr Thomas Coke, the great Wesleyan missionary leader, made the first of his eighteen voyages across the Atlantic, to the West Indies, and initiated a missionary enterprise in which the Church Missionary Society and other societies afterwards co-operated.

But it was within the Church of England that the greatest efforts were made. After much protestation and lobbying, an Act of Parliament had been passed which enabled the Church of England to commence its colonial and missionary episcopate. But this did not meet the needs of those vast overseas territories which were as yet unevangelized and unchurched. Such a shortcoming was a particular concern for members of the Clapham Sect. They started a campaign to introduce into the Charter of the East India Company measures for the religious and moral improvement of the inhabitants of India; and, more specifically, to empower and require the Company to send out fit and proper persons to act as schoolmasters and missionaries. They failed to achieve their objective in 1793, and it took a further twenty years of pressure and persistence before the Charter of 1813 guaranteed liberty to propagate the Christian faith. It was a major step forward. William Wilberforce was convinced that the foundation stone had been laid 'of the greatest edifice that ever was raised in Asia'.[32]

In its concern for the church-worldwide, the Clapham brotherhood also engaged in attempts to open up new regions to Christian influence, and to improve the lot of various disadvantaged groups and societies. Wilberforce was one of the early members of the African Association, which was established in 1788 to send out explorers. Within less than three weeks of the passing of the Abolition Bill in 1807, the men of Clapham founded the African Institution, of which the main object was to promote civilization in Africa by providing 'example to enlighten the minds of the natives, and instruction to enable them to direct their industry to proper objects'. As the slave trade did not cease with its official abolition, the Institution was soon transformed into an anti-slavery society. But the most notable example of the Clapham Sect missionary interest was the engagement of almost all the Clapham fraternity in an initiative in 1799 which was to have worldwide and lasting importance of considerable magnitude.

When the Eclectic Society had its discussions on the possibility of a Church of England mission to the 'heathen' there was by no means a unanimously enthusiastic response; in fact only two or three out of seventeen present – probably Charles Simeon, Thomas Scott and Basil

Woodd – favoured any definite attempt being made. Here was an echo of the recent reception given to the proposal of William Carey at a Baptist ministers' meeting that consideration should be given to the Baptist responsibility to the heathen; for Carey had been told in a forthright way by the chairman to sit down. In the case of the Eclectic members, the majority expressed apprehension about the reaction of the bishops, shrank from seeming to interfere with the SPCK and the SPG, doubted the possibility of recruiting men, or urged the claims of the church at home. Undaunted, the two or three persisted, and long afterwards Basil Woodd wrote across his manuscript notes of the discussion, 'This conversation proved the foundation of the Church Missionary Society.' It was on Friday, 12 April 1799 that the public meeting was held in a first-floor room in a hotel in Aldersgate, The Castle and Falcon, which established The Society for Missions in Africa and the East, later to be renamed the Church Missionary Society: a society which was to become the largest missionary organization in the world.[33] It was the same hotel in which, four years earlier, the London Missionary Society had been founded.

In the first years of its life the new society faced daunting difficulties. Although I have spoken of the birth of a missionary awareness at this time, it was limited to a quite small number of the bolder and more visionary members of the denominations involved; there was no wave of missionary enthusiasm which engulfed English Christendom, as is sometimes implied. Such a great event as the departure of William Carey for India in 1793 was only seen to be momentous many years later. At the time the 'consecrated cobbler' was mostly the subject of sneers or indifference. The new society started with much discouragement; the glamour of it as a pioneer enterprise was only recognized in retrospect, after it had acquired great stature. For many years no bishop joined it and no British missionaries could be found. The only suitable candidate who offered his services, and who would have been joyfully accepted, the brilliant Senior Wrangler Henry Martyn, went to India as an East India Company chaplain because of difficulties and restrictions to which a professed missionary would have been subject. By the time the society was ten years old, it had sent out only five missionaries, all Germans, of whom one was dead, one had been dismissed, and three were still at work.

Also, the whole concept of work among native peoples in far off lands was not familiar. When Simeon called for chaplains for India the response was good. Clergy were ready to travel to the uttermost ends of the earth in order to work among white men, but to serve among peoples of other cultures and native religions was an almost unheard-of-thing. There was 'no missionary literature, no missionary tradition; the whole scheme seemed vague and nebulous, and not a man would come forward'.[34]

The committee was without experience and had no precedents from which to seek guidance. Many mistakes were made. When a mission was begun in Sierra Leone the untrained missionaries lingered near the coast, appalled at the dangers of the country and the difficulties of the language. One of them caused a scandal by engaging in the slave trade. When a mission was inaugurated among the Maoris of New Zealand there were interminable delays, and some of the missionaries had to be dismissed for trading in liquor and guns.

Then there was tragedy, hardship and loss, as in 1823. In that year, of seven new schoolmasters and five wives who landed at Sierra Leone, ten died within eighteen months, and there were also the deaths of three other missionaries and two chaplains and their wives. The society was fortunate that, with so many, and such grave, problems in its early years it was served by able leaders, including the wise John Venn, the sensitive Thomas Scott, the able and conscientious Josiah Pratt, and the fervent, eloquent and diplomatic Edward Bickersteth.

The founders of the CMS saw the new society as supplementary to the SPCK and the SPG. It was necessary partly because of the different churchmanship of the older societies, partly because, by the late eighteenth century, they concentrated almost exclusively on the British plantations in America and the West Indies, and partly because they had become apathetic and ineffective. But the Evangelicals viewed the SPCK and the SPG as part of a total global mission. When there was a sudden and marked expansion of the SPG in the second and third decades of the century and onwards, it was described by Pratt with unfeigned joy and unreserved sympathy. The CMS committee was also careful not to intrude into what might be SPG fields of labour.

Despite the innumerable setbacks, and the continuing problems, the work of the society progressed in varying degrees in India, Sierra Leone and New Zealand, and new mission fields were opened, including Ceylon (1818), Egypt (1826), British Guiana (1827) and Abyssinia (1830).

In the meantime High Churchmen were not idle. The Hackney Phalanx was once more to the fore. Its sympathies lay with the SPCK and the SPG, because they were rooted and grounded in the established church, and they were identified with a High Church tradition. On the initiative of the Phalanx, a committee was set up in 1810 to help revitalize the SPCK, largely by organizing local diocesan committees. The whole initiative was with the sanction and under the direction of the bishops. In 1814 Joshua Watson became the Treasurer of the SPCK. He also laboured energetically for the SPG, and strove to link the two societies together as closely as possible. Like the SPCK, the SPG was in urgent need of new men and new ideas; it had degenerated into a board for holding various trust funds, and it had lost the verve and vision of former times. Its total income was only about £8,000 per year, of which less than £500 came from donations or subscriptions. By the time of Watson's death in 1855 this had increased to more than £82,000, mainly due to an enormous increase in subscriptions, and to frequent collections in churches.[35]

It was in the sphere of world mission that the extent of common ground between the Clapham and Clapton Sects was perhaps most clearly demonstrated. In the campaign which led to Parliament authorizing the admission of missionaries to India and to the creation of a small establishment of one bishop and three archdeacons, the Evangelicals took the lead, but they were supported by the High Church Hackney Phalanx members. And it was one of the most able and energetic members of the Phalanx, T. F. Middleton, who was appointed as the first bishop; a move accepted graciously, albeit with disappointment, by the Evangelicals. The Clapham Sect members, the Saints and the members of the Phalanx maintained a degree of co-operation despite an abortive attempt, instigated by Christopher Wordsworth and Reginald Heber, to bring about the union of the CMS and the SPG. Perhaps the main contribution of Watson and his associates was to help in placing mission on the agenda of every bishop; it was no mean achievement, and it married nicely with the more voluntaristic policy of the Evangelicals.

Although Evangelicals in the Church of England were *ex animo* loyal members of their chosen church, thoroughly believed in episcopacy and liturgical worship, and set a high value on establishment, a number of them were prepared to co-operate with Dissenters in some pan-evangelical ventures in the late eighteenth century and the early nineteenth century. Such joint non-denominational projects as the Religious Tract Society, founded in 1799, and the British and Foreign Bible Society, founded in 1804, did not compromise the loyalty of the Anglican participants to the established church. The London

Missionary Society had been almost exclusively the work of Dissenting evangelicals; the support of Anglican Evangelicals having been unsuccessfully sought. The two new societies were supported by both Anglican and Dissenting evangelicals.

The Religious Tract Society had as its aim the distribution of Christian literature for the benefit of Christians and as a tool for evangelism. It was soon playing an important part in the domestic mission of the church. Anglican Evangelicals such as Charles Simeon, Thomas Biddulph, Legh Richmond and Richard Cecil contributed tracts; Legh Richmond served as a Secretary to the Society, and Zachary Macaulay was a member of the first committee.

The British and Foreign Bible Society was even more impressive, both in the quality and the quantity of what it produced and distributed, and in the support it attracted. It was the first pan-evangelical institution to win the patronage of most evangelicals in a full range of denominations. Church of England Evangelicals were encouraged to participate in it because it was perceived by many of them as having one, uncomplicated objective, to distribute the Bible; because it restricted the Bibles circulated to those established by public authority; and because it insisted that its committee should be composed of an equal number of Anglicans and Dissenters. Even though some Evangelicals, most notably Charles Simeon, hesitated to support it, it was not long before they were in a minority, and it was established as the largest and most ambitious of the great pan-evangelical organizations. It was viewed as an essentially Christian business venture which did not impinge upon denominational interests or autonomy.

Nevertheless, from the start the Bible Society was vigorously opposed by some High Churchmen. They saw it as a challenge to the authority of the SPCK, and they feared that unwary clergymen would be drawn into what was patently an evangelical organization, upholding evangelical interests. Co-operation with Dissenters was anathema to such churchmen, as it implied the abandonment of a distinctively Anglican ecclesiology. It was a denial of the concept of a single, national, established church, and a threat to church order. The confrontation was especially intense in Cambridge, where an auxiliary of the Society was established despite entrenched resistance and disapproval.

By the third decade of the nineteenth century the conflict with High Churchmen was superseded by contention over the continental practice of distributing Bibles containing the Apocrypha. The Edinburgh and

Glasgow auxiliaries withdrew from the Bible Society because the parent body in London, while agreeing not to circulate the Apocrypha with Society Bibles, would not withdraw all support from the continental societies which still elected to print Apocryphal Bibles at their own expense. Other Scottish auxiliaries ended their contributions to the parent body; and this sometimes heated debate spread throughout all the auxiliaries.

Just as the agitation was subsiding, the Society was further disrupted by the Socinian or Test controversy, in which some supporters demanded a test of faith which would weed out unorthodox members. Again, those for and against were set fiercely in opposition to each other. The climax was reached in 1831 at Exeter Hall in London, when the anti-Test party, consisting of many Anglican Evangelicals, and virtually all the evangelical Dissenters, defeated the pro-Test party which was composed almost entirely of those belonging to either the English or Scottish establishments. Largely failing in their persistent attempts to assert their view, the pro-test party established the Trinitarian Bible Society.

Nonetheless, despite these and other disputes, the progress in the space of little more than one generation in confronting the challenge of global mission was most impressive. The churches in 1832 were poised for impending massive advances in extending Christian mission into many of the unevangelized regions of the world. In the following century and a half missionaries were to penetrate vast tracts of formerly unreached parts of the habitable world, and a significant proportion of this outreach was to be accomplished by English men and women, or by others sent out and supported by English societies. It has been suggested that the worldwide advance of Christianity went hand-in-hand with the triumphant march of colonialism, imperialism and national commercial interests, and even that Christianity rode on the back of these secular interests, or simply aided and abetted them. Certainly, even in these early pioneer days of missionary outreach situations arose in which questions of British colonial policy were impossible to avoid, as with the slavery issue in the West Indies,[36] the treatment of indigenous peoples in South Africa[37] and the interrelation of Christianity, slavery, commercial activity and 'the civilization process' in Africa as a whole.[38] A thorough examination of British nineteenth- and twentieth-century missionary activity, which I clearly cannot undertake within the limits of this present study, seems to reveal a considerable intertwining of these various, and often disparate, interests, but generally appears to exonerate the missionaries, their societies, supporters and supporting churches from complicity in the process of colonial exploitation, and to emphasize how noble was the missionary enterprise as a whole. It conferred immense, unmeasurable benefits on the receiving peoples and nations. It demanded a quality of life and a measure of self-sacrifice from countless missionaries which has left a lasting and imperishable testimony to the power of the Christian message to transform lives. It produced a saga of dedicated service which would reflect honour and credit on any nation. Certainly it suffered from shortcomings, and it was tarnished by association with ideals less pure and worthy than those which were at its heart. Yet, in total, it remains as a remarkable record of human endeavour under the inspiration of a life-transforming faith.

9

The Churches in England Transformed

The churches in England in 1832 presented a marked contrast to the churches which had emerged from the bloodless Revolution of 1688, and also to the churches which, less than a hundred years ahead, were to emerge from the extremely bloody First World War. With hindsight we can see that the one hundred and fifty years of history which I have reviewed was a prelude to the modern era of English church history. The main contours were established. A framework of tolerance allowed for a variety of religious traditions to establish themselves, and to be widely accepted by the English people at large. This embraced a range of Christian traditions, but also increasingly encompassed a strong representation of all the other major world religions as well as some more bizarre and exotic 'fringe' religions. Then, as an aspect of this, there was the entrenchment of Nonconformity and Roman Catholicism in the period from 1689 to 1832, which provided a foundation for the impressive growth and multiplication of non-Church of England Protestant traditions as well as the quite remarkable blossoming of Roman Catholicism in the succeeding century and a half, and the important minority presence of the Orthodox Church. Within Protestantism itself evangelicalism and High Churchmanship, which had started to assume such importance before 1833, were to develop and make massive contributions to the religious history of the country. And the modern evangelical movement, which had been born in the eighteenth century, was destined to be vigorous both within most of the denominations and in the form of pan-evangelicalism. The 1828–1832 re-definition of the relationship of the various churches to the state was to be further refined and elaborated as the religious scene became more complex and as English society became more 'secular'. This entailed Church of England institutional renewal, which may be viewed within 'a wider, utilitarian, government-sponsored movement to increase the efficiency of institutions';[1] a process which included the professionalization of the clergy and the episcopate, and the increasingly important part played by the laity in the life and governance of the church. A similar re-adjustment was to take place of the previously assumed association of Christianity, and more especially Protestantism, with an emerging distinctive British identity. A degree of urban, industrial, working-class alienation from institutional religion, of which there were signs in the eighteenth century and early nineteenth century as a consequence of the process of industrialization and urbanization was, during the ensuing century and a half, to be an ever more important element in the total religious, or non-religious, English scene. And, lastly, 'secularism', 'rationalism' and atheism, the first tender shoots of which had appeared in the period 1689–1832, were to assume a greater significance, and become more central to the whole religious life of the nation. These were the main features of English religious life which the period covered by this book bequeathed to the future. As I conclude my survey I will therefore take a brief look forward, so that the relevance of what I have covered in the preceding chapters may be more clearly understood because it is set within the total historical context of the churches in England throughout the last three hundred years and more.

From ancien regime *to the modern state*

In 1800 the Church of England was secure. The state was confessional, with the established church 'accorded exclusive endorsement as the spiritual and theological basis in the ordering of society. Political groups saw it as their highest duty to maintain the union of throne and altar. The church established by law was . . . effectively governed by Parliament as a kind of lay assembly, and had been ever since the suspension of the Convocations in 1717. As the 'bulwark of the Reformation' the church was regarded, both popularly and by ruling opinion, as the repository of Protestant virtue, the guarantor of order and morality, and – strange notion to modern understanding – as the guardian of political liberty'.[2] All of this was to start to crumble from 1828 onwards. The combination of the Repeal of the Test and Corporation Acts in 1828, the Catholic Emancipation Act of 1829 and the Reform Act of 1832 changed the situation for ever. These three measures represented a revolution as significant in its way as the Revolution of 1688. They set in motion trends which were irreversible. They sounded the death knoll for the *ancien régime*. They changed the ground rules which governed the status and standing of the established church, and they helped to establish a principle of 'democracy' which was to effect a revolution in the way the country was to be governed. But it was only the beginning of a process. Still, in 1832, all Members of Parliament were Christians, and almost entirely members of the Church of England. Non-Anglicans were barred from acquiring degrees at Oxford and Cambridge. Civil divorce was virtually unobtainable. Taking a wider view, Christianity itself in its various institutional forms was to all appearances safe, despite periodic, and largely unco-ordinated, onslaughts. The Christian faith in its orthodox form was widely accepted as normative and not questioned; and most publishers refused to produce works such as Strauss's *Life of Jesus* for fear of prosecution for blasphemy. Forty years later the change was startling. Men of all faiths, and soon men of no faith, might enter Parliament and the universities; and divorce could be obtained from a division of the High Court. 'It was possible publicly to deny the most basic tenets of Christianity and still remain within the law; and to query the accuracy and even the authority of the Bible, to doubt the reality of miracles and of hell and still remain a beneficed clergyman, and even a bishop. In its influence in state and society, the Church, though still a partner, was no longer an equal, still less a dominant partner; while the Anglican Church in Ireland was actually disestablished.'[3]

Nonetheless, despite this general picture of declining influence – of 'secularization' and of the changing role in society of the churches as a whole including the Nonconformists and the Roman Catholics – Victorian England was exceedingly religious.

> Its churches thrived and multiplied, its best minds brooded over divine metaphysic and argued about moral principle, its authors and painters and architects and poets seldom forgot that art and literature shadowed eternal truth or beauty, its legislators professed outward and often accepted inward allegiance to divine law, its men of empire ascribed national greatness to the providence of God and the Protestant faith. The Victorians changed the face of the world because they were assured . . . Part of their confidence was money, a people of increasing wealth and prosperity, an ocean of retreating horizons. And part was of the soul. God is; and we are his servants, and under his care, and will do our duty.[4]

Both the elements of Christian vitality, revival and renewal and those of underlying decline and erosion can be seen to have had their origins in the long eighteenth century, and even further back.

A brief consideration of a somewhat random selection of Christian leaders and opponents of the Christian faith who were alive in 1832 will give a feel of the new religious world which was being inaugurated. Anthony Ashley Cooper, the seventh Earl of Shaftesbury, was at the beginning of a career which would engage the Church of England in some of the central issues arising out of industrialization and urbanization. William Ewart Gladstone had entered Parliament in 1832. His career was to embrace a personal move from Evangelicalism to High Churchmanship, and to involve responsibility for such contentious policies as the abolition of compulsory church rates, the disestablishment of the Irish Church, and the establishment of a combined Catholic and Protestant university in Ireland. John Henry Newman, John Keble and Edward Bouverie Pusey were about to spearhead the Oxford Movement, and to reinvigorate Anglican High Churchmanship in such a way that the effects were to last until the present day. And such dedicated High Churchmen as Charles Lowder (born 1820) and Alexander Mackonochie (born 1825) were to serve sacrificially in an unrelenting effort to bring the gospel to deprived and disadvantaged people in the urban slums. Then there were John Ludlow, Frederick Denison Maurice, Charles Kingsley and Thomas Hughes, and all that they were to represent and accomplish in the Christian Socialist movement, as well as the stir they were to generate as a consequence of some of their less conventional beliefs. Such giants of Nonconformity as Robert William Dale (born 1829) and George Muller (born 1805) were to epitomize a vibrant, self-confident Nonconformist denominationalism; and it was only two years before Charles Haddon Spurgeon, that prince of nine-teenth-century preachers, was to see the light of day, and five years before D. L. Moody was to be born. Far away in Rome Nicholas Wiseman presided quietly and uncontroversially over the English College, but was to be at the centre of a great religious and political storm when the Roman Catholic hierarchy was restored in England in 1850, and when he was appointed cardinal and the first Archbishop of Westminster. In contrast, William Booth (born 1829) was to found a society which, in its structure, ethos and strategy was to characterize much of the extra-ecclesiastical activity of the late nineteenth century and the twentieth century. It was in the same spirit that George Williams (born 1821) founded the Young Men's Christian Association. And, to round off this portrait gallery of future 'moulders of public opinion' and contributors to a much changed religious scene in a very different age to come, I include Charles Darwin, Karl Marx and Charles Bradlaugh, each of whom, in different ways, was to cast a massive rock into the religious pool.

The Church of England

The first change which was pending in 1832 was institutional reorientation. 'To enter England in the 1830s through her Church door is to confront immediately a new set of conditions in the age-old Church-State relationship.'[5] Both Anglicans and non-Anglicans were acutely aware that a fundamental alteration had taken place. The opponents of the church were anxious to push their new-found advantages as far and as quickly as possible in order to achieve further rights, and in order to bring about disestablishment; and churchmen were keen to reappraise their position, and to formulate various defenses for the continuance of the establishment. The onslaught on the privileges, property and prerogatives of the Church of England gathered momentum in the 1820s and the 1830s. 'A formidable coalition – English dissenters, Irish Catholics and middle-class radicals, under the leadership of worldly Whigs – launched a wide-ranging attack on the Anglican monopoly of public life. One by one the citadels fell: parliament; the corporations; the universities; the Irish executive.'[6]

Foremost among the early Church of England champions were the affronted Tractarians. The 1833 Assize Sermon of John Keble was a clarion call for the church to reaffirm its catholicity and independence in the face of attack and the evils of Erastianism; and it was rapidly followed by Tracts which called upon all true churchmen to join the crusade in support of 'the Church in danger'. The battered and bruised Church of England was reminded of the ideal church-state relationship expounded by Richard Hooker: in which the state was a Christian community ruled by a godly king; in which all citizens were members of Christ's church; and in which church and state were but aspects of the one coherent unified society. The Tractarians tried to impart a new vision of what should be, and what was possible; fully aware of the perils of perishing for a people who had no vision.

Thomas Mozley wrote of the Church of England as 'folding its robes to die with what dignity it could'. But all was not lost. Indeed, the position was perhaps not as dire as it was portrayed by the prophets of doom. The church still had a strong hold upon countless people at all levels in the population at large; it also had many friends in the newly constituted House of Commons, as well as in the House of Lords. Because of its latent and pervasive grip on the affections and loyalty of a diffuse, numberless but large, body of the population, and because of its continued great influence in Parliament and throughout the establishment as a whole, the fears of churchmen were not speedily realized, and there was an anticlimax for about forty years.

The Church of England was able to escape with a meagre harvest of change and reform. Although Peel instituted an ecclesiastical commission in 1835, with the brief to redeploy the wealth of the church; although in 1836 an act was passed which eliminated the troublesome business of the payment of tithes in kind; and although in the same year a new system of civil registration relieved Nonconformists of the need to be married in church; most of the remaining Dissenting disabilities, including the bitterly resented imposition of a compulsory church rate, were unredressed until after the Second Reform Act of 1867. But the day of reckoning was merely being postponed. Most thinking men and women, friends and foes alike, probably appreciated that the fears of the period 1828 to 1832 were neither unreasonable nor irrelevant. They 'were excited by forces in the country whose demands would not be for ever frustrated by the limitations of the electoral system'.[7]

Such forces were ominous and threatening to the Church of England as established. There were the mass desertions to the Nonconformist denominations, which had already begun, and which were to become much more pronounced within a short time. There was the readiness of the aggrieved Irish Catholics to resort to violence, and to assert their rights, especially whenever their priesthood felt that their spiritual interests were at stake. There was the emergence of a newly-assertive, self-confident middle class, the product of an expanding economy, which contested aristocratic dominance, many of whom were not loyal members of the Church of England, or even active members of any church. There was the impact of such 'new' disciplines as biblical criticism and geology, and the 'crisis of faith' which this heralded, as it reinforced the agnosticism of the eighteenth-century *philosophes*. And there was the secularization of the European mind which 'subjected religious institutions to utilitarian criteria'.[8]

From within the Church of England perhaps the most radical and far-reaching reaction to the assaults on the status and standing of the established church came from the pen of that disturber of the church's peace and complacency, Thomas Arnold. In 1833, in a pamphlet entitled *Principles of Church Reform*, he attempted 'to cut through the ambiguity of a national church set in a pluralist society', and advocated 'the inclusive method, whereby all Christians would once again be embraced within the national Church'.[9] But the means proposed to achieve this end appeared to alarmed and infuriated churchmen as being nothing less than pernicious and extreme Erastianism. For he proposed that the church should be made comprehensive enough to encompass the widest possible range of Christian, and indeed non-Christian, views, and he aligned himself with some of the more rabid radicals in suggesting that such comprehensiveness would then allow church property to be applied 'to strictly public purposes, to schools, hospitals, almshouses, or something of the sort'.[10] In the eyes of his detractors he displayed a distressing disregard for dogmatic niceties. With his emphasis upon tolerance, morality and social utilitarianism, he was regarded as a propagator of that *bête noire* of Evangelicals and High Churchmen alike, liberalism.

This brings us to another characteristic of incipient modernity: the development of religious parties and pressure groups. The 1830s witnessed the emergence of the modern political party system, with the ever clearer concentration of power in the hands of the Prime Minister, with an inner 'Cabinet', a House of Commons increasingly dominated by two opposing parties, and this whole edifice supported by an emergent professional civil service. The eighteenth century had seen the commencement of this process, but it reached its apogee in the second quarter of the nineteenth century. Likewise, there was, to some extent, a parallel ecclesiastical development with the Evangelicals and High Churchmen, and perhaps the Broad Churchmen, assuming an ever-clearer identity in the Church of England, and the Nonconformist denominations as well as the Catholics also displaying distinct characteristics, with ever more formal organization and more elaborate national and local bureaucratic structures. And, of course, as in the political sphere, such developments had their origins in the eighteenth century.

Among the parties within the Church of England in the first two decades of the nineteenth century Evangelicals were the most integrated and dynamic; their confidence raised by the quite remarkable growth in their numbers, both in absolute terms and as a proportion of the total church of which they were a part. The phenomenal transformation since their very uncertain and vulnerable early life in the second quarter of the eighteenth century, of which they were justifiably proud, bore fruit in the eighteenth and nineteenth centuries. They experienced internal divisions and some decline in influence during the 1820s and 1830s, but the Victorian era was to be the great time of Anglican Evangelical dominance and influence in certain selected towns, with the notable ministries of Francis Close (1797–1882) in Cheltenham, Hugh McNeile

(1795–1879) in Liverpool, Hugh Stowell (1799–1865) in Manchester, and William Pennefather (1816–73), William Champneys (1807–75) and William Cadman in London. For fifty years there was also a note-worthy Evangelical influence in national movements of reform and ecclesiastical affairs, with the work of Lord Shaftesbury, Charles Sumner (1790–1874) as Bishop of Winchester, and John Bird Sumner (1780–1862) as Bishop of Chester and then Archbishop of Canterbury being of particular importance. Evangelicals also distinguished them-selves in evangelistic and missionary endeavour at home and abroad. Outstanding contributions came from those already mentioned in their various urban situations, and from Wilson Carlile with the founding of the Church Army in the last two decades of the century. And on the world scene Henry Venn (1796–1873) took a leading part in the progress of the Church Missionary Society, with a countless host of mostly unsung heroes of the faith giving themselves in service in an ever widening circle of countries of the world, and not infrequently at the cost of their own health and lives.

Evangelicalism in general, of which the Anglican version was but a part, was the quintessential expression of a popular Protestant culture which flourished throughout the Victorian era. The nineteenth was 'the great century of English Protestantism, the era of the Evangelical and Nonconformist revivals, when the religion of the Reformation influenced and moulded the lives of as high a proportion of the popula-tion at as deep a level as in any previous era of English history'.[11]

For the first five and a half decades of the twentieth century this buoyant Evangelicalism gave way to decline and negativity, in which there was preoccupation with campaigns against High Church ritualism and the revision of the Prayer Book, internal divisions between the more conservative Evangelicals and a blossoming Evangelical Liberalism, and little of the creative evangelism, social involvement and missionary activity of the former period.

The post-Second World War years brought a new Evangelical thrust forward, symbolized by such prominent and influential Evangelicals as Max Warren, John Stott and George Carey; by the Evangelical Anglican Conferences at Keele (1967) and Nottingham (1977), in which Evangelicals attempted to grapple with the issues facing them and the church as a whole; by a new sense of social responsibility as expressed in such ventures as the Shaftesbury Project; a renewed sense of vitality, as demonstrated in the vigorous life of the Inter-Varsity Fellowship (later the Universities and Colleges Christian Fellowship), the Charismatic Movement and such well-supported events as the Billy Graham Crusades and the Spring Harvest gatherings; and the responsible involvement in worldwide Christian mission, as depicted in the founding and flourishing of TEAR Fund. And those late twentieth-century Evangelicals who had sufficient historical awareness were as conscious as any of their forebears that their roots were in the eighteenth century and early nineteenth century, in the lives and labours of those whom I have considered in the present study.[12]

Present day High Churchmen trace the modern phase of their history back to Richard Hooker, to William Laud, the seventeenth-century Caroline Divines, to Bishop Thomas Ken and the Nonjurors, and to the Hutchinsonians and the Hackney Phalanx; but also, in a very special way, to the Oxford Movement and the subsequent development of Anglo-Catholicism.

Although in certain respects the Oxford Movement inherited a long and distinguished tradition, in many aspects of its teaching and practice it diverged from the older High Churchmanship and caused ideological division. It was especially divisive in its ambiguous attitude to the authority, standing and teaching of the Church of England, and in the warmth of welcome which some of its members gave to the teaching and decrees of the Roman Catholic Church. And, of course, it caused the greatest consternation when this was made explicit with the publication in 1838 of Tract 80 on *Reserve in Religious Teaching* and, more especially, in the same year, with Richard Hurrell Froude's *Remains*, in which he fiercely condemned the Reformation. Concern was raised to fever pitch with the circulation in 1841 of Newman's *Tract 90*, in which he asserted that the Thirty-Nine Articles, 'the offspring of an uncatholic age, are, through God's good providence, at least not uncatholic, and may be subscribed by those who aim at being Catholic in heart and doctrine', and with the publication in 1844 of W. G. Ward's *The Ideal of a Christian Church*, the sting of which was the claim that the author could keep his place in the English church while holding and teaching all Roman doctrine. To cap this Romeward bias there were the very much publicized secessions to the Roman church, headed in 1845 by John Newman.[13]

In the following one hundred years there were various manifestations of High Church vitality and creativity, as well as painful divisions and much violent opposition. There was a somewhat uneasy period of adjustment between the secession of Newman and the birth of Liberal Catholicism under Charles Gore and Henry Scott Holland forty years later. This subsequent new phase of modern High Churchmanship was heralded with the publication in 1889 of *Lux Mundi. A Series of Studies in the Religion of the Incarnation*, edited by Gore. It shook the religious world by the manner in which it attempted 'to put the Catholic faith into its right relation to modern intellectual and moral problems'.[14] Many of the assertions contained in the book caused consternation, as they appeared to critics to yield too much to modern biblical critics, but indignation was largely reserved for the kenotic theory to which the editor gave credence in an aside in his essay on the problem of Christ's human knowledge. In the face of the prevailing belief in the omniscience of Christ, Gore insisted that Christ revealed God 'through, and under conditions of, a true human nature'.[15] In his incarnation he showed no signs of transcending the science or history of his day, and he never attempted to reveal his eternal divinity by statements on what happened in the past or were to happen in the future. The tone set by *Lux Mundi* was perpetuated and became part of the High Church tradition out of which the present day High Churchmanship has been forged. At the time the new, liberal, approach was energetically opposed by H. P. Liddon and others, and the tension between the conservative and liberal wings of Anglican High Churchmanship continued throughout the next century, and became particularly acute in the latter part of the century.

Other developments of major importance in the latter half of the nineteenth century included the establishment of religious communities; the flourishing of neo-Gothic church architecture as the only recognized authentic setting for traditional Catholic worship, in which William Butterfield was supreme; the serious study of ceremonial and the serious attention given to hymnology, where John Mason Neale was the dominant figure, and *The Ecclesiologist* the most effective organ; the outstanding attempts at urban evangelism, by the slum priests in London and other cities; and the magnificent attempt to promote overseas mission, especially through the Universities' Mission to Central Africa.

A further high peak for Anglo-Catholicism, as it was by then termed, was the astonishing response to a series of post-First World War congresses. They attracted massive support, engendered a sense of triumph, were pitched at a high level of intensity and exuberance, and gave expression to a visionary type of Anglican Catholicism. But they ceased in 1933 as quickly as they had begun in 1920. The inter-war years were also a period of Anglo-Catholic theological restatement, with *Essays Catholic and Critical* (1926) edited by Edward Gordon Selwyn, and *The*

Gospel and the Catholic Church (1936) by Arthur Michael Ramsey, being the most important publications.

In the post-Second World War era the high points were the Mission to London of 1949, headed by the High Church Bishop of London, J. W. C. Wand, under the title, 'Recovery Starts Within'; the superlative leadership of Michael Ramsey in various capacities, and in particular as Archbishop of Canterbury; and the remarkable contribution of some High Churchmen to the task of world mission, most notably in South Africa, with the work of G. H. Clayton, Ambrose Reeves, Joost de Blank and Trevor Huddleston providing special support and inspiration in the struggle for human rights.

At the end of the century the achievements were marred by the same internal wrangles between the liberals, represented, for example, by the Affirming Catholicism movement, and the more conservative High Churchmen, which had beset the movement for a century and more. Both groups, and Anglican Catholics as a whole, like the Evangelicals, looked back on the history I have reviewed in this present book, for examples to follow, for dangers to avoid, and for inspiration in their walk of faith.[16]

Lastly, there were the Broad Churchmen, or Liberals. Again, they had their roots in the pre-1833 era. In its essence Liberalism represented anti-dogmatism; a concern to stress tolerance, to avoid divisive, or potentially divisive, issues, and to emphasize what is held in common between different Christian traditions and points of view, and later even between Christianity and other faiths; and these have remained distinctive characteristics. Associated with this has been the championing of the right of each and every individual to hold their own opinions, even on matters as vital as religion, without let or hindrance. Although such convictions were characteristic of the Noetics in the 1820s, and acquired a coherence and authority at that time which may allow us to identify that decade as having given birth to the modern phase of Christian Liberalism, it is an attitude of mind which has a long and distinguished history prior to the nineteenth century.

In its post-Reformation manifestation the appearance of an explicit ecclesiastical liberalism was part of the 'passage to modernity' which had four main hallmarks: 'the acceptance of the use of reason in free enquiry, instead of unquestioning acceptance of authority in religion; the rise of critical historical attitudes towards the past, including the Bible and the creeds; the collapse of the metaphysical view of reality, that is, the view which claims to comprehend all that is natural, and all that is supernatural, in a general system of reality and being; and the primacy of "subjectivity", that is, the feeling, knowing human self, in all discussion of the nature of truth and how it can be known'.[17] The Noetics and other liberals at the time looked back especially to Locke's *An Essay concerning Human Understanding* (1689), to William Paley, not with reference to his moral philosophy and utilitarianism, which they abhorred, but to him as the author of *A View of the Evidences of Christianity* and of *Natural Theology*, and to Joseph Butler, with a special importance being given to his *Analogy*.

We have encountered isolated examples of the characteristic liberal approach to theological matters throughout the long eighteenth century. In the course of the nineteenth century the works of A. P. Stanley, D. F. Strauss's *Life of Jesus*, significantly translated into English in 1846 by the 'liberal' novelist George Eliot, Charles Lyell's *Principles of Geology*, Robert Chambers' *Vestiges of the Natural History of Creation* (1844) and Charles Darwin's *Origin of Species* (1859) all helped to foster a liberal disposition. *Essays and Reviews* (1860) provided a platform for the public demonstration of how some leading Christian scholars attempted to cope with the impact of modern knowledge in a 'liberal' spirit; and this paved the way for a similar undertaking with the publication of *Lux Mundi* (1889). Bishop J. W. Colenso achieved notoriety, by his 'liberal' treatment of the Pentateuch.

The twentieth century has witnessed an almost continuous stream of English liberalism from within the church itself. There was the surge of English biblical criticism in the early years of the century, embodied in such works as S. R. Driver's *Introduction to the Literature of the Old Testament* (published in its eighth edition in 1891, but influential in the opening years of the new century) and the *Encyclopaedia Biblica* (1899–1903), edited by T. K. Cheyne and J. S. Black; the influence of Adolf von Harnack, especially as contained in his book translated into English as *What is Christianity* (1904), and the writings of T. R. Glover, W. R. Inge, William Sandy, B. H. Streeter and Hastings Rashdall; the 'New Theology' expounded in particular by R. J. Campbell in the early part of the century; and the publication of *Foundations* (1912), with its declared purpose to communicate a theology which was in harmony with modern science, philosophy and scholarship. In the inter-war years there were the liberal views expressed by Bishop Hensley Henson and the work of the Modern Churchmen's Union, which reached a climax of public recognition at the Girton Conference in 1921. In the post-

Second World War period there was the influential teaching of E. W. Barnes, especially as expounded in *The Rise of Christianity* (1947); the work of the Cambridge theologians in the 1960s, and the furious debate surrounding John A. T. Robinson's *Honest to God* (1963); and, finally, the widening influence of liberalism within all Christian denominations in the closing decades of the century, with a prominent part being played in this by Bishop David Jenkins, the book of essays edited by J. Hick in 1977 under the title *The Myth of God Incarnate*, and the impact upon Christian opinion of the teaching of Don Cupitt, Dennis Nineham and Maurice Wiles.

As with Evangelicalism and High Churchmanship, a placing of Liberal thought within a long historical timescale, including the period 1688 to 1833, helps to give a more balanced perspective and appreciation of what at any one time was under debate; and likewise, a study of the churches in the long eighteenth century is enlightened by an awareness of what has followed on from that period to the present day. The same is true of developments in Nonconformity.

The Nonconformists

The constitutional reforms of the years 1828–35 created hope and expectation among Nonconformists. For the first time in their history it appeared that their disabilities might soon be removed. Before the end of 1833 the Protestant Dissenting Deputies, together with other Dissenting bodies, had compiled a minimum programme of five points:

1. a legal registration of births, marriages and deaths, dissenting registers not having the same standing in the courts as parish registers;
2. the right to marry in dissenters' chapels;
3. the right of burial according to nonconformist forms in parochial cemeteries;
4. the removal of university tests;
5. the abolition of church rates.

These were not unrealistic expectations, but only the first two had been achieved by the end of the decade, and it was to be several more decades before any substantial relief was forthcoming. Nonconformity was not a very formidable force in the 1830s, notwithstanding the numerical gains of the previous fifty years; it lacked national coherence. The residual strength of the establishment, and the extent of its innate reluctance to concede to Nonconformists any more than expediency required, together with resistance to any further parliamentary reform, meant that a further protracted period of Nonconformist pressure was necessary before any more major concessions were granted. Thus, the tension between the Church of England, which still retained almost all its former privileges, and Nonconformity, which still suffered many of its previous religious, political and social disadvantages, continued, and was a feature of Victorian religious life at national and local levels.

Nevertheless, despite the persisting constraints which it had to endure, Victorian Nonconformity quite rapidly acquired a remarkable power and vibrancy; and it speedily advanced until it enjoyed a higher profile in the life of the nation than ever before. There was always the sense of religious, political and social inferiority, but Nonconformists could no longer be treated as an insignificant and unimportant conglomeration of enthusiastic sectarians; they had become a force in the land. 'The public prominence of Victorian Protestant Nonconformity was turbulent and full of controversy, both within the Nonconformist community itself and in the relationship between Nonconformity as a whole and the rest of the social, political and religious culture of Victorian Britain. But, in sheer numbers, in religious vitality, in its centrality to political debate, and in its contribution to the social, cultural and ethical *mores* of the era, Victorian Nonconformity was an integral and inescapable ingredient in national life.'[18]

Although the statistics of the 1851 census of religious affiliation were subject to criticism, two conclusions were almost inescapable. First, as the organizer of the census and the author of the report accompanying its presentation succinctly stated, it was 'apparent that a sadly formidable portion of the English people are habitual neglecters of the public ordinances of religion'. Secondly, of those who did attend a Christian place of worship almost half were Nonconformists or Roman Catholics. There were both urban and rural areas in England in which Nonconformity was the religious majority, and this included twenty out of the twenty-nine towns which the Census had identified as the main manufacturing districts. For the Nonconformists as a whole, and for the more radical members among them who campaigned not only for the rights of the Dissenters but for the disestablishment of the Church of England, the message was clear. The census had 'finally laid to rest any possibility of basing the claims of the established church upon the assumption that the Church of England was, in any active sense, the church of even a passable majority of the English people . . . If establishment were still to be defended, it would have to be on grounds other than that of the Church of England being the majority religious choice.'[19]

The message about Nonconformity was also abundantly clear. If about half the Christian worship in the country was Nonconformist, it was intolerable and a scandal that the Nonconformists should labour under the disabilities which beset them, and be treated as second-class citizens. The census sharpened one of the fundamental questions faced by Victorians in respect of their religious life, namely 'whether representative government was compatible with an established church, that is, how religious inequality could be married to political equality'.[20] And, in the second half of the century, the powerful presence and influence of Nonconformity increased.[21] This included a more pronounced political involvement. 'Nonconformists had established their position as the greatest single power behind the Liberal Party as once the landed gentry had been behind the Tories, aristocrats had been behind the Whigs and Trade Unions would in turn be behind the Labour Party.'[22] Through this political channel Nonconformity made its voice heard, as it did through its own newspapers and pulpits. It was the voice of the skilled artisan and the increasingly important and influential lower middle classes.

There was an inevitability about the freeing of Nonconformity from the shackles which had bound it for centuries, although the establishment held out for as long as possible. In 1900 there was still not a single Nonconformist in the House of Lords; it was not until 1918 that a reigning British sovereign attended a Nonconformist service; and only in 1920 would Free Churchmen be admitted at Oxford for higher degrees in divinity. Throughout the twentieth century the Nonconformists moved inexorably towards a more recognized and central role in national life. They were subject, like all the Protestant churches, to a massive decline in membership, and to the corrosive effects of 'secularization' but, compared with the past they were far more able to participate in the religious life of the country, and they provided some of the century's leading theologians and church historians, such as P. T. Forsyth, C. H. Dodd and F. F. Bruce; they made indispensable contributions to religious debates, ecclesiastical affairs and inter-church events through the Free Church Federal Council as well as through the national bodies of the separate Nonconformist denominations; and they exercised a major influence in political, social and cultural life through a host of able and articulate leaders, both lay and ordained. It was a strange and astonishing transformation from the obscurity and marginality which was their lot at the time of the 1688 Revolution.

The Roman Catholics

The two decades after 1833 saw a continuation and escalation of the increase in the number of Roman Catholics, largely as a consequence of the influx of Irish Catholics. This was accompanied by greater clericalization, which had been a feature of the previous four decades. Within such a setting there 'came the rise into prominence of Nicholas Wiseman (a supreme Ultramontane and "Roman"), the influx of a number of Anglican converts of decidedly Ultramontane and Roman sympathies, and the introduction to Britain of a number of key missionary orders – especially the Rosminians, the Passionists, the Redemptorists and the Oratorians'.[23] The missionary orders were particularly effective in transforming the devotional ethos of English Catholicism; and much credit for this must go to the charismatic leadership of the two Italian missionaries Luigi Gentile and Dominic Barberi. But the local priests, or 'missionary priests' as they were known, since canon law did not recognize Catholic parishes until 1918, were also crucial to this whole process of growth and transmutation.

The expansion of Catholicism in England caused alarm and heightened anti-Catholic sentiment which, as we have seen, had never been far beneath the surface of society. It burst out afresh in 1850, when Pope Pius IX issued a Bull by which England was constituted an ecclesiastical province of the Roman Catholic Church, and Cardinal Wiseman, with undue haste and inappropriately forthright and triumphalist language, spoke of 'Catholic England' being 'restored to its orbit in the ecclesiastical firmament'. Such an event, and such 'Papal Aggression', as it was universally called, was astonishing so soon after English Catholicism had consisted of a small, much-maligned, and little regarded minority.

The character of English Catholicism was further changed and diversified in the 1880s and 1890s with the advent of a new generation of 'liberals'. They became part of a loose network of Catholic thinkers known as Modernists, in which George Tyrrel, Friedrich von Hügel and George Jackson Mivart were prominent. But the liberal teaching ran counter to the somewhat strict and increasingly authoritarian Ultramontane Catholicism, and the liberals were severely rebuffed, especially in the two Papal Encyclicals of 1907 condemning Modernism.

'Unlike the other major denominations in Victorian Britain, Roman Catholicism did not enter the twentieth century with a *de facto* theological pluralism within its own bounds. On the contrary, it retained a position of doctrinal orthodoxy and theological unity which set it sharply apart from the other major denominations.'[24] Rich variety within unity was promoted by such talented Roman Catholic leaders as Cardinal Archbishops Wiseman, Manning and Vaughan, by the widespread influence in their different spheres of G. K. Chesterton, Hilaire Belloc, Ronald Knox, Frederick Copleston, Evelyn Waugh and Graham Greene, and by the archbishopric of Cardinal Basil Hume.

In the late 1950s and in the 1960s, however, with 'greater social mobility, the social upheaval of urban renewal (and consequent decline of the urban 'ghettos'), the coming of the welfare state, and the public diversification of Roman Catholicism during and after the Second Vatican Council',[25] British Roman Catholicism experienced a double crisis. It was suddenly confronted with decline and the tensions of internal pluralism; and the shock was in no small part the result of having been so disciplined and conservative for so long. Such traumas were also accompanied by the twentieth-century ecumenical movement, by dialogue between Protestants and Roman Catholics, and by the trenchant questioning of orthodoxy by such powerful writers as Hans Küng. It was a most disturbing time.

All these changes of fortune are best understood in the light of traits I have identified in the long eighteenth century.

Secularization, scepticism, agnosticism and atheism

Every English religious tradition was fundamentally affected by the process of secularization which took root in the seventeenth and eighteenth centuries, accelerated throughout the nineteenth century and was to become even more pronounced during the course of the twentieth century.

There has been an extended debate among sociologists about the meaning of the word 'secularization', and some have even concluded that it is meaningless.[26] To the sociologist David Martin, the 'whole concept appears as a tool of counter-religious ideologies which identify the "real" element in religion for polemical purposes and then arbitrarily relate it to the notion of a unitary and irreversible process.' The word, he says, 'should be erased from the sociological dictionary'.[27] Undoubtedly the subject is infested with doctrinaire bias and presuppositions, and it is a large and somewhat nebulous idea. But it should not be discarded. 'By the nature of historical science, vagueness, blurred edges, recognition of the unchartable mystery in human motives and attitudes and decisions, are no necessary obstacle to an authentic though broad judgment in history.'[28] And there is statistical evidence to indicate a general reduction in the extent to which previously accepted Christian symbols, doctrines and institutions have lost their prestige, influence and attraction. As we have previously seen there were wails and lamentation when the 1851 religious survey revealed that about 30% of the population who were capable of going to church or chapel did not do so. But this meant that 70% did go; a figure which appears as almost sublimely rosy when compared with the 10% or 12% one hundred years later; especially as this latter figure includes the Roman Catholics, whose numbers had soared in the nineteenth and twentieth centuries, and whose attendance at services is greater in proportion to the total membership than among Protestants.

From the point of view of the number of worshippers it is difficult to determine when decline first began, and whether the mid-nineteenth-century census measured a long process of decline which had been temporarily reversed during the Victorian era, or whether it revealed a high level of religious participation which was reaching its climax before the very definite decline during the twentieth century. The former seems the most likely explanation, for there is evidence that the rot had set in more than a century before. As far as the Church of England is concerned, during the period 1740 to 1830 there may, as we have previously noted, even have been an *absolute* decline of numbers despite the rapid growth in the total population of the country.[29] And there was not compensation for this in the additional numbers of worshippers represented by the Methodists and the other Protestant Dissenters. Most importantly, by the early eighteenth century a new urban, industrial, plebian culture was emerging which was largely out of touch with the institutional church. It represented a distinct sub-culture, with its own life-style, rituals, festivals and superstitions. It was 'remarkably robust, greatly distanced from the polite culture', and it 'no longer acknowledged, except in perfunctory ways, the hegemony of the Church'.[30] But such alienation must not be exaggerated. The claim of A. F. Winnington-Ingram that the church of God has not lost the great towns because it never had them[31] must, at the very least, be highly qualified.

Mark Smith and others have made a convincing case for at least questioning the 'pessimistic view' of the eighteenth and nineteenth centuries 'as an arena in which struggling churches fought a losing battle to impose an essentially middle-class religiosity on a working-class culture characterized by mass indifference'. He rightly claims that a number of local studies, including his own, have 'drawn attention to the vitality of church life in an urban environment where the predominantly voluntaristic nature of church affiliation seems to have produced a particularly dynamic form of religious culture'.[32] What he and other historians attest on the basis of their research certainly challenges any facile and all-embracing generalizations. Even if there was a widespread alienation of the urban industrial working class from organized religion from an early stage in the process of industrialization, there were enough exceptions to this in specific towns and situations to make it questionable if this was as extensive as has been generally portrayed in the past.

It is also highly significant that, whatever the extent of the decline in attendance at public worship, there remained a widespread belief in God among the population as a whole.[33] This paradox, of widespread 'religious' or quasi-religious 'beliefs' alongside non-attendance at places of worship appears to have been characteristic of modern industrial society. A kind of urban, industrial, working-class folk religion has persisted even up to the present day. Perhaps the long Christian tradition of the country, and such comparatively recent phenomena as the eighteenth-century revival, the Oxford Movement and its aftermath, and the surge in religious intensity during the Victorian era all contributed to a residual Christian, or at least religious, disposition. Such persistent 'religious' beliefs and orientations, although they are not made explicit or articulated in any very coherent manner, are a manifestation of the non-institutional, 'privatization of religion' which can be seen as one of the characteristics of religion in a 'post-Christian' era.

The lessening of attendance at public worship, and the seeming growth in religious apathy or indifference among the population of England as a whole has also been accompanied by a proliferation of various new sects and religious movements, and by revival and renewal movements within existing religious traditions. Considerable numbers of people have been attracted to a multiplicity of these, such as Christian Science, the Mormons, Jehovah's Witnesses, Scientology, Transcendental Meditation (the cult of the Maharishi), the Hari Krishna Movement and the Divine Light Mission of Maharaj Ji, as well as to dynamic eruptions within traditional Christianity such as Pentecostalism, the Jesus Movement, the Charismatic Movement and the

House Church Movement. Some sociologists contend that these manifestations of religious vitality are a denial of secularization, while others maintain that they are transient phenomena, with little widespread influence within society as a whole, and can therefore be discounted as in any significant way lessening the remorseless march of secularization. But they cannot be dismissed so lightly. They may indicate that profound religious experience is finding new and unfamiliar forms of expression in a modern, and to a considerable extent anomic, society.

A variant of the privatization of religion has been the development of liberalism and 'freethinking'. 'From the moment that European opinion decided for toleration, it decided for an eventual free market in opinion . . . A free market in some opinions became a free market in all opinions.'[34] And in this process 1688–69 may, in retrospect, be seen as a gentle opening of the floodgates. As we have observed, from then onwards Socinianism, Arianism and Unitarianism started to take a hold on small but increasingly large sections of the churches in England; and this was followed by the radical thinkers of the late eighteenth and early nineteenth centuries. Such questioning of previously sacrosanct beliefs provided a foundation for the biblical criticism, the conflicts of science and faith, so-called, and the 'crisis of faith' of the mid-Victorian age. In 1869 T. H. Huxley coined the word 'agnostic' to designate himself as one who did not deny God's existence, but could not agree with Christians in purporting to know what could not be known. 'His doctrine was ontologically neutral.'[35]

The process of drift into an age of doubt and disbelief in relation to traditional Christian dogmas was becoming well-advanced by the late nineteenth century.

> In the years 1860–80 contemporaries were agreed that the tone of society in England was more 'secular'. By that they meant the atmosphere of middle-class conversation; the kind of books which you could find on a drawing-room table, the contents of the magazines to which educated men subscribed whether they were religious or irreligious, the appearance of anti-Christian books on bookstalls at the railway station, the willingness of devout men to meet undevout men in society and to honour them for their sincerity instead of condemning them for their lack of faith.[36]

In the closing decades of the century George Holyoake, Charles Bradlaugh and Annie Besant publicly proclaimed their agnosticism or atheism; and such bodies as the British Secular Union gave organizational expression to unbelief. As the new century opened, and as it unfolded, agnosticism hardened into atheism, and at times it became almost fashionable in certain circles to decry dogma; relativism and latitude became virtuous, while doctrine and the declaration of ulti-mates were castigated as undesirable and uncharitable. All of this was a far cry from the prevailing ethos of the long eighteenth century. But it was not so far removed from the freethinking of that small band of philosophers, scholars and theologians in the early eighteenth century whose impact was perhaps as much long-term as it was immediate. 'Confident in the powers of human reason alone, men like John Toland (1670–1722), Anthony Collins (1676–1729) and Thomas Woolston (1670–1733) went beyond the classical synthesis of rational and revealed truth as expounded by the Natural Theologians to adopt the theology of Deism or even, in a heavily disguised and ironic form, out-right atheism.'[37] They, and sympathizers with a similar cast of mind and spiritual disposition, probably had no conception of the crop which, in the fullness of time, the seeds they sowed would produce. As we have seen in this chapter, the same can be said of a host of others in the long eighteenth century.

Abbreviations

AHR	*American Historical Review*
BJS	*British Journal of Sociology*
CH	*Church History*
DR	*Downside Review*
ECS	*Eighteenth Century Studies*
ED	*Enlightenment and Dissent*
H	*History*
HEI	*History of European Ideas*
HJ	*Historical Journal*
HT	*History Today*
JAH	*Journal of American History*
JBS	*Journal of British Studies*
JEH	*Journal of Ecclesiastical History*
JMH	*Journal of Modern History*
JRH	*Journal of Religious History*
LH	*Literature and History*
MH	*Midland History*
MethH	*Methodist History*
NH	*Northern History*
PH	*Parliamentary History*
PP	*Past and Present*
RMS	*Renaissance and Modern Studies*
SCH	*Studies in Church History*
TRHS	*Transactions of the Royal Historical Society*
TUHS	*Transactions of the Unitarian Historical Society*
VS	*Victorian Studies*

Bibliography

Ackroyd, Peter, *William Blake*, London 1995

Abbey, Charles J. and Overton, John H., *The English Church in the Eighteenth Century*, 2 vols, London 1878

Acheson, A.R., 'The Evangelicals in the Church of Ireland, 1784–1859', Belfast Ph.D 1967

Addleshaw, G.W.O., *The High Church Tradition*, London 1941

Albers, J., 'Seeds of Contention: Society, Politics and the Church of England in Lancashire, 1689–1790', Yale Ph.D 1988

Allen, W.O.B. and McClure, E., *Two Hundred Years. The History of the SPCK 1698–1898*, London 1898

Anson, Peter, *The Call of the Cloister. Religious Communities and Kindred Bodies in the Anglican Communion*, London 1955

Anstey, Roger, *The Atlantic Slave Trade and British Abolition 1760–1810*, London 1975

Armstrong, Anthony, *The Church of England, the Methodists and Society 1700–1850*, London 1973

Ashton, N., 'Horne and Heterodoxy: The Defence of Anglican Beliefs in the Late Enlightenment', *EHR*, October 1993, pp. 895–919

Aveling, J.C.H., *The Handle and the Axe. The Catholic Recusants in England from the Reformation to Emancipation*, London 1976

Avis, P.D.L., *Anglicansim and the Christian Church – Theological Resources in Historical Perspective*, Edinburgh 1989

Bahlman, D.W.R., *The Moral Revolution of 1688*, New Haven 1957

Baker, Eric W., *A Herald of the Evangelical Revival. A Critical Enquiry into the Relation of William Law to John Wesley and the Beginnings of Methodism*, London 1948

Baker, Frank, *John Wesley and the Church of England*, London 1970

Baker, W.J., 'The Attitudes of English Churchmen, 1800–1850, towards the Reformation', Cambridge Ph.D 1966

Balleine, G.R., *A History of the Evangelical Party in the Church of England*, London 1908

Barry, J., 'The Parish in Civic Life: Bristol and its Churches 1640–1750' in Wright, S.J. (ed), *Parish, Church and People*, London 1988

Bateman, Josiah, *The Life of the Right Revd Daniel Wilson*, London 1860

Baxter, John, 'The Great Yorkshire Revival 1792–6: a study of mass revival among the Methodists' in Michael Hill (ed), *A Sociological Yearbook of Religion in Britain* 7, London 1974, pp. 46–76

Beardsley, Frank G., *A History of American Revivals*, 2nd revd and enlarged edn, New York 1912

Bebb, E. D., *Nonconformity and Social and Economic Life 1660–1800. Some Problems of the Present as they appeared in the Past*, Philadelphia 1935

Bebbington, D. W., *Evangelicalism. A History from the 1730s to the 1980s*, London 1989

Becker, Howard, *Systematic Sociology on the Basis of the Beziehungslehre und Gebildelehre of Leopold von Wiese*, New York 1932

Beddard, R. A. (ed), *The Revolution of 1688*, Oxford 1991

Bennett, G. V., *White Kennett 1660–1728*, London 1957

Bennett, G. V., 'Conflict in the Church' in G. Holmes (ed), *Britain after the Glorious Revolution*, London 1969

Bennett, G. V., *The Tory Crisis in Church and State 1688–1730. The Career of Francis Atterbury Bishop of Rochester*, Oxford 1975

Bennett, G., 'The Era of Party Zeal 1702–14' in L. Sutherland and L. Mitchell (eds), *The History of the University of Oxford, Vol V: The Eighteenth Century*, Oxford 1986

Benson, F. J., *The Life of the Revd John William de la Flechiere*, London 1817

Berger, Peter L., *The Sacred Canopy*, New York 1967

Berger, Peter, *A Rumour of Angels*, New York 1969

Berman, David, *A History of Atheism in Britain: From Hobbes to Russell*, London 1988

Best, G. F. A., 'The Protestant Constitution and its Supporters, 1800–1829', *TRHS*, fifth series, 8, 1985, pp. 105–27

Best, G., 'The Constitutional Revolution, 1828–32, and its Consequences for the Established Church', *Theology*, 62, 1959, pp. 226–34

Best, G., *Temporal Pillars. Queen Anne's Bounty, the Ecclesiastical Commissioners and the Church of England*, Cambridge 1964

Black, Jeremy (ed), *Britain in the Age of Walpole*, Basingstoke 1984

Black, J. and Gregory, J. (eds), *Culture, Politics and Society in Britain 1660–1800*, Manchester 1991

Bossy, John, *The English Catholic Community 1570–1850*, London 1975

Boswell, James, *The Life of Samuel Johnson together with A Journal of a Tour to the Hebrides*, 3 vol edn, London 1888

Bradley, I. C., 'The Politics of Godliness: Evangelicals in Parliament, 1784–1832', Oxford D Phil. 1974

Bradley, Ian, *The Call to Seriousness: The Evangelical Impact on the Victorians*, London 1976

Bradley, J., 'The Anglican Pulpit, the Social Order, and the Resurgence of

Toryism during the American Revolution', *Albion*, 21, 1989, pp. 361–88

Bradley, J., *Religion, Revolution and English Radicalism*, Cambridge 1990

Bradley, J. E., 'Whigs and Nonconformists: "Slumbering Radicalism" in English Politics, 1739–1789', *ECS*, 9, 1, 1975, pp. 1–27

Braithwaite, William C., *The Beginnings of Quakerism*, London 1912

Braithwaite, William C., *The Second Period of Quakerism*, London 1919

Bready, J. Wesley, *England Before and After Wesley: The Evangelical Revival and Social Reform*, London 1939

Brent, Richard, *Liberal Anglican Politics. Whiggery, Religion, and Reform 1810–1842*, Oxford 1987

Bridenbaugh, C., *Mitre and Sceptre. Transatlantic Faiths, Ideas, Personalities, and Politics 1689–1775*, New York 1962

Briggs, Asa, *The Age of Improvement*, London 1959

Briggs, Asa (compiler), *How They Lived. An Anthology of original documents written between 1700 and 1815*, Oxford 1969

Brilioth, Yngve, *The Anglican Revival. Studies in the Oxford Movement*, London 1925

Brooke, John, *King George III*, London 1972

Brose, O., *Church and Parliament. The Reshaping of the Church of England 1828–60*, Stanford and London 1959

Brown, Ford K., *Fathers of the Victorians: The Age of Wilberforce*, Cambridge 1961

Brown, Kenneth D., *A Social History of the Nonconformist Ministry in England and Wales 1800–1930*, Oxford 1988

Brown, Raymond, *The English Baptists of the Eighteenth Century*, London 1986

Brown, Richard, *Church and State in Modern Britain 1700–1850*, London 1991

Brown-Lawson, A., *John Wesley and the Anglican Evangelicals of the Eighteenth Century*, Edinburgh 1994

Brunner, D., 'The Role of the Halle Pietists in England (c.1700–c.1740)', Oxford D Phil. 1988

Bullock, F.W.B., *Voluntary Religious Societies 1520–1799*, St Leonards on Sea 1963

Bunting, T. P., *The Life of Jabez Bunting*, 2 vols, London 1859, 1887

Burgon, J. W., *Lives of Twelve Good Men*, London 1891

Burke, Edmund, *Reflections on the Revolution in France*, Oxford 1993

Burnet, G., *History of His Own Time*, new edn London 1850

Burns, Arthur R., 'The Diocesan Revival in the Church of England, c.1825–1865', Oxford D Phil. 1990

Bushaway, Bob, *By Rite. Custom, Ceremony and Community in England 1700–1880*, London 1982

Butler, Joseph, *The Analogy of Religion*, London 1736

Cadogan, W. B., *The Life of the Revd William Romaine*, London 1821

Cairns, Earle E., *An Endless Line of Splendor. Revivals and Their Leaders from the Great Awakening to the Present*, Wheaton 1986

Campbell, Ted, *The Religion of the Heart: A Study of European Religious Life in the Seventeenth and Eighteenth Centuries*, Columbia 1991

Carey, S. Pearce, *William Carey*, London 1923

Carpenter, S. C., *Church and People, 1789–1889: A History of the Church of England from William Wilberforce to 'Lux Mundi'*, London 1933

Carpenter, S. C., *The Protestant Bishop. Being the Life of Henry Compton, 1632–1713, Bishop of London*, London 1956

Carpenter, S. C., *Eighteenth Century Church and People*, London 1959

Carson, John S., *God's River in Spate*, Belfast 1958

Carter, G., 'Evangelical Seceders from the Church of England, c.1800–50', Oxford D Phil. 1990

Carus, William, *Memoirs of the Life of the Revd Charles Simeon with a Selection from his Writings and Correspondence*, London 1847

Carwardine, Richard, *Transatlantic Revivalism: Popular Evangelicalism in Britain and America, 1790–1865*, Westport, Connecticut 1978

Cecil, David, *The Stricken Deer: Life of William Cowper*, London 1929

Chadwick, Owen, *The Victorian Church*, 2 vols, London 1966, 1970; reissued London 1987

Chadwick, Owen, *The Secularization of the European Mind in the Nineteenth Century*, Cambridge 1975

Champion, J., *The Pillars of Priestcraft Shaken. The Church of England and its Enemies 1660–1730*, Cambridge 1992

Chilcote, Paul Wesley, *John Wesley and the Women Preachers of Early Methodism*, New Jersey 1991

Christie, Ian R., *Wars and Revolutions. Britain 1760–1815*, London 1982

Christie, I. R., *Stress and Stability in Late Eighteenth-Century Britain: Reflections on the British Avoidance of Revolution*, Oxford 1984

Church, John E., *Quest for the Highest*, Exeter 1981

Church, Leslie F., *The Early Methodist People*, London 1948

Church, Leslie F., *More about the Early Methodist People*, London 1949

Church, R. W., *The Oxford Movement. Twelve Years 1833–1845*, London 1892

Churton, E., *Memoir of Joshua Watson*, 2 vols, Oxford 1861

Clark, G. Kitson, *Churchmen and the Condition of England. A study in the development of social ideas and practice from the Old Regime to the Modern State*, London 1973

Clark, J. C. D., *English Society 1688–1832. Ideology, social structure and political practice during the ancien regime*, Cambridge 1985

Clark, J. C. D., *Revolution and Rebellion. State and Society in England in the Seventeenth and Eighteenth Centuries*, Cambridge 1986

Clark, J. C. D., 'England's Ancien Regime as a Confessional State', *Albion*, 21, 1989

Clarke, B. F. L., *The Building of the Eighteenth-Century Church*, London 1963

Clarke, W. K. Lowther, *Eighteenth Century Piety*, London 1944

Clarke, W. K. Lowther, *A History of the SPCK*, London 1959

Clegg, H., 'Evangelicals and Tractarians. An investigation of the connecting links between the two movements in the Church of England in the earlier part of the last century and a consideration of how, and how far, these links came to be broken', Bristol MA 1965

Cockshut, A.O.J. (ed), *Religious Controversies of the Nineteenth Century*, London 1966

Cohn, Norman, *The Pursuit of the Millenium*, London 1970

Cole, G. A., 'Doctrine, Dissent, and the Decline of Paley's Reputation 1805–25', *ED*, 6, 1987, pp. 19–30

Coombs, P. B., 'A History of the Church Pastoral-Aid Society, 1836–1861', Bristol MA 1960

Colley, Linda, *Britons. Forging the Nation 1707–1837*, London 1992

Conybeare, W. J., *Essays Ecclesiastical and Social*, London 1855

Coomer, Duncan, *English Dissent under the Early Hanoverians*, London 1946

Cornish, F. Warre, *The English Church in the Nineteenth Century*, 2 vols, London 1910

Corsi, P., *Science and Religion. Baden Powell and the Anglican Debate 1800–60*, Cambridge 1988

Coupland, R., *William Wilberforce*, Oxford 1923

Coward, Barry, *The Stuart Age*, London 1980

Cowherd, Raymond G, *The Politics of English Dissent. The Religious Aspects of Liberal and Humanitarian Reform Movements from 1815 to 1848*, New York 1956

Cragg, George G., *Grimshaw of Haworth*, London 1947

Cragg, G., *From Puritanism to the Age of Reason*, Cambridge 1950

Cragg, G. R., *The Church and the Age of Reason 1648–1789*, Harmondsworth 1960

Craig, A. G., 'The Movement for the Reformation of Manners 1688–1715', Edinburgh Ph.D 1980

Crawford, Michael, 'Origins of the Eighteenth Century Evangelical Revival: England and New England Compared', *JBS*, 26, 1987, pp. 361–97

Creed, John Martin and Boysmith, John Sandwith (eds), *Religious Thought in the Eighteenth Century Illustrated from Writers of the Period*, Cambridge 1934

Cross, M., 'The Church and Local Society in the Diocese of Ely, *c.*1630–*c.*1730', Cambridge Ph.D 1991

Cross, F.L. and Livingstone, E.A. (eds), *The Oxford Dictionary of the Christian Church*, Oxford 1974

Cruickshanks, Eveline (ed), *Ideology and Conspiracy: Aspects of Jacobitism, 1689–1759*, Edinburgh 1982

Cruickshanks, E. and Black, J. (eds), *The Jacobite Challenge*, Edinburgh 1988

Cuming, G. J., *A History of Anglican Liturgy*, London 1969

Currie, R., Gilbert, A. and Horsley, L., *Churches and Churchgoers*, Oxford 1977

Curtis, T. C. and Speck, W. A., 'The Societies for the Reformation of Manners. A Case Study in the Theory and Practice of Moral Reform', *LS*, 3, 47, 1987, pp. 45–63

Dallimore, Arnold, *George Whitefield. The life and times of the great evangelist of the eighteenth century revival*, 2 vols, Edinburgh 1970

Dallimore, Arnold, *A Heart Set Free. The Life of Charles Wesley. Evangelist, Hymn-writer Preacher*, Co. Durham 1988

Dallimore, Arnold, *The Life of Edward Irving, the Fore-runner of the Charismatic Movement*, Edinburgh 1983

Davidson, Edward H., *Jonathan Edwards. The Narrative of a Puritan Mind*, Boston 1966

Davie, Donald, *A Gathered Church. The Literature of the English Dissenting Interest, 1700–1930*, London 1978

Davies, G. C. B., *The Early Cornish Evangelicals 1735–1760*, London 1951

Davies, G. C. B., *The First Evangelical Bishop*, London 1958

Davies, Horton, *Worship and Theology in England. From Watts and Wesley to Maurice, 1690–1850*, London 1961

Davies, Rupert E., *Methodism*, Harmondsworth 1963; 2nd revd edn London 1985

Davies, Rupert E., Rupp, Gordon and George, A. Raymond (eds), *A History of the Methodist Church in Great Britain*, 4 vols, London 1965–88

Derry, John W., *Politics in the Age of Fox, Pitt and Liverpool. Continuity and Transformation*, London 1990

de Waal, E., 'New Churches in East London in the Early Eighteenth Century', *RMS*, 9, 1965, pp. 98–114

Dewey, C., *The Passing of Barchester*, London 1991

Ditchfield, G., 'The Priestly Riots in Historical Perspective', *TUHS*, 20, 1991, pp. 3–16

Ditchfield, G. M., 'Anti-Trinitarianism and Toleration in Late Eighteenth-Century British Politics: The Unitarian Petition of 1792', *JEH*, 42, 1991, pp. 39–67

Ditchfield, G. M. and Keith-Lucas, Bryan (eds), *A Kentish Parson. Selections from the Private Papers of the Revd Joseph Price Vicar of Brabourne, 1767–1786*, Kent 1991

Drury, John (ed), *Critics of the Bible 1724–1873*, Cambridge 1989

Drysdale, A. H., *History of the Presbyterians in England. Their Rise, Decline, and Revival*, London 1889

Duffy, E., 'Over the Wall: Converts from Popery in Eighteenth-Century England', *DR*, 94, 1976, pp. 1–25

Duffy, E., 'Primitive Christianity Revived: Religious Renewal in Augustan England', *SCH*, 14, 1976, pp. 287–300

Duffy, Eamon (ed), *Challoner and his Church. A Catholic Bishop in Georgian England*, London 1981

Dunne, Tom (ed), *The Writer on Writers*, Cork 1987

Edwards, David L., *Christian England*, 3 vols, London 1981, 1983, 1984

Edwards, Jonathan, *Jonathan Edwards on Revival*; a reissue of *A Narrative of Surprising Conversions* (1736), *Distinguishing Marks of a Work of the Spirit of God* (1741) and *An Account of the Revival in Northampton in 1740–42 in a Letter* (1743), Edinburgh 1965

Ella, George Melvyn, *William Cowper Poet of Paradise*, Darlington 1993

Elliott-Binns, L. E., *The Evangelical Movement in the Church of England*, London 1928

Elliott-Binns, L. E., *The Early Evangelicals: A Religious and Social Study*, London 1953

Ervine, W. J. C., 'Doctrine and Diplomacy: Some aspects of the life and thought of Anglican Evangelical Clergy 1797–1837', Cambridge Ph.D 1979

Evans, E., 'Some Reasons for the Growth of English Rural Anti-Clericalism c.1750–c.1830', *PP*, 66, 1975, pp. 84–109

Evans, Eric J., *The Forging of the Modern State. Early Industrial Britain 1783–1870*, London and New York 1983

Evershed, W., 'Party and Patronage in the Church of England, 1800–1945', Oxford D Phil. 1986

Every, George, *The High Church Party 1688–1718*, London 1956

Fawcett, Arthur, *The Cambuslang Revival*, London 1971

Ferguson, J. F., *An Eighteenth-Century Heretic: Dr Samuel Clarke*, Kineton 1976

Findon, John C., 'The Nonjurors and the Church of England, 1689–1716', Oxford D Phil.1978

Finney, Charles G., *Lectures on Revivals of Religion*, New York 1988

Flew, R. Newton and Davies, Rupert E. (eds), *The Catholicity of Protestantism*, London 1950

Flindall, R. P. (ed), *The Church of England 1815–1948. A Documentary History*, London 1972

Fox, L. P., 'The work of the Revd Thomas T. Biddulph, with special reference to his influence on the Evangelical Movement in the West of England', Cambridge Ph.D 1953

Furneaux, Robin, *William Wilberforce*, London 1974

Garbett, Cyril, *In an Age of Revolution*, London 1952

Garnett, Jane and Matthew, Colin (eds), *Revival and Religion since 1700. Essays for John Walsh*, London 1993

Gash, Norman, *Aristocracy and People. Britain 1815–1865*, London 1979

Gascoigne, John, 'Anglican Latitudinarianism and Political Radicalism in the Late Eighteenth Century', *H*, 71, 1986, pp. 22–38

Gascoigne, J., *Cambridge in the Age of the Enlightenment*, Cambridge 1989

Gaustad, Edwin S., *The Great Awakening in New England*, New York 1957

George, M. Dorothy, *London Life in the Eighteenth Century*, Harmondsworth 1966

Gibson, D. (ed), *A Parson in the Vale of White Horse. George Woodward's Letters from East Hendred 1753–61*, Gloucester 1983

Gibson, William, *The Year of Grace*, London 1909

Gibson, William, *Church, State and Society, 1760–1850*, London 1994

Gibson, William, *The Anglican Achievement*, 1994

Gilbert, Alan D., *Religion and Society in Industrial England: Church, Chapel and Social Change 1740–1914*, London 1976

Gilbert, Alan D., *The Making of Post-Christian Britain. A History of the Secularization of Modern Society*, London 1980

Gill, Sean, *Women and the Church of England from the Eighteenth Century to the Present*, London 1994

Gill, Stephen, *William Wordsworth. A Life*, Oxford 1989

Gilley, S. W., 'Evangelical and Roman Catholic Missions to the Irish in London, 1830–1870', Cambridge Ph.D 1970

Gilley, S., 'Christianity and Enlightenment', *HEI*, I, 1981, pp. 103–21

Gilley, Sheridan, *Newman and his Age*, London 1990

Gilley, Sheridan and Sheils, W.J. (eds), *A History of Religion in Britain. Practice and Belief from Pre-Roman Times to the Present*, Oxford and Cambridge, USA 1994

Gillies, John (compiler), *Historical Collections relating to Remarkable Periods of the Success of the Gospel*, Kelso 1845

Gillispie, Charles Coulston, *Genesis and Geology. A Study in the Relations of Scientific Thought, Natural Theology, and Social Opinion in Great Britain, 1790–1850*, New York 1951

Gillispie, Charles C., 'The Work of Elie Halévy: A Critical Appreciation', *JMH*, XXII, 3, September 1950, pp. 232–49

Gladstone, William Ewart, *Correspondence on Church and Religion*, selected and arranged by D. C. Lathbury, 2 vols, London 1910

Gordon, James M., *Evangelical Spirituality: from the Wesleys to John Stott*, London 1991

Gore, Charles (ed), *Lux Mundi*, London 1889

Gowland, D. A., *Methodist Secessions. The origins of Free Methodism in three Lancashire towns*, Manchester 1979

Green, V. H. H., *Religion at Oxford and Cambridge. A History c.1160–1960*, London 1964

Gregory, J., 'Archbishop, Cathedral and Parish: The Diocese of Canterbury 1660–1800', Oxford D Phil. forthcoming

Grell, Ole Peter, Israel, Jonathan I. and Tyacke, Nicholas (eds), *From Persecution to Toleration. The Glorious Revolution and Religion in England*, Oxford 1991

Gunter, Stephen W., *The Limits of 'Love Divine': John Wesley's Response to Antinomianism and Enthusiasm*, Nashville 1989

Haakonssen, Knud (ed), *Enlightenment and Religion. Rational Dissent in Eighteenth-Century Britain*, Cambridge 1996.

Halévy, E., *A History of the English People in the Nineteenth Century*, 6 vols, 1912, ET London 1949

Halévy, Elie, *The Birth of Methodism in England*, ed and with an introductory chapter, 'Elie Halévy, Methodism and Revolution' by B. Semmel, Chicago 1971

Hammond, J. L. and B., *The Town Labourer, 1760–1831*, London 1917

Handy, Robert T., *A History of the Churches in the United States and Canada*, Oxford 1976

Hardman, Keith J., *Charles Grandison Finney 1792–1875. Revivalist and Reformer*, Darlington 1987

Hardy, R. Spence, *Life of Grimshaw*, London 1860

Harrison, G. Elsie, *Son to Susanna: The Private Life of John Wesley*, London 1937

Harrison, J. F. C., *The Second Coming. Popular Millenarianism 1780–1850*, London 1979

Harrison, P., *'Religion' and the Religions in the English Enlightenment*, Cambridge 1990

Hart, A. Tindal, *The Life and Times of John Sharp Archbishop of York*, London 1949

Hastings, Adrian, *The Church in Africa 1450–1950*, Oxford 1994

Haweis, T., *The Life of William Romaine*, London 1797

Haydon, C., 'Anti-Catholicism in Eighteenth-Century England, c.1714–c.1780', Oxford D Phil. 1985

Haydon, Colin, *Anti-Catholicism in Eighteenth-Century England, c.1714–80*, Manchester 1993

Haykin, Michael A. G., *One Heart and One Soul. John Sutcliff of Olney, his friends and his times*, Darlington 1994

Hayton, D., 'Moral Reform and Country Politics in the Late Seventeenth-Century House of Commons', *PP*, 128, 1990, pp. 48–91

Heitzenrater, Richard P., *Wesley and the People Called Methodists*, Nashville 1995

Heitzenrater, Richard P. (ed), *Diary of an Oxford Methodist – Benjamin Ingham, 1733–4*, Durham, NC 1985

Hellmuth, E. (ed), *The Transformation of Political Culture*, Oxford 1990

Hempton, David, 'Evangelicalism and Eschatology', *JEH*, 31, 2, 1980, pp. 179–94

Hempton, David, *Methodism and Politics in British Society 1750–1850*, London 1984

Hempton, David, *Religion and Political Culture in Britain and Ireland from the Glorious Revolution to the Decline of Empire*, Cambridge 1996

Henderson, G. D., *Presbyterianism*, Aberdeen 1954

Hennell, M., *John Venn and the Clapham Sect*, London 1958

Henriques, Ursula, *Religious Toleration in England 1787–1833*, London 1961

Hill, Michael, *A Sociology of Religion*, London 1973

Hilton, Boyd, *The Age of Atonement. The Influence of Evangelicalism on Social and Economic Thought 1785–1865*, Oxford 1988

Hirschberg, D., 'The Government and Church Patronage in England, 1660–1760', *JBS*, 20, 1980–81, pp. 112–13

Hobbes, Thomas, *Leviathan*, ed Richard Tuck, Cambridge 1991

Hobsbawm, E. J., 'Methodism and the Threat of Revolution in Britain', *HT*, February 1957, pp. 115–24.

Hobsbawm, E. J., *The Age of Revolution*, London 1962

Hole, Charles, *The Early History of the Church Missionary Society*, London 1896

Hole, R., *Pulpits, Politics and Public Order in England 1760–1832*, Cambridge 1989

Holmes, Geoffrey (ed), *Britain after the Glorious Revolution 1689–1714*, Basingstoke 1969

Holmes, Geoffrey, *The Trial of Doctor Sacheverell*, London 1973

Holmes, Geoffrey, *Politics, Religion and Society in England, 1679–1742*, London 1986

Holmes, Geoffrey, *The Making of a Great Power. Late Stuart and early Georgian Britain 1660–1722*, London 1993

Holmes, Geoffrey and Szechi, Daniel, *The Age of Oligarchy. Pre-industrial Britain 1722–1783*, London 1993

Holt, Geoffrey, *The English Jesuists in the Age of Reason*, Tonbridge Wells 1993

Hugh, Evan, *Charles Simeon of Cambridge*, London 1977

Howse, Ernest Marshall, *Saints in Politics: The 'Clapham Sect' and the Growth of Freedom*, London 1953

Hudson, N., *Samuel Johnson and Eighteenth-Century Thought*, Oxford 1988

Hutton, William Holden, *William Laud*, London 1895

Hutton, William Holden, *The English Church from the Accession of Charles I to the Death of Anne (1625–1714)*, London 1903

Hylson-Smith, Kenneth, *The Evangelicals in the Church of England 1734–1984*, Edinburgh 1989

Hylson-Smith, Kenneth, *High Churchmanship in the Church of England from the Sixteenth Century to the Late Twentieth Century*, Edinburgh 1993

Hylson-Smith, Kenneth, *The Churches in England from Elizabeth I to Elizabeth II*. Vol I, *1558–1688*, London 1996

Innes, J., Review Article: 'Jonathan Clark, Social History and England's "Ancien Regime"', *PP*, 115, May 1987, pp. 165–200

Isaac, Robert and Wilberforce, Samuel, *The Life of William Wilberforce*, 5 vols, London 1838

Itzkin, E. S., 'The Halévy Thesis – A Working Hypothesis? English Revivalism: Antidote for Revolution and Radicalism 1789–1815', *CH*, 44, 1975, pp. 47–56

Jay, E., 'Anglican Evangelicalism and the Nineteenth-Century Novel', Oxford D Phil. 1975

Jaeger, Muriel, *Before Victoria. Changing Standards and Behaviour 1787–1837*, London 1956

Jones, J. R., *Country and Court. England 1658–1714*, London 1978

Jones, M. G., *The Charity School Movement*, Cambridge 1938

Jones, M. G., *Hannah More*, Cambridge 1952

Jones, R. Tudur, *Congregationalism in England 1662–1962*, London 1962

Jones, Rufus, *The Later Periods of Quakerism*, 2 vols, London 1921

Keeble, N. H., *The Literary Culture of Nonconformity in Later Seventeenth-Century England*, Leicester 1987

Kent, John, 'Methodism and Revolution', *MethH* 12, 1973–74, pp. 136–44

Kent, John H. S., *The End of the Line ? The Development of Christian Theology in the Last Two Centuries*, London 1978

Kent, John H. S., *The Unacceptable Face. The Modern Church in the Eyes of the Historian*, London 1987

Kenyon, J. P., *Revolution Principles: the Politics of Party 1687–1720*, Cambridge 1977

Kidder, Richard, *The Life of the Reverend Anthony Horneck*, London 1698

Kiernan, V., 'Evangelicalism and the French Revolution', *PP*, 1, February 1952, pp. 44–56

Kinnear, M., 'The Correction Court in the Diocese of Carlisle, 1704–56', *CH*, 59, 1990

Knight, Frances, 'The Hanoverian Church and Anglicanism in Transition: Some Recent Perspectives', *HJ*, 36, 3, 1993, pp. 745–52

Knight, Frances, *The Nineteenth-Century Church and English Society*, Cambridge 1995

Knox, Ronald A., *Enthusiasm. A Chapter in the History of Religion with Special Reference to the XVII and XVIII Centuries*, Oxford 1950

Koch, Kurt, *The Revival in Indonesia*, Grand Rapids 1972

Lambert, Frank, 'Pedlar in Divinity: George Whitefield and the Great Awakening, 1737–1745', *JAH*, 77, 1990, pp. 812–37

Lambert, Frank, 'The Great Awakening as Artifact: George Whitefield and the Construction of International Revival, 1739–1745', *CH*, 60, June 1991, pp. 223–46

Langford, Paul, *A Polite and Commercial People. England 1727–1783*, Oxford 1992

Lanternari, Vittorio, *The Religions of the Oppressed. A Study of Modern Messianic Cults*, London 1963

Laqueur, T., *Religion and Respectability. Sunday Schools and Working Class Culture 1780–1850*, New Haven 1976

Laycock, J.W. (memorials compiled by), *Methodist Heroes in the Great Haworth Round 1734–1784*, Keighley 1909

Lecky, William Edward Hartpole, *A History of England in the Eighteenth Century*, 7 vols, London 1892

Lemay, J. A. Leo (ed), *Deism, Masonry and the Enlightenment*, Delaware 1987

Lewis, Donald, *Lighten their Darkness*, Westport, Connecticut 1986

Lewis, Donald Munro, 'The Evangelical Mission to the British Working Classes: A study of the growth of Anglican support for a pan-evangelical approach to evangelism with special reference to London 1828–1860', Oxford D Phil.1981

Lewis, I. M., *Ecstatic Religion. An Anthropological Study of Spirit Possession and Shamanism*, Harmondsworth 1971

Leys, M. D., *Catholics in England 1559–1829. A Social History*, London 1961

Linnan, J. E., 'The Evangelical Background of J.H. Newman, 1816–1826', Louvain DTh. 1965

Livingstone, David N., *Darwin's Forgotten Defenders. The Encounter Between Evangelical Theology and Evolutionary Thought*, Grand Rapids 1987

Loane, Marcus L., *Oxford and the Evangelical Succession*, London 1951

Loane, Marcus L., *Cambridge and the Evangelical Succession*, London 1952

Locke, John, *An Essay Concerning Human Understanding*, abridged and edited by John W. Yolton, Everyman edn, London 1961

Lossky, Nicholas, *Lancelot Andrewes the Preacher (1555–1626). The Origins of the Mystical Theology of the Church of England*, Oxford 1991

Lovegrove, D., *Established Church, Sectarian People. Itinerancy and the Transformation of English Dissent 1780–1830*, Cambridge 1988

Luckmann, Thomas, *The Invisible Religion*, New York 1967

Luker, David, 'Revivalism in Theory and Practice: the Case of Cornish Methodism', *JEH*, 37, 1986, pp. 603–19

McClatchey, Diana, *Oxfordshire Clergy 1777–1869. A Study of the Established Church and the Role of the Clergy in Local Society*, Oxford 1960

McCord, Norman, *British History 1815–1906*, Oxford 1991

Machin, G. I. T., *Politics and the Churches in Great Britain 1832 to 1868*, Oxford 1977

McLoughlin, William G., *Modern Revivalism*, New York 1955

MacMath, Fiona (ed), *The Faith of Samuel Johnson. An anthology of his spiritual and moral writings and conversations*, London 1990

Malcolmson, Robert W., *Life and Labour in England 1700–1780*, London 1981

Manning, Bernard L., *The Hymns of Wesley and Watts*, London 1942

Marshall, Dorothy, *Eighteenth Century England*, London 1962

Marshall, W. M., 'The Administration of the Dioceses of Hereford and Oxford 1660–1760', Bristol Ph.D 1978

Marshall, W., 'Episcopal Activity in the Hereford and Oxford Dioceses, 1660–1760', MH, 8, 1983

Martin, David, *The Religious and the Secular*, London 1969

Martin, David, 'The Denomination', BJS, XIII, 1962, pp. 1–14

Martin, R. H., 'The Pan-Evangelical Impulse in Britain 1798–1830; with special reference to Four London Societies', Oxford D Phil. 1974

Martin, R. H., *Evangelicals United: Ecumenical Stirrings in Pre-Victorian Britain 1795–1830*, Metuchen, NJ and London 1983

Mather, F. C., 'High Churchmanship Reconsidered: Some Variations in Anglican Public Worship 1714–1830', JEH, 36, 2 April 1985, pp. 255–283

Mather, F. C., *High Church Prophet. Bishop Samuel Horsley (1733–1806) and the Caroline Tradition in the Later Georgian Church*, Oxford 1992

Mathew, David, *Catholicism in England. The Portrait of a Minority: Its Culture and Tradition*, London 1955

Maxson, Charles H., *The Great Awakening in the Middles Counties*, Gloucester, Mass. 1978

Maynard, W. B., 'Pluralism and Non-Residence in the Archdeaconry of Durham, 1774–1856', NH, 26, 1990, pp. 103–30

Meacham, S., *Henry Thornton of Clapham 1760–1815*, London 1964

Member of the House of Shirley and Hastings, *Life and Times of Selina, Countess of Huntingdon*, 2 vols, London 1839

Middleton, Erasmus, *Biographia Ecclesiastica*, Vol IV, London 1816

Miller, John, *James II. A Study in Kingship*, Hove 1977

Mitchison, R., 'Pluralities and the Poorer Benefices in Eighteenth-Century England', HJ, 5, 1962

Moffatt, James, *The Presbyterian Churches*, London 1928

Monod, Paul Kleber, *Jacobitism and the English People, 1688–1788*, Cambridge 1989

Monod, René, *The Korean Revival*, London 1969

Moore, E. R., 'John Bird Sumner, Bishop of Chester, 1828–48', Manchester MA 1976

More, Paul Elmer and Cross, Frank Leslie (compilers and eds), *Anglicanism. The Thought and Practice of the Church of England Illustrated from the Religious Literature of the Seventeenth Century*, London 1935

Morgan, Derec Llwyd, *The Great Awakening in Wales*, London 1988

Morgan, J. J., *The 'Fifty-nine Revival in Wales*, London 1909

Morgan, J. Vyrnwy, *The Welsh Revival*, London 1909

Morgan, M., 'Rational Religion and the Idea of the University: A study of the Noetics 1800–36', Adelaide Ph.D 1991

Morris, R. J., 'Voluntary Societies and British Urban Elites, 1780–1850: an Analysis', *HJ*, 26, 1983, pp. 95–118

Moule, Handley C. G., *Charles Simeon*, London 1892

Moule, Handley C. G., *The Evangelical School in the Church of England*, London 1901

Munson, James, *The Nonconforrmists: In Search of a Lost Culture*, London 1991

Murray, Nancy, 'The Influence of the French Revolution on the Church of England and its Rivals, 1789–1802', Oxford D Phil. 1975

Napthine, D. and Speck, W. A., 'Clergymen and Conflict 1660–1763', *SCH*, 20, 1983, pp. 231–51

Neill, Stephen, *Anglicanism*, Harmondsworth 1958

Neill, Stephen, *A History of Christian Missions*, Harmondsworth 1964

Newbigin, Leslie, *The Other Side of 1984*, Geneva 1983

Newell, A. G., 'Studies in Evangelical Prose Literature: Its rise and decline', Liverpool Ph.D 1976

Newman, John Henry, *Apologia Pro Vita Sua: Being a History of his Religious Opinions*, Everyman edn, London 1912

Newton, John, *An Authentic Narrative*, London 1764

Newton, John, *Cardiphonia*, London 1780

Newton, J., *Memoirs of the Revd W. Grimshaw*, London 1799

Niebuhr, Richard H., *The Social Sources of Denominationalism*, New York 1929

Nockles, Peter, 'Continuity and Change in Anglican High Churchmanship 1792–1850', Oxford D Phil. 1982

Nockles, Peter B., *The Oxford Movement in Context. Anglican High Churchmanship 1760–1857*, Cambridge 1994

Noll, Mark A., Bebbington, David W. and Rawlyk, George A. (eds), *Evangelicalism. Comparative Studies of Popular Protestantism in North America, the British Isles, and Beyond, 1700–1990*, New York and Oxford 1994

Norman, E. R., *Church and Society in England, 1770–1970: a historical study*, London 1976

Norman, Edward, *Roman Catholicism in England: from the Elizabethan Settlement to the Second Vatican Council*, Oxford 1985

Nuttall, Geoffrey F. (ed), *Philip Doddridge 1702–51. His Contribution to English Religion*, London 1951

Nuttall, Geoffrey F. and Chadwick, Owen (eds), *From Uniformity to Unity 1662–1962*, London 1962

Obelkevich, J., *Religion and Rural Society. South Lindsey 1825–75*, Oxford 1979

Obelkevich, Jim, Roper, Lyndal and Samuel, Raphael (eds), *Disciplines of Faith. Studies in Religion, Politics and Patriarchy*, London 1987

O'Brien, Patrick, and Quinault, Roland (eds), *The Industrial Revolution and British Society*, Cambridge 1993

O'Brien [Durden], Susan, 'A Study of the First Evangelical Magazines, 1740–1748', *JEH*, 27, July 1976, pp. 255–75

O'Brien, S., 'Transatlantic Communication and Influence during the Great Awakening, 1730–60', Hull Ph.D 1978

O'Brien [Durden], Susan, 'A Transatlantic Community of Saints: The Great Awakening and the First Evangelical Network, 1735–1755', *AHR*, 91, 1986, pp. 811–15

O'Day, R. and Heal, F. (eds), *Princes and Paupers in the English Church 1500–1800*, Leicester 1981

Oliver, W. H., *Prophets and Millenialists*, Auckland 1978

Ollard, S. L., *A Short History of the Oxford Movement*, London 1915

Orchard, S. C., 'English Evangelical Eschatology, 1790–1850', Cambridge Ph.D 1968

Orr, J. Edwin, *The Second Evangelical Awakening in Britain*, London 1949

Orr, J. Edwin, *The Second Evangelical Awakening in America*, London 1952

Otto, Rudolf, *The Idea of the Holy. An Inquiry into the non-rational factor in the idea of the divine and its relation to the rational*, Oxford 1923

Overton, John H., *Life in the English Church (1600–1714)*, London 1885

Overton, John H., *The English Church in the Nineteenth Century 1800–1833*, London 1894

Overton, J. H. and Relton, F., *The English Church from the Accession of George I to the End of the Eighteenth Century (1714–1800)*, London 1906

Padwick, Constance E., *Henry Martyn Confessor of the Faith*, London 1922

Park, J. A., *Memoir of the Late William Stevens*, London 1859

Parsons, Gerald (ed), *Religion in Victorian Britain*, 4 vols, Manchester 1988

Patten, John A., *These Remarkable Men: The Beginning of a World Enterprise*, London 1945

Pattison, M., 'Tendencies of Religious Thought in England, 1688–1750' in H. Nettleship (ed), *Essays*, 2 vols, II, Oxford 1889, p. 43

Pedersen, Susan, 'Hannah More meets Simple Simon: Tracts, Chapel Books and Popular Culture in Late-Eighteenth Century England', *JBS*, 25, 1986, pp. 84–113

Perkin, Harold, *The Origins of Modern English Society 1780–1880*, London 1969

Piette, Maximin, *John Wesley in the Evolution of Protestantism*, London 1938

Piggin, Stuart, *Making Evangelical Missionaries 1789–1858*, London 1984

Plumb, J. H., *England in the Eighteenth Century*, Harmondsworth 1950

Plummer, Alfred, *The Church of England in the Eighteenth Century*, London 1910

Plumptre, E. H., *The Life of Thomas Ken Bishop of Bath and Wells*, 2 vols, London 1890

Podmore, Colin John, 'The Role of the Moravian Church in England: 1728–1760', Oxford D Phil. 1994

Pollard, Arthur and Hennell, Michael, *Charles Simeon 1759–1836*, London 1964

Pollock, John, *Wilberforce*, London 1977

Poole-Connor, E. J., *Evangelicalism in England*, London 1951

Pope, Liston, *Millhands and Preachers: A Study of Gastonia*, New Haven 1942

Pope, R., 'The Eighteenth-Century Church in Wirral', Lampeter MA 1971

Porter, R., 'The Enlightenment in England' in R. Porter and M. Teich (eds), *The Enlightenment in National Context*, Cambridge 1981

Porter, Roy, *English Society in the Eighteenth Century*, Harmondsworth 1982

Portus, Garnet V., *Caritas Anglicana*, London 1912

Pratt, John H., *The Thought of the Evangelical Leaders: Notes on the Discussions of the Eclectic Society London during the Years 1798 to 1814*, London 1956

Rack, H., ' "Christ's Kingdom not of this World": The Case of Benjamin Hoadly versus William Law Reconsidered', *SCH*, 12, 1975, pp. 275–91

Rack, H. D., 'Religious Societies and the Origins of Methodism', *JEH*, 38, 1987, pp. 582–89

Rack, *Reasonable Enthusiast. John Wesley and the Rise of Methodism*, London 1989

Rattenbury, J.Ernest, *The Evangelical Doctrines of Charles Wesley's Hymns*, London 1941

Rawlyk. G. A. and Noll, M. A. (eds), *Amazing Grace: Evangelicalism in Australia, Britain, Canada and the United States*, Grand Rapids and Montreal 1993

Reardon, Bernard M. G., *Religious Thought in the Nineteenth Century illustrated from writers of the period*, Cambridge 1966

Reardon, Bernard M. G., *Religious Thought in the Victorian Age. A Survey from Coleridge to Gore*, London 1971

Reardon, Bernard M. G., *From Coleridge to Gore*, London 1971

Reardon, Bernard M. G. (ed), *Roman Catholic Modernism*, London 1979

Redwood, John, *Reason, Ridicule and Religion. The Age of Enlightenment in England 1660–1750*, London 1976

Rennie, I. S., 'Evangelicalism and English Public Life, 1823–1850', Toronto Ph.D 1962

Reynolds, J. S., *The Evangelicals at Oxford 1735–1871*, Oxford 1953

Rice, Hugh A. L., *Thomas Ken, Bishop and Non-Juror*, London 1958

Robbins, Keith (ed), *Protestant Evangelicalism: Britain, Ireland, Germany and America c.1750–c.1950*, Oxford 1990

Robe, James, *Narrative: Revival of Religion*, Glasgow 1840

Rosell, Garth M. and Dupuis, A.G (eds), *The Memoirs of Charles Finney. The Complete Restored Text*, Michigan 1989

Rosman, Doreen M., 'Evangelicals and Culture in England, 1790–1833', Keele Ph.D 1978

Rosman, D., *Evangelicals and Culture*, London 1984

Rouse, Ruth and Neill, Stephen Charles (eds), *A History of the Ecumenical Movement 1517–1948*, 2nd edn London 1967

Rowdon, H. H., *The Origins of the Brethren 1825 to 1850*, London 1967

Rowell, Geoffrey, *Tradition Renewed. The Oxford Movement Conference Papers*, London 1986

Rowlands, J. H. L., *Church, State and Society. The Attitudes of John Keble, Richard Hurrell Froude and John Henry Newman 1827–1845*, Worthing 1989

Royle, Edward, *Radical Politics 1790–1900. Religion and Unbelief*, London 1971

Royle, E., *Victorian Infidels: The Origins of the British Secularist Movement 1791–1866*, Manchester 1974

Royle, Edward and Walvin, James, *English Radicals and Reformers 1760–1848*, Brighton 1982

Rudé, George, *The Crowd in History, 1730–1848*, New York 1964

Rule, John, *Albion's People. English Society 1714–1815*, London 1992

Rule, John, *The Vital Century. England's Developing Economy, 1714–1815*, London 1992

Rupp, E. G., *Religion in England 1688–1791*, Oxford 1986

Rycroft, P., 'Church, Chapel and Community in Craven, 1764–1851', Oxford D Phil. 1988

Ryle, J. C., *Christian Leaders of the Eighteenth Century*, London 1885; reissued Edinburgh 1978

Sack, James J, *From Jacobite to Conservative. Reaction and Orthodoxy in*

Britain c.1760–1832, Cambridge 1993

Samuel, D. N., *The Evangelical Succession in the Church of England*, London 1979

Scott, John, *The Life of the Revd Thomas Scott*, London 1822

Scott, Thomas, *The Force of Truth*, London 1835

Seeley, M., *The Later Evangelical Fathers*, London 1879

Semmel, Bernard, *The Methodist Revolution*, London 1973

Shepherd, T. B., *Methodism and the Literature of the Eighteenth Century*, London 1940

Shuler, J., 'The Pastoral and Ecclesiastical Administration of the Diocese of Durham 1721–71', Durham Ph.D 1975

Simon, John S., *John Wesley and the Methodist Societies*, 2 vols, London 1921, 1923

Simon, John S., *John Wesley and the Advance of Methodism*, London 1925

Simon, John S., *John Wesley The Master Builder*, London 1927

Simon, John S., *John Wesley. The Last Phase*, London 1934

Simon, John S., *The Revival of Religion in England in the Eighteenth Century*, London *c.*1907

Skeats, H.S. and Miall, C.S., *History of the Free Churches of England 1688–1891*, London 1891

Smith, A. G., *Henry Martyn*, London 1892

Smith, Alan, *The Established Church and Popular Religion 1750–1850*, London 1971

Smith, M. A, 'Religion in Industrial Society. The Case of Oldham and Saddleworth, 1780–1865', Oxford D Phil. 1987

Smith, Mark, *Religion in Industrial Society. Oldham and Saddleworth 1740–1865*, Oxford 1994

Smyth, C. H., *Simeon and Church Order*, Cambridge 1940

Soloway, R., *Prelates and People. Ecclesiastical Social Thought in England 1783–1852*, London 1969

Southey, Robert, *The Life and Works of William Cowper*, 8 vols, London 1854

Southey, Robert, *The Life of John Wesley*, London edn 1903

Speck, W. A., *Tory and Whig. The Struggle in the Constituencies 1701–15*, London 1970

Speck, W. A., *Stability and Strife. England 1714–1760*, London 1977

Spooner, W. A., *Bishop Butler*, London 1901

Spring, D., 'The Clapham Sect', VS, 5(1), 1963

Spurr, John, *The Restoration Church of England 1646–1689*, New Haven and London 1991

Stanley, Arthur Penrhyn, *Life and Correspondence of Dr Arnold*, London 1844

Stanley, Brian, *The Bible and the Flag. Protestant missions and British imperialism in the nineteenth and twentieth centuries*, Leicester 1990

Stanley, Brian, *The History of the Baptist Missionary Society 1792–1992*,

Edinburgh 1992

Stephen, James, *Essays in Ecclesiastical Biography*, London 1860

Stephen, Leslie, *English Thought in the Eighteenth Century*, London 1876

Stevenson, George J., *The History of City Road Chapel London and its Associations*, London and New York 1872

Stiles, Andrina, *Religion, Society and Reform 1800–1914*, London 1995

Stock, Eugene, *The English Church in the Nineteenth Century*, London 1910

Stock, Eugene, *History of the Church Missionary Society: its Environment, its Men and its Work*, 3 vols, London 1899; vol 4, London 1916

Stoughton, J., *Religion in England 1800–1850*, 2 vols, London 1884

Stoughton, John, *History of Religion in England from the Opening of the Long Parliament to 1850*, London 1901

Stout, Harry S., *The Divine Dramatist. George Whitefield and the Rise of Modern Evangelicalism*, Grand Rapids 1991

Summerville, C.J., 'The Destruction of Religious Culture in Pre-industrial England', *JRH*, London 1988

Sutherland, L. S. and Mitchell, L. G. (eds), *History of the University of Oxford*, Vol V, Oxford 1986

Swift, Rowland C., *Lively People. Methodism in Nottingham 1740–1979*, Nottingham 1982

Sydney, Edwin, *Life and Ministry of Samuel Walker*, London 1838

Sykes, N., *Edmund Gibson, Bishop of London, 1669–1748*, London 1926

Sykes, Norman, *Church and State in England in the Eighteenth Century*, Cambridge 1934

Sykes, N., *William Wake, Archbishop of Canterbury*, 2 vols, Cambridge 1957

Sykes, N., *From Sheldon to Secker*, Cambridge 1959

Sykes, N., 'Ecumenical Movements in Great Britain in the Seventeenth and Eighteenth Centuries' in R.Rouse and S. Neill (eds), *A History of the Ecumenical Movement 1517–1948*, 2nd edn London 1967, pp. 152–62

Tawney, R. H., *Religion and the Rise of Capitalism*, London 1944

Taylor, S., 'Church and State in England in the Mid-Eighteenth Century: The Newcastle Years 1742–62', Cambridge Ph.D 1987

Taylor, S., 'Walpole and the Church', *PH*, 7, 1988, pp. 51–77

Taylor, S., 'Whigs, Bishops and America: The Politics of Church Reform in Mid-Eighteenth Century England', *HJ*, 36, 2, 1993

Telford, John, *Wesley's Veterans. Lives of the early Methodist preachers told by themselves*, 7 vols, London n.d.

Thomas, Keith, *Religion and the Decline of Magic. Studies in Popular Beliefs in Sixteenth- and Seventeenth-Century England*, London 1971

Thomas, T. (ed), *The British: Their Religious Beliefs and Practices 1800–1986*, London 1988

Thomis, Malcolm I., and Holt, Peter, *Threats of Revolution in Britain 1789–*

1848, London 1977

Thompson, E. P., *The Making of the English Working Class*, Harmondsworth 1968

Thompson, E. P., *Customs in Common*, London 1991

Thompson, H. P., *Into All Lands. The History of the Society for the Propagation of the Gospel in Foreign Parts 1701–1950*, London 1951

Thompson, K. A., *Bureaucracy and Church Reform: The Organizational Response of the Church of England to Social Change 1800–1965*, Oxford 1970

Thomson, David, *England in the Nineteenth Century (1815–1914)*, Harmondsworth 1950

Tidball, Derek J., *Who are the Evangelicals? Tracing the roots of the modern movements*, London 1994

Townsend, G., 'Religious Radicalism and Conservatism in the Whig Party under George I: The Repeal of the Occasional Conformity and Schism Acts', *PH*, 7, 1988, pp. 24–44

Townsend, W. J., Workman, H. B. and Eayrs, George (eds), *A New History of Methodism*, London 1909

Tracey, Joseph, *The Great Awakening. A History of the Revival of Religion in the time of Edwards and Whitefield*, 1842; reissued Edinburgh 1976

Treasure, Geoffrey, *Who's Who in Early Hanoverian Britain (1714–1789)*, London 1991

Troeltsch, E., *The Social Teaching of the Christian Churches*, 1912, ET (2 vols) London 1931

Tulloch, John, *Movements of Religious Thought in Britain during the Nineteenth Century*, London 1885

Turberville, A. S., *English Men and Manners in the Eighteenth Century*, Oxford 1926

Turberville, A. S. (ed), *Johnson's England. An Account of the Life and Manners of his Age*, Oxford 1933

Turner, John Munsey, *Conflict and Reconciliation. Studies in Methodism and Ecumenism in England 1740–1982*, London 1985

Tyerman, L., *The Oxford Methodists*, London 1873

Tyerman, L., *Wesley's Designated Successor*, London 1882

Tyerman, L., *The Life and Times of the Revd John Wesley founder of the Methodists*, 3 vols, London 1871

Tyerman, L., *The Life of George Whitefield*, 2 vols, London 1876

Underwood, A. C., *A History of the English Baptists*, London 1947

Urdank, Albion M., *Religion and Society in a Cotswold Vale. Nailsworth. Gloucestershire, 1780–1865*, California 1990

Vaisey, D. (ed), *The Diary of Thomas Turner 1754–65*, Oxford 1984

Valenze, D., *Prophetic Sons and Daughters. Female Preaching and Popular Religion in Industrial England*, Princeton 1975

Varley, E. A., *The Last of the Prince Bishops. William Van Mildert and the High Church Movement of the early nineteenth century*, Cambridge 1992

Venn, John, *Memoir of Henry Venn*, London 1834

Vidler, Alec R., *The Church in an Age of Revolution. 1789 to the Present*, Harmondsworth 1961

Virgin, P., *The Church in an Age of Negligence 1700–1840*, Cambridge 1989

Vulliamy, C. E., *John Wesley*, 3rd edn London 1954

Walsh, J., 'The Yorkshire Evangelicals in the Eighteenth Century, with special reference to Methodism', Cambridge Ph.D 1956

Walsh, J., 'Methodism and the Mob in the Eighteenth Century', *SCH*, 8, 1972, pp. 213–27

Walsh, J., 'Religious Societies: Methodist and Evangelical 1738–1800', *SCH*, 23, 1986, pp. 279–302

Walsh, John, Haydon, Colin and Taylor, Stephen (eds), *The Church of England c.1689–c.1833. From Toleration to Tractarianism*, Cambridge 1993

Wand, J. W. C.(ed), *The Anglican Communion. A Survey*, London 1948

Wand, J. W. C., *The High Church Schism. Four Lectures on the Non-Jurors*, London 1951

Ward, W. R., 'The Tithe Question in England in the Early Nineteenth Century', *JEH*, 16, 1965, pp. 67–81

Ward, W. R. (ed), *The Early Correspondence of Jabez Bunting 1820–1829*, London 1972

Ward, W. R., *Religion and Society in England 1790–1850*, London 1972

Ward, W. R., 'The Religion of the People and the Problem of Control 1790–1850', *SCH*, 8, 1972, pp. 237–57

Ward, W. R., 'The Relations of Enlightenment and Religious Revival in Central Europe and in the English-speaking World', *SCH*, subsidia 2, 1979, pp. 281–305

Ward, W. R., *The Protestant Evangelical Awakening*, Cambridge 1992

Ward, W. R., *Faith and Faction*, London 1993

Warne, Arthur, *Church and Society in Eighteenth-Century Devon*, Newton Abbot 1969

Waterman, A. M. C., 'A Cambridge "Via Media" in Late Georgian Anglicanism', *JEH*, 42, 1991, pp. 419–36

Waterman, A. M. C., *Revolution, Economics and Religion. Christian Political Economy 1798–1833*, Cambridge 1991

Watkin, E. I., *Roman Catholicism in England from the Reformation to 1950*, Oxford 1957

Watson, J. Steven, *The Reign of George III 1760–1815*, Oxford 1960

Watts, Michael R., *The Dissenters*. Vol I: *From the Reformation to the French*

Revolution, Oxford 1978

Watts, Michael R., *The Dissenters*. Vol II: *The Expansion of Evangelical Nonconformity*, Oxford 1995

Wearmouth, Robert F., *Methodism and the Working-class Movements of England 1800–1850*, London 1937

Wearmouth, Robert F., *Methodism and the Common People of the Eighteenth Century*, London 1945

Weber, Max, *The Protestant Ethic and the Spirit of Capitalism*, 1904–5, ET1930, 2nd edn London 1976

Weber, Max, *General Economic History*, New York 1963

Weber, Max, *The Sociology of Religion*, London 1965

Webster, A.B., *Joshua Watson: the Story of a Layman, 1771–1855*, London 1954

Weisberger, Bernard A., *They Gathered at the River: The Story of the Great Revivalists and Their Impact Upon Religion in America*, Boston 1958

Welsby, Paul A., *Lancelot Andrewes 1555–1626*, London 1964

Werner, Julia Stewart, *The Primitive Methodist Connexion. Its Background and Early History*, Wisconsin 1984

Wesley, Charles, *The Journal of the Revd Charles Wesley*, 2 vols, with introduction and notes by Thomas Jackson, London 1849

Wesley, John, *The Journal* ed Nehemiah Curnock, 8 vols, London 1938

Wesley, John, *The Letters* ed John Telford, 8 vols, London 1931

Wesley, John, *The Works of John Wesley* ed Thomas Jackson, 14 vols, London 1829–31

White, B.R., *The English Baptists of the Seventeenth Century*, London 1983

White, R.J., *The Age of George III*, London 1968

Whitefield, George, *The Works of George Whitefield*, 6 vols, London and Edinburgh 1771

Whitefield, George, *Journals*, with an Introduction by Iain Murray, Edinburgh 1960

Whiteley, J.H., *Wesley's England. A Survey of XVIIIth Century Social and Cultural Conditions*, London 1938

Whittingham, Richard, *The Works of the Revd John Berridge AM*, London 1833

Whyte, Alexander, *Characters and Characteristics of William Law*, London 1907

Wickham, E.R., *Church and People in an Industrial City*, London 1957

Wickham-Legg, J., *English Church Life from the Restoration to the Tractarian Movement*, London 1914

Wigley, John, *The Rise and Fall of the Victorian Sunday*, Manchester 1980

Wilkinson, John T., *Hugh Bourne 1772–1852*, London 1952

Wilkinson, John T., *1662 and After*, London 1962

Willey, Basil, *Seventeenth Century Background*, London 1950

Williams, Basil, *The Whig Supremacy 1714–1760*, Oxford 1962

Williams, W., *Welsh Calvinistic Methodism. A Historical Sketch*, London 1872

Wilson, B. R., *Sects and Society*, London 1961

Wilson, B. R., *Religion in a Secular Society*, Harmondsworth 1966

Wilson, B. R., *Patterns of Sectarianism*, London 1967

Wilson, B. R., *Contemporary Transformations of Religion*, Oxford 1976

Wolffe, J., *The Protestant Crusade in Great Britain 1829–60*, Oxford 1991

Wolffe, John (ed), *Evangelical Faith and Public Zeal. Evangelicals and Society in Britain 1780–1980*, London 1995

Wood, A. Skevington, *The Inextinguishable Blaze*, Exeter 1960

Woodforde, James, *The Diary of a Country Parson* ed J. Beresford, 5 vols, Oxford 1968

Woodward, Josiah, *An Account of the Rise and Progress of the Religious Societies in the City of London*, London 1701

Woodward, Sir Llewellyn, *The Age of Reform 1815–1870*, Oxford 1962

Worrall, B. G., *The Making of the Modern Church. Christianity in England since 1800*, London 1988

Worsley, Peter, *The Trumpet Shall Sound. A Study of 'Cargo' Cults in Melanesia*, London 1957

Wright, S. J. (ed), *Parish, Church and People: Local Studies in Lay Religion 1350–1750*, London 1988

Wrightson, K. and Levine, D., *Poverty and Piety in an English Village. Terling 1525–1700*, New York 1979

Wykes, D., ' " The Spirit of Persecutors Exemplified": The Priestly Riots and the Victims of the Church and King Mobs', *TUHS*, 20, 1991, pp. 17–39

Yinger, Milton J., *Religion, Society and the Individual*, New York 1957

Young, B., ' "Orthodoxy Assail'd": An Historical Examination of some Metaphysical and Theological Debates in England from Locke to Burke', Oxford D Phil. 1990

Notes

In general, works will be referred to only by author and shortened title. Details of date and publication will be found in the Bibliography.

Introduction

1. Clark, *Revolution and Rebellion*, p. 2.
2. See Brown, *Church and State in Modern Britain*, ch. 3.
3. Ibid., p. 30.
4. See Watson, 'The don rewriting history' in *The Observer*, 31 January 1988, to which the present comments are greatly indebted.
5. See Clark, *English Society*, p. x.
6. Innes, Review Article: 'Jonathan Clark, Social History and England's "Ancien Regime"'.
7. Ibid., p. 173.
8. Ibid., p. 174.
9. Ibid., p. 185.
10. Special mention should be made of his influential book, *A Polite and Commercial People*.
11. Recent works of note include Cruickshanks (ed), *Ideology and Conspiracy*; Cruickshanks and Black (eds), *The Jacobite Challenge*; and Monod, *Jacobitism and the English People*.
12. See especially, *Britons*.
13. Rule, *Albion's People*, p. xiii.
14. Strachey, 'Cardinal Manning' in *Eminent Victorians*, quoted in Clarke, *Eighteenth Century Piety*, p. 1.
15. Quoted in Clarke, ibid., p. 1.
16. Abbey and Overton, *The English Church in the Eighteenth Century*, p. 4.
17. Overton and Relton, *The English Church from the Accession of George I to the End of the Eighteenth Century*, p. 1, quoted in Walsh, Haydon and Taylor (eds), *The Church of England*, p. 1.
18. Bradley, *Religion, Revolution and English Radicalism*, p. xi.
19. The following comments owe much to Walsh and Taylor, 'Introduction: the Church and Anglicanism in the "long" eighteenth century' in Walsh, Haydon and Taylor (eds), *The Church of England*, pp. 2, 3.
20. See, for example Gregory, 'The eighteenth-century Reformation: the pastoral task of Anglican clergy after 1689' in Walsh, Haydon and Taylor (eds), *The Church of England*, pp. 67–85, and 'Archbishop, Cathedral and Parish: The Diocese of Canterbury 1660–1800'.

21. Clark, *English Society*.
22. Nockles, 'Continuity and Change in Anglican High Churchmanship 1792–1850' and *The Oxford Movement in Context*.
23. Rycroft, 'Church, Chapel and Community in Craven, 1764–1851'.
24. Smith, 'Religion in Industrial Society. The Case of Oldham and Saddleworth 1780–1865' and *Religion in Industrial Society*.
25. Urdank, *Religion and Society in a Cotswold Vale*.
26. Warne, *Church and Society in Eighteenth-Century Devon*.
27. Ward, 'The eighteenth-century Church: a European view' in Walsh, Haydon and Taylor (eds), *The Church of England*, pp. 285–98.
28. Gilbert, *Religion and Society in Industrial England,* and *The Making of Post-Christian Britain*.
29. Norman, *Church and Society in England, 1770–1970*.
30. See in particular Ashton, 'Horne and Heterodoxy: The Defence of Anglican Beliefs in the Late Enlightenment'; Bradley, *Religion, Revolution and English Radicalism*; Gascoigne, *Cambridge in the Age of the Enlightenment*; Hole, *Pulpits, Politics and Public Order in England*; Knight, 'The Hanoverian Church and Anglicanism in Transition: Some Recent Perspectives'; Monod, *Jacobitism and the English People*; Sack, *From Jacobite to Conservative*; Taylor, 'Church and State in England in the Mid-Eighteenth Century: the Newcastle Years, 1742–1763'.
31. See especially, Gascoigne, 'Anglican Latitudinarianism and Political Radicalism in the Late Eighteenth Century', and *Cambridge in the Age of the Enlightenment*.
32. See especially Cruickshanks and Black (eds), *The Jacobite Challenge*, and Monod, *Jacobitism and the English People*.
33. See in particular Hylson-Smith, *High Churchmanship in the Church of England*; Nockles, *The Oxford Movement in Context*; Mather, *High Church Prophet*; Varley, *The Last of the Prince Bishops*.
34. See especially Corsi, *Science and Religion*; Brent, *Liberal Anglican Politics*.
35. See Bebbington, *Evangelicalism*; Hilton, *The Age of Atonement*; Hylson-Smith, *The Evangelicals in the Church of England*.
36. See especially as a good summary Watts, *The Dissenters*, and for the Roman Catholics Aveling, *The Handle and the Axe*, and Bossy, *The English Catholic Community*.
37. See especially Walsh, 'The Yorkshire Evangelicals in the Eighteenth Century, with special reference to Methodism'; Walsh, 'Methodism and the Mob in the Eighteenth Century'; and Walsh, 'Religious Societies: Methodist and Evangelical 1738–1800'.
38. See in particular Ward, 'The relations of enlightenment and religious revival in central Europe and in the English-speaking world'; Ward, *The Protestant Evangelical Awakening*; and Ward, *Faith and Faction*.
39. See in particular Rack, 'Religious Societies and the Origins of Methodism';

Rack, *Reasonable Enthusiast*; and Rack, 'Survival and Revival: Bennet, Methodism and Old Dissent' in Robbins (ed), *Protestant Evangelicalism*, pp. 1–23.

40. See especially Podmore, 'The Role of the Moravian Church in England: 1728–1760'.

41. These are too numerous to mention here. They will appear in footnotes throughout the book.

42. As with the local studies, these are too prolific to be listed here, but they will appear throughout the text.

43. Hylson-Smith, *The Churches in England from Elizabeth I to Elizabeth II*, Vol. I: *1558–1688*.

44. For works on church and state, see n. 30 above.

45. Gilbert, *Religion and Society*, p. vii.

46. Thompson, *The Making of the English Working Class*, p. 385.

47. Weber first focussed the attention of sociologists on the distinction between church and sect in his seminal work *The Protestant Ethic and the Spirit of Capitalism*, as well as in his *General Economic History*, and in *The Sociology of Religion*. Weber's pupil Troeltsch elaborated on the basic conceptual framework provided by his mentor in his monumental work *Social Teaching of the Christian Churches*. Becker built on the ideas of Weber and Troeltsch, especially in his *Systematic Sociology*. Other sociologists have made contributions to the debate, including Niebuhr, *The Social Sources of Denominationalism*; Pope, *Millhands and Preachers*; Yinger, *Religion, Society and the Individual*; Wilson, *Sects and Society*, and *Patterns of Sectarianism*; Martin, 'The Denomination'; and Berger, *The Sacred Canopy*.

48. Speck, *Stability and Strife*, p. 88.

1. The Post-Revolution Church of England

1. Holmes, *The Making of a Great Power*, p. 212.

2. Among such must be numbered all the Whig historians, as well as most recent historians.

3. Most notably J. C. D. Clark and those who support him.

4. Holmes (ed), *Britain after the Glorious Revolution*, pp. 18,19.

5. Jones, *Country and Court*, p. 256.

6. Beddard, 'Introduction: The Protestant Succession' in Beddard (ed), *The Revolution of 1688*, pp. 9,10.

7. Beddard, 'The Unexpected Whig Revolution of 1688' in Beddard (ed), op. cit., p. 19.

8. Jones, *Country and Court*, p. 257.

9. Townsend, 'Religious Radicalism and Conservatism in the Whig Party under George I', p. 24.

10. Speck, *Tory and Whig*, p. 1.
11. For a discussion of these matters, and in addition to those sources to which reference has just been made, see Bennett, *White Kennett 1660–1728*; Bennett, 'Conflict in the Church'; Bennett, *The Tory Crisis in Church and State 1688–1730*; Bennett, 'The Era of Party Zeal 1702–14'; Bradley, 'Whigs and Nonconformists: "Slumbering Radicalism" in English Politics, 1739–1789'; Bradley, 'The Anglican Pulpit, the Social Order, and the Resurgence of Toryism during the American Revolution'; Bradley, *Religion, Revolution and English Radicalism*.
12. The account in this section is indebted to Bennett, 'Conflict in the Church'.
13. Spurr, *The Restoration Church of England*, p. 379.
14. Holmes, *The Trial of Dr Sacheverell*, p. 22. This is book to which the present section owes much.
15. See especially Holmes, *The Making of a Great Power*, and Rupp, *Religion in England*.
16. Holmes, *The Making of a Great Power*, p. 358.
17. Holmes, *The Trial of Dr Sacheverell*, p. 23.
18. This whole section is indebted to Monod, *Jacobitism and the English People*.
19. Ibid., p. 139.
20. Rupp, *Religion in England*, p. 14. This is a book to which this section owes much.
21. Monod, *Jacobitism and the English People*, pp. 140, 141.
22. Rupp, *Religion in England 1688–1788*, p. 19.
23. Bennett, 'Conflict in the Church', p. 155.
24. See in particular Hylson-Smith, *High Churchmanship in the Church of England*; Nockles, *The Oxford Movement in Context*; Mather, *High Church Prophet*; and Varley, *The Last of the Prince Bishops*.
25. What follows is based on Peter Nockles, 'Church Parties in the pre-Tractarian Church of England 1750–1833: the "Orthodox" – some problems of identity' in Walsh, Haydon and Taylor (eds), *The Church of England*, pp. 334–59, as the characteristics he identifies can, with modifications and additions which I note, be applied to the previous sixty-one years.
26. This is a term which has been used by theologians from at least the early thirteenth century. It expresses the belief that the sacraments operate in an essentially objective manner, and are not dependent for their efficacy on the subjective attitudes of either the minister or the recipient.
27. The comments in this present section are indebted to Jeffrey S. Chamberlain, 'Portrait of a High Church clerical dynasty in Georgian England: the Frewens and their world' in Walsh, Haydon and Taylor (eds), *The Church of England*, pp. 299–316.

28. Ibid., pp. 300, 301.
29. Ibid., pp. 309, 310.
30. Rupp, *Religion in England*, p. 56.
31. Bennett, *The Tory Crisis in Church and State 1688–1730*, p. 80.
32. Holmes, *The Trial of Dr Sacheverell*, p. 30.
33. Ibid, p. 32.
34. Bennett, 'The Era of Party Zeal', p. 61.
35. Bennett, 'Conflict in the Church', p. 170.
36. Ibid, p. 171.
37. Rupp, *Religion in England*, p. 88.
38. Quoted in ibid, pp. 91–93.
39. The comments in this section owe much to Rack, ' "Christ's Kingdom not of this World"'.
40. Rack, art.cit., p. 283.
41. Quoted in Rupp, *Religion in England*, p. 96.
42. See glossary of terms.
43. Ibid., p. 33.
44. The remarks in this present section owe much to Walsh and Taylor, 'Introduction' to Walsh, Haydon and Taylor (eds), *The Church of England*, as do the footnote references.
45. Walsh and Taylor, ibid., p. 36, with reference to Sykes, *Church and State*, pp. 268, 283.
46. See, for instance, Young, '"Orthodoxy Assail'd"'.
47. See, for example, Cragg, *From Puritanism to the Age of Reason*, p. 81; D. Greene, 'The Via Media in an Age of Revolution: Anglicanism in the Eighteenth Century' in P. Hughes and D. Williams (eds), *The Varied Pattern*, Toronto 1971, pp. 312–13.
48. Sykes, *Church and State*, p. 343, quoted in Gascoigne, *Cambridge in the Age of the Enlightenment*, p. 5.
49. Martin Fitzpatrick, 'Latitudinarianism at the Parting of the Ways: a Suggestion' in Walsh, Haydon and Taylor (eds), *The Church of England*, p. 211.
50. This present section owes much to Tuck, 'Introduction' in Hobbes, *Leviathan*.
51. See glossary of terms.
52. Tuck, p. xxiii.
53. Young, '"Orthodoxy Assail'd"'.
54. Locke, *An Essay Concerning Human Understanding*, p. 17.
55. Ibid., pp. 39,40.
56. Ibid., p. 46.
57. Ibid., p. 412.
58. Rupp, *Religion in England*, p. 250.
59. See glossary of terms.

60. The following exposition of the teaching and influence of Samuel Clarke owes much to Gascoigne, *Cambridge in the Age of Enlightenment*, and Ferguson, *An Eighteenth-Century Heretic*.
61. Gascoigne, *Cambridge in the Age of Enlightenment*, p. 117.
62. Ferguson, *An Eighteenth-Century Heretic*, p. 226.
63. Ibid., p. 229.
64. Holmes, *The Making of a Great Power*, p. 370.
65. Key works for the topics covered in this section are Gascoigne, *Cambridge in the Age of Enlightenment*; Harrison, *'Religion' and the Religions in the English Enlightenment*; R.H. Popkin, 'The Deist Challenge' in Grell, Israel and Tyacke (eds), *From Persecution to Toleration*, pp. 195–216.
66. Gascoigne, *Cambridge in the Age of the Enlightenment*, p. 2.
67. Ibid., p. 2.
68. See Popkin, 'The Deist Challenge' in Grell, Israel and Tyacke (eds), *From Persecution to Toleration*, p. 196.
69. Elliott-Binns, *The Early Evangelicals*, p. 92.
70. Sykes, *Church and State*, p. 345.
71. Holmes, *The Making of a Great Power*, pp. 369, 370.
72. For these quotations see Sykes, *Edmund Gibson, Bishop of London*, pp. 245–247. This is a book to which this present section is greatly indebted.
73. Sykes, *Church and State*, p. 346.
74. Rupp, *Religion in England*, p. 270.
75. Butler, *The Analogy of Religion*, p. 229, quoted in Avis, *Anglicanism and the Christian Church*, p. 281.
76. Holmes, *The Making of a Great Power*, p. 37.
77. Israel, J.I., 'William III and Toleration' in Grell, Israel and Tyacke, *From Persecution to Toleration*, p. 161.
78. Holmes, *The Making of a Great Power*, p. 368.
79. Quoted in Ward, *The Protestant Evangelical Awakening*, p. 15.
80. Israel, J.I., 'William III and Toleration' in Grell, Israel and Tyacke, *From Persecution to Toleration*, p. 161.
81. Holmes, *The Making of a Great Power*, pp. 352, 353.
82. Dr Williams' Library, London, MS. 34.4 (Evans List), to which reference is made in Holmes, *The Making of a Great Power*, p. 353.
83. Paul Langford, 'Convocation and the Tory Clergy, 1717–61' in Cruickshanks and Black (eds), *The Jacobite Challenge*, p. 107.
84. Virgin, *The Church in an Age of Negligence*.
85. Although there is not much to draw upon for a clear picture of eighteenth-century and early nineteenth-century 'popular religion' and parochial life, works which help include Thomas, *Religion and the Decline of Magic*; Bushaway, *By Rite*; Hempton, *Religion and Political Culture in Britian and Ireland*; Obelkevich, *Religion and Rural Society*,

and diaries such as that of James Woodforde.

86. See Davies, *Worship and Theology in England*.
87. Virgin, *The Church in an Age of Negligence*, p. 3.
88. This present section owes much to Walsh and Taylor, 'Introduction' to Walsh, Haydon and Taylor (eds), *The Church of England*.
89. Sykes, *Church and State*, p. 93.
90. Ibid., p. 120, quoted in Walsh and Taylor, 'Introduction' to Walsh, Haydon and Taylor (eds), *The Church of England*, p. 5.
91. Warne, *Church and Society in Eighteenth-Century Devon*, p. 12. This book is the basis of the present comments.
92. Ibid., p. 34.
93. Marshall, 'The Administration of the Dioceses of Hereford and Oxford 1660–1760'.
94. See Walsh and Taylor, 'Introduction' to Walsh, Haydon and Taylor (eds), *The Church of England*, p. 5.
95. See, for example, Virgin, *The Church in an Age of Negligence*, pp. 195 and 258.
96. In addition to the works already noted, some of the relevant works include Albers, 'Seeds of Contention'; Cross, 'The Church and Local Society in the Diocese of Ely, c.1730'; Helmuth (ed), *The Transformation of Political Culture*; Marshall, 'The Administration of the Dioceses of Hereford and Oxford 1660–1760'; McClatchey, *Oxfordshire Clergy 1777–1869*; O'Day and Heal (eds), *Princes and Paupers in the English Church*; Rycroft, 'Church, Chapel and Community in Craven, 1764–1851'.
97. The following details and comments owe much to Virgin, *The Church in an Age of Negligence*.
98. See Barry Coward, *The Stuart Age*, pp. 442, 443.
99. Warne, *Church and Society in Eighteenth-Century Devon*, p. 37.
100. For a discussion of these matters see, for instance, O'Day and Heal (eds), *Princes and Paupers*.
101. See, for example, comments on these matters in Paul Langford, 'The English Clergy and the American Revolution' in Helmuth (ed), *The Transformation of Political Culture*.
102. See Virgin, *The Church in an Age of Negligence*, pp. 192, 259.
103. Smith, *Religion in Industrial Society*.
104. Walsh and Taylor, 'Introduction' to Walsh, Haydon and Taylor (eds), *The Church of England*, p. 8.
105. Vivianne Barrie-Curien, 'The Clergy in the Diocese of London in the Eighteenth Century' in Walsh, Haydon and Taylor (eds), *The Church of England*, p. 101.
106. Mark Smith, 'The Reception of Richard Podmore: Anglicanism in Saddleworth 1700–1830' in Walsh, Haydon and Taylor (eds), *The*

Church of England, p. 113.

107. Walsh and Taylor, 'Introduction' to Walsh, Haydon and Taylor (eds), *The Church of England*, pp. 10,11.

108. Barrie-Curien, art. cit., p. 96.

109. Ibid., p. 95.

110. Jeremy Gregory, 'The Eighteenth-Century Reformation: the Pastoral Task of Anglican Clergy after 1689' in Walsh, Haydon and Taylor (eds), *The Church of England*, p. 71.

111. McClatchey, *Oxfordshire Clergy*, p. 146.

112. Duffy, 'Primitive Christianity Revived', p. 292.

113. C. E. Davies, 'The enforcement of religious uniformity in England, 1668–1700, with special reference to the Dioceses of Chichester and Worcester', Oxford D Phil. 1983, p. 1.

114. Ibid., pp. 1,2.

115. Rycroft, 'Church, Chapel and Community in Craven', p. 134.

116. Ibid.

117. The present description and comments on the religious societies owe much to Rack, 'Religious Societies and the Origins of Methodism'. The most important contemporary account is Woodward, *An Account of the Rise and Progress of the Religious Societies*.

118. Woodward, op. cit., p. 23.

119. Quoted in Curtis and Speck, 'The Societies for the Reformation of Manners', p. 46.

120. Curtis and Speck, art.cit., p. 50.

121. Williams, *A sermon preached at Salters Hall to the societies for reformation of manners*, quoted in Curtis and Speck, art.cit, p. 50.

122. Heitzenrater, *Wesley and the People Called Methodists*, p. 22.

123. Ibid., p. 22.

124. Harrison, *The Second Coming*, p. xiii.

125. Ibid.

126. Bushaway, *By Rite*, p. 22.

127. Richard Burton (pseud for Nathaniel Crouch), *The Apprentices Companion*, London 1681, pp. 2,3, quoted in Malcolmson, *Life and Labour in England*, p. 14.

128. Hempton, *Religion and Political Culture*, p. 13.

129. Ibid., p. 15.

130. Thomas, *Religion and the Decline of Magic*, p. 761.

131. Ibid.

132. See ibid., pp. 189–97, and Malcolmson, *Life and Labour in England*, p. 84.

133. Gill, *Women and the Church of England*, p. 53.

134. See ibid.

2. *The Dissenters in an Age of Toleration*

1. Quoted in Jones, *Congregationalism in England*, p. 105.
2. Quoted ibid., p. 105.
3. The comments in this opening section owe much to Grell, Israel and Tyacke (eds), *From Persecution to Toleration*, and Watts, *The Dissenters*, Vol I.
4. 'Introduction' to Grell, Israel and Tyacke (eds), *From Persecution to Toleration*, p. 12.
5. Watts, *The Dissenters*, Vol I, p. 263.
6. Sacheverell, *The Perils of False Brethren*, 1709, reprinted Exeter 1974, p. 36; quoted in Watts, *The Dissenters*, Vol I, p. 263.
7. See Bebb, *Nonconformity and Social and Economic Life*, p. 35.
8. Watts, *The Dissenters*, Vol I, p. 270.
9. See Bradley, *Religion, Revolution and English Radicalism*, p. 93, and Watts, *The Dissenters*, Vol I, pp. 267–89.
10. Holmes, *The Making of a Great Power*, p. 356.
11. For this section on Devonshire, see Warne, *Church and Society in Eighteenth-Century Devon*, pp. 93f.
12. Ibid., p. 93, and see Carpenter, *Eighteenth Century Church and People*, p. 173 and 172.
13. Warne, *Church and Society in Eighteenth-Century Devon*, p. 94.
14. For Presbyterianism in this period see especially Bradley, *Religion, Revolution and English Radicalism*; Drysdale, *History of the Presbyterians in England*, London 1889; Grell, Israel and Tyacke (eds), *From Persecution to Toleration*; Nuttall and Chadwick (eds), *From Uniformity to Unity*; Rupp, *Religion in England*; Skeats and Miall, *History of the Free Churches of England 1688–1891*; and Watts, *The Dissenters*, Vol I, as well as articles and theses to which reference will be made.
15. Drysdale, *History of the Presbyterians in England*, p. 443.
16. For details of Presbyterian demography, see Watts, *The Dissenters*, Vol I, pp. 270f. For information on the Dr John Evans list, and generally on the number and distribution of Dissenters in the early eighteenth century, see Watts, pp. 491–510; and on the Revd Josiah Thompson list, as well as the Evans list, see Bebb, *Nonconformity and Social and Economic Life 1660–1800*, p. 37, n.1.
17. Drysdale, *History of the Presbyterians in England*, p. 501.
18. Ibid., p. 506.
19. Watts gives a full account of this whole matter, *The Dissenters*, Vol I, pp. 371f.
20. A useful account of Presbyterian and other Dissenting preaching in this period can be found in Skeats and Miall, *History of the Free Churches of England*, an old, but still helpful, source of information.

21. Jones, *Congregationalism in England*, p. 109.
22. This present section owes much to Watts, *The Dissenters*, Vol I, pp. 268f.
23. Commentators rely quite heavily on the Dr John Evans list. See Jones, *Congregationalism in England*, p. 466, and n.16 above.
24. Jones, *Congregationalism in England*, p. 127.
25. Manning, *The Hymns of Wesley and Watts*, p. 81.
26. Ibid., p. 82.
27. Ibid., p. 83.
28. Jones, *Congregationalism in England*, p. 132.
29. The list given by Jones is as follows: Dartmouth (1668–1691) under John Flavell; Gloucester (1696–1712), James Forbes; Newington Green (1675?–1706?), Charles Morton; Rathmell (1670–1698), Richard Frankland; Oswestry (1690–1700), James Owen; Shrewsbury (1680?–1715?), Francis Tallents and James Owen; Warrington (1697?–1746), Charles Owen. For the influence of Dissenting academies in promoting rationalism see David L. Wykes, 'The contribution of the Dissenting academy to the emergence of Rational Dissent' in Haakonssen (ed), *Enlightenment and Religion*.
30. A. P. Davis, *Isaac Watts*, pp. 13,14, quoted in Watts, *The Dissenters*, Vol I, p. 370.
31. R. Thomas,'Philip Doddridge and Liberalism in Religion' in Nuttall (ed), *Philip Doddridge*, p. 122.
32. W. T. Whitley, *A History of the British Baptists*, p. 163, quoted in Underwood, *A History of the English Baptists*, p. 118.
33. Skeats and Miall, *History of the the Free Churches of England*, pp. 125, 131.
34. Brown, *The English Baptists of the Eighteenth Century*, pp. 2, 12, 15, 32.
35. The following statistics are culled from Watts, *The Dissenters*, Vol I, pp. 269, 270.
36. B. R. White, 'The Twilight of Puritanism in the years before and after 1688' in Grell, Israel and Tyacke (eds), *From Persecution to Toleration*, p. 322.
37. Ibid., p. 325.
38. See Brown, *The English Baptists of the Eighteenth Century*, p. 21.
39. 'Therefore let us leave the elementary doctrine of Christ and go on to maturity, not laying again a foundation of repentance from dead works and of faith toward God, with instruction about ablutions, the laying on of hands, the resurrection of the dead, and eternal judgment.'
40. J. Ivimey, *History of the Baptists*, 4 vols, Vol III, pp. 228ff., 428 ff., quoted in Underwood, *A History of the English Baptists*, p. 118.
41. Brown, *The English Baptists in the Eighteenth Century*, p. 10.
42. Ibid., p. 11.
43. The following comments owe much to Hugh Trevor-Roper, 'Toleration and Religion after 1688' in Grell, Israel and Tyacke (eds), *From Persecution to Toleration*, pp. 389–408.

44. Rupp, *Religion in England*, p. 142.
45. Skeats and Miall, *History of the Free Churches of England*, p. 121.
46. Braithwaite, *The Second Period of Quakerism*, p. 175. This is a book to which the present section is inevitably indebted, as it remains the fullest account of Quakerism in the period under review.
47. Watts, *The Dissenters*, Vol I, p. 285.
48. Rupp, *Religion in England*, p. 184.
49. Of the works on James II the most relevant to our particular focus of interest is Miller, *James II. A Study in Kingship*.
50. Aveling, *The Handle and the Axe*, p. 245.
51. Ibid., pp. 248, 249.
52. Colley, *Britons*, p. 18.
53. Ibid., p. 18.
54. Ibid., p. 20.
55. Monod, *Jacobitism and the English People*, p. 7.
56. Haydon, *Anti-Catholicism in Eighteenth Century England*, p. 256.
57. Ibid., p. 259.
58. Ibid. p. 246.
59. Watkin, *Roman Catholicism in England*, p. 103.
60. Matthew, *Catholicism in England*, p. 132.
61. J. Bossy, 'English Catholics after 1688' in Grell, Israel and Tyacke (eds), *From Persecution to Toleration*, p. 370.
62. Holmes and Szechi, *The Age of Oligarchy*, p. 91, with reference to Bossy.

3. The Churches in England c.1735 to c.1791

1. Walsh and Taylor, 'Introduction' in Walsh, Haydon and Taylor (eds), *The Church of England*, p. 12.
2. Rupp, *Religion in England*, p. 289.
3. Chadwick, *The Secularization of the European Mind in the Nineteenth Century*, p. 14.
4. S. Halifax (ed), *The Works of Joseph Butler*, Vol II, pp. lxxv, lxxvi, quoted in Wood, *The Inextinguishable Blaze*, p. 15.
5. G. Berkeley, *Discourse Addressed to Magistrates and Men in Authority*, pp. 41ff., quoted in ibid., p. 15.
6. Porteous and Stinton (eds), *The Works of Thomas Secker*, Vol V, p. 29, quoted in ibid., p. 16.
7. Quoted in Holmes and Szechi, *The Age of Oligarchy*, p. 102.
8. Quoted in Hylson-Smith, *Evangelicals in the Church of England*, p. 6.
9. W. R. Ward, 'The eighteenth-century Church: a European View' in Walsh, Haydon and Taylor (eds), *The Church of England*, p. 285.
10. Currie, Gilbert, Horsley (eds), *Churches and Churchgoers*, p. 23.
11. Davies and Rupp (eds), *A History of the Methodist Church in Great*

Britain, Vol 1, p. xxii.

12. Gilbert, *Religion and Society in Industrial England*, p. vii. This is a book to which the present section is greatly indebted.

13. Ibid., p. 12.

14. Rupp, *Religion in England*, p. 493.

15. Lovegrove, *Established Church, Sectarian People*, p. 8

16. Ibid., p. 9.

17. Davies and Rupp (eds), *A History of the Methodist Church in Great Britain*, Vol I, p. xxiii.

18. Taylor, 'Church and State in England in the Mid-Eighteenth Century', pp. 132–3, to which reference is made in Taylor, 'Whigs, Bishops and America', p. 333, an article to which the present comments are indebted.

19. J.S. Macauley and R.W.Greaves (eds), *The Autobiography of Thomas Secker, Archbishop of Canterbury*, p. 126, quoted in Mather, *High Church Prophet*, p. 8.

20. Warne, *Church and Society in Eighteenth-Century Devon*, p. 34.

21. Quoted in Davies and Rupp (eds), *A History of the Methodist Church in Great Britain*, Vol 1, pp. xxiii, xxiv.

22. John Wesley, *Works*, vii, *Sermons* iii, p. 179, quoted in Warne, *Church and Society in Eighteenth-Century Devon*, p. 50.

23. See, for example, McClatchey, *Oxfordshire Clergy 1777–1869*; Mitchison, 'Pluralities and the Poorer Benefices in Eighteenth-Century England'; and Virgin, *The Church in an Age of Negligence 1700–1840*.

24. Lovegrove, *Established Church, Sectarian People*, p. 10.

25. Ibid.

26. Mitchison, 'Pluralities and the Poorer Benefices in Eighteenth-Century England', p. 190.

27. Maynard, 'Pluralism and Non-Residence in the Archdeaconry of Durham, 1774–1856'.

28. Lovegrove, *Established Church, Sectarian People*, p. 13.

29. J. Albers, ' "Papist traitors" and "Presbyterian rogues": religious identities in eighteenth-century Lancashire' in Walsh, Haydon and Taylor (eds), *The Church of England*, p. 319.

30. Gascoigne, 'Anglican Latitudinarianism and Political Radicalism', p. 22.

31. Martin Fitzpatrick, 'Latitudinarianism at the Parting of the Ways: a Suggestion' in Walsh, Haydon and Taylor (eds), *The Church of England*, p. 209.

32. The present comments in this section owe much to Waterman, 'A Cambridge "Via Media" in Late Georgian Anglicanism' .

33. Art. cit., p. 422.

34. Ibid.

35. See Introduction, n.31.

36. Good reviews of the various movements to which reference is made can

be found in the books and articles listed in n. 30 of the Introduction.

37. For descriptions and comments on the other forms of churchmanship and their political, social and religious consequences see the books by Hylson-Smith, Nockles, Mather, Varley, Corsi, Brent, Bebbington and Hilton listed in nn. 33, 34 and 35 of the Introduction.

38. See especially Bebbington, *Evangelicalism*, and Hylson-Smith, *The Evangelicals in the Church of England*.

39. See in particular Hylson-Smith, *High Churchmanship in the Church of England*.

40. For descriptions and comments on Hutchinsonianism see especially Nockles, *The Oxford Movement in Context*.

41. Ibid., p. 13.

42. Mather, *High Church Prophet*, p. 10.

43. Ibid., p. 13.

44. Varley, *The Last of the Prince Bishops*, p. 41.

45. MacMath (ed), *The Faith of Samuel Johnson*, p. 3.

46. Hudson, *Samuel Johnson and Eighteenth-Century Thought*, p. 203.

47. Ibid., pp. 84,85.

48. Nockles, *The Oxford Movement in Context*, p. 185.

49. Chamberlain, 'Portrait of a High Church Clerical Dynasty in Georgian England: the Frewens and their World' in Walsh, Haydon and Taylor (eds), *The Church of England*, p. 315.

50. Watts, *The Dissenters*, Vol I, pp. 384, 386.

51. Gilbert, *Religion and Society in Industrial England*, pp. 32, 33.

52. Machin, *Politics and the Churches in Great Britain*, p. 4.

53. Bebb, *Nonconformity and Social and Economic Life*, p. 35.

54. Wilkinson, *1662 and After*, p. 115.

55. Elliott-Binns, *The Early Evangelicals*, p. 109.

56. The following comments owe much to Gilbert, *Religion and Society in Industrial England*, and Bebb, *Nonconformity and Social and Economic Life*, and they in turn rely quite heavily on the lists of Dr John Evans and the Revd Josiah Thompson. The calculations of Bebb, and to a certain extent Gilbert, have been questioned by Bradley, *Religion, Revolution and English Radicalism*.

57. See Gilbert, *Religion and Society in Industrial England*, pp. 33–36.

58. Bradley, *Religion, Revolution and English Radicalism*, p. 93.

59. Gilbert, *Religion and Society in Industrial England*, p. 36.

60. Watts, *The Dissenters*, Vol I, p. 451.

61. H. Rack, 'Survival and Revival: John Bennet, Methodism and Old Dissent' in Robbins (ed), *Protestant Evangelicalism*, p. 2.

62. See Tyerman, *The Life of George Whitefield*, Vol II, pp. 113–14; *Baptist Quarterly*, iv, 1928–29, p. 70; x, 1940–41, p. 283; *Broadmeads Records*, p. 306, to which reference is made in Watts, *The Dissenters*, Vol I, p. 451.

63. T. Jackson, *Life of Charles Wesley*, 2 vols, London 1841, Vol I, pp. 363, 416, 464, to which reference is made in Watts, *The Dissenters*, Vol I, p. 451.

64. Newton, *The Causes and Reasons of the Present Declension among the Congregational Churches*, London 1766, pp. 9–10, to which reference is made in Watts, *The Dissenters*, Vol I, p. 451.

65. Rack, 'Survival and Revival: John Bennet, Methodism and Old Dissent' in Robbins (ed), *Protestant Evangelicalism*, p. 3.

66. Ibid., p. 3.

67. Drysdale, *History of the Presbyterians in England*, p. 520.

68. Quoted in Watts, *The Dissenters*, Vol I, p. 472.

69. Ibid., p. 469.

70. Jones, *Congregationalism in England*, p. 141, and quoting from Humphreys, *The Correspondence and Diary of Philip Doddridge, DD*, 5 vols, London 1829–1831, Vol IV, p. 414. The present section owes much to this work by Jones.

71. Jones, *Congregationlism in England*, pp. 160, 161.

72. Ibid., p. 161.

73. This present section is indebted to Skeats and Miall, *History of the Free Churches of England*; Underwood, *A History of the English Baptists*; and Watts, *The Dissenters*, Vol I.

74. Underwood, *A History of the English Baptists*, p. 160.

75. Quoted in Ibid., p. 160.

76. Quoted in Watts, *The Dissenters*, Vol I, p. 459.

77. Watts, *The Dissenters*, Vol I, p. 459, quoting from R. and S. Wilberforce, *Life of William Wilberforce*, London 1838, iii, p. 389.

78. Wilkinson, *1662 and After*, p. 136.

79. Braithwaite, *The Second Period of Quakerism*, p. 524.

80. Jones, *The Later Periods of Quakerism*, Vol I, pp. 30, 31.

81. Duffy, 'Introduction' in Duffy (ed), *Challoner and his Church*, p. xiii.

82. Pollen and Burton, 'Introduction' to Kirk, *Biographies of English Catholics, 1700–1800*, London 1909, p. ix, quoted in Williams, 'Change or Decay? The Provincial Laity 1691–1781' in Duffy (ed), *Challoner and his Church*, p. 28.

83. Ibid., p. 28, quoting Newman, *Sermons Preached on Various Occasions*, London 1857, pp. 199–201.

84. Hume, 'Foreword' in ibid., p. ix. See also Aveling, *The Handle and the Axe*; Bossy, *The English Catholic Community*; and Matthew, *Catholicism in England*.

85. See White, *The Age of George III*, and Norman, *Roman Catholicism in England*.

86. White, *The Age of George III*, p. 186, quoted in Haydon, 'Anti-Catholicism in Eighteenth-Century England, c.1714 – c.1780', p. 311.

87. Norman, *Roman Catholicism in England*, pp. 54–56, quoted in Haydon, p. 311.

88. Black, 'An Age of Political Stability?' in Black (ed), *Britain in the Age of Walpole*, quoted in Haydon, p. 312.

89. Colley, *Britons*.

90. Haydon, 'Anti-Catholicism in Eighteenth-Century England, c.1714–c.1780', p. 312.

91. Colley, *Britons*, p. 326.

92. Aveling, *The Handle and the Axe*, p. 258.

93. Duffy, 'Challoner 1691–1781: A Memoir' in Duffy (ed), *Challoner and his Church*, p. 7.

94. Bossy, *The English Catholic Community*, pp. 303f.

95. Hume, 'Foreword' in Duffy (ed), *Challoner and his Church*, p. ix.

96. Duffy, 'Introduction' in ibid., pp. xiii, xiv.

97. Hempton, *Religion and Political Culture*, pp. 15, 16.

98. Bushaway, *By Rite*, p. 87, quoted in ibid., p. 16.

99. Hempton, *Religion and Political Culture*, p. 17.

100. Ibid., p. 18.

4. *The Evangelical Revival: The Methodists*

1. Cohen, *The Pursuit of the Millennium*.

2. See, for example, Lanternari, *The Religion of the Oppressed*; Lewis, *Ecstatic Religion*.

3. Knox, *Enthusiasm*.

4. For example McLoughlin, *Modern Revivalism*.

5. See especially, Edwards, *A Narrative of Surprising Conversions*.

6. Ibid., p. 9.

7. Ibid., pp. 12–15.

8. Whitefield, *Journals*, 1738–41, pp. 459, 460.

9. Ibid., p. 464.

10. Tyerman, *Life of George Whitefield*,Vol I, pp. 424, 425.

11. *Evangelical Library Bulletin*, No 20, p. 5, quoted in Wood, *The Inextinguishable Blaze*, p. 66.

12. Walsh, '"Methodism" and the Origins of English-Speaking Evangelicalism' in Noll, Bebbington and Rawlyk (eds), *Evangelicalism*, p. 20.

13. This section owes much to the work of Ward who has greatly helped to give scholars of the early Protestant revival movements of the eighteenth century not only an Anglo-American context, but a European perspective. See especially *The Protestant Evangelical Awakening*, and *Faith and Faction*, but also 'The relations of enlightenment and religious revival in central Europe and in the English-speaking world'.

14. Ward, *The Protestant Evangelical Awakening*, p. 57.

15. Ibid., p. 62.
16. Ibid.
17. Walsh,'"Methodism" and the Origins of English-Speaking Evangelicalism' in Noll, Bebbington and Rawlyk (eds), *Evangelicalism*, p. 20.
18. The present description of the revival in Scotland owes much to Fawcett, *The Cambuslang Revival* and to Robe, *Narrative: Revival of Religion*.
19. Robe, *Narrative*, pp. 217, 218.
20. Ibid., pp. 41, 42.
21. Williams, *Welsh Calvinistic Methodism*, p. 5.
22. O'Brien, 'A Transatlantic Community of Saints', p. 811.
23. Ibid., p. 813.
24. Crawford, 'Origins of the Eighteenth-Century Evangelical Revival', p. 397.
25. Walsh,'"Methodism" and the Origins of English-Speaking Evangelicalism in Noll, Bebbington and Rawlyk (eds), *Evangelicalism*, p. 19.
26. See Lambert, 'Pedlar in Divinity' and Stout, *The Divine Dramatist*.
27. Stout, *The Divine Dramatist*, p. xvi.
28. Ibid., p. xviii.
29. For the life and teaching of George Whitefield, see especially Whitefield, *Journals*, 1738–41; Tyerman, *Life of George Whitefield*, and Dallimore, *George Whitefield*.
30. Whitefield, *Journals*, 1738–41, p. 77.
31. Ibid., p. 87.
32. Ibid., p. 88.
33. Ibid., p. 88.
34. Ibid., pp. 88, 89.
35. See Podmore, 'The Role of the Moravian Church in England', p. 4.
36. Ibid., p. 4.
37. Ibid., pp. 5,6.
38. Whitefield, *Journals*, 1738–41, p. 193.
39. Ibid., pp. 203, 204.
40. See *The Works of John Wesley*, Vol VIII, p. 269.
41. Ibid., Vol VIII, p. 269.
42. Ibid., Vol VIII, p. 252.
43. Heitzenrater, *Wesley and the People Called Methodists*, p. 104.
44. Ibid., p. 105.
45. *The Works of John Wesley*, Vol VIII, p. 258.
46. Ibid., p. 259.
47. Church, *More about the Early Methodist People*, p. 141.
48. Wesley, *The Journal*, Vol VI, p. 221.
49. See Stevenson, *History of City Road Chapel*, p. 28.
50. Wesley, *The Journal*, Vol I, pp. 467–9, quoted in Watts, *The Dissenters*, Vol I, p. 361.

51. See in particular Whitefield, *Journals*; Wesley, *The Journal* and Telford, *Wesley's Veterans*.

52. Rack, *Reasonable Enthusiast*, p. 214.

53. For the theological differences between the Wesleys and Whitefield see especially Dallimore, *George Whitefield* and Rack, *Reasonable Enthusiast*.

54. Knox, *Enthusism*, p. 496, quoted in Wood, *The Inextinguishable Blaze*, p. 87.

55. Wood, *The Inextinguishable Blaze*, p. 188.

56. Wesley, *Poetical Works*, Vol VI, p. 63, quoted in Wood, *The Inextinguishable Blaze*, p. 188.

57. Watson, 'Whitefield and Congregationalism', *Transactions of the Congregational Historical Society*, Vol 8, No 4, 1922, p. 175, used as a source in Bebbington, *Evangelicalism in Modern Britain*, p. 29.

58. Davies and Rupp (eds), *A History of the Methodist Church in Great Britain*, Vol 1, p. 292.

59. Ryle, *Christian Leaders of the Eighteenth Century*, p. 31.

60. Quoted in Elliott-Binns, *The Early Evangelicals*, p. 135.

61. See Walsh, 'Methodism at the End of the Eighteenth Century' in Davies and Rupp (eds), *A History of the Methodist Church in Great Britain*, Vol 1, p. 292.

62. *Life and Times of the Countess of Huntingdon*, Vol II, pp. 483f., quoted in Davies and Rupp (eds), *A History of the Methodist Church in Great Britain*, Vol 1, p. 292.

63. A. Harding, 'The Countess of Huntingdon and Her Connexion in the 18th Century', Oxford D Phil. 1992, 'Conclusion'.

64. Turner, *Conflict and Reconciliation*, p. 22.

65. Ibid., p. 25.

66. Rack, *Reasonable Enthusiast*, p. 200.

67. *Minutes of Conference*, 1, pp. 95, 96, quoted in Simon, *John Wesley The Master Builder*, pp. 277, 278.

68. Davies and Rupp (eds), *A History of the Methodist Church in Great Britain*, Vol 1, p. 167.

69. Quoted in Bebbington, *Evangelicalism*, p. 153. For a modern edition of *A Plain Account of Christian Perfection*, from which the quotation is taken, see Halycon C. Blackhouse (ed), *A Plain Man's Guide to Holiness*, London 1988.

70. Ibid.

71. Rack, *Reasonable Enthusiast*, p. 395.

72. See ibid., p. 337.

73. See especially Beardsley, *A History of American Revivals*; Cairns, *An Endless Line of Splendor*; Carwardine, *Transatlantic Revivalism*; Gaustad, *The Great Awakening in New England*; McLoughlin, *Modern*

Revivalism; Maxson, *The Great Awakening in the Middle Colonies*; Orr, *The Second Evangelical Awakening in America*; Weisberger, *They Gathered at the River*.

74. See in particular Cairns, *An Endless Line of Splendor*; Carson, *God's River in Spate*; Church, *Quest for the Highest*; Evans, *The Welsh Revival of 1904*; Finney, *Lectures on Revivals of Religion*; Gibson, *The Year of Grace*; Koch, *The Revival in Indonesia*; Monod, *The Korean Revival*; Morgan, *The 'Fifty-nine Revival in Wales*; Morgan, *The Welsh Revival*; Orr, *The Second Evangelical Awakening in Britain*.

75. For a discussion of these matters see, for example, Cohn, *The Pursuit of the Millennium*; McLoughlin, *Modern Revivalism*; Wearmouth, *Methodism and the Common People of the Eighteenth Century*; Wilson, *Religion in Secular Society*; Worsley, *The Trumpet Shall Sound*.

76. See Valenze, *Prophetic Sons and Daughters*.

77. William Holland, *Short Account of the Work of the Lord in England*. MS in the Moravian archives in London.

78. See such books as Halévy, *A History of the English People in the Nineteenth Century*, Vol I, *England in 1815*; Tawney, *Religion and the Rise of Capitalism*; Thompson, *The Making of the English Working Class*; Weber, *The Protestant Ethic and the Spirit of Capitalism*.

79. For the character, lifestyle, role and significance of women preachers and lay leaders, see especially Gill, *Women and the Church of England* and Valenze, *Prophetic Sons and Daughters*.

80. For this summary see David Hempton, ' "Popular Religion" 1800–1986' in Thomas (ed), *The British*.

81. *Journal of the Revd Charles Wesley*, p. 86.

82. MS letter from Sarah Middleton to Charles Wesley. This and the quotations from the early converts which are used in the paragraphs which follow are to be found in the Methodist Archives, now located in Manchester. In all of them the original spelling and grammar are retained.

83. MS letter from William Barber to Charles Wesley, 1741.

84. Telford, *Wesley's Veterans*, Vol III, p. 11.

85. MS letter from Nathaniel Hurst to Charles Wesley, 1741.

86. MS letter from Elizabeth Hinson to Charles Wesley, 25 May 1740.

87. MS letter from Samuel Webb to Charles Wesley.

88. Ibid.

89. MS letter from Martha Sones to Charles Wesley, 1 June 1740.

90. William Holland, *Short Account of the Work of the Lord in England*. MS in the Moravian archives in London.

91. MS letter from Mrs Clagget to Charles Wesley.

92. MS letter from Sarah Middleton to Charles Wesley.

93. Ibid.

94. 'Memoir of Brother John West', *Moravian Messenger*, 1875.

95. MS letter from Maria Price to Charles Wesley, 18 May 1740.
96. MS letter from E.Bristow to Charles Wesley, 12 April 1740.
97. Otto, *The Idea of the Holy*.
98. Ibid., p. 33.
99. MS letter from Martha Sones to Charles Wesley, 1 June 1740.
100. Gunter, *The Limits of 'Love Divine'*, p. 276.
101. Ibid., p. 276.
102. See the list of works under these various authors in the bibliography.

5. *The Evangelical Revival: The Church of England*

1. Much in this chapter is based on my previous work, *The Evangelicals in the Church of England from 1734 to 1984*.
2. The term Evangelical, and its various derivatives, will be used from now onwards as an accepted shorthand for Evangelicals in the Church of England. It will be distinguished from the more general term 'evangelical', in lower case, which refers to all those, including the Church of England Evangelicals, who shared a recognizably similar set of theological beliefs.
3. Smyth, *Simeon and Church Order*, p. 6.
4. For the Cornish Evangelicals see especially Davies, *The Early Cornish Evangelicals*.
5. *The Works of George Whitefield*, Vol II, p. 44.
6. For the life of Samuel Walker see Davies, *The Early Cornish Evangelicals*; Elliott-Binns, *The Early Evangelicals*; Ryle, *Christian Leaders in the Eighteenth Century*; and Sydney, *Life and Ministry of Samuel Walker*.
7. Wesley, Letters, Vol III, p. 152.
8. For the life and teaching of Thomas Adam, see Elliott-Binns, *The Early Evangelicals*, pp. 131f., 159f., 314f., 454f.
9. Quoted in Sydney, *Life and Ministry of Samuel Walker*, p. 224.
10. Tyerman, *Life and Times of John Wesley*, Vol III, London 1871, p. 636, quoted in Turner, *Conflict and Reconciliation*, p. 12.
11. Turner, *Conflict and Reconciliation*, p. 12.
12. For the life and teaching of William Romaine see in particular Cadogan, *The Life of the Revd William Romaine*; Elliott-Binns, *The Early Evangelicals*; Haweis, *The Life of William Romaine*; Loane, *Oxford and the Evangelical Succession*; and Ryle, *Christian Leaders of the Eighteenth Century*.
13. For the life of William Grimshaw see especially Balleine, *A History of the Evangelical Party in the Church of England*; Elliott-Binns, *The Early Evangelicals*; Hardy, *Life of Grimshaw*; Middleton, *Biographia Ecclesiastica*; and Wesley, *Journal*, Vol IV.
14. Cited in Ryle, *Christian Leaders in the Eighteenth Century*, p. 119.
15. See Wesley, *Works*, Vol XII, p. 355.

16. Letter from Samuel Walker to Charles Wesley, cited in Ryle, *Christian Leaders in the Eighteenth Century*, p. 130.
17. Cited in Ryle, *Christian Leaders in the Eighteenth Century*, pp. 124–126.
18. Hardy, *Life of Grimshaw*, p. 232.
19. Ryle, *Christian Leaders in the Eighteenth Century*, pp. 127,138.
20. For the life and teaching of John William Fletcher see in particular Benson, *The Life of the Revd John William de la Fléchière*; Elliott-Binns, *The Early Evangelicals*; Loane, *Cambridge and the Evangelical Succession*; Ryle, *Christian Leaders in the Eighteenth Century*; and Tyerman, *Wesley's Designated Successor*.
21. Quoted in Elliott-Binns, *The Early Evangelicals*, p. 210.
22. Ibid., p. 300.
23. For the life of Henry Venn see especially Elliott-Binns, *The Early Evangelicals*; Loane, *Cambridge and the Evangelical Succession*; Ryle, *Christian Leaders in the Eighteenth Century*; and Venn, *Memoir of the Revd Henry Venn*, London 1834.
24. For the life of John Berridge, see in particular Elliott-Binns, *The Early Evangelicals*; Loane, *Cambridge and the Evangelical Succession*; Ryle, *Christian Leaders in the Eighteenth Century*; and Wood, *The Inextinguishable Blaze*.
25. Works which examine these and related phenomena include Knox, *Enthusiasm* and Lewis, *Ecstatic Religion*.
26. For the life of James Hervey see especially Elliott-Binns, *The Early Evangelicals* and Tyerman, *The Oxford Methodists*.
27. For the lives of these Evangelicals see especially Balleine, *A History of the Evangelical Party in the Church of England*; Elliott-Binns, *The Early Evangelicals*; Reynolds, *The Evangelicals at Oxford 1735–1871*; and *The Dictionary of National Biography*.
28. Bebbington, *Evangelicalism*, p. 3.
29. Quoted in Elliott-Binns, *The Early Evangelicals*, p. 392.
30. Quotations in ibid., p. 392.
31. For the life and work of John Newton see especially Loane, *Oxford and the Evangelical Succession*; Newton, *An Authentic Narrative* and *Cardiphonia*; and Ryle, *Christian Leaders in the Eighteenth Century*.
32. B. Hindmarsh, ' "I am a Sort of Middle-Man". The Politically Correct Evangelicalism of John Newton' in Rawlyk and Noll (eds), *Amazing Grace*, p. 36.
33. Hindmarsh, art. cit., p. 37.
34. Ibid., p. 45.
35. For the life of William Cowper see in particular Cecil, *The Stricken Deer*; Ella, *William Cowper Poet of Paradise*; and Southey, *The Life and Works of William Cowper*.
36. For the life of Hannah More see especially Jones, *Hannah More*.

37. Ibid., p. 100.
38. See Weber, *The Protestant Ethic and the Spirit of Capitalism, General Economic History* and *The Sociology of Religion*.
39. See Troeltsch, *Social Teaching of the Christian Churches*.
40. See John Wesley's sermon on 'The Use of Money', first preached in 1744 and published in 1760 (sermon L in Works of John Wesley, London 1872).
41. See Niebuhr, *The Social Sources of Denominationalism*.
42. See Martin, 'The Denomination'.
43. See Wilson, *Sects and Society* and *Patterns of Sectarianism*.

6. *The Church of England: From One Revival to Another*

1. Carpenter, *Church and People, 1789–1889*.
2. See especially Gill, *William Wordsworth*.
3. For a discussion of these matters see, for example, Halévy, *A History of the English People in the Nineteenth Century*, Vol I, *England in 1815*; Perkin, *The Origins of Modern English Society*; and Thompson, *The Making of the English Working Class*.
4. Opening lines of Dickens, *A Tale of Two Cities* (1859).
5. Ward, *Religion and Society in England 1790–1850*, p. 1.
6. Gilbert, *Religion and Society*, p. 27.
7. Ibid., p. 28.
8. Kiernan, 'Evangelicalism and the French Revolution', p. 45.
9. Currie, Gilbert and Horsley, *Churches and Churchgoers*, p. 104.
10. Rycroft, 'Church, Chapel and Community in Craven, 1764–1851'.
11. Smith, *Religion in Industrial Society*, p. 243. This is an excellent analysis of the subject it examines.
12. Rycroft, 'Church, Chapel and Community in Craven, 1764–1851', pp. 7,8.
13. Ibid., p. 7.
14. Ward, 'The Tithe Question in England in the Early Nineteenth Century', p. 67.
15. Evans, 'Some Reasons for the Growth of English Rural Anti-Clericalism', p. 84.
16. Ibid., p. 94.
17. Ward, 'The Tithe Question in England in the Early Nineteenth Century', p. 69.
18. *The Extraordinary Black Book*, London 1831, p. 21, quoted in Evans, 'Some Reasons for the Growth of English Rural Anti-Clericalism'.
19. See Evans, art.cit.
20. Chadwick, *The Victorian Church*, Vol I, p. 26.
21. Ibid., p. 27.
22. Nockles, *The Oxford Movement in Context*, p. 44. This is an important

work in the subject it covers.

23. These are the characteristics listed by Mather in *High Church Prophet*.
24. This list is given in Nockles, *The Oxford Movement in Context*, p. 149.
25. Quoted in Mather, *High Church Prophet*, pp. 206, 207.
26. Nockles, *The Oxford Movement in Context*, p. 210.
27. For the life and teaching of Samuel Horsley, see especially Mather, *High Church Prophet*.
28. Varley, *The Last of the Prince Bishops*, p. 9.
29. The following account of the life of Joshua Watson and the Hackney Phalanx is greatly indebted to Webster, *Joshua Watson*. For the life of Joshua Watson see also Churton, *Memoir of Joshua Watson*, p. 9.
30. Varley, *The Last of the Prince Bishops*, p. 106.
31. Charles Daubeny, *Guide to the Church*, London 1829, quoted in Reardon, *Religious Thought in the Victorian Age*, p. 34.
32. Webster, *Joshua Watson*, ch.5.
33. Ibid., ch.6.
34. Stock, *History of the Church Missionary Society*, Vol I, p. 38.
35. Stoughton, *Religion in England from 1800 to 1850*, Vol I, p. 114.
36. H. P. Liddon, *Life of E. B. Pusey*, London 1893, Vol I, p. 235, quoted in Carpenter, *Church and People 1789–1889*, p. 29.
37. Gladstone, *Correspondence*, Vol I, p. 8.
38. Carpenter, *Church and People 1789–1889*, p. 28.
39. See William Romaine, *Christian Guardian*, London 1809.
40. See Coombs, 'A History of the Church Pastoral-Aid Society, 1836–1861' and Gilbert, *Religion and Society in Industrial England*, for discussion on the numerical strength of the Evangelicals.
41. Anstey, *The Atlantic Slave Trade and British Abolition 1760 1810*, pp. 157–99, quoted in Hilton, *The Age of Atonement*, p. 8.
42. Hilton, op. cit., p. 8.
43. Ward, *Religion and Society 1780–1850*, p. 5.
44. For the life and teaching of Charles Simeon see especially Carus, *Memoirs of the Life of the Revd Charles Simeon*; Loane, *Cambridge and the Evangelical Succession*; and Moule, *Charles Simeon*.
45. G. O. Trevelyan, *The Life and Letters of Lord Macaulay*, London 1876, Vol I, p. 67.
46. Moule, *Charles Simeon*, pp. 77, 78.
47. Letter quoted in Carus, *Memoirs of the Life of the Revd Charles Simeon*, p. 780.
48. For the life of William Wilberforce see in particular Coupland, *William Wilberforce*; Furneaux, *William Wilberforce*; Pollock, *Wilberforce*; and Isaac and Wilberforce, *The Life of William Wilberforce*.
49. Quoted in Carpenter, *Church and People 1789–1889*, p. 30.
50. For an account of the Clapham Sect and the Saints, see especially Stephen,

Essays in Ecclesiastical Biography; and Howse, *Saints in Politics*. For a thorough analysis and critique, see in particular Bradley, 'The Politics of Godliness'; Bradley, *The Call to Seriousness*; and Brown, *Fathers of the Victorians*.

51. For the life of Henry Thornton see Meacham, *Henry Thornton of Clapham 1760–1815*.

52. For the life of John Shore, Lord Teignmouth, see Josiah Pratt, *Sketch of the life of the late Right Honourable Lord Teignmouth*, London 1834; and Lord Teignmouth, *Memoir of the Life and Correspondence of John, Lord Teignmouth*, 2 vols, London 1843.

53. For the life of Zachary Macaulay see Vicountess Knutsford, *Life and Letters of Zachary Macaulay*, London 1900.

54. For the life of James Stephen see Caroline Stephen, *The Right Honourable Sir James Stephen*, London 1906; and Leslie Stephen, *The Life of Sir James Fitzjames Stephen, Bart, KCIS*, London 1895.

55. For the life of Charles Grant see Thomas Fisher, *A Memoir of the Late C. Grant, Esq.*, London 1833; and Morris, *The Life of Charles Grant*, London 1904.

56. Jones, *Hannah More*, p. 91.

57. Ibid., p. 139.

58. The following comments owe much to Bradley, 'The Politics of Godliness' and *The Call to Seriousness*.

59. David Hempton, 'Evangelicalism and Reform c.1780–1832' in Wolffe (ed), *Evangelical Faith and Public Zeal*, p. 20.

60. Ibid., p. 21.

61. Bebbington, *Evangelicalism*, p. 71.

62. See Anstey, *The Atlantic Slave Trade*, p. 126.

63. Ibid., p. 239.

64. Ibid., pp. 405, 406.

65. For the life of Thomas Fowell Buxton see Buxton (ed), *Memoirs of Sir Thomas Fowell Buxton*, London 1850.

66. Bradley, 'The Politics of Godliness', p. 192.

67. Hammond, *The Town Labourer, 1760–1832*, p. 216.

68. Brown, *Fathers of the Victorians*, p. 5.

69. Neill, *Anglicanism*, p. 243.

70. Bradley, 'The Politics of Godliness', p. iii.

71. Ibid., p. iv.

72. *Edinburgh Review* 1838, p. 167, quoted in Howse, *Saints in Politics*, p. 131. The comments in this section owe much to Howse's book, pp. 129–31.

73. Examples include Hannah More, *Thoughts on the Importance of the Manners of the Great to General Society* (1788), *An Estimate of the Religion of the Fashionable World* (1790), *Village Politics by Will Chip*,

and *Cheap Repository Tracts* (1795–98), including *Black Giles the Poacher* and *The Shepherd of Salisbury Plain*; Legh Richmond, *Annals of the Poor* (1809, 1810), including *The Dairyman's Daughter*; and Mary Sherwood, *The Fairchild Family* (1813, 1842, 1847), and *The Lady of the Manor* (1825–9).

74. Dickey, 'Going about and doing good': Evangelicals and Poverty c.1815–1870' in Wolffe (ed), *Evangelical Faith and Public Zeal*, pp. 45, 46.

75. As examples, see Bradley, 'The Politics of Godliness' and *The Call to Seriousness*; Brown, *Fathers of the Victorians*; and Bready, *England Before and After Wesley*.

76. See *The Works of the Revd Sydney Smith*, London 1854, Vol I, p. 209, quoted in Newell, 'Studies in Evangelical Prose Literature: Its rise and decline', p. 53.

77. Macaulay, *History of England*, London 1849, Vol I, p. 161, quoted in ibid., p. 54.

78. Rosman, 'Evangelicals and Culture in England, 1790–1833', p. 198.

79. Edward Royle, 'Evangelicals and Education' in Wolffe (ed), *Evangelical Faith and Public Zeal*, p. 120.

80. Ibid, p. 120.

81. Watts, *The Dissenters*, Vol II, *The Expansion of Evangelical Nonconformity*, p. 58.

82. Ibid.

83. Laqueur, *Religion and Respectability*, 1976, quoted in Watts, *The Dissenters*, Vol II, p. 59.

84. Laqueur, op. cit., quoted in Watts, *The Dissenters*, Vol II, p. 59.

85. Carwardine, *Transatlantic Revivalism*, pp. 80, 193.

86. Jones, *Congregationalism in England*, p. 164 and D.G.Evans, 'The Growth and Development of Organized Religion in the Swansea Valley, 1820–1890', University of Wales Ph.D 1978, p. 347, cited in Watts, *The Dissenters*, Vol II, pp. 60, 61.

87. Watts, op. cit., p. 63.

88. Elliott-Binns, *Religion in the Victorian Era*, p. 47.

89. Newman, *Apologia Pro Vita Sua*, p. 288.

90. Elliott-Binns, *Religion in the Victorian Era*, p. 470.

91. Keith W. Clements, *Lovers of Discord*, London 1988, p. 6. This is a book to which the present section is greatly indebted.

92. Ibid., p. 6.

93. Ibid., p. 10.

94. Gillispie, *Genesis and Geology*, p. 4.

95. Ibid., p. 96.

96. See Livingstone, *Darwin's Forgotten Defenders*, 1987.

97. Vidler, *The Church in an Age of Revolution*, p. 39.

98. Waterman, 'A Cambridge "Via Media" in Late-Georgian Anglicanism',

to which reference is made in Nockles, *The Oxford Movement in Context*, p. 29.

99. Brilioth, *The Anglican Revival*, p. 78.
100. Gilley, *Newman and his Age*, p. 42.
101. Brilioth, *The Anglican Revival*, p. 79.
102. Reardon, *From Coleridge to Gore*, pp. 43.
103. Ibid., pp. 43, 44.
104. Nockles, *The Oxford Movement in Context*, p. 273.
105. Stanley, *Life of Dr Arnold*, pp. iii, iv.
106. Quoted in ibid., p. iv.
107. Reardon, *From Coleridge to Gore*, p. 57.
108. Ibid., p. 16.
109. Mill, *Dissertations and Discussions*, London 1867, i, pp. 330 and 394, quoted in ibid., p. 60.
110. Reardon, *From Coleridge to Gore*, pp. 66, 67.
111. Stiles, *Religion, Society and Reform*, p. 1.
112. Ibid., p. 20.
113. Smith, *Religion in Industrial Society*, p. 272.
114. Ibid., p. 272.
115. Urdank, *Religion and Society in a Cotswold Vale*, p. 100.
116. Stiles, *Religion, Society and Reform*, p. 28.
117. Valenze, *Prophetic Sons and Daughters*, pp. 91, 92.
118. Harrison, *The Second Coming*, p. 39.
119. E.Peacock, *Notes and Queries*, 2nd series, i (1856), p. 415, quoted in Thomas, *Religion and the Decline of Magic*, p. 666, and in Harrison, *The Second Coming*, p. 41.
120. Harrison, *The Second Coming*, p. 50.
121. Ibid, p. 52.
122. Ibid.
123. Ibid., pp. 5,6.

7. *Dissenters and Roman Catholics: The Road to Emancipation*

1. Watts, *The Dissenters*, Vol II., p. 1. This is a work to which the present chapter is greatly indebted.
2. Lovegrove, *Established Church, Sectarian People*, p. 14.
3. See McCord, *British History 1815–1906*, p. 122; and also Gilbert, *Religion and Society in Industrial England*, ch.2.
4. Watts, *The Dissenters*, Vol II, pp. 23, 29.
5. W.R. Ward, 'Church and Society in the First Half of the Nineteenth Century' in Davies, George and Rupp (eds), *A History of the Methodist Church in Great Britain*, Vol 2, pp. 26, 27.
6. Watts, *The Dissenters*, Vol II, p. 36.

7. Ibid., p. 126.
8. Ibid., p. 129.
9. Ibid., p. 132.
10. Lovegrove, *Established Church, Sectarian People*, p. 14.
11. See Watts, *The Dissenters*, Vol II, pp. 58–63.
12. Cowherd, *The Politics of English Dissent*, p. 22. This is a book to which the present section owes much.
13. Evans, 'Some Reasons for the Growth of English Rural Anti-Clericalism', p. 84.
14. David Hempton, 'Evangelicalism and Reform c.1780–1832' in Wolffe (ed), *Evangelical Faith and Public Zeal*, pp. 26, 27.
15. Greville, *A Journal of the Reigns of King George IV and King William IV* ed Henry Reeve, London 1875, I, p. 198, quoted in Cowherd, *The Politics of English Dissent*, p. 34.
16. See Orchard, 'English Evangelical Eschatology, 1790–1850'; Soloway, *Prelates and People*, pp. 34,35; and Ward, *Religion and Society in England*, p. 2.
17. See, for a discussion of this, Cohn, *The Pursuit of the Millennium*, and Knox, *Enthusiasm*.
18. Bebbington, *Evangelicalism*, p. 62.
19. See ibid., p. 62.
20. Frere, *A Combined View of the Prophecies of Daniel, Esdras, and St John*, 2nd edn, London 1815, pp. ivf., 210–16, especially p. 212, quoted in Bebbington, *Evangelicalism*, p. 82.
21. For the life and teaching of Edward Irving see especially Dallimore, *The Life of Edward Irving*, and Orchard, 'English Evangelical Eschatology, 1790–1850'.
22. Dallimore, *The Life of Edward Irving*, p. 32.
23. Stock, *History of the Church Missionary Society*, Vol I, p. 282.
24. Sheridan Gilley, 'Edward Irving: Prophet of the Millennium' in Garnett and Matthew (eds), *Revival and Religion since 1700*, p. 107.
25. Ibid.
26. See especially Rowdon, *The Origins of the Brethren 1825 to 1850*.
27. E. Swedenborg, *The True Christian Religion*, London 1771, 1883 edn, para. 779, quoted in Harrison, *The Second Coming*, p. 73.
28. See Ackroyd, *William Blake*.
29. Harrison, *The Second Coming*, pp. 219, 220.
30. Gowland, *Methodist Secessions*.
31. Davies, *Methodism*.
32. J. Walsh, 'Methodism at the end of the Eighteenth Century' in Davies and Rupp (eds), *A History of the Methodist Church in Great Britain*, Vol 1, p. 80.
33. Gowland, *Methodist Secessions*, p. 3.

34. Ibid., p. 3.
35. Ibid., pp. 4,5.
36. Ward (ed), *The Early Correspondence of Jabez Bunting 1820–1829.*
37. Watts, *The Dissenters*, Vol II, p. 408.
38. Ibid., p. 625.
39. For the life of Hugh Bourne see especially Wilkinson, *Hugh Bourne 1772–1852.*
40. Quoted in ibid., p. 34.
41. The description is taken from a pamphlet he wrote entitled *Observations on Camp Meetings, with an Account of a Camp Meeting held on Sunday, May the 31st, 1807, at Mow, near Harriseahead* (Newcastle-under-Lyme, 1807). Reprinted in Walford, pp. 119–25, quoted in ibid., pp. 46–48.
42. Quoted in ibid., p. 36.
43. Gilbert, *Religion and Society*, p. 31.
44. Davies, *Methodism*, pp. 137,138 (page nos refer to original edn).
45. See Gilbert, *Religion and Society*, p. 31.
46. Halévy, *A History of the English People in the Nineteenth Century*, Vol I, *England in 1815*, p. 387.
47. See, for example, Hammond and Hammond, *The Town Labourer*, chs 10–12; Wearmouth, *Methodism and the Common People of the Eighteenth Century*; and Kiernan, 'Evangelicalism and the French Revolution'. For the present comments, see Semmel, 'Introduction' in Halévy, *The Birth of Methodism in England*, p. 1. Relevant works on the interpretation of Methodism, and related subjects, included Gillispie, 'The Work of Elie Halévy: A Critical Appreciation'; Hobsbawm, 'Methodism and the Threat of Revolution in Britain' . See also the severe criticism in John Kent, 'M. Elie Halévy and Methodism', *Proceedings of the Wesley Historical Society*, 34, pt 8, December 1964, pp. 189f.
48. Hobsbawm, 'Methodism and the Threat of Revolution in Britain', quoted in Watts, *The Dissenters*, Vol II, p. 373.
49. Watts, *The Dissenters*, Vol II, p. 374, quoting Thompson, *Making of the English Working Class*, pp. 49, 50, 419, 428–29.
50. Semmel, 'Introduction' in Elie Halévy, *The Birth of Methodism in England*, p. 1.
51. Alan D. Gilbert in O'Brien and Quinault (eds), *The Industrial Revolution and British Society*, p. 94.
52. Ibid., p. 98.
53. Hempton, 'Evangelicalism and Reform c.1780–1832' in Wolffe (ed), *Evangelical Faith and Public Zeal*, p. 24.
54. Hempton, *Religion and Political Culture*, p. 32.
55. Ibid.
56. Ibid., p. 27.
57. Kiernan, 'Evangelicalism and the French Revolution', p. 45.

58. Pedersen, 'Hannah More meets Simple Simon', p. 109.
59. Gilbert, *Religion and Society*, p. 37.
60. Jones, *Congregationalism in England 1662–1962*, p. 194.
61. Cowherd, *The Politics of English Dissent*, p. 20.
62. Jones, *Congregationalism in England 1662–1962*, p. 194.
63. Davies, *Worship and Theology in England*, pp. 94, 95. This is a book to which the points made in the present paragraph are indebted.
64. Gibson, *Church, State and Society, 1760–1850*, p. 160.
65. Gilbert, *Religion and Society*, p. 37.
66. See Brown, *The English Baptists of the Eighteenth Century*, p. 106.
67. Underwood, *A History of the English Baptists*, p. 157.
68. *The Monthly Repository of Theology and General Literature*, X, 1815, p. 320, quoted in Brown, *The English Baptists of the Eighteenth Century*, p. 108.
69. Quoted in Brown, op. cit., p. 109.
70. Underwood, *A History of the English Baptists*, p. 161.
71. Quoted in ibid., p. 184.
72. Gilbert, *Religion and Society*, p. 36, who draws upon the careful analysis of these growth processes made by J.S. Rowntree in *Quakerism Past and Present: being an inquiry into the causes of its decline . . .*, London 1859, pp. 68–88.
73. Watts, *The Dissenters*, Vol II, p. 99.
74. Jones, *The Later Periods of Quakerism*, Vol I, p. 323.
75. Ibid., p. 335.
76. See Gilbert, *Religion and Society*, pp. 32–36.
77. Ibid., p. 36.
78. Quoted in Wilkinson, *1662 and After*, p. 135.
79. See Watts, *The Dissenters*, Vol II, p. 488.
80. Wilkinson, *1662 and After*, p. 136.
81. The quotations are made in Drysdale, *History of the Presbyterians in England*, pp. 537,538.
82. Gilbert, *Religion and Society*, p. 42.
83. See Parsons, 'Victorian Roman Catholicism: Emancipation, Expansion and Achievement' in Parsons (ed), *Religion in Victorian Britain*, Vol I, *Traditions*, p. 150, n.1.
84. Matthew, *Catholicism in England*, p. 150, a book to which this present section is indebted.
85. Gilley, 'The Roman Catholic Church in England, 1780–1940' in Gilley and Sheils (eds), *A History of Religion in Britain*, p. 351.
86. Ibid., p. 348.
87. Aveling, *The Handle and the Axe*, p. 321.
88. Ibid.
89. Henriques, *Religious Toleration in England*, p. 136.

90. Colley, *Britons*, p. 328.
91. Davies, George and Rupp (eds), *A History of the Methodist Church in Great Britain*, Vol 2, p. 17.
92. Colley, *Britons*, p. 328.

8. *Overseas Mission, 1689–1883*

1. Neill, *A History of Christian Missions*, pp. 224, 225. This is a book to which this whole chapter is greatly indebted.
2. For these quotations see ibid., p. 225.
3. Robert T. Handy, *A History of the Churches in the United States and Canada*, p. 1.
4. Ibid., p. 3.
5. For the history of the SPCK see especially Clarke, *A History of the SPCK*, and Craig Rose, 'The Origins and Ideals of the SPCK 1699–1716' in Walsh, Haydon and Taylor (eds), *The Church of England*, pp. 172–190.
6. Rose, 'The origins and ideals of the SPCK 1699–1716' in Walsh, Haydon and Taylor (eds), *The Church of England*, p. 180.
7. Ibid., p. 180.
8. Clarke, *A History of the SPCK*, p. 21.
9. Sykes, *William Wake, Archbishop of Canterbury*, Vol II, p. 220.
10. For the founding of the SPG see especially Thompson, *Into All Lands*.
11. Neill, *A History of Christian Missions*, p. 226.
12. Thompson, *Into All Lands*, p. 44.
13. Ibid., p. 44.
14. Ibid., p. 45.
15. Quoted in Neill, *A History of Christian Missions*, p. 227.
16. Walsh and Taylor, 'Introduction' in Walsh, Haydon and Taylor (eds), *The Church of England*, pp. 15,16.
17. Thompson, *Into All Lands*, p. 36.
18. Norman Sykes, 'Ecumenical Movements in Great Britain in the Seventeenth and Eighteenth Centuries' in Rouse and Neill (eds), *A History of the Ecumenical Movement 1517–1948*, p. 153.
19. Ibid., p. 154.
20. Gallicanism can be defined as the 'collective name for the body of doctrine which asserted the more or less complete freedom of the Roman Catholic Church, especially in France, from the ecclesiastical authority of the Papacy.' Cross and Livingstone (eds), *The Oxford Dictionary of the Christian Church*, p. 548.
21. Quoted in Sykes, 'Ecumenical Movements in Great Britain in the Seventeenth and Eighteenth Centuries' in Rouse and Neill (eds), *A History of the Ecumenical Movement 1517–1948*, p. 155.
22. Martin, Schmidt, 'Ecumenical Activity on the Continent of Europe in the

Seventeenth and Eighteenth Centuries in Rouse and Neill (eds), *A History of the Ecumenical Movement 1517–1948*, p. 102.

23. Neill, *A History of Christian Missions*, pp. 243, 244.

24. Ibid., p. 253.

25. George Smith, *The Life of William Carey*, London 1909, p. 12, quoted in Brown, *The English Baptists in the Eighteenth Century*, p. 116.

26. Ibid., p. 117.

27. Ibid., pp. 117,118.

28. Bebbington, *Evangelicalism*, p. 41.

29. Elizabeth Elbourne, 'The Foundation of the Church Missionary Society: the Anglican Missionary Impulse' in Walsh, Haydon and Taylor (eds), *The Church of England*, p. 247.

30. Neill, *A History of Christian Missions*, p. 261.

31. Elbourne, art.cit., p. 247.

32. Correspondence of Wilberforce, Vol II, p. 271, quoted in Howse, *Saints in Politics*, p. 94.

33. For the history of the early years of the Society, see Hole, *The Early History of the Church Missionary Society*, and Stock, *History of the Church Missionary Society*.

34. Balleine, *A History of the Evangelical Party in the Church of England*, p. 127.

35. See C.F. Pascoe, *Two Hundred Years of the SPG*, pp. 831,832, referred to in.Webster, *Joshua Watson*, p. 115.

36. See Stanley, *The Bible and the Flag*, pp. 85–91.

37. Ibid., pp. 91–98.

38. See Hastings, *The Church in Africa 1450–1950*.

9. *The Churches in England Transformed*

1. Knight, *The Nineteenth-Century Church and English Society*, pp. 10, 11.

2. Edward Norman, 'Church and State since 1800' in Gilley and Sheils (eds), *A History of Religion in Britain*, p. 277.

3. Antony Lentin, 'Anglicanism, Parliament and the Courts' in Parsons (ed), *Religion in Victorian Britain*, Vol II, *Controversies*, p. 89.

4. Chadwick, *The Victorian Church*, Vol I, p. 1.

5. Brose, *Church and Parliament*, p. 1.

6. Dewey, *The Passing of Barchester*, p. 1.

7. Clark, *Churchmen and the Condition of England 1832–1885*, p. 65. This is a book to which the present comments are much indebted.

8. Dewey, *The Passing of Barchester*, p. 2.

9. Brose, *Church and Parliament*, pp. 28,29.

10. Arthur Penryhn Stanley, *The Life and Correspondence of Thomas Arnold*, p. 297 (letter of 4 February 1837), quoted in Brose, *Church and Parlia-*

ment, p. 30.

11. Gilley, 'The Roman Catholic Church in England, 1780–1940' in Gilley and Sheils (eds), *A History of Religion in Britain*, p. 346.

12. For the Evangelicals see especially Bebbington, *Evangelicalism*, and Hylson-Smith, *Evangelicals in the Church of England 1734–1984*.

13. For the Oxford Movement see in particular Brilioth, *The Anglican Revival*; Church, *The Oxford Movement*; Hylson-Smith, *High Churchmanship in the Church of England*; Nockles, *The Oxford Movement in Context*; Ollard, *A Short History of the Oxford Movement*; Rowell (ed), *Tradition Renewed*; and Rowlands, *Church, State and Society*.

14. Gore (ed), *Lux Mundi*, Preface, p. vii.

15. Gore, 'The Holy Spirit and Inspiration' in Gore (ed), *Lux Mundi*, p. 360.

16. For a broad history of High Churchmanship in the Church of England see Hylson-Smith, *High Churchmanship in the Church of England*.

17. Clements, *Lovers of Discord*, pp. 5,6.

18. Parsons, 'From Dissenters to Free Churchmen: The Transitions of Victorian Nonconformity' in Parsons (ed), *Religion in Victorian Britain.* Vol I, *Traditions*, p. 68.

19. Ibid., p. 70 .

20. Chadwick, *The Victorian Church*, Vol I, p. 6.

21. See especially Bebbington, *The Nonconformist Conscience* and Munson, *The Nonconformists*.

22. Munson, *The Nonconformists*, p. 6.

23. Parsons, 'Victorian Roman Catholicism: Emancipation, Expansion and Achievement' in Parsons (ed), *Religion in Victorian Britain*. Vol I, *Traditions*, p. 153.

24. Ibid., p. 179. For Roman Catholic Modernism see especially Reardon (ed), *Roman Catholic Modernism*.

25. Parsons, ibid., p. 181.

26. For a discussion of the concept and process of secularization see Berger, *The Sacred Canopy*; Berger, *A Rumour of Angels*; Hill, *A Sociology of Religion*, ch. 11; Luckmann, *The Invisible Religion*; Martin, *The Religious and the Secular*; Wilson, *Religion in Secular Society*, and Wilson, *Contemporary Transformations of Religion*.

27. Martin, *The Religious and the Secular*, pp. 1, 16, 22.

28. Chadwick, *The Secularization of the European Mind*, p. 3.

29. See Gilbert, *Religion and Society*, p. 27.

30. Thompson, *Customs in Common*, p. 64.

31. A.F. Winnington-Ingram, *Work in Great Cities*, London 1896, p. 22, quoted in Perkin, *The Origins of Modern English Society*, p. 202.

32. Smith, *Religion in Industrial Society*.

33. Modern surveys and analyses include B.G. Sandhurst, *How Heathen is Britain?*, London 1946; *The ITA Opinion Research Centre Survey of*

Popular Attitudes, London 1970; and Peter Brierley, '*Christian England'.What the English Church Census Reveals*, London 1991.

34. Chadwick, *The Secularization of the European Mind in the Nineteenth Century*, p. 21.

35. James R. Moore, 'Freethought, Secularism, Agnosticism: The Case of Charles Darwin' in Parsons (ed), *Religion in Victorian Britain*. Vol I, *Traditions*, p. 308.

36. Parsons, 'Reform, Revival and Realignment: The Experience of Victorian Anglicanism' in Parsons (ed), *Religion in Victorian Britain*. Vol I, *Traditions*, p. 37.

37. Edward Royle, 'Secularists and Rationalists, 1800–1940' in Gilley and Sheils (eds), *A History of Religion in Britain*, p. 406.

Some Key Dates

1689 Joint sovereignty in England offered to William and Mary. The Toleration Act. Bill of Rights.

1690 Archbishop Sancroft deprived for refusing the oaths to William and Mary. Locke, *An Essay concerning Human Understanding*.

1695 Lifting of the Stuart censorship of the press.

1696 Jacobite rebellion; plot to assassinate William III. John Toland's *Christianity not Mysterious* published; also Frances Atterbury's *Letter to a Convocation Man*.

1699 The Society for Promoting Christian Knowledge founded.

1700 Frances Atterbury, *The Rights, Powers and Privileges of an English Convocation*.

1701 Bill of Settlement providing for a Protestant Hanoverian succession to the throne and imposing many new restrictions on the royal prerogative. Foundation of the Society for the Propagation of the Gospel in Foreign Parts.

1702 Death of William III, accession of Anne.

1704 Queen Annes's Bounty for the relief of poor clergy.

1707 Union of England and Scotland.

1709 Dr Henry Sacheverell preaches at St Paul's on the text 'In peril among False Brethren'. Whigs vote to impeach him.

1710 Trial of Sacheverell. Sacheverell riots in London. Lords find Sacheverell guilty but impose a light sentence which causes widespread rejoicing and shocks the Whigs. Frances Atterbury elected Prolocutor of the Lower House of Convocation. Griffith Jones begins his ministry in Wales.

1711 Fifty new Churches Act for London passed. Convocation prorogued causing the High Church party to be bitterly frustrated. Occasional Conformity Act.

1712 Last judicial trial for witchcraft in England.

1713 Atterbury made Bishop of Rochester.

1714 Schism bill to stamp out Dissenting schools and academies.

1715 General Election gives the Whigs a great majority. Serious pro-Jacobite riots in London. The Pretender's standard raised in Scotland. Tenison succeeded by Wake as Archbishop of Canterbury.

1717 Benjamin Hoadley, the Whig Bishop of Bangor, preaches his sermon 'My

Kingdom is not of this world' before George I and provokes the 'Bangorian controversy'.

1719 Repeal of the Occasional Conformity bill and the Schism bill. Act for Quieting and Establishing Corporations. The Salters' Hall meeting on subscription.

1722 News of the Jacobite conspiracy involving Frances Atterbury made public. The establishment of the Herrnhut settlement.

1723 Atterbury goes into exile.

1727 Death of George I, accession of George II. London Dissenting ministers (Presbyterian, Independent and Baptist) appoint a General Committee of the Three Denominations.

1728 William Law, *A Serious Call to a Devout and Holy Life.*

1729 John Wesley becomes tutor of Lincoln College and leader of the Oxford 'methodist' society.

1730 The Deist Matthew Tindal publishes *Christianity Old as Creation.*

1732 The Protestant Dissenting Deputies formed as a parallel lay organization to the Protestant Dissenting Ministers.

1733 Or perhaps 1734; George Thomson begins his 'evangelical' ministry in Cornwall.

1734 The start of the Northampton revival in America.

1735 Howell Harris begins his ministry in Wales, as does Daniel Rowland at about this time.

1736 George Whitefield starts his preaching ministry.

1738 Conversion of Charles and John Wesley.

1739 Wesley and Whitefield begin open air preaching at Bristol.

1740 The beginning of the Great Awakening in America.

1742 The revival at Cambuslang and Kilsyth in Scotland.

1745 The Young Pretender heads a Jacobite uprising (finally routed at Culloden, 16 April 1746).

1760 James, the Old Pretender, dies. The Pope and all other Catholic powers refuse to recognize Charles Edward Stuart as 'Charles III', signalling the virtual end of the Jacobite cause.

1770 The foundation of the General Baptist New Connexion. The Minutes of the Methodist Conference on predestination.

1771 The Feathers Tavern meeting on subscription.

1778 Catholic Relief Act.

1779 Dissenting ministers and schoolmasters relieved from subscription to the 39 Articles.

1780 Gordon Riots against the Catholic Relief Act.

1781 Countess of Huntingdon's Connexion separates from the Church of England.

1782 Charles Simeon becomes curate-in-charge of Holy Trinity, Cambridge, in which capacity he remains for fifty-four years.

1783 The foundation of the Eclectic Society. Robert Raikes publishes an account of his Sunday School.

1787 Hannah More, *Thoughts on the Manners of the Great* published.

1790 Burke's *Reflections on the Revolution in France.*

1791 Thomas Paine, *Rights of Man*, Part 1.

1792 Foundation of the Baptist Missionary society.

1794 Thomas Paine, *Age of Reason.* The foundation of the London Missionary society.

1797 William Wilberforce, *Practical View of the Prevailing Religious System of Professed Christians.* The formation of the Methodist New Connection.

1799 Church Missionary Society founded. The foundation of the Religious Tract Society.

1802 William Paley, *Natural Theology.*

1804 British and Foreign Bible Society founded.

1807 Slave trade abolished in British territories.

1811 The Primitive Methodists founded. Foundation of the National Society.

1813 Foundation of the Methodist Missionary Society.

1814 Joshua Watson resigns from his business and devotes himself full time to church matters.

1815 The foundation of the Methodist Bible Christian Society.

1818 Parliament votes £1m for church building.

1819 Peterloo Massacre.

1820 Death of George III, George IV succeeds.

1823 Irish Catholic Association established by O'Connell.

1828 Repeal of the Test and Corporation Acts.

1829 Roman Catholic Emancipation granted.

1830 George IV dies, accession of William IV. Charles Lyell, *Principles of Geology.*

1831 *The Extraordinary Black Book.*

1832 Reform Act.

1833 John Keble's Assize Sermon.

Glossary

Many of these definitions are indebted to Cross and Livingstone (eds), *The Oxford Dictionary of the Christian Church (ODCC)* or to Holmes, *The Making of a Great Power (H)*.

Advowson The right to appoint a clergyman to a parish or other ecclesiastical benefice (*ODCC*).

Anabaptist One who denies the validity of infant baptism and asserts that re-baptism of adults baptized in infancy is necessary.

Antinomianism A view that the grace of God working in a believer sets that person free from the need to observe the moral law.

Archdeacon A clerical post in the Church of England (and other churches) with authority delegated from the bishop for the exercise of general disciplinary supervision of the clergy, oversight of financial matters and the care of the fabric and fittings in the churches of the Archdeaconry. The duties usually include the induction of priests to new benefices and the admission of church-wardens to their offices.

Arius/Arianism Following Arius (*c.*280–*c.*336), Arians hold that Christ, though created by God before his physical birth on earth, had not co-existed with God from eternity. He was therefore 'more than man but less than God' *(H)*.

Arminianism A term applied to those who rejected predestination and were anti-Calvinist.

Athanasius/Athanasian Creed Athanasius (*c.*296–373) was a leading champion of the orthodox faith (as proclaimed by the Council of Nicaea in 325) in opposition to the teaching of Arius.

Diggers A sect which emerged during the Commonwealth period. The members believed that part of their calling was to dig in a specified area in order to promote a communistic mode of life.

Erastianism The belief that the church should be subordinate to the state.

Eusebius 'Father of Church history'. His most celebrated work (*c.*260) is his *Ecclesiastical History*.

Fifth Monarchists A sect which arose in the mid-seventeenth century which was distinguished by its aim of bringing in the 'fifth monarchy' to succeed the empires of Assyria, Persia, Greece and Rome (*ODCC*).

French prophets A section of the French Huguenot refugees in England, prominent especially in the early part of the eighteenth century, who spoke in tongues, claimed to receive revelations and displayed gifts of healing.

Gnosticism A form of Christian heresy which came into prominence as early as the second century AD. It took various forms, but had certain features in common. It emphasized secret knowledge of the way of salvation was revealed via the apostles, from whom it was derived by a secret tradition, or through a direct revelation given to the leader of the particular Gnostic sect concerned. The systems of teaching ranged from those which embodied genuine philosophical speculation to those which were a strange mixture of mythology and magical rites, with but a slender admixture of Christian elements.

Levellers A seventeenth-century political and religious group which opposed kingship and advocated complete religious freedom and a wide extension of the suffrage.

Long eighteenth century The period from 1688/89 to the 1830s.

Pan-evangelicalism Joining together or co-operation of those from various Christian traditions who recognize that they share basic beliefs which distinguish them as evangelicals.

Ranters There has been some debate as to whether they were a fanatical religious group of the mid-seventeenth century who stressed personal revelation and were anti-authority in any guise, or whether the term just indicates a tendency of various groups and individuals to move in that direction at that time.

Rector An incumbent who was entitled to the whole of the tithes of a parish (*ODCC*).

Rural Dean In the Church of England, a clergyman who is appointed by the bishop of the diocese to exercise a measure of leadership and encourage some coordination among parishes in the Rural Deanery concerned.

Seekers A seventeenth-century religious group which believed that no true church had existed since the spirit of Antichrist invaded the institutional church, and they simply waited for the true church to emerge.

Tithes In early times the clergy were maintained by receiving one-quarter of the offerings of the laity, with the remaining three-quarters going to the upkeep of the fabric of the church, to the relief of the poor, and to the bishop. This was superseded by the payment of a tenth part of all the produce of the lands (ODCC).

Vicar In the Church of England, the priest of a parish in which the tithes have been appropriated. It goes back to the time when, for instance, monasteries were given responsibility for providing the priest.

Index